Introduction to Library Public Services

Recent Titles in Library and Information Science Text Series

INTRODUCTION TO LIBRARY PUBLIC SERVICES

Seventh Edition

G. Edward Evans and
Thomas L. Carter

Library and Information Science Text Series

LIBRARIES
UNLIMITED
A Member of the Greenwood Publishing Group

Westport, Connecticut • London

Library of Congress Cataloging-in-Publication Data

Evans, G. Edward, 1937–
  Introduction to library public services / G. Edward Evans
and Thomas L. Carter. — 7th ed.
      p. cm. — (Library and information science text series)
  Includes index.
  ISBN 978–1–59158–596–1 (alk. paper)—
  ISBN 978–1–59158–595–4 (pbk. : alk. paper)
  1. Public services (Libraries) 2. Reference services (Libraries)
3. Library circulation and loans. I. Carter, Thomas L. II. Title.
  Z711.B63 2009
  025.5'2—dc22   2008037445

British Library Cataloguing in Publication Data is available.

Library of Congress Catalog Card Number: 2008037445
ISBN: 978–1–59158–596–1
      978–1–59158–595–4 (pbk.)

First published in 2009

Libraries Unlimited, 88 Post Road West, Westport, CT 06881
A Member of the Greenwood Publishing Group, Inc.
www.lu.com

Printed in the United States of America

The paper used in this book complies with the
Permanent Paper Standard issued by the National
Information Standards Organization (Z39.48–1984).

10 9 8 7 6 5 4 3 2 1

Contents

List of Illustrations

FIGURES

TABLE

Preface to the Seventh Edition

It did not seem as if eight-plus years had passed since the last edition of this book appeared. At least not when we began to think about what changes should take place in the new version. However, it quickly became crystal clear that public services had indeed changed—in rather dramatic ways in some areas and more slowly in others, but many modifications had taken place.

A person need only look through the previous editions to observe just how vast the changes have been since the first edition came out in the 1970s. Comparing the last edition with this one will demonstrate how quickly services have evolved. We have no doubt that the pace will only accelerate in the coming years.

The roles of support staff, as well as volunteers, have become an ever more critical part in providing high-quality library public services. They form, in many instances, the image of the library in the mind of the general public, as they are most frequently the first individuals the user encounters on a library visit. For some individuals, they are almost the only staff that the user interacts with. We are also aware that in difficult economic times such staff sometimes are asked to assume greater administrative/management roles, including becoming unit heads. Frequently a "support" person is in charge of the circulation or document delivery service. Even when not the unit's administrator, individuals tend to provide better service when they have an understanding of underlying purposes as well as some of the major issues confronting their unit/service activities. Thus, our purpose in this edition is assist support staff and volunteers to gain a broad understanding of the nature, purposes, and challenges of library public services.

Although it is natural, given the primary market for this text, that our examples and discussion emphasize U.S. library practices and services, we have drawn on material from other English-speaking parts of the world. While

practices do vary from country to country, the basic underlying concepts/
concerns are surprisingly global. Also, we believe that looking broadly at
how others provide a service or activity may motivate us to ponder these approaches and perhaps improve our services.

There are four completely new chapters in this edition. Chapter 2 explores
the issues of staffing and training for public service duties. Chapter 3 deals
with the concepts of "customer service" and "quality service." In Chapter 14, we
examine special services (programming) as well as looking at some examples
of such services—the topic of special services could and has filled many books
longer than this one, so our coverage is very selective. The final chapter (16)
covers the importance of assessment and its relationship to quality service.

Much has changed since 1999, the publication date of the last edition. We
also believe that support staff have played an increasingly important role during the intervening years since the last edition appeared. Given the current
(2008) economic conditions, we fully expect their role will expand even further.
Thus, we have rewritten the other chapters to reflect where libraries are in
the twenty-first century. Needless to say, that means there is an even greater
emphasis on technology and the World Wide Web. As we did in the previous
edition, we risk instant obsolescence by including numerous Web site URLs in
the text as well as in the suggested readings.

As always, we owe a debt of gratitude to the authors of all the books and
articles that address library services that we drew on in preparing this edition.
We also know the text would be much the poorer if not for the many comments, ideas, and suggestions we received from the following individuals who
read one or more of the chapter drafts.

Tony Amodeo—Reference Collection Coordinator, Loyola Marymount
University

Cynthia Becht—Head of Archives and Special Collections, Loyola Marymount University Library

Clare Castleberry—Interlibrary Borrowing Manger, Saint Mary's College
of California

Debbie Holbrook—Director of the Coconino County Community College
Library

Heidi Holland—Director of Flagstaff-Coconino County Public Library
and former Head of Outreach Services

Karla Kelly—Collections Registrar, Museum of Northern Arizona

Karen Lee—Professor, Diablo Valley College

Alle Porteer—Document Delivery Manager, Saint Mary's College of
California

Errol Stevens—recently retired Head of the Archives and Special Collections Department, Loyola Marymount University Library

Ava Stone—recently retired Director of the Flagstaff-Coconino County
Public Library

Steve Stonewell—Reserves Manager, Saint Mary's College of California

Sharon Walters—Access Services Department Head, Saint Mary's College of California

Volney White—recently retired School Library Media Specialist, Flagstaff, AZ

Our very special thanks to Margaret Saponaro (Manager of Staff Learning and Development, University of Maryland Libraries) and Sachi Yagu (Head of Public Services, Loyola Marymount Libraries) who read the entire manuscript and provided invaluable advice from start to finish.

G. Edward Evans
Harold S. Colton Library & Archives
Museum of Northern Arizona
Flagstaff, Arizona

Thomas L. Carter
Dean of Libraries
Saint Mary's College of California
Moraga, California

Chapter 1

Introduction

I thought I'd find myself at the library.
> —Alvin Schrader, 2007

The Economic Impact Study confirms that SFPL is a critical force for San Francisco.
> —Friends of the San Francisco Public Library (SFPL), 2008

You might wonder, in today's technology-oriented world, if libraries are either relevant or viable. Today's popular press might have you believing that if something is not on the Internet and/or profit focused (such as pop-up ads on so-called "free" Web sites) it must be of limited information value. Certainly there is merit in the idea that people's information-seeking behavior has changed and benefited as a result of recent advancements in technology. What is also certain is that a large percentage of what one finds on free Internet sites is incorrect and in some cases fraudulent. As library staff members we are well aware that one of the ways of assuring yourself of getting good information is to use your local library services.

A library's primary function is to provide access to information considered useful or valuable to the society in which it exists. What a great many people don't realize is just how long libraries have been performing this function. One of the earliest recorded libraries was uncovered by an archaeologist in the city of Ur, dating to about 2850 B.C. Thus, libraries have almost a 5,000 year history of not only providing access to information but meeting and adapting to new technologies.

Some people today may doubt that libraries have much of a future. We disagree; we believe they still and will have a major role to play in the information cycle and in providing essential services to today's societies. They provide open and generally free access to the entire world of knowledge, not just a segment

1

of it. Further, we agree with the following: "Reports of the death of paper, rampant in the 1990s, were evidently greatly exaggerated. The paperless office never materialized; nor, yet, have e-books. People still print letters and flip through pages of magazines" (*The Economist*, 2007, p. 72).

In 2003, Ann Okerson offered her thoughts about the digital library. Her view was that there are eight "eternal verities" about library collections and services that remain valid today and will continue to do so into the future. Most of the truths relate to services in some manner. These truths were: content is selectable; content is collectable; libraries retain information for the long term; collections grow and require some type of space; long-term retention requires preservation of some type; libraries expect to be around for a very long time; libraries exist to meet users information needs; today's information is worldwide and so are libraries to help assure worldwide preservation of information/knowledge. She concluded her article by writing, "May we all go boldly together where no libraries have gone before" (p. 285). We believe her views are accurate and to the point—that libraries will indeed go successfully and boldly forward into the future.

There is some data that suggest such a positive view of the viability of libraries is realistic. In late 2006, Cree and Yoon reported that public library circulation in 2005 increased by 1.8 percent. That may not seem like a very large increase; however, when it occurs at a time when the popular press reports on "deserted libraries" and that people no longer read or use libraries, it is indeed significant. During the same year communities also increased their expenditures on library services by 5.1 percent. Another study in late 2006 (9libraries. info) reported that a group of public libraries had demonstrated they provide a 4-to-1 "return on investment" to their service communities. That is to say, the libraries created an annual economic impact on the community that was four times greater than the amount the communities invested in library services. Almost any investor would be pleased with that level of return and would continue to invest in the service.

This is as good a place as any to insert a word or two about words referring to the individuals who access libraries and their services. Words such as *patron*, *client*, *user*, and *customer* appear in library literature as references to such people. The labels have even generated a modicum of heat among the people who use one of the variations. "Patron" is one of the longest-standing terms; however, for some people that label is thought of as demeaning to libraries as well as to their staffs. (One can view patronage as suggesting something is unable to exist on its own and requires a special person[s] to underwrite its existence.) "Customer," although it is in many ways the most appropriate term—as in "customer service"—is viewed by some in the field as too profit or commercially oriented to use for a public service/good like a library. "Client" also carries a stigma of commercialism for some—lawyers or brokers have clients, not a library. "User," for a few people, suggests a person with some bad habits. So, where does this leave us? Based on our years of library and archival experience, we believe either "customer" or "user" best reflect what public services are all about. After some debate, we have elected to employ "user" in this work to refer to the people who come to the library or access online library services.

ROLE AND PHILOSOPHY OF PUBLIC SERVICES

Libraries have a long history of adapting to change, and one of the keys to their longevity has been their focus on service to the primary and secondary user community. We are not suggesting that today's service philosophy—equal service to all primary users—has been in place all that long. Just as the contents of libraries have changed over time, so has the service philosophy evolved.

For the vast majority of their history, libraries served a very small segment of the people in their societies. The earliest libraries catered to government officers and religious leaders and essentially contained administrative materials (one can imagine how many clay tablets—rarely with more than a few square inches of writing surface—one would need for even a short poem). During the time scrolls were the dominant information technology, the topical range of materials increased (in addition to government data, there were plays, histories, etc., within libraries), as did the number of individuals who could read and were given access to libraries. However, that number was still only a small percentage of the total population. The Dark and Middle Ages brought about a narrowing of access—very few people could read, including royalty. Also, the new "technology" of the time, books (called a codex), were literally chained down in libraries due to their value—both because of their content and the cost of producing a handwritten book. Most of the books produced during this time were religious in character. With the arrival of movable type and the printing press, information materials began the explosion that continues to this day. As the reading public expanded, so did the growth of libraries, their range of collection content, and their steady shift from restricted to open access for everyone.

Looking at library history, we see that libraries have served and continue to serve their publics, parent institutions, and society in four basic ways. First, libraries meet society's information needs by *acquiring* the materials deemed valuable or useful to some or all the people. Second, they provide a physical location and an environment for *storing and preserving* those items. Third, libraries add value to the items acquired by *organizing* them in some manner to make access more efficient. Fourth, the library's staff improves access by *providing assistance* to individuals in locating desired information. All these functions involve public service personnel to a greater or lesser degree.

With the exception of some private libraries (including almost all corporate libraries), most U.S. libraries operate with an open-access policy. Today's open-access debate often revolves around what services should be available to which category of user as well as whether the access/service is free or fee-based. The traditional view ("traditional" for roughly the last 100 years) was that service should be free. That position slowly changed during the last half of the twentieth century. Most of that change was the result of technology to some degree. For example, libraries could not afford to underwrite the volume of copying that took place with the advent of the photocopier—they had to recover at least some of the costs. (To a large extent, the debate today is more about how much of the new costs a library should attempt to recover rather than if it should try to do so.) The databases libraries now subscribe to charge a fee based on some combination of factors, which almost always includes a service population size factor—registered borrowers, student FTE (full-time equivalent), researchers, and so on. In such cases, the question may be, do we limit access, and how must we limit access in order to stay within our contract/license agreements? We will be exploring these issues, and many others, in greater depth in the following chapters.

Traditionally, libraries divided their activities into two broad categories: technical and public services. Technical functions were and are those that secure and prepare materials for use. Public service functions are those that involve direct daily contact with the users.

In this book we cover the role, purpose, and philosophy related to each of the major functional areas of public service. Our hope is that both beginning professionals and support staff will find the material of use in gaining an understanding of the many facets of public service, as well as how these facets relate to one another to provide a complete public service program. Our primary purpose in this book is to describe the current basic elements of the various aspects that make up library public services.

Although libraries come in a variety of "flavors"—academic, corporate, public, school, and special at the very broadest level—they all share, regardless of category, the same basic functions. What makes the difference between types is their environment/parent organization. Except in rare instances, a library is normally part of a larger parent organization—university, business, city, school district, or museum, for instance. It is how the library modifies its basic services and functions to fit its user community's needs that place it into one of these categories. Throughout this book we attempt to provide a general focus rather than attempting to treat library category-specific variations. However, when the activity is unique to one or more institutional categories we do cover the specifics. Some examples of narrower focus are children's services, reserve collections, and special/archival collections. One reason for the more general approach is there are a number of texts that address category-specific environments.

Educational institution libraries often start as a collection of donated materials in the corner of a classroom. Even today, many school libraries depend upon book donations. One of the world's great research libraries, Harvard's Widener Library, started with a donation of a few books from John Harvard. Many public libraries developed from reading societies where a few people joined together to buy and have access to more books than they could buy individually. Over time these cooperatives evolved into the "free" public library.

Earlier we mentioned the evolution in thinking about who might have access to library services and how often; one example of such thinking/evolution comes from the eighteenth and early nineteenth centuries. In their early days, U.S. college libraries were only open a few hours each week. Generally, students had to have permission to examine a book in the library. Even that use required the direct supervision of a professor. As colleges grew in size and attitudes and teaching methods changed, hours and access increased. User assistance is an even more recent phenomenon. Public libraries began staffing reference desks in the late nineteenth century. It was not until 1914 that Harvard business students recommended creating a reference department, and it was the late 1930s before Widener Library provided even minimal reference assistance (Carpenter, 1986, p. 2). As late as World War II, some financial officers and library boards questioned the need for reference assistance.

An even newer form of service (relatively speaking) is an expansion of the one-on-one reference assistance to providing group teaching sessions of "library/bibliographic" skills. Such instruction serves two purposes: it teaches people how to use information sources independently, and allows existing staff to assist an ever-increasing user base and/or devote more time to complicated questions. The instruction also normally focuses on one or two specific sources of immediate interest to the user rather than on an overview of all services and resources. Corporate (special) libraries frequently provide needed information directly to individuals rather than requiring the person to find the information. There are several reasons for this. One major reason is that the staff-to-user ratio is much higher than in other types of libraries. Such ratios allow for more personalized service. Another reason is the product and profit orientation of the organization. It is more cost effective for experts to locate the necessary information and deliver it to the end user. With the advent of online databases, special librarians realized that they should do more end user training to address the employees' need to search for information from their desktops or while on the road in both company and commercial databases.

For library public service staff, there are two broad goals. The first is to provide access to informational materials; the second is to provide assistance to users in identifying desired appropriate materials. The *Code of Ethics* of the American Library Association (ALA) (http://www.ala.org/ala/oif/state mentspols/codeofethics/codeethics.htm) summarizes the overall philosophy of library public service. It identifies the key service elements—collections, suitable loan conditions and service policies, and staff who are knowledgeable and who provide unbiased service to all. (Do check out this Web resource.)

During periods of restricted or shrinking budgets, implementing or maintaining appropriate services creates several challenges. Maintaining high levels of service is an obvious challenge when there is a hiring freeze and resigning staff cannot be replaced. A less obvious, but very important challenge is maintaining staff morale, especially when staff members know services could be better. Yet another challenge is maintaining the traditional concept of free services, even with a reasonably good budget.

Free library service has been the tradition in most countries. In the past, users from outside the primary service population occasionally paid a fee for a service that was free to the primary group. Today, technology is slowly changing some aspects of that practice. No one thinks twice about charging or paying for photocopies. Years ago the idea of paying for an interlibrary loan (ILL) or document delivery was a topic of heated debate. Today such charges to libraries and users are fairly common. Each new information technology seems to generate added and often unexpected costs for the library. More and more of these costs are being passed on to the person requesting the information or using the service. A newer typical charge is for printing material from online databases and the Internet. Initially libraries did not charge for such printing, but as the volume of printing has increased, more and more libraries have started charging for each page printed just as they did with photocopying.

Not all technological developments result in passing on costs to users, at least not yet. One such example, which we explore in more depth in Chapter 6, are the statewide resource-sharing networks (OHIONET for instance) that allow end users to generate their own document delivery requests. Although free to end users, such programs do add significant costs to library operations. Although not a direct charge to the individual, several countries pay fees to the authors whose books circulate from a public library. Public lending right (PLR) fees exist in a number of countries, including Canada and the United Kingdom. U.S. authors have at times attempted to have a PLR program implemented in the United States, with no success to date. Presently PLR national pools (funds from the government) pay the fees to the authors, not monies collected from libraries or readers. However, it is not inconceivable that in the future the fees might be a direct tax on libraries and borrowers. Although completely free library services are becoming a thing of the past, libraries still offer many free services, and charges seldom recover the full cost of any of the services provided.

You may recall, if you checked out the ALA's *Code of Ethics* site, that "appropriate . . . collections" was one of the important elements of an ideal library public service program. Generally, the collection decisions are the responsibility of librarians with substantial input from the user community. Although the content of the collection is beyond the scope of this book, how the collection is managed and maintained is a topic we cover.

Another ALA document, the *Library Bill of Rights* (http://www.ala.org/ala/oif/statementspols/statementsif/librarybillrights.htm), provides additional insight into what public service policies ought to address. Again, assuming you looked at the Web page, you noted that the *Code* and *Bill* address many of the same topics. In terms of collections, it makes the point that collections should include all points of view on a topic and that complaints about collection content should have a review procedure that is fair and objective. Essentially, the document lays out the parameters for providing free, balanced, accurate information to all comers. (As with the *Code of Ethics*, we strongly suggest you review the *Bill of Rights*.)

Many libraries have built upon the ALA's documents or ones generated by other professional information groups and posted their positions where anyone can view the policy. Below are some library Web sites that address user-access policies:

> http://www.waukesha.lib.wi.us/about/staff.shtml
> Waukesha Public Library—"Our Staff and Customer Service Policy"
> http://www.newtonplks.org/libplcy.html
> Newton Kansas Public library—"Library Policy Statements"
> http://www.library.american.edu/about/students/rights.html
> American University—"User Bill of Rights"
> http://www.scils.rutgers.edu/~pack501/njrights.html
> "Bill of Rights for New Jersey Library Users"
> http://www.nlc.state.ne.us/freedom/lbrpart2.html
> "A Fresh Look at the Library Bill of Rights"—Nebraska Library Commission
> http://www.asla.org.au/policy/p_bor.htm
> "Policy Statement—School Library Bill of Rights"—Australian School
>   Library Association

As you can see, the issues regarding public access to library services cover almost library types and occur in almost all countries.

An interesting public service concept was reported in *Library Management* (Yap and Yeo, 2007). CARE (Courtesy, Attentiveness, Responsiveness, and Effectiveness) is a program/concept being implemented in the National University of Singapore. The idea is to take "a customer focus approach and with clearer understanding of our users' needs, we worked hard to integrate our services into *their* workflow and use targeted promotions to create awareness of our services" (p. 67).

Today, "customer service" is once again a common mantra for almost all organizations. The concept has had cyclical history over the past 100 years. For libraries, it has always been the primary emphasis. A few years ago, Albrecht and Zemke (2002), suggested that there are three major dimensions to customer/user service—"help," "fix," and "value-added." Libraries have been and are, or should be, effective on all three dimensions. Answering reference questions, such as "What is a good video about geology?"—is an aspect of the "help me" dimension. A caller saying she/he cannot log into a certain database because of a password or other technical issue is a form of a "fix-it" service. Libraries have been providing "value-added" services for almost as long as they have existed—they organize information materials in ways to make the material more easily accessible.

Today's libraries realize they face new and serious competition in what had been an almost monopolistic service area. Obviously the biggest competitor is the Internet (it is also in many ways a great asset for libraries) and sites such as Google and Yahoo!, not to mention emerging Web 2.0 technologies and resources. What libraries must do is find an effective means to differentiate their information services from the Googles and Yahoos of the Internet world that offer only unevaluated information (or even the wikis that offer user generated/moderated content). The key is to show that the differences that exist *do* matter in the long run. This may not be an easy process when it comes to the Millennial Generation (individuals born after 1980).

Millennials are the first generation of people who grew up in what seems to be a totally wired world. Internet, e-mail, cell phones, instant messaging, iPods, you name it and there is probably one or more computer chips in it. Occasionally this generation is referred to as "digital natives" (Prensky, 2001) because they have never known a world without computers. Even in less developed countries, computers and cell phones are impacting societies. All the other generations, Gen Xers, Boomers, and the like, are essentially digital immigrants—people who have had to come to grips with how to use the "new" technologies as they were forced to change behaviors and even their thought patterns. Digital natives do not think of technology as "new" but simply a natural part of their environment. They also don't always realize the older generations often have concerns about technology's increasing role in society. Because Millennials generally prefer/expect immediate responses and apparently have little regard/understanding about the validity of the information they retrieve, they represent a major challenge for libraries. To be able to attract and hold such users will require new approaches to our services.

We suggest that careful thought and planning of new services will, in time, prove the value of library services to the Millennium Generation. However, it will take "thinking outside the traditional boxes" of library services. A good starting point for that thinking process is to ponder the special nature/characteristics of service (see below). Further, we urge our readers to do the same while reading this book. It will only be through such thinking that significant changes in service can and will take place.

Points to Ponder Regarding Quality Service and Millennials

- Service only exists at the point of delivery—Millennials expect instantaneous results
- Quality exists during the delivery process, it can not be assured prior to that time—Millennials expect consistent performance
- If it is of poor quality, it cannot be called back—Millennials are use to "what you see is what you get" and make judgments accordingly
- It (quality service) is a one-on-one process—high touch rather than high tech
- It is not something you can put on display like a book or video; it does or doesn't happen during the delivery process—Millennials have high expectations and don't revisit disappointing sites very often
- It is intangible, it is an experience—Millennials are comfortable with virtuality
- It can-not be traded, sold, shared, or experienced by anyone but the recipient—Millennials are fans of trading and sharing
- It cannot be stored for future use—Millennials expect to come back to a service time and time again and experience the same results
- It is highly subjective, "in the eye of the beholder,"—Millennials are into sharing their views on matters with the world (using sites such as MySpace)
- Its quality declines as additional people become involved in its delivery—Millennials are no more fond of being shifted from one person to another when seeking service than any other generation

---

If you have the time, you might like to explore a free online program called Learning 2.0 (http://plcmclearning.blogspot.com; Farkas, 2007). It contains a number of technology learning modules (23 topics) focusing on Web 2.0 that may keep you up to date on what digital natives are doing and talking about.

BASIC FUNCTIONS OF PUBLIC SERVICES

Public services revolve around circulation and reference activities. As the principal operations of public services, *circulation* and *reference* involve direct contact with customers and responsibility for their needs. The only reason for the existence of most libraries is to serve a specific group of people. Users judge a library on the basis of their experience with public services. Every public transaction adds to or detracts from the library's image. (Think about the above points.) Keeping this in mind, especially when it is busy and the pressure builds, is difficult; yet this is when library personnel must try hard-est to provide top-notch service.

The *circulation* function consists of four fundamental tasks:

1. Charging out materials to borrowers
2. Checking in returned materials
3. Returning materials to their proper places in the library
4. Carrying out necessary housekeeping tasks in such a way as to keep the collection in good order

Circulation usually also involves assessing and collecting fines and fees. This is an activity that can create strong emotions on both sides of the service counter. (Chapter 8 covers circulation operations.)

Answering questions and assisting people in identifying useful material is the focal point of reference service. Inquiries can be simple directional ques-tions such as, "Where are the restrooms?" or "Which computers provide Web access?" They can be information questions such as "Where are the craft books?" that sometimes morph into reference questions upon further probing (as you learn the true nature of the query was to find an article on the history of calligraphy.) They can also be research questions that require several hours or even days to answer properly, if at all. (Not long ago one of the authors had to try to answer, "What is the design of the tattoo behind the left ear of a White Mountain Apache male, which he gets when he becomes an elder?" That might not seem like an actual question, but it was; after several days of searching we never did find an illustration or description of the design, just that it was done.) Other responsibilities of reference service may include instruction in using library resources, compiling bibliographies or research guides, and ob-taining interlibrary loans. (Chapters 4, 5, and 7 cover most of these activities.)

Document delivery service—DDS (aka interlibrary loan or ILL)—is a coop-erative activity that, at least in theory, is capable of expanding the walls of the library to encompass the world's library collections. UNESCO's Universal Availability of Publications (UAP) Program expands on the concept. The goal of UAP is to have any publication available to any person anywhere in the world. The practical limits of DDS make its scope much smaller, but the potential for expanding customers' access to other libraries' collections is still great and is an important public service. (DDS activity is covered in Chapter 7.)

Reserve activities serve to both limit and expand access to the library's col-lections. They limit access in the sense that materials placed on reserve often do not circulate outside the library. If they do circulate out of the library, their loan periods are shorter (24 hours to one week) than for items in the general collection. The service expands access by assuring that high-demand items are available to many people for at least a brief period. Educational libraries (school and academic libraries) seldom can buy enough copies of materials instructors want their students to read, view, or hear. The reserve system is one effective way to assure equitable access to one or two copies of a required item. (Chapter 9 covers this activity.)

Special collections may be nothing more than a few unusual items of local interest kept in a room or office with limited public access. On the other hand, archives and research libraries may have collections of rare and costly items larger than many collections of school districts and public libraries. The primary purpose of special collections is to provide for the proper care and handling of items of unusual interest or value. At the same time, they permit controlled public access to the items. Often these collections contain objects normally found in a museum, such as paintings, furniture, and other works of art. Occasionally they contain manuscripts and operational records of organizations. In such cases they have an archival function. Some public libraries (and a few academic libraries) serve as a city's archive, housing public records that are no longer active. A special collections area requires a higher level of security and environmental control (temperature and humidity) than the rest of the library to preserve items stored there. (Chapter 13 covers special collections.)

Serials are publications that *may* arrive in the library on a regular basis and require special handling. ("May" is an important word in today's digital environment, as very often a library now provides access to more electronic versions of journals and magazines than they receive in paper.) Each serial usually focuses on a single topic, such as gardening or biochemistry, or on a type of reader (for example, for young women, *Seventeen* magazine). For readers, serials represent the source of the most current vetted and printed information. Because of their currency they are often in high demand (for example, newspapers and daily financial publications). From the point of view of the staff, serials, especially newspapers and magazines, generate considerable work and numerous problems regardless of the format. At the same time, staff members recognize the value the public places on these publications and make every effort to ensure quality service. (Chapter 10 addresses the problems and issues of serials work for the public service staff.)

Media services handle a variety of nonprint formats, two of which circulate at high rates especially in public libraries—video and audio recordings. Media collections present interesting challenges for the staff. Learning to use the equipment well enough to teach the public its proper use and handling takes time and effort. Maintaining software and hardware in good working condition requires skill and patience. Today there is also a need to upgrade and maintain a wide variety of computer equipment. Legal issues related to use of software must be understood and the staff must ensure that library use complies with the applicable law. (Chapter 11 covers these and other media issues.)

Government information sources are not widely used by the public. Nevertheless, government information represents a major source of current data on a variety of topics. Almost every governmental body issues or posts on the Web at least a few publications, if nothing more than an annual budget. Most national governments issue both official publications (material that records governing activities) and items designed to assist citizens in their daily activities. For the public to fully exploit this information resource, the library staff must understand how to provide access to the wealth of material available. Special libraries collect a variety of government information, including documents from regulatory agencies, legislation, public laws, and the *General*

Accounting Office Reports in a variety of formats. The federal government has dramatically scaled back its paper distribution of these resources. Libraries must develop a timely system to scan Internet resources for information and preserve the information. (Chapter 12 covers different types of government information.)

Library security is an important aspect of public service. Every library has users with poor memories, who may forget to return library materials. However, there are both amateur and professional thieves who prey on libraries. Although the public may not realize it, books and other library materials are valuable community commodities. Library materials cost substantial sums to acquire, process, maintain records for, and store—much more than the price paid in a retail outlet. Further, especially in academic libraries, the bulk of the information is not replaceable, which leads to loss of access to information. Books go out of print rapidly, and publishers often print a very limited edition for scholarly books. As if thieves were not enough, various disasters can rob a library of valuable information. Natural and man-made disasters can destroy thousands of items in a short period. And there are also "quiet" disasters, such as insect infestations and the kind of deterioration of materials that time, uncontrolled environmental factors, and the bad habits of humans can cause. Constant vigilance, staff and customer education, and good planning are the best antidote to these threats to the library. (Chapter 15 covers these aspects of library security in depth.)

We have added several new chapters to this edition. Chapter 2 examines staffing public service points/desks with both paid and volunteer personnel. Chapter 3 explores in some depth the overarching issues of what is effective "customer service." Chapter 14 looks at issues related to programming and marketing activities, which are increasingly becoming factors in high-quality library service. Finally, Chapter 16 addresses the question related to assessing/determining the quality of service; this is something funding bodies, especially federal and state government agencies, are now demanding from agencies that receive funds.

SUMMARY

Libraries, media centers, learning resource centers, and information centers exist to provide service. The kind and degree of service will vary from library to library. At one end of the spectrum is the "archive-museum" library, which provides only research and preservation services. At the other end is the information brokerage, which locates and delivers specific pieces of information to its customers.

Throughout their long history, libraries have focused on providing access to information that they acquire, organize, and store; this is how they have adapted to a constantly changing environment. The library service philosophy evolved over time from very limited access to open access for all. While technology has brought about a host of changes in the services provided, it has not changed the idea that any authorized person should have access to courteous, professional, unbiased service.

Chapter Review Material

1. Thinking about the changes that have occurred in libraries over time, what do you think are the requirements for libraries to prosper in the digital world?
2. What are the four ways libraries serve their societies?
3. What are the two major goals for public service staff?
4. What document is the basis for most public services policies in the United States? What are their key elements?
5. What are the 10 characteristics of customer service?

REFERENCES

Albrecht, Karl, and Ron Zemke. 2002. *Service America in the New Economy.* New York: McGraw-Hill.

Carpenter, Kenneth E. 1986. *The First 350 Years of the Harvard University Libraries.* Cambridge, MA: Harvard University Press.

Cree, Charity, and Mijung Yoon. 2006. "Public Library Circulation and Expenditures Increase in 2005," *American Libraries* 37, no. 10: 38–39.

The Economist. 2007. "Flat Prospects," 382 (March 17): 72.

Farkas, Meredith. 2007. "A Roadmap to Learning 2.0," *American Libraries* 38, no. 2: 26.

Friends of the San Francisco Public Library. 2008. *One Dollar In, More Than Three Out.* http://www.friendsandfoundation.org/press_release.cfm?id=41.

9libraries. 2006. "Economic Benefit Study Released November 29, 2006." http://9libraries.info.

Okerson, Ann.2003. "Asteroids, Moore's Law, and the Star Alliance," *Journal of Academic Librarianship* 29, no. 5: 280–285.

Prensky, Marc. 2001. "Digital Natives, Digital Immigrants." *On the Horizon* 9, no. 5: 1–6.

Schrader, Alvin M. 2007. "I Thought I'd Find Myself at the Library," *PNLA* 72, no. 1: 4–9.

Yap, Sylvia, and Gabriel Yeo. 2007. "Reaching Out, Building Bonds," *Library Management* 28, no. 8/9: 569–576.

SUGGESTED READINGS

Barack, Lauren. 2005. "Library Offers Instant Research Buddy," *School Library Journal* 51, no. 10: 19.

Condon, Scott. 2005. "Public Libraries, Public Funding, Public Good," *Alki* 21, no. 1: 22–24.

Cooper, Tom. 2007. "Are We Helping the Information Have-Nots?" *Public Libraries* 46, no. 1: 18–19.

Day, Rosalie. "Information Networks Building Social Networks," *Australasian Public Library Information Services* 20, no. 4: 153–169.

Eiselstien, June. 2003. "College Access Programs and Services," *Public Libraries* 42, no. 3: 184–187.

Ford, Charlotte E., and Annabel Stephens. 2007. "Alabama Public Library Services to the Hispanic Community," *Alabama Librarian* 57, no. 1: 6–19.

Gupta, Dinesh, and Jambhekar Ashok. 2002. "Which Way Do You Want to Serve Your Customers?" *Information Outlook* 6, no. 7: 26–32.

Kostiak, Adele. 2002. "Valuing Your Public Library," *Bottom Line* 15, no. 4: 159–162.

Kretzmann, John P., and John L. McKnight. 2005. *Discovering Community Power.* Evanston, IL: School of Education and Social Policy, Northwestern University.

Robinson, Michael. 2008. "Digital Nature and Digital Nurture: Libraries, Learning, and the Digital Native," *Library Management* 29, no. 1/2: 67–76.

Young, Timothy G. 2007. "The Young Visitors: Introducing Children to the Research Library Through Exhibitions." *College & Research Libraries News* 68, no. 4: 235–238.

Zemke, Ron, and John A. Woods. 1998. *Best Practices in Customer Service.* New York: AMACOM.

Chapter 2

Staffing

The best thing our library has going for it is the staff.
—Alan Kaye, 2006

Recruiting and working with volunteers requires a time investment, but it pays off in building advocates for the library program.
—Sue W. McGown, 2007

Quality service requires adequate funding and reasonable physical facilities; however, even the most generously funded libraries with beautiful new facilities will not be able to provide quality service without staff members who are highly service-oriented. Gaining the services of the best and brightest people is a process that requires thoughtful planning. When it comes to hiring people who will provide outstanding service, you must think and plan even more carefully. People are the key to providing successful service—people who are thoughtfully selected, people who are given proper support and ongoing training, and, most importantly, people who really do like people.

Hire happy people. That may sound platitudinous and rather silly. However, research has shown (*Harvard Business Review*, 2007) it does in fact make a difference in customer service and satisfaction. "The bigger the employee's smile, the happier the customer. That is the conclusion of new research from Bowling Green and Penn State Universities. . . . If a manger wants employees to deliver service with a smile, they can do better than mandate it. They should create an environment that encourages genuine smiles" (p. 24).

Sometimes those of us working in libraries forget that our users/customers are our real employers. These are the people who really fund our paychecks. Providing them with the best possible service within our power is the least we can do. Those of our nominal employers who believe, as did those who David Drickhamer (2006) wrote about, will have quality service. He suggested that managers who "believe as a matter of faith that if they take care of their employees—offering continuous training, regularly assessing performance, and treat them with same respect with which they would like to be treated—those employees will help deliver superior performance. Lo and behold, it's true" (p. 42).

CATEGORIES OF INFORMATION SERVICE PERSONNEL

Like libraries, the categories of library staff are variable. A general rule is the larger the library, the more complex its structure and the number of staff categories one encounters. Some very small libraries operate solely on the basis of volunteers; others may have one or two people who have had some education in library operations. At the other end of the spectrum are places like the Library of Congress with dozens of different staff categories. In the vast middle ground are libraries with just a few categories. We divide staff into two types—full- or part-time.

Full-time staff in mid-range libraries consists of professionals (librarians and perhaps some other nonlibrary personnel such as information technology or IT), support or paraprofessionals, and clerical staff. All play a vital role in providing high-quality user services. We firmly believe, and practice, that there is no such thing as second-class or less important job categories in a library. Everyone's role is important; even when at times you may wonder if what you are asked to do really contributes much, if anything, to the overall service.

Librarians

In today's information world, the differences between a librarian and a paraprofessional are probably most apparent in the human resources (HR) department rather than within the library. The reason for HR's ability to differentiate between the two is that it maintains the job descriptions, position holder's name, and salary classifications. None of these attributes are apparent on a daily basis in the library. "On the floor," especially for the users, it is almost impossible to know who holds what job title. For many users, anyone working in the library is a librarian. William Curran (2006) indicated that three-quarters of the libraries in his survey reported that the need for paraprofessionals to perform tasks once done by librarians had increased over the prior five years, and that they also expected the trend would continue for at least five more years. Curran noted, "A redefinition of roles and expectations is needed. The level of competencies in information technology as well as the constant upgrading of equipment create expectations on the part of library users and invite professional and paraprofessional staff into a new routine of duties and responsibilities" (p. 30).

Individuals holding positions designated as "librarian" generally have a master's degree in library science (MLS). "Generally" is an important word in the preceding sentence. School libraries, when they have a librarian, usually require that the individual hold a teaching certificate with some coursework in librarianship. Many large research libraries have bibliographic/subject librarians or administrators who may hold a graduate degree in their assigned subject area. Finally, some librarians may have satisfied a frequent phrase in position advertisements—"MLS or equivalent required." Just what is "equivalent" varies from institution to institution. However, the vast majority of librarians do in fact have an MLS degree.

Paraprofessional/Support Staff

If the definition of librarian appears rather vague, deciding on a label and required background of those holding nonlibrarian positions in libraries is even fuzzier. Years ago, Elin Christianson (1973) reported on the various labels used to designate nonlibrarian personnel as well as attitudes about those labels. The list included clerk/clerical, library aide, library associate, library assistant, library clerk, library technician, nonprofessional, paraprofessional, supportive/support, and subprofessional. The only label that did not elicit at least a few negative responses from those holding such positions was library technician. Paraprofessional had only a few negative comments, and today there probably would be none, given the raise of groups such as paralegals.

A long-running journal for people in these ranks was *Library Mosaics* and its editorial staff consistently used the label paraprofessional. (We were saddened to see it cease publication at the end of 2005. However, its back files have a wealth of information for anyone interested in this field.) Perhaps COLT (Council on Library/Media Technicians—http://colt.ucr.edu) and/or LSSIRT (the ALA's Library Support Staff Interests Round Table—http://www.ala.org/ala/lssirt/lssirt.cfm) will fill in the void left by the passing of *Library Mosaics*. As you probably noted, there were three different labels discussed in Chapter 1. Clearly there is still no consensus as to what the label should be. This is probably due to a lack of agreement about what training/education is required to hold such positions. We personally prefer either paraprofessional or support staff.

Support staff members are the backbone of library services. Without them few libraries could offer the variety and quality of services that they do. "According to the 2004 statistics from the National Center for Education Statistics (NCES) 230,843 workers are employed in U.S. academic and public libraries. Of these, 160,150 (69%) are library support staff" (ALA LSSCP, 2008, http://www.ala-apa.org/certification/supportstaff.html). Clearly the total number of support staff is even greater when one adds in those in school and special libraries.

What type of background is called for to fill nonlibrarian positions that now often perform duties and carry responsibilities that were once the sole domain of MLS holders? Like so many questions, the answer is, it depends. Ideally individuals who perform such work would have, and many do have, extensive education, training, and library experience. Without doubt, having a degree from a program that focuses on library and information services, in all their forms, is very valuable. Someone who has the ability, interest, and desire to grow and learn on the job can also fill such positions in time. While having a supervisor who encourages and trains people is a wonderful asset, a person can independently gain the requisite knowledge and skills through workshops, online opportunities, and formal classes. (There are some entry-level positions that require no prior library experience or knowledge, that are clerical in nature and should not carry the label paraprofessional or library technician.)

People usually think of their work in one of two ways—as a job or as a career. Job-oriented individuals only focus on the assigned duties. They often perform those responsibilities at an extremely high level and are a very valuable organizational resource. However, when their work shift ends, so does their interest in the organization. They have other interests. Career-oriented people, on the other hand, have a strong interest in their organization as well as an interest in the field in general. They are quick to volunteer to take on new tasks, especially those that offer an opportunity to learn a new skill or gain new knowledge. Because of their interest in the organization, they offer suggestions for improvements and accept committee assignments willingly. It is our opinion that the career-oriented individuals form the core of paraprofessional ranks. We also must note that career-oriented individuals, when overworked and undersupported, can quickly become job-oriented. This is something that all good supervisors attempt to avoid and try to point out to more senior managers when they observe such mistreatment.

For the career-oriented person the LSSIRT, described earlier, has created the *Task Force on Career Ladders* (1999). This document, as well as the companion *Continuing Education & Training Opportunities* (2000) publication, are useful to review and should be thoughtfully considered. As the *Career Ladders* work indicates, "career development shifts the responsibility to the individual and away from the organization" (p. 4). It goes on to point out that libraries have an obligation in this area as well, such as providing opportunities for skill development, promotions, and the chance to put new skills to use.

A key point was made in the LSSIRT *Training* statement (2000): "Although there has been rapid development of electronic databases, the Internet, and other resources, there has not been nearly enough training for the staff who must use these resources" (p. 4). It goes on to suggest one need is that "there should be standard core competences for all levels of support staff" (p. 5). The Support Staff Section of the Connecticut Library Association developed a competency list—both for all staff and for some areas of service, for example public services (http://ctlibraryassociation.org/archive/class.html). Many of their general staff competencies are ones you would expect to find in any list of desirable staff traits—positive attitude toward users, being open to change, having good communication skills, and being willing and able to work independently. Below are the 11 competencies for public service staff:

- Ability to introduce users to all library services
- Ability to use the entire library collection to satisfy user requests
- Knowledge of the library's circulation system and public access catalog
- Knowledge of fine and fee policies and cash and security procedures
- Knowledge of basic reference and information resources and referral procedures
- Knowledge of available community resources
- Knowledge of library copyright requirements

- Knowledge of library classification systems with the ability to do shelving and shelf reading
- Familiarity with reader's advisory issues and resources
- Familiarity with ILL procedures
- Ability to deal with disruptive patrons and emergency situations

We address all of these competencies in the remaining chapters of this book.

The ALA is undertaking a certification program for support staff. You can check this program out at www.ala-apa.org/certification/supportstaff.html.

Other Full-Time Staff

There are a variety of full-time employees who work in libraries but do not fall into the above two categories. The most obvious are clerical staff such as receptionists and secretaries. These are job categories that only require general office skills—a person does not need to have any prior background in library operations to carry out the job functions. Other clerical positions might include processing and mailing notices to users (overdue and document delivery information, for example) or maintaining order in the current magazine and newspaper area.

You are likely to encounter at least one bookkeeper whose only special "library" knowledge is the concept of encumbrance; even that is not unique to the library environment. Someone with a general background in bookkeeping can quickly step into a library administrative office and handle the budget record–keeping activities. Only if the person is to handle the financial records for the acquisitions department would she/he need to understand the principles of encumbering funds. In larger libraries, there may be some IT staff that handle networking/server maintenance, and the like, and who have no responsibility for specific library technologies. The very largest libraries are likely to have other professional positions, such as fundraising specialists, training officers, marketing and public relations people, or HR personnel who may or may not have an MLS. (We cover part-time and volunteer personnel later in this chapter.)

Shannon Hoffman (1993) suggested that clerical staff provide general office skills, while shelvers (or part-time personnel) perform a variety of very routine but essential tasks. She further proposed that "paralibrarians" would be a preferable term for those with library training but less than an MLS. "This title is a title that would command respect and understanding by the public. Now is the time for the librarians to give more support to paraprofessionals and establish them with an appropriate title. By this means librarians can project themselves forward in the quest for professionalism" (p. 10). Certainly in today's environment it is indeed difficult to determine just who is a "librarian."

Our reason for covering all library staff in our discussion is technology or information communication technology (ICT). Over the years that this book has been available (1971 to the present), there has been a profound shift in staffing patterns, as technology has become an ever more dominant feature in the daily work patterns of library staff. ICT has in fact become so integrated to the work flow that when the system has problems, or "goes down," work almost comes to a complete stop. It has changed work requirements, skills, and who does what. It has also made the case for "cross-training" and/or teamwork crystal clear, thus further blurring job distinctions. Libraries are increasing use of "empowered teams" that are composed of a variety of job categories. (Empowered teams have decision-making powers.) ICT and other factors have resulted in a flattening of the traditional hierarchy of library organizations.

One impact of a changing economic picture and new technologies is that library staff sizes have remained relatively constant in spite of increased user demands and expectations. Technology allows public service personnel to handle changing and, in a few cases, increased workloads without additional people. Occasionally, it has allowed some libraries to shift positions from technical to public services.

Today's libraries require a much wider variety of skill sets than they did even 5 or 10 years ago. Budget restraints in turn create situations in which public service staff must be able to fill in for one another (cross-training). Technology also brings with it the need for constant training, as it seems to change every day.

We agree with the ideas expressed by Michael Gorman (1987) in what he called the "drift down" theory of organization:

- No professional should do a task that can be performed by a paraprofessional
- No paraprofessional should do a task that can be performed by a clerical staff member
- No human being should do a task that can be performed by a machine (p. 158)

STAFFING PROCESS

Selecting appropriate staff, regardless of category—full-time, part-time, and even volunteers—requires significant time, planning, and effort. Although few libraries have an HR unit, library staff do become involved in the HR process on an operational level. Because of that fact, we have included a short discussion of the major HR issues. During your career, you are likely to be involved in all of the issues we cover from time to time—from selection to retirement. Understanding some of the key points of the recruitment and selection process is useful when you are looking for a job as well as when you are asked to serve on a search committee. When you become a supervisor, you will need to have a sense of what goes into a job description, how to orient and train new people, and how to handle the inevitable performance appraisal process.

HR departments expect and require library staff involvement, to some degree, in a number of key steps in the staffing process. Those steps are some variation of the following:

- Determining needs/succession planning
- Job design

- Recruitment
- Selection
- Orientation and training
- Evaluation
- Coaching and discipline
- Resignation and termination

Determining staffing needs is usually the responsibility of senior managers and consists of two lists. One is a wish list of positions that would be wonderful to have, if only funding were available; it is often a long list and it is a special occasion when a new FTE is finally funded. The second and shorter list covers expected vacancies—retirements, promotions, and resignations. It is up to the library to keep HR informed of expected vacancies. Knowing in advance what positions may become vacant and the timing may assist HR in doing some combination recruiting for several units, which should stretch limited advertising dollars and generate a stronger pool of candidates.

It almost goes with saying that the job design/description (JD) is the foundation for getting the best and brightest people. The U.S. Department of Labor suggests a process for developing job descriptions and deciding upon the proper selection instruments. The suggested process starts with the library's organizational goals that a particular job is to assist in fulfilling. (Note: every staff member holds a separate "position"; however, several people may hold the same "job"—for example, document delivery assistant.) Designing a job requires answering questions such as, "What activities are necessary to accomplish organizational goals?" Answering this apparently simple question is usually more complex than you might expect. It requires detailed information in order to be useful. Your goal is to be as comprehensive as possible in listing the tasks. Being too brief or broad only creates more work later in the process. For example, a response for a circulation service point should be more than "check out materials." It should cover all aspects of the work, such as checking the user's borrowing status, providing answers to questions about item availability or items the person could not locate, and deactivating security tags. Such detail is essential for developing sound job descriptions as it helps you identify the necessary skills and knowledge to successfully perform the work.

Another step is establishing job success criterion (JSC). JSCs are the keys to selecting the right person for the right position. This is also the most difficult and subjective of the steps in the model. While the goal of the process is simple to state—"What distinguishes successful from unsuccessful performance in the position?"—it is difficult to carry out. What constitutes success will vary from library to library and from time to time as the work changes. For example, being courteous to users is always important, but what if a person is courteous while providing incorrect information? What about a person who is great with users but is unwilling or unable to work well with other staff members? Thinking through the JSCs for a job makes it much easier to select the right person for the position. JSCs allow you to develop the best questions to ask the candidates, those that most accurately reflect the skills and knowledge needed for success.

Job specifications (JS) are the skills, traits, knowledge, and experience that, when combined, result in successful performance. JSs are what you see in job descriptions and advertisements, such as educational background or degree required, years of experience, and a list of the specific skills sought. From a legal point of view, these items must be BFOQ (bona fide occupational qualifications). Merely saying they are will not satisfy a court, if you are challenged. You must be able to prove that they are the skills, knowledge, and experience, a person ought to possess to succeed. You might like to have someone with a high school diploma, but can you prove that it is essential to succeed in the work? If you can't, don't make it a requirement; make it "desirable."

Having completed the above steps, you can decide what "instruments" you should use to assist in deciding which applicants to call in for an interview. Some instruments are ones that you know well—application forms, names of references, and letters of interest. Others that are less common are various tests of basic required skills—often handled by HR in order to winnow out individuals who don't possess the skill needed—such as a certain level of error-free keyboarding. Library skills tests, such as alphabetizing or ordering call numbers, are handled by the library. Whatever instruments you select, you must have a clear link back to the JSC and JS in the event that you are challenged in court.

Recruitment

Once you develop the JD, HR can commence the search for suitable applicants. Many large libraries conduct national searches for their librarian and other professional positions while drawing on the local labor market for their paraprofessional and clerical positions. Advertisements for openings ought to provide the basic job description information and indicate where and when a person should apply.

The search often begins as an internal process; that is, an announcement of a vacancy goes to the library's staff. In some organizations, the policy is to interview any internal candidates before going outside. More often, the search is both internal and external—with the internal applicant(s) having the advantage of knowing more about the nature of the open position and being a known quantity to the employer (often, but not always, a good thing). U.S. employers must place advertisements or recruit in places where persons in the "protected categories" (Civil Rights Acts) are likely to see position announcements.

Selecting the Pool

Most recruiting efforts generate a larger pool of applicants than it is feasible to interview. Deciding who to interview draws on information produced by the selection instruments you identified. The most common place to begin the sorting process is the application form and cover letter (when you apply for a position, keep this fact in mind; how carefully you prepare these documents often decides your chances of getting interviewed). Some of the factors to look for are if the person has the required skills, how carefully their materials are presented, and if the person supplies all the required information. A "gross" sorting of applicants just using basic issues such as those listed above usually will reduce the pool by a substantial number. A further reduction, if necessary, can be done by asking how many of the "desirable" skills/abilities the applicant possesses. Having a final interview pool of three to six people is likely to produce a person to whom you would like to make an offer. Because the selection process involves a substantial amount of subjectivity, having developed sound JSCs and JSs will assist in keeping the process as objective as possible.

Interviewing

We devote some space to the interview process because it will come into play when applying for a position and when you serve on a search committee. In both instances, it requires an understanding of the process as well as a good deal of practice to become effective as an interviewee or interviewer. What follows applies to both sides of the interview table.

A sound interview process has six important elements. First, there is the need to plan the process. Beyond the obvious—such as timing and place—some of the key planning issues are length of the interview, who to involve in the interview, the questions to ask, if there should be a tour, and how much time to devote to answering candidates' questions. As a candidate, you should also plan your questions about the position and institution.

The second element, and perhaps the most critical in a legal sense, is to carefully review the interview questions for their compliance with antidiscrimination laws; this is an area where HR staff can be of great assistance. You also want to have consistency and comparability of information about each candidate. Maintaining consistency in the questions and in the structure of the entire process for all the candidates is critical when it comes time to assess each one and make a final selection. Your questions *must* be job related. If you can't link each question to the job description, don't ask it. Asking a few open-ended questions gives candidates an opportunity to respond more fully and demonstrate some of their skills.

Below are a few examples of legal open-ended questions that could apply to a variety of vacant library positions:

- What would do you think your (current or former) supervisor would tell a friend about you?
- What are some of the special skills you would bring to this job?
- Tell us about who and what has motivated your work efforts in the past?
- Have you performed the work entailed by this position before? If so, when? Do you see any significant differences between then and now?
- Give the candidate a real-life situation and ask how the person would handle it. (The situation ought to relate to the work the person would be doing)
- What things do you like the most about your current position? What do you like the least?

- Tell us about one of the major accomplishments you made in your present position
- Tell us about the goals you set for yourself in terms of work
- What does the term "service" mean to you?
- What are some new work skills or knowledge that you believe would improve your performance on the job?
- What are your current career plans? Do you see them changing in the next three years? What do you envision for yourself over the long term?

The third element is having a segment of time when the candidate is given a clear sense of what the available position actually does and an overview of the library's operation and mission. Also, having some time to explain the relationship of the library to its parent body helps candidates make an informed decision should an offer be made. It is also the time for the candidate to ask the search committee questions.

A fourth element in the process is the "personal impact" of both the candidate and the interviewers on one another. Creating a relaxed and friendly atmosphere at the outset helps candidates become less nervous and thus more effective during the formal interview. Things such as tone of voice, eye contact, personal appearance and grooming, posture, and gestures on the part of both candidate and interviewer influence both parties. Keep in mind, in a culturally diverse community, the meanings of the above may be very, very different. For example, lack of eye contact does not always mean the person is the "shifty-eyed character" of English novels.

Related to impact is how the interviewer responds to the applicant (the fifth element). Interviewers must be careful to control any nonverbal behavior that may encourage or discourage the applicant in an inappropriate way. Not showing an interest in what the candidate is saying will discourage the person from expanding on her/his thoughts, and this may well carry over to the remainder of the interview. Anyone with extensive interviewing experience understands just how difficult controlling those two behaviors can be at times.

The final element is to assess the interview data fairly and equitably for all the interviewees. Some of the issues that can cause unfair processing are:

- Stereotyping the "right" person for the position
- Using different levels of importance for various attributes by different members of a search committee
- Overusing visual clues about the candidate that are not job-related
- Not recognizing "contrast effects"—that is, when a strong candidate follows a very weak candidate, the contrast makes the stronger applicant look even stronger than she/he may be

Here are some suggestions to keep in mind when you are being interviewed:

- Take some time to research the library and its parent organization ahead of time, their Web sites can tell you a great deal about them

- Generate a few questions about the library based on your research and your own interests
- If you did not receive a full position description, don't be shy about asking for one; take time to think of questions about the position
- Spend some time thinking about the answers you might give to questions that are likely to be part of the interview (for example, what interests you about this particular position? What do you consider your strengths and your weaknesses? What does the term "service" mean to you?)
- Dress appropriately
- Be on time
- Be certain to have the interviewer's/chairperson's name and its correct pronunciation
- Remember that your "body language" also reflects your interest and attentiveness
- Taking time to think before answering complex questions is appropriate—thinking before speaking is always a good idea
- When asked a multi-part question, be sure to cover all the parts; asking for clarification or for repetition of such questions is appropriate
- Asking how any personal or potentially illegal question(s) *relate to job performance* is appropriate; however, be sure to ask in a nonconfrontational manner, as the question may be job-related
- Thank the interviewer(s) for the opportunity to interview for the position
- Asking about the anticipated time frame for on the decision of who will be hired is appropriate
- To learn from each interview experience, jot down a few post-interview notes about some of the high and low points of the interview
- Even if you decide during the interview process that this is not the position for you, send a follow-up thank-you note to the chair of the search committee, position supervisor, or head of HR (whichever is most appropriate), thanking them for their time and for giving you an opportunity to meet with them

Earlier, we mentioned the care you need to take when asking applicants questions because it is illegal to pose queries on certain topics that could lead to discriminatory hiring practices. What should you do if you are asked inappropriate questions, and is this likely to happen? An article by Marilyn Gardner (2007a) indicates it happens more often than you'd expect, especially with medium- and small-sized organizations, in part because people are not aware they are doing anything wrong. In her article she quotes John Petrella, an employment lawyer: "It happens all the time. . . . It's really easy for employers to get in trouble. It's really easy to run afoul of the antidiscrimination laws" (p. D1). The article goes on to address what to do if you are asked improper questions and offers different approaches to consider before you respond to such questions. First, ask yourself, and perhaps the interviewer, "Is this question related to the position I'm applying for?" Remember, the question could be appropriate if it is clearly job related. At the same time you might want to consider, "Do I really want to work for an organization that asks such questions?" You do have the choice of not answering the question knowing it might cause you not to get an offer. You can of course answer the question and then inquire as to the relevance of the question to the position. There is a reasonable chance that you will have to deal with this issue at some point in your career, as an interviewee—try not to do it when you are the interviewer.

We would like to include a few final words about staffing and providing quality service to all. Hall and Grady (2006) made several very significant points about providing library service to a diverse user community and staffing patterns that may or may not reflect diversity:

> We have to recognize that the whole process of information access and mediation, especially in the context of public libraries, brings up issues around hierarchy, privilege, and access. The question of who is behind that desk dispensing information and who is in front of it seeking information is in many ways a question of power. . . . Hiring in a manner that reflects this diversity and empowering staff to participate in collection development and create and offer programming is not about truism. . . . It's about seeing the payoff in increased visits, circulation, and funding opportunities. (pp. 45–46)

STAFF DEVELOPMENT, TRAINING, AND RETENTION

Once a person has been selected and has accepted the position, you should develop a plan for orienting the individual to both the position and the library. Sometimes people forget that the first few days on the job set a pattern for the new person that can be either negative or positive. Essentially, these first few days are critical to fitting in, retention, and the person's views about the library as well as its long-term training/development program. A well-thought-out orientation, including the training required for the position, will make it more likely that you will retain the person. Too often the first days focus only on the activities of the position; that is natural as in most cases the position has been vacant for a month or more and work has stacked up. If you fall into this trap, you may find yourself having a higher staff turnover than anyone would like.

Generally, the first week should be equally divided between position training and learning about the library and its parent organization. For most people, the first days on a new job are stressful and confusing. The common practice of taking the "new person" around to meet everyone, assuming there are more than a dozen people to meet, leaves the individual with a blur of faces, a few names (rarely connected to the right face), and a vague sense of what others do. Breaking the process up over several days gives the new person a better chance to absorb information and make meaningful connections. Starting with the "home" unit and working out through units that feed into and receive output from the home unit allows the new person to gain a sense of where her/his position fits in the scheme of things and how it is important to library operations. After that you can move on to other units to allow the person to gain an overall picture of operations. Linking a new person to someone at their level in the workgroup (a mentor) provides a personal connection for clarification or for questions that the person might be afraid to ask their supervisor, lest they be thought of as silly. It also helps the mentors by giving them recognition and the motivation to check over those points that are often taken for granted. One institution with a well-thought-out orientation program is the University of Washington (http://www.washington.edu/admin/hr/pod/newemp/).

Retention

A major concern for today's organizations is retaining their best people. Nora Spinks (2005) offered some interesting thoughts about generational differences and their impact on retention: "If you were a child in the 50s (a Boomer), you saw that working hard was a strategy that led to success. Loyalty was rewarded with long-term employment through to retirement. However, if you were a child in the 70s or 80s (a Nexus), you saw adults working hard and getting laid off, downsized or reengineered out of a job anyway. Employment tenure was out of your control, employers offered you a job as long as they felt you were of value, then let you go" (p. 11).

For many employers, their lack of "loyalty" to long-term staff is coming back to haunt them. "Why should I have any loyalty to the organization if it has none to me?" is a question in the minds of many workers today. For many of them, all it takes is hint of staffing changes—real or imagined—or something perceived to be a threat, and people start looking for other employment and in many cases actually leaving. They have experienced or heard of organizations that announce staff reductions and say in effect to the staff, "We don't need you but fully expect you to give a 100 percent work effort until the day you are terminated." When that happens, the outcome is what you would expect—performance declines and people leaving as quickly as possible. Although the pattern is primarily seen in for-profit organizations, staff reductions in force (RIFs) are not unheard of in libraries.

Another retention factor that is just gaining the attention of researchers is "new-job regrets." This is something that about 25 percent of newly hired people experience (Gardner, 2007b). All too often the regrets arise from the employer overselling the nature of the position or some other aspect of the environment. If you properly followed the steps we outlined above and the individual had a copy of the job description prior to accepting the offer, there should be few problems related to the nature of the work. Where you may unknowingly oversell is when you really need to fill the position and fall into the trap of making the institution, opportunities, benefits, and so forth better than they actually are. In the long run, overselling or misrepresenting the position makes for very unhappy people—both the new hire and yourself. When the remorse is very strong, the probability that the person will quit is extremely high.

Training and Development

One key method for gaining and retaining staff loyalty, is to have programs that give ample opportunities for staff to grow and develop. Without doubt this will help with the long-term retention of the best and brightest people. You have two basic training/development areas to consider—specific job-related skills and career development competencies and opportunities.

We all know that libraries face a rapidly changing technological environment. Keeping staff current with the changes related to their activities is a major challenge, especially when budgets are static. It is also crystal clear that failing to maintain staff skills will result in users receiving poorer service, which in turn leads to user dissatisfaction. Technology carries with it two financial challenges—acquiring and upgrading requisite technology and funding staff training.

Certainly training and development goes beyond technological issues. Some of the other major areas include training for individuals moving into supervisory positions and keeping staff up to date on changing professional standards. Other areas for public service personnel are handling "problem" users, customer service, disaster recovery, emergency procedures, security, and changing legal issues.

Professional associations can and do provide excellent training opportunities. Annual conventions often have workshops and other continuing education programs as part of their overall program. Unfortunately, there are very few such organizational opportunities for support staff; this seems to be changing, at least with the ALA, where the annual conference started a "conference within a conference" for support staff. (The primary reason is that there is limited financial assistance for support staff travel. In addition, their salaries are substantially lower, making it difficult for many of them to pay for such opportunities on their own. Thus, groups such as COLT have difficulty attracting enough people to a workshop to make the effort worthwhile.) As more educational institutions and professional bodies extend the range of distance education programs, training opportunities are increasing for support staff—particularly via "Webinars" and video conferencing. Notable examples of these training opportunities are the SirsiDynix Institute (http://www.sirsidynixinstitute.com/), the "Soaring to Excellence" series (http://www.dupagepress.com/COD/index.php?id=980), or the programs available through OCLC's WebJunction (http://www.webjunction.org).

In addition to concerns about funding, libraries face the problem of limited staffing, at least in most services. When staff is limited, it becomes difficult to have employees away at training programs for any length of time. Some jurisdictions are so short-sighted that they refuse to give time off to attend training programs even when the staff member is willing to pay for the program—short-sighted because in time the staff member's services become less and less effective.

Singer and Goodrich (2006) outlined five critical factors for retaining and motivating library staff. These are principles for a supervisor to exemplify and to help employees perform as well.

- Focus: employees know what they need to do and what is expected of them
- Involvement: people support most what they help create
- Development: opportunities for learning and growth are encouraged
- Gratitude: recognition of good performance (formal and informal)
- Accountability: employees are responsible for their performance or lack thereof (pp. 62–63)

PERFORMANCE APPRAISAL

Singer and Goodrich's last point regarding accountability directly links to performance appraisal. Performance assessment takes two forms—ongoing daily review with occasional corrective action and an annual overall assessment.

In terms of corrective action, you should discuss poor performance as situations arise. Trying to avoid unpleasant interactions regarding performance and letting problems "slide" only hurts everyone in the long run. Being told that something was/is amiss during the annual performance review when it is too late to take corrective action causes anger, frustration, and poorer performance down the road. Furthermore, other employees will notice the lack of any corrective action and they are likely to conclude you don't really care about quality performance. When that happens, they are likely to let their work performance slide. By the time that happens, you face a highly complex situation that will be difficult to resolve. Finally, service to users also suffers, and that in turn can lead to a serious lack of user support.

There are some steps you can follow when you do need to take corrective action that can help make the process as effective as possible. Start by stating the purpose of the session; even if the situation has the potential for confrontation, speak calmly. Plan on letting the employee talk as much as possible. *Listening* is the key to having a successful session. Too often, there is a tendency to start planning one's response rather than listening and trying to *hear* what the person is saying. Silence, even a long one, serves a good purpose—it lets both parties think about what is taking place. Setting a time limit for the session can defeat the purpose of the session; it may take time to get the central issue(s). Expect the employee to be unhappy, upset, and probably argumentative, as well as the possibility that she/he may engage in a personal verbal attack on you. It is important, if difficult, not to take the attack very personally; above all do *not* respond in kind. Total resolution is not the only indication of a successful session. Sometimes it takes a series of sessions to reach a complete resolution. Try to end the session on a positive note and, if appropriate, schedule a follow-up session.

Your goal is to be as consistent as possible in your evaluations. Standards should not shift from one week to the next or, worse yet, vary from one employee to another. Remember you should be evaluating outcomes rather than the process (as long as the process does not cause trouble or problems for others). You shouldn't hold a new employee as closely accountable for an error as an older, experienced person. This does *not* mean that you ignore the newcomer's problem. Naturally, a person lacking the skill to do a task needs additional training rather than criticism. If the training does not work, then other adjustments will be necessary, including the different but occasionally necessary step of termination.

Something to consider before taking corrective steps is to think about your personal biases that might color your judgment of people and their performance. If the matter is serious, look at prior annual appraisals before moving ahead. When it is clear something should be done, think about the next appraisal (keeping in mind any and all personal biases), and then begin the counseling process. Keep in mind this may require further serious steps, especially if a person has a negative review for two years in succession. It is always wise to work collaboratively with HR in these situations.

Annual performance reviews are something that most people endure and almost never look forward to, much less enjoy. Neither the givers nor the recipients have great faith in the process or that much good will come out of what many view as an ordeal.

Probably the biggest challenge, and where the difficulty lies, is in the dual nature of the review process. Although most HR departments attempt to keep it to a single purpose, performance enhancement, the reality that is there is sometimes an unofficial but real link to salary increases. The dual purpose is well documented, but most clearly articulated by Saul Gellerman (1976). Essentially the single process attempts to handle behavioral issues (work performance) and administrative issues (compensation and occasional promotions). The two purposes are almost diametrically opposed in character. To be effective in improving performance, the process should be open and candid. From an administrative perspective it should be closed and secretive. Trying to accomplish both in a single process is a challenge to say the least. Almost every employee believes the salary aspect is the dominant factor. (See the Further Readings section at the end of this chapter for more about this complex and rather unpopular aspect of work life.)

If you give constant honest feedback throughout the year—both praise and correction—the annual review will be as painless and stress-free as possible. There is no way to remove the salary component as long as the parent organization, directly or indirectly, uses reviews as part of its salary deliberations/considerations.

In spite of your best efforts, there will be times when disciplinary action must take place. Needless to say, such action only follows after a number of counseling sessions have failed to resolve the issue. In the United States, HR units label the process "progressive discipline." What the process consists of is a series of steps that become progressively more severe and can end with termination. Most of the time, the process never reaches the termination stage as the parties resolve the issue earlier. The sooner you address performance issues, the less likely it is you will have to go through the stress of a formal grievance procedure.

PART-TIME STAFF

There is a tendency to pay little attention to part-time staff in the literature. We think this is unfortunate as often the work of part-timers is critical to quality public service—just think about those who reshelve collections materials, most of whom are part-time people, and the impact on quality of service.

Students

Although you will encounter part-time people in almost any job category, there are two very common part-time groups in libraries—student assistants and volunteers. These two groups, especially students in educational library settings, may come close to the equivalent of full-time staff in terms of hours worked. (A 2005 survey by the Association of Research Libraries [ARL] noted that the average number of student workers exceed, by a slight margin, the average number of full-time personnel in public services.) For many libraries, quality service would not be possible without the aid of part-time students and volunteers. The work such individuals perform should receive the same attention and thought you give to full-time jobs.

Almost all libraries associated with educational institutions make extensive use of student labor. No matter what type of library—college, school, or university—the students have, or should have, the proper handling of their studies as their primary objective. Working in the library, even for pay, is much lower priority and that fact must be kept in mind when using student labor. Many public libraries also use students for positions such as "pages"/stack maintenance personnel. (One of this book's authors, while in high school, began his library career as a page for the branch librarian who had read books to him during "story hours.") At public libraries, unlike at academic institutions, the part-time students are viewed as any other part-time staff members, except that perhaps they are given a little slack during exam periods.

Looking at the early literature about using students as employees, you probably would come away with the view that student workers are too much trouble and not the worth the effort. The focus then was on the limitations/problems of employing students. Such an emphasis may have been necessary to work out the issues. We believe part of the problem did and can lie in not spending enough time on preplanning and developing true job descriptions for what the students will do. What is clear today is that educational libraries are very dependent on such labor.

Beyond the obvious benefit of having valuable work accomplished at a modest cost, students bring several benefits to the library. One benefit, in our view, is that as peers/classmates they are often viewed as more approachable than the full-time staff. This is especially true when the student body's cultural composition and that of the full-time staff is markedly different. Student employees are much more likely to have a sound idea of what technologies students use and how and when they use the technologies. Such information can be of great value when planning a new service or a different approach to an old one. Yet another benefit is that students can assist full-time staff in understanding "where the students are coming from"—they relate more effectively to the primary service population. Finally, they are the pool from which to recruit individuals to our field.

Certainly you need recognize the generational differences regarding work expectations and the workplace when adding students to the staffing mix.

There only a few of us "Traditionalists" (born before 1945) still working in libraries, and most of us are working as volunteers rather than as paid staff. Such individuals worked in highly structured workplaces for almost all their careers and are comfortable with a hierarchical system. They believe in hard work, commitment, and loyalty.

"Boomers" (1946–1964) are the largest of the generations in the workplace as well as in the population. They are now mostly in the senior positions in libraries. When they entered the workforce, there was great competition for available jobs; further, they faced a highly competitive work environment for much of their careers. Generally they are less inclined to teamwork, in the sense of the term today. They were also the first generation to experience significant layoffs, which often reinforced their need to be competitive and independent.

Generation X (1965–1980) is a much smaller cohort. These are the people who will begin to fill the senior positions in libraries as Boomers retire—a process that is now under way. They grew up pretty much on their own—with two working parents or in a single-parent home—sometimes referred to as latchkey children. Generally, they are very independent, having strong doubts about authority and loyalty. Often they value their "free" time more highly than doing extra work to earn more money, even when that work might lead to a promotion. They are much more comfortable with self-managed teams than are the Boomers.

Millennials (1981–1999), the most recent group to enter the workforce, are even fewer in number than Generation X. This generation will not face strong competition for positions given their small numbers; in fact it is likely the employers will be ones facing competition. They were the first generation to grow up in a technology-filled world—it was not new, it was just the way world was. Technology is something they are comfortable with; they expect it to work properly and on demand. Their expectation of a quick response often carries over into their workplace expectations. Employers are finding that Millennial generation employees have little patience when it comes to waiting for promotions and are quick to leave organizations. Teams have been a natural part of their growing up in school via highly structured group activities such as sports, so work teams do not seem unnatural to them.

When you have a mix of generations in the workplace, as do most libraries, there are motivation challenges to address. With large numbers of student workers, you add to the complexity. You will probably need to employ different approaches for the students than you do with the older full-time staff.

Just as you want to retain full-time staff, you want to retain student workers for as long as possible. There is the obvious built-in student turnover; however, keeping the best workers for as long as possible lowers your training costs as well as some of your supervision costs. One step to take, even if it is not well implemented with the full-time staff, is to create student work teams. As noted above, Millennials are team-oriented and need little assistance fitting into team duties and responsibilities. Consider building teams around a set of duties rather than scheduled work times. In the past, a duties approach was difficult at best and often impossible. What with texting, cell phones, e-mail, and the like, students are "in touch" all the time. A team that seldom has more than one member on duty at any time can still be very effective in today's technological environment.

Teams need leaders, and this provides you with opportunities for promotion and rewards. With multiple work schedules, there may be opportunities for assistant leaders. Such a structure may also allow you to create a "student career ladder" with appropriate pay differentials.

Regardless of how you structure the work, students should be held just as accountable for the quality of their work as full-time staff. (This also applies to volunteer workers.) Having different standards of accountability can and probably will lead to major morale problems and low-quality overall performance for the library.

Sound mentoring is effective in recruiting people to our field. Students tend to be open to mentoring when it focuses on issues they perceive as relevant. If for nothing more than helping them to learn appropriate work behavior and dress, this is useful activity. We have only touched on a few of the benefits of using student workers. We highly recommend you spend some time reviewing Kimberly B. Sweetman's *Managing Student Assistants* (New York: Neal-Schuman, 2007). Although its primary focus is on academic libraries, it has much to offer anyone thinking about or using student employees.

Volunteers

Library volunteers play a growing role in daily operations. They are likely to become even more common as more and more of the Boomer generation retires. Many small libraries (rural, school, and church) are totally dependent on volunteers, with perhaps a retired person with library experience taking a lead role. Other libraries may be less dependent on volunteer assistance, but still use such services for important tasks.

During the late 1990s, there was a major effort to increase volunteerism in the United States Although there is less government emphasis today, volunteer service hours grow steadily. In the last edition of this book, we mentioned what was then a new youth volunteer program in the St. Paul Public Library. Looking at the library's Web site it is clear the program is very vigorous and more diverse as of late 2007.

No matter what value you place on the work, as of 2007, many granting agencies currently allow you to use a $17.93 per hour rate for valuing volunteer service, and the annual contribution is in the billions of dollars. While volunteer work is increasing there is concern about being able to retain volunteers. Daniel Kadlec (2006, p. 76) reported that "Nearly 38 million Americans who had volunteered in a nonprofit in the past didn't show up last year . . . That is a waste of talent and desire." The "last year" in the quote was 2005. Organizations cannot waste such potential people power. As Boomers retire, they take with them a vast amount of experience and, perhaps more importantly, institutional memory that is very valuable. You will find frequent stories in the professional literature about library staff members retiring and then returning as volunteers. Losing such people because the volunteer activities have not been properly planned is/would be very sad.

You have a vast pool of talented, energetic, and motivated volunteers to tap into and, hopefully, retain. Volunteers can become highly committed to a library's organizational goals, given the proper environment, even if they never worked in a library. Part of that environment is thinking about volunteers as just as important to quality service as any paid staff member.

Begin your thinking and planning for volunteers by considering a few basic questions:

- Should we use volunteers? (A very key question to ponder)
- Where could we use volunteers?
- How would we use them?
- Would the tasks be meaningful for volunteers?
- Who would supervise the volunteers?
- Would we have one person in charge of the overall program?
- Do we have or can we create meaningful volunteer rewards?

Dale Freund (2005) explored the question of whether volunteers should be used in libraries. He believed that when done properly and for the right reasons, the answer is yes. Essentially, success hinges on your thinking through questions such as the above and creating a plan.

There are three major volunteer categories to think about, at least in the United States. One is the "short-term" volunteer. These are people who will work on special projects or events, but have no interest in a regular commitment, such as coming in one day per week for a few hours. Some library examples are an annual book sale, disaster recovery efforts, or a capital fundraising campaign. A second category is the "commitment" volunteer. These are people who have a strong interest in the area in which they seek volunteer opportunities. They expect to gain gratification, knowledge, and useful skills as well as a sense of accomplishment from the work they perform. For most libraries, these are the people who form the backbone of a successful long-term volunteer program. They are also the group that requires the most careful planning and needs the most meaningful work to perform.

Finally, there are "volunteers" who engage in the activity because of some outside pressure rather than any personal desire. You may be able to transform some of these people into committed volunteers, but only through careful planning. There are two significant sources of outside pressure—the workplace and school. Many for-profit organizations, while not making volunteering mandatory, make it very clear they expect employees to engage in some form of volunteer work. Such organizations normally have a very broad definition of what constitutes volunteer work and how that activity counts in the performance review process. A few colleges and universities have gone so far as to make volunteer work a graduation requirement. Most don't go that far, but they do encourage students to volunteer, often through such means as adding it to the student's transcript, offering credit for the approved activities. They have been rather successful, for example, in 2005, more than 3.3 million college students engaged in service to some nonprofit organization and averaged just under 100 hours per student (Pope, 2006, p. A1).

Where do you begin your search for volunteers? Your recruiting efforts will not take place in the same venues as for paid staff. There are five major places to explore; each requires a somewhat different approach both in the message and where to place that message. The pools are:

- Retirees
- Students
- Homemakers
- Employed people
- Unemployed people (most hope to gain a marketable skills or perhaps secure a paid position with the organization)

Reaching out to students, the employed, and the unemployed is relatively easy as you have organizations to contact that will assist in getting your message out. Retirees are a little more challenging; however, senior centers and other locations that offer senior programs are a good starting point. Homemakers are the biggest challenge; in this case school libraries have an inside track on getting great volunteers.

The best way to develop a cadre of committed volunteers is to start with job descriptions, using the same method as you do for paid staff positions. Doing this provides a solid base for everyone about the "whats and hows" of the position(s). Surprises such as "I don't want to make photocopies" are much less likely when the person had an opportunity to review a JD indicating photocopying was part of the job. As with paid positions, the JD should outline duties and experience/skills sought. (Note: after preparing the descriptions it is wise to consult with the HR department to explore any issues such as injury and liability coverage for volunteers.)

When it comes to volunteers, you rarely have a pool of "applicants" to interview—you are happy to have someone interested in the position. That notwithstanding, the interview is just as important for volunteers as it is for paid staff. This is the opportunity to assess skills, motivation, and the nature of the work by both parties.

Motivation is critical for volunteers, if you expect to keep them. Years ago, William M. Marston (1979) identified four basic personality types (the concept has taken on a number of labels over the years). Marston's original labels—dominance (D), influencing (I), steadiness (S), and conscientiousness (C)—are as good as any. People of type D personality are action-oriented—get something done, seek quick results, solve the problem now. "I"s are socially oriented; they are verbal and enjoy interacting with people; being liked is important to them. "S"s are dependable and steady; they prefer to focus on one task at time and whenever possible they want a workplace where they can concentrate on the task at hand. "C"s are focused on standards/procedures in addition to being very detail-oriented. The following also applies to any group of employees, especially part-timers.

Take some time to think about yourself in light of the above, and then think about your volunteers and where you think each one fits into the categories. Here are some tips regarding how you might want to interact with the various types. If you have a "D" personality, your usual style works well with "D" volunteers. When it comes to "I"s, be less formal than you normally are. Take your time when working with "S" volunteers. Be certain to present facts/evidence when working with your "C"s.

If you are an "I" type person, avoid your usual "small talk" with "D" volunteers. Obviously, being yourself works well with your "I" type volunteers. Go against your normal style and be rather formal at first and stay focused on activities when starting off "S" volunteers. With "C"s, drop your normal approach and just deal with facts.

If you are an "S," maintain your confidence in how to do things when working with "D" volunteers—they can be a challenge for you. Be more open than usual when working with "I" volunteers; remember they are people-oriented. "S" volunteers will call for more than your usual level of support/encouragement. Even if no "standard" exists, you must firm about what you require when working with "C"s, especially when they think it is nonstandard.

Finally, if you are a "C," be less fact-oriented than usual, just hit the main/high points when working with "D" volunteers. Although it may require lots of effort on your part, try to be as informal as possible, while conveying the facts, when working with "I"s. Be patient and present facts/issues completely when working with "S" volunteers. Being yourself is fine when it comes working with "C"s.

Just as is the case with paid staff, providing lots of positive feedback is essential for volunteers. However, this does not mean you shouldn't correct problems with volunteer performance. When it does become necessary, do it in as positive a manner as possible. (Volunteers can be quick to leave if they don't think their efforts are appreciated.) Forgetting to thank them each time they come in can be, and often is, viewed as being taken for granted and cause for leaving.

Generally, volunteers require more initial training and development than paid staff. This is particularly true when the volunteer has retired from a somewhat similar paid position—for example, a retired school librarian volunteering in an archive. They need time to unlearn years of past practices and/or modify beliefs about "how things should be done." Too often the supervisor's assumption is that such people have done this before and therefore need very little training. It may be a while before it becomes apparent that that was a poor assumption and work must be redone.

There is no doubt that volunteers provide wonderful assistance to thousands of libraries, as our opening quotation by Sue McCown suggests; however, there are a few areas in which tension can arise between volunteers and paid staff. One obvious area is a fear/concern about job security, especially where funding is tight or hiring freezes are in place. Paid staff may harbor unstated worries that their jobs may be in jeopardy, especially if some of the volunteers have prior library experience. We are unaware of any documented case where paid staff lost their jobs because of the availability of volunteers. However, we do know of instances where layoffs took place because of funding problems and sometime later the organization restarted a service based on volunteer help. When starting a volunteer program you should address this concern openly and honestly with the paid staff.

Another challenge is when volunteers and paid staff perform the same task(s), something to avoid whenever possible. When it does happen, performance assessment becomes a significant issue. There may be strong resentment of the volunteers apparent freedom to come and go with little or no notice and the appearance that they are held to a lower work standard. Paid staff may also think/observe the volunteer(s) receiving encouragement/praise for work they believe is less than standard, or at least a lower standard than they are expected to deliver. Your managerial creativity and ingenuity will face great challenges when you try to provide that extra level of encouragement to volunteers and retain their services, while not undermining staff morale.

SUMMARY

Many years ago John D. Rockefeller is supposed to have said, "I will pay more for the ability to deal with people than any other ability under the sun." Whether he said that or not, the sentiment is the key to having quality library services; hire top-notch people and retain their services and loyalty. To be able to do that you need to follow sound people-planning practices and thoughtfully design their work activities.

It may not seem likely right now that you will need much of the information in this chapter; however, we anticipate that paraprofessionals will play an ever-growing role in quality library services. Those roles will call for greater involvement in personnel matters, from, how to select the right person, to how to supervise and motivate team members whether they are full- or part-time or volunteers.

Chapter Review Material

1. What are the typical employee categories in most libraries?
2. Which label do you prefer for nonlibrarian positions in libraries? Explain your preference.
3. What are the major steps in the staffing process?
4. Why is the job description such an important document?
5. In what ways do student workers differ from other library employees?
6. Do you think volunteers are more or less valuable to libraries? Explain your position.

REFERENCES

Association of Research Libraries. 2005. *ARL Statistics Interactive Edition.* http://www.fisher.lib.virginia.edu/arl.

Christianson, Elin. 1973. *Paraprofessional and Nonprofessional Staff in Special Libraries.* New York: Special Library Association.

Curran, William. 2006. "The 8Rs and Training Needs." *Argus* 35, no. 2: 29–33.

Drickhamer, David. 2006. "Putting People First Pays Off." *Material Handing Management* 61, no. 6: 42, 44–45.

Freund, Dale. 2005. "Do Volunteers Belong in the Library?" *Rural Libraries* 25, no. 1: 19–41.

Gardner, Marilyn. 2007a. "Job Interviewers: What Can They Legally Ask?" *Arizona Daily Sun*, July 29: D1, D4. (Also printed as "What You Need to Know about What They Can Ask," *Christian Science Monitor*, July 23, 2007.)

———. 2007b. "New-Job Regrets: Should You Go or Stay?" *Arizona Daily Sun*, Sunday, August 12: D1, D4.

Gellerman, Saul. 1976. *Management of Human Resources.* New York: Holt Rinehart.

Gorman, Michael. 1987. "The Organization of Academic Libraries in the Light of Automation," *Advances in Library Automation and Networking.* Greenwich, CT: JAI Press.

Hall, Tracie D., and Jenifer Grady. 2006. "Diversity, Recruitment, and Retention: Going from Lip Service to Foot Patrol," *Public Libraries* 45, no. 1: 39–46.

Harvard Business Review. 2007. "Service With a Very Big Smile." 85, no. 5: 24.

Hoffman, Shannon L. 1993. "Who Is a Librarian?" *Library Mosaics* 4, no. 4: 8–11.

Kadlec, Daniel. 2006. "The Right Way to Volunteer." *Time* 168, no. 10 (September 4): 76.

Kaye, Alan. 2006. "Library Profile: Roddenbery Memorial Library," *E-news@PLA* 9, no. 8. http://www.ala.org/ala/pla/plamemonly/plaenewsletter/2006archive/27oct2006.cfm

Marston, William M. 1979. *Emotions of Normal People.* Minneapolis, MN: Persona Press.

McGown, Sue W. 2007. "Valuable Volunteers." *Library Media Connection* 26, no. 2: 10–13.

Pope, Justin. 2006. "College Volunteers Skyrocket." *Arizona Daily Sun*, October 16: A1, A7.

Singer, Paula, and Jeanne Goodrich. 2006. "Retaining and Motivating High Performing Employees," *Public Libraries* 45, no. 1: 58–63.

Spinks, Nora. 2005. "Talking about My Generation," *Canadian Healthcare Manager* 12, no. 7: 11–13.

Support Staff Interest Round Table. 1999. *Task Force on Career Ladders.* Chicago: American Library Association.

———. 2000. *Task Force on Access to Continuing Education & Training Opportunities.* Chicago: American Library Association.

SUGGESTED READINGS

Armstrong, Sharon, and Madelyn Applebaum. 2003. *Stress-Free Performance Appraisals.* Franklin Lakes, NJ: Career Press.

Bliss, Elizabeth S. 2006. "Staffing the Small Public Library," *Rural Libraries* 26, no. 1: 7–28.

Chon, John M., and Ann L. Kelsey. 2004. *Staffing the Modern Library: A How-To-Do-It Manual.* New York: Neal-Schuman.

Davenport, Thomas. 2005. *The Care and Feeding of Knowledge Workers.* Boston: Harvard Business School Press.

Division of Library Development, Connecticut State Library. 1997. *Guidelines for Using Volunteers in Libraries.* http://www.cslib.org/volguide.htm

Driggers, Preston, and Eileen Duma. 2002. *Managing Library Volunteers.* Chicago: American Library Association.

Evans, G. Edward. 2004. *Performance Management and Appraisal: How-to-Do-It.* New York: Neal-Schuman.

Giesecke, Joan, and Beth McNeil. 2005. *Fundamentals of Library Supervision.* Chicago: American Library Association.

Goodrich, Jeanne. 2005. "Staffing Public Libraries: Are There Models or Best Practices?" *Public Libraries* 44, no. 5: 277–281.

Holcomb, Jean M. 2006. "The Annual Performance Evaluation: Necessary Evil or Golden Opportunity?" *Law Library Journal* 98, no. 3: 569–574.

Hurt, Tara Ludlow, and Deborah Stansbury Sunday. 2005. "Career Paths for Paraprofessionals: Your Ladder to Success," *Library Mosaics* 16, no. 1: 8–11.

Kutzik, Jennifer S. 2005. "Are You the Librarian?" *American Libraries* 36, no. 3: 32–34.

Miller, Corey E., and Carl Thornton. 2006. "How Accurate Are Your Performance Appraisals?" *Public Personnel Management* 35, no. 2: 153–162.

Oblinger, Diana. 2003. "Boomers, GenXers, & Millennials: Understanding the New Students," *EDUCAUSE Review* 38, no. 4: 37–47.

Osa, Justlina, Syliva Nyana, and Clara Ogbaa. 2006. "Effective Cross-Cultural Communication to Enhance Reference Transactions," *Knowledge Quest* 35, no. 2: 22–24.

Parsons, Martha. 2005. "Are Library Support Staff Up to the Challenge?" *Library Mosaics* 16, no. 3: 18–19.

Reed, Sally G. 1994. *Library Volunteers—Worth the Effort: A Program Manager's Guide.* Jefferson, NC: McFarland.

Smith, Sandra. 2004. "From Beginnings to B.R.A.I.N.C.E.L.L.S.: Training at Denver Public Library," *Colorado Libraries* 30, no. 2: 18–20.

Stanley, Mary J. 2008. *Managing Library Employees.* New York: Neal-Schuman.

Todaro, Julie, and Mark L. Smith. 2006. *Training Library Staff and Volunteers to Provide Extraordinary Customer Service.* New York: Neal-Schuman.

Tunstall, Pat. 2006. "The Accidental Supervisor," *Public Libraries* 45, no. 3: 50–57.

Uchitelle, Louis. 2006. *The Disposable American: Layoffs and Their Consequences.* New York: Knopf.

Chapter 3

Customer Service

Excellence in customer service leads to greater use of library services, better coordination with other departments, and a greater chance of ensuring the security of library funding.

—Debbie Schachter, 2006

The new wisdom has become: "Only customers judge quality: all other judgments are essentially irrelevant."

—E. Stewart Saunders, 2007

Libraries have a long history of providing services and for much of the last 100 years the focus has been on good customer service. One need only go back to the work of S. R. Ranganathan (an Indian scholar/mathematician/librarian) who played a leading role in developing modern librarianship in India. His *Five Laws of Library Science* (1931) was and still is the most succinct statement about what to consider when creating a collection or service that truly serves the end user—books are for use; every reader his book; every book its reader; save the reader's time; and a library is a growing organism. These laws have a very clear customer focus as well as being essential to providing economical service(s). Since its first publication, Ranganathan's basic concepts have proven their viability time and time again as well as their applicability to varying areas of the field. For example, Alireza Noruzi (2004) published a paper titled "Application of Raganathan's Laws to the Web," illustrating just how viable those five short statements are for the field:

1. Web resources are for use.
2. Every user his or her Web resource.
3. Every Web resource its user.
4. Save the time of the user.
5. The Web is a growing organism.

In the business world, the concept of customer service dates from at least the nineteenth century and the desire of retail stores, hotels, and restaurants to develop loyal customers who would provide repeat business and encourage their friends and colleagues to shop, sleep, or eat at the particular establishment. Beginning in the 1980s, many retail businesses paid renewed attention to customer service because market research indicated it was an effective way to attract and retain customers. Much research and hundreds of articles and books have been devoted to better meeting customer needs, and libraries began to pick up on the findings of this research and adapt these practices to improving their own customer service.

In this chapter, we explore the history and philosophy of customer service, why it is significant to libraries, and its applicability to public services. Further, we examine the importance of involving customers in library planning and decision-making processes, and the advantages to the library of doing so. We look at the relationship between service quality and customer satisfaction as well as how to determine quality service. We cover how to create a plan for developing a customer service program and present examples from the literature of successful customer service programs. Naturally we address technology and its increasing role in meeting our customers' needs, including those users who have special needs (such as enhanced monitors for those with visual impairments). Finally, we delve into training issues and the elements of a training program to promote good customer service practices and attitudes in the public service staff.

PHILOSOPHY OF CUSTOMER SERVICE

Given that libraries have a long tradition of being service organizations, it may seem odd to have a separate chapter on customer service in a book about library public services. However, since the 1990s there has been a strong movement among libraries to improve service by borrowing customer services techniques developed by the business community in the 1980s and 1990s.

As we noted earlier, attracting and retaining customers through programs specifically designed to produce loyalty to an organization's product or service became a popular marketing trend in the 1980s. Every organization needs repeat customers to survive and prosper. However, customers tend to remain loyal only as long as they are satisfied with the quality of the service or product provided. If these do not measure up or keep pace with changing customer preferences or needs, then repeat use cannot be ensured (Hernon et al., 1999). As Jurewicz and Cutler (2003) observed, "We have seen it in our own lives that as customer habits have changed, savvy businesses have changed their service strategies in an attempt to anticipate customer needs. . . . Too busy to go the mall? Buy from a catalog online and we'll send it to your door. Need to know when to update your online auction bid? Sign up for our service and we'll notify you. Want to know where your package is? Check our website and we'll track it for you" (p. 2).

Many businesses, such as supermarkets, car washes, hair salons, hotels, and restaurants, adopted customer service programs to attract and retain customers. One example of such practices in the not-for profit environment are college and university "heritage/legacies" programs, through which children of alumni have preference for admission.

Besides the service ethic present in libraries, economics is another motive towards adopting successful customer service methods. Academic, school, and public funding authorities are facing tighter financial situations, and evidence of good customer service helps libraries argue more strongly for support when budget priorities are decided, as our opening quotation from Debbie Schachter (2006) suggests. Satisfied customers are also more liable to support library funding. Another driving force, also influenced by economics and discussed in our chapter on assessment (Chapter 16), is the increased pressure of accountability on the part of publicly supported agencies. Libraries may address accountability with documentation of the outcomes of service programs, how they contribute to the mission of their parent institutions, and evidence of good customer service, at a minimum based on their level of satisfaction.

One may view customer service interactions as either transaction-based or relationship-based. "Transaction-based" service occurs at point of need; for example, when a person checks out a book or video. This is the kind of service that most organizations, including libraries, typically focus on. However, the realization that building loyalty is the best way to retain customers has caused many organizations to focus on "relationship-based" service. This is seen most clearly in the relationship that the public services staff sometimes develop with their user communities. Establishing a relationship with our customers through learning their reading or viewing interests allows us to recommend new titles as they arrive or new Web sites or databases. In academic institutions, librarians often develop collegial relationships with faculty and are able to offer specialized assistance with their research and teaching. Many Web 2.0 initiatives, described later in this chapter, are aimed at personalizing library services in an effort to make them more useful and attractive to library customers. Doing so increases the library's usefulness to its customers and their perceived value of library services.

We examined different labels currently in use for those who use library services in Chapter 1. Here we briefly mention some additional concerns about the word "customer." One issue is that it implies payment for a product or service, and, in a library context, implies that libraries are businesses. However, most library users do not pay for the services and resources they receive from libraries, at least not as directly as in a commercial transaction. For example, undergraduate college students often have their tuition paid for by their parents (who are usually not library customers), and faculty do not pay to use the library but in fact are paid by the institution to use it. Anyone, not just local taxpayers, may and does make use of many public library services without any payment. Students in elementary, middle, and high school have free access to school library/media center materials. However, libraries do in fact charge for some services, such as photocopies. The fees for "special services" are increasing in libraries as the pressure to engage in cost recovery mounts, thus blurring the distinction between free and fee and customer and patron.

The idea that libraries are businesses is anathema to many library staff as well the general public. It implies a paradigm shift. Businesses exist for the bottom line, to make a profit, and libraries clearly are not in the money-making business (usually far from it). Libraries provide intellectual value to their users, only some of whom pay for it through taxes, tuition, or user fees. This intellectual value, many argue, is a public good that enriches communities beyond dollars and cents. Equating (or reducing) libraries to the level of a capitalist enterprise transforms libraries from cultural icons to something like transitory storefronts.

We don't argue that libraries are a societal good whose value goes far beyond any measure that can be derived by cost analysis or return on investment. However, it is also true that libraries are under enormous pressure today to demonstrate evidence of accountability. As Weingand (1997) states, "librarians who flinch at the word *customer* are operating out of an outmoded paradigm. This older paradigm portrays the library as a "public good," with as high a ranking on the 'goodness' scale as the national flag, parenthood, and apple pie. As a public good, the library 'should' receive public support. However, today's library is in increasingly tight competition for declining resources, and unless it adopts and masters the language and techniques of its competitors, it faces a future of declining support and significance" (p. 3).

In their "Top Ten Assumptions for the Future of Academic Libraries and Librarians" (Association of College and Research Libraries [ACRL], 2008) the ACRL Research Committee listed as number seven, "As part of the 'business of higher education,' students will increasingly view themselves as 'customers' of the academic library and will demand high-quality facilities, resources, and services attuned to their needs and concerns." Another rationale, from a public library perspective, is provided by Walters (1994) when she states that "good service will result in customers voting for bond elections, contributing private dollars, and volunteering to support libraries. Poor service will result in lost elections and lost funding. It is as simple as that. Good customer service pays" (p. 1).

You may or may not agree with Weingand's and Walter's perspectives, which have taken on greater urgency with the appearance of information providers like Google and Amazon; however, borrowing and adapting the principles of customer satisfaction from the corporate world is a pragmatic way to improve library services and better serve our customers. It is also a way to demonstrate to those demanding accountability the value of the library to their organization and community.

Despite the reservations expressed above, and the authors' decision not to use the term "customer" throughout this text, in this chapter we will employ Hernon and Altman's (1998) definition that library "customers are the people who actually use, or are likely to use, the library's services" (p. 5), and we will explore the positive aspects about the customer paradigm for libraries. Many service organizations have begun focusing on relationship-based customer service as a way of distinguishing themselves. As Saunders (2007) observes, "Imposing a business model on libraries has been beneficial for library management" (p. 24). It is important for library staff to know what our customers want and need from our libraries, and how they value the resources and services they receive. The reason for this, summarized by Schachter (2006, p. 8), is that "Excellence in customer service leads to greater use of library services, better coordination with other departments, and a greater chance of ensuring the security of library funding." The following section describes some ways to assess your customers' needs in order to better satisfy them and provide quality service.

HOW TO DETERMINE CUSTOMER NEEDS AND SATISFACTION

In the chapter on assessment, we describe a number of data-gathering instruments used by libraries for various kinds of assessment. The following are the methods, quantitative and qualitative, used most often by libraries to ascertain customer needs and satisfaction.

Surveys

Surveys or questionnaires are the data-gathering methodologies most often used to ascertain customer needs and satisfaction (or dissatisfaction). Although most library staff are not trained in survey methodology, it is easy to find examples in the library literature of customer surveys conducted by all types of libraries. Survey instruments may be administered via the Web, mailed, emailed, or distributed in person to library customers. A survey can reach more people than interviews and focus groups, for example, and provides a more valid and reliable statistical sample.

LibQUAL+ (http://www.libqual.org/) is an assessment tool developed jointly by the ARL and Texas A&M University to measure library users' satisfaction. The survey is based on an earlier instrument, called SERVQUAL, developed to measure customer satisfaction in businesses. The instrument gathers users' opinions about service quality and is administered via the Web. The survey utilizes "gap analysis" to identify shortfalls (that is, the gap) that may exist between the level of services received and the level expected. Libraries have found LibQUAL+ to be particularly useful in enabling them to identify specific changes they need to make in specific services. For example, the University of Pittsburgh administered the study in 2002, and a major source of customer dissatisfaction was lack of complete journal runs. The library addressed this by purchasing digital back files for many journals, instituting document delivery for faculty and graduate students, and providing a shuttle connection to the off-site storage facility (Saunders, 2007). As of March 2007, more than 1,000 libraries have used LibQUAL+, including colleges and universities, community colleges, health sciences libraries, law libraries, and public libraries (Joubert and Lee, 2007).

As an aside, there may be something of a disconnect between how users think of customer service and instruments such as LibQUAL+. Instruments developed by librarians often include, unintentionally, library jargon that gets in the way of interpreting the results accurately. This issue is explored by an article titled "Academic Library Customer Values" that will appear in a late 2008 issue of *Library Management.*

Interviews

Interview data gathering involves an interviewer asking questions of one or more individuals, usually one participant at a time. Carefully structured questions limit the range of responses for interviewees to the areas of interest and make data analysis easier. Interviewing has gained increased popularity as library staff members have become more familiar with focus group methodology.

Focus Groups

Used by businesses since the 1920s, focus groups are essentially group interviews. They involve open-ended questions/topics that are designed to generate in-depth discussions with small groups, usually between six and ten individuals. The participants are purposely selected and led (ideally) by a trained facilitator, although resources do not always make this possible. The groups explore a predefined topic in a nonthreatening and semistructured setting. The goal is to obtain data about a single topic or limited range of topics from a user's perspective. The entire group answers questions together (Walden, 2006).

Libraries frequently employ focus groups to determine customer satisfaction and to explore the reasons behind their satisfaction or dissatisfaction with the services. While focus groups can provide a rich source of qualitative data about library services, the methodology is labor-intensive to perform, limiting its wider use. Focus groups are frequently used in conjunction with surveys to gather both qualitative and quantitative data about service.

Observation

Observation of customer behavior and staff behavior has been a popular data-gathering method since at least the 1960s. One popular method, called unobtrusive observation, involves someone (referred to in the business world as a "secret shopper") posing as a customer and asking typical questions in a reference or other service setting, then judging the quality of the staff member's response. Some libraries have used extensive observation programs, including videotaping, to assess service behavior and quality. However, observation is most commonly used informally by managers seeking quick information about customer service interactions.

In addition to the above-mentioned methodologies, customer requests and complaints are also an important source of information about their wants and needs. These requests or complaints may be made informally to library staff while they are assisting users or more formally through suggestion boxes, Web sites, or other Web 2.0 communication vehicles. Repeated requests or suggestions for particular services or resources should be taken seriously by the library administration.

CUSTOMER SERVICE PLAN

The most effective way to establish and maintain a customer service ethic is to plan for it. A good plan can improve customer relations and internal operations by refocusing them on customer needs. A service plan also empowers frontline staff to meet customer needs by giving them the flexibility to say "yes" to requests.

Hernon and Whitman (2001, pp. 77–87) offer the following steps towards mobilizing a service plan:

1. *Take control of the factors that influence service quality and satisfaction.* This involves understanding the factors that influence how service quality is defined, achieved, and assessed and how these factors relate to the mission of the library. Generally the development of a service plan begins with a vision or mission statement affirming the service tradition of the library. This is important to let customers know and help library staff to remember the service nature of the institution. For a customer service plan to work it is important for service to be part of library culture. At one end, where service is present but at a minimum level, the culture may be task oriented, focused on efficient completion of routine duties. At the other end, where customer satisfaction is the primary goal, administration and staff direct their energies toward that goal. There are points between the two polls, and libraries should be striving towards the service end.

2. *Set expectations for customers based on what can reasonably be delivered.* The library should explicitly define its customers' expectations so that it is in a position to meet them. A service plan should include an assessment of a library's market to determine customer wants and needs. It is important not to assume what customers want from the library. Next, library staff determines what services the organization will or is able to offer or needs to refocus on in order to meet those customer needs. It is important to listen to customers, but not to the exclusion of good sense, marketplace changes, and other developments. Some expectations revealed by customer surveys may be unrealistic, given available human and financial resources. For example, free babysitting was identified by library staff at a library customer service seminar as one of the top five services requested by customers that the library was not able to offer (Schroer, 2003). Service boundaries that are completely undefined will lead to staff frustration. Over the long term, this situation can lead to burnout as staff are not able to fulfill the wishes of every customer. An important contribution frontline staff can make to the development of the service plan is helping to set realistic service goals.

3. *Define the relationship between the customer and the library.* This could take the form of a simply worded pledge to customers guaranteeing their satisfaction. A formal service plan also includes the standards of expected performance or outcomes against which the actual

performance will be measured. For example, "Customers may expect to receive items requested through interlibrary loan within three to five days."

4. *Empower employees to satisfy customers.* Staff have a critical role in delivering service, and empowering them to make decisions should be part of all public services staff orientation and training. Frontline staff working under guidelines defined by school districts or city hall are probably least likely to be able to be empowered by library administrations.

5. *Ask for customer feedback.* Evaluating and measuring how well service is being delivered requires one or more feedback loops. We discussed some of the ways to do this above in the section on determining customer needs and satisfaction, and it is important to use these data to monitor policies, services, and operations.

6. *Respond to customers individually and collectively.* The results of assessment efforts and the library's complaint procedure should be shared with individuals and/or groups, along with the library's proposed or actual response to them (pp. 77–87).

Wehmeyer and colleagues (1996) distilled from the literature the following items of consensus about customer service plans.

- *Frontline staff are vital to the plan's success.* Frontline staff are usually the only library employees customers see, so their responsibility for the success of customer service is key. Experienced frontline staff know what reasonable service is given the circumstances of a particular library, and their input should be an integral part of developing the plan. Also, staff who are involved in the planning process tend to become invested in the program, and for the plan to succeed, staff must have a genuine commitment to customer service.

- *Service is a product.* Great service not only enhances the reputation of an organization, but adds value to the organization's services by enabling customers to use the resources effectively.

- *Understand your customer.* Formal research such as surveys and focus groups is important in helping the organization determine which services are important to its customers.

- *There is no quick fix.* Long-term, reliable, and effective customer service depends on regularly reviewing procedures, careful planning, and employee training (p. 174).

One segment of the population that public libraries, especially, need to remember to address is the poor. The *ALA Handbook of Organization* (ALA, 2007) begins its section on services to the poor with these words:

The American Library Association promotes equal access to information for all persons, and recognizes the urgent need to respond to the increasing number of poor children, adults, and families in America. These people are affected by a combination of limitations, including illiteracy, illness, social isolation, homelessness, hunger, and discrimination, which hamper the effectiveness of traditional library services. Therefore it is crucial that libraries recognize their role in enabling poor people to participate fully in a democratic society, by utilizing a wide variety of available resources and strategies (p. 54).

Many public libraries serve neighborhoods with poor residents who may have different needs for library services than their more affluent neighbors. However, the service needs of the poor may be difficult to ascertain through the methods identified above. Per capita book circulation is usually lower in poor neighborhoods, partly because of high illiteracy rates and because families fear incurring late fines or lost book charges. They often do not have stable mailing addresses or phone numbers. And the poor may be suspicious of attempts to "help" them.

Not including the poor in researching customer needs, however, risks marginalizing them further by not meeting their special needs. Libraries with significant poor populations must make extra efforts to connect with their customers by making repeated attempts in multiple formats to communicate.

Holt (2006) proposes the following steps to finding out what our poor customers need in terms of quality services and delivering them:

- Solicit information from members of poor households about the services they want and need
- Organize quality services based on the information gathered; for example, thematic book bags or boxes (going to the doctor, caring for a pet, telling time, etc.) that parents or children can check out without spending time at the online public access catalog (OPAC) or browsing the shelves
- Decide the limits of the services you will provide. For example, are GED and adult literacy classes appropriate for your clientele? If so, where do you shelve the materials and offer such programs?
- Deliver services at times convenient to users. Maybe the five-day work week in poor neighborhoods needs to be Wednesday through Sunday
- Deliver services at the right locations. If branch facilities are too small, where in the neighborhood can you offer programs? If public libraries want to attract kids, school visits are in order
- Make partnerships with agencies who know their neighborhoods and constituencies; for example, day cares, senior residences, and churches
- Publicize services in neighborhood venues like billboards, buses and rapid transit vehicles and stops, and ethnic and satellite radio stations
- Recognize that kids lead. Kids lead their parents in the selection of foods, study locations, and places that offer experiences they want

- Organize family experiences. For example, one library obtained a grant to pay for buses and organized evening family visits to a children's museum that waived fees to get new users
- Organize performance venues for kids. When kids perform, lots of adults attend (p. 184–185).

Two interesting examples of customer service plans are the National Agricultural Library (http://www.nal.usda.gov/about/policy/customerservice.shtml) and the State Library of Western Australia (http://www.slwa.wa.gov.au/custserv.html).

SERVICE QUALITY

An important aspect of customer service is service quality. According to Hernon and Nitecki (2001), service quality has been defined from at least four perspectives:

- *Excellence.* Although the mark of an uncompromising student and high achievement, the attributes of excellence may change dramatically and rapidly. Excellence is often externally defined
- *Value.* It incorporates multiple attributes, but quality and value are different constructs—one the perception of meeting or exceeding expectations and the other stressing benefit to the recipient
- *Conformance to specifications.* It facilitates precise measurement, but users of a service may not know or care about internal specifications
- *Meeting and/or exceeding expectations.* This definition is all-encompassing and applies across service industries, but expectations change and may be shaped by experiences with other service providers (p. 690).

Many library science researchers interested in service quality focus on the last definition. Quality is usually assessed employing "gap analysis"; that is, determining the gap between customers' expectations for a particular service or for the library in general, and the customer's perceptions about the library and its services. Service quality is "a means of reducing the gap between customer expectations and needs" (Hernon and Altman, 1996, p. 57). If the gap between expectations and perceptions is too great, this is defined as poor service. This model offers greater utility for decision making and planning than simple satisfaction surveys.

Both service quality and customer satisfaction may be ends in themselves, and often are, but quality is often the antecedent of customer satisfaction. Better quality service usually results in higher levels of customer service. Determining and trying to improve the quality of the services offered is therefore an important part of a commitment to customer service. A paradigm of excellent service quality encourages library staff to identify customer expectations and desires and commit the resources necessary to satisfy high-priority expectations.

Each library needs to determine for itself how to define quality customer service. Zeithaml and colleagues (1990, pp. 22–23) identify 10 dimensions of service quality:

- *Tangibles.* Appearance of physical facilities, equipment, personnel, and communication materials
- *Reliability.* Ability to perform the promised service dependably and accurately
- *Responsiveness.* Willingness to help customers and provide prompt service
- *Courtesy.* Politeness, respect, and friendliness of contact personnel
- *Empathy.* Caring and individualized attention that the firm provides its customers
- *Competence.* Required skills and knowledge to perform the service, believability, and honesty of the service provider
- *Security.* Freedom from danger, risk, or doubt
- *Access.* Approachability and ease of contact
- *Communication.* Keeping the customers informed in language they can understand and listening to them
- *Understanding the customer.* Making the effort to know customers and their needs

Each of the above dimensions has a number of variables contributing to good quality performance. For example, a survey of librarians and students by Hernon and Altman (1996, p. 71) revealed the following components of good quality communication:

- Ability to communicate with staff in other units of the library
- Ability to determine what the customer needs
- Ability to negotiate the library system and records (for example, the OPAC and Web page) to assist customers
- Conducting the reference interview beyond the initial question asked
- Offering referral
- Using follow-up questions inviting users to return

Customers will have different expectations regarding each dimension and component of quality service, and library staff cannot meet each one. Priorities will have to be established based on a particular library's customer needs and resources.

A distinction should be made between service quality and customer satisfaction. Customer satisfaction is only one component, albeit an important one, of service quality. Certainly our customers are the best judge of whether, and how much, they are satisfied with library services. But is it also true that "only customers judge quality: all other judgments are essentially irrelevant," as Saunders (2007) stated in our opening quotation? If a customer is satisfied with a reference transaction, but the answer she received is wrong, is this quality service?

One useful way to look at this question, taken from the service marketing literature, is described by William Edgar (2006). Edgar acknowledges that relying on customers' assessments of service satisfaction is applicable to libraries, but that it should not be the sole means by which a library measures its service. Customer assessment is valuable in evaluating the "functional component" of service; that is, a subjective measure of how a service is delivered ascertained through customers' own perceptions. This describes the manner in which staff handle a service transaction, and customer evaluation here is very important; however, this should be supplemented by an assessment of what Edgar calls the "technical component" of services, a more objective measure of what services customers receive from a library. This would include the accuracy of a reference answer, the quality of the library's book and journal collections, and the usability of the OPAC. Because of their training and experience, library staff are often much better equipped than their customers to judge the technical quality of the resources and services delivered. Library customers would be hard put to place a value on the library's collection, or judge whether the reference staff member consulted the best available sources to answer a reference question.

In our chapter on assessment, we describe many ways libraries work to evaluate the quality of their operations. The idea of determining quality has been extended from numbers measuring inputs and outputs to the relationship between customers and the library. Outcomes measurement (described in Chapter 16) is one way of describing this relationship, and customer satisfaction is another way. Customer assessment should be employed along with outcome measures in order to determine a balanced picture of a library's service quality. As Omidsalar and Omidsalar (1999) observe, "libraries cannot afford to place single-minded devotion to customer service at the foundation of their existence. They have to balance the momentary wants of their patrons with their best estimation of the long-term needs of a reading culture" (p. 25).

TECHNOLOGY AND CUSTOMER SERVICE

One of the strategies businesses are using to improve customer satisfaction is using technology to enable customers to shop for products and services. Libraries are also using technology to empower their customers to "shop" for services. Libraries are using the Internet and their Web sites as a major part of their information delivery systems. Library Web sites have gone from simply linking to their OPAC to offering online reference services, blogs, RSS feeds, wikis, meeting room reservations, digital newsletters, and various commercial and in-house databases, among other things.

The emergence of Web 2.0 tools allows new opportunities for libraries to provide services and satisfy changing customer needs and expectations. Web 2.0 refers to the evolution of the Web to being user-centered in that it allows users to create, change, and publish dynamic online content. It is essentially not a Web of textual publication but rather a Web of multimedia communication. In a library context, sometimes termed Library 2.0, these tools allow customers to participate in creating the resources and services they want.

Maness (2006) describes the following elements of Library 2.0:

- It is user centered. Users participate in the creation of the content and services they view within the library's Web presence, OPAC, etc. The creation of content is dynamic, and the roles of library staff and users sometimes overlap

- It provides a multimedia experience. Both the collections and services of Library 2.0 contain video and audio components

- It is socially rich. The library's Web presence includes users' presences

- It is communally innovative. This is perhaps the single most important aspect of Library 2.0. It rests on the foundation of libraries as a community service, but understands that as communities change, libraries must not only change with them; they must allow users to change the library

As library customers change, from the technologies they use to their demographics and expectations, libraries need to change along with them. Web 2.0 tools allow libraries the flexibility to adapt to changing environments.

Michael Stephens (2006) lists some of the uses libraries are making of Web 2.0 "social software" tools "in creating conversations, connections, and community":

- *Openness.* Libraries use weblogs to generate dialogue and tell the human story of the library.
- *Ease of use.* Libraries use instant messaging to perform virtual reference instead of hard-to-use proprietary platforms.
- *Innovation.* Libraries create subject-based wikis where users can suggest resources and ask questions.
- *Social interaction.* Comment-enabled weblogs allow users to get involved with library planning and programs.
- *Creation of content.* A library offers space and digital tools to create audio and video presentations, stories and more. (See the Public Library of Charlotte and Mecklenburg County's "ImaginOn" program for a good example: http://www.imaginon.org/index.asp).
- *Sharing.* A library feeds RSS content from various sources to other web pages within the local community.
- *Decentralization.* A librarian creates a Google Maps mash-up of the routes of library delivery vehicles.
- *Participation.* The library begins a wiki for its strategic plans, inviting all staff and users to participate in a vision for the future.
- *Trust.* Librarians release control of their data and utilize "radical trust" with their users and each other. Staff blog freely and informally (p. 32).

No doubt more tools like those described above are forthcoming.

As you might guess, allowing our customers into library resources that were formerly the exclusive domain of library staff is not without controversy. Some argue that we are in danger of deprofessionalizing libraries by allowing too much creative participation by our users. Web 2.0 technology is most effective if viewed as supplementing, not replacing, traditional library expertise. For example, allowing users to "tag" entries in our OPACs with their own descriptors, comments, reviews, and ratings does not replace the cataloging expertise required to assign controlled vocabulary subject headings. Tagging does, however, offer an additional means for customers to discover the contents of our OPACs and improves their utility. Using Web 2.0 tools is a customer-centered paradigm that seeks to reduce barriers to information, increase library knowledge of customer wants and needs, and improve customer satisfaction with library services and resources.

Providing access to Web 2.0 productivity tools (for example, Google Docs & Spreadsheets) has a dual advantage for libraries, especially small libraries. Online productivity software allows library users to write resumes, create newsletters, share documents, and do other tasks usually performed by Microsoft Office or Apple suites. And the online software allows them to create, store, access, and share their documents online for free, anywhere they can access a network connection. Empowering people to customize their own Web-based services in this way can be an important to step to lessening the technology gap between haves and have-nots, and will certainly create a loyal base of library supporters who utilize these services. Offering online productivity software is also an advantage for the library. It can be expensive to keep up with new versions of commercial office productivity software (e.g., Microsoft and Apple), both the software and hardware requirements, and providing access to, and training in, the alternative free software can allow the library to provide user services they could not otherwise afford (Gordon and Stephens, 2007).

In adapting new technology libraries need to be careful to avoid "technology lust" for new tools just because they are new. Technology is a tool; it is never a good reason to employ it just because you can. Tools should be adopted selectively, to meet identified customer needs, and should be regularly evaluated as part of the library's assessment program.

An example of the use of technology to meet identified customer needs is offered by the Contra Costa County Library (Butler and Kantor-Horning, 2007). Located in the eastern portion of the San Francisco Bay Area, Contra Costa County has the largest commuter population west of the Mississippi River. As part of developing a strategic plan, the library gathered information from the community in order to help identify library priorities. Among the findings, community members identified "the capacity for easy, independent exploration when using the library." In response, the library successfully implemented an online library card registration and e-Card service. The service allows county residents to log into the library Web site and register for immediate access to an electronic library card, which also serves as preregistration for the full-access library card. Customers obtain immediate access to all the library's virtual services and resources, and the e-Card database interfaces with the registered user database so the staff only maintains one database for all users. The new service was publicized to media outlets and local agencies and featured on the library home page. In the first year of the new service, about 3,500 customers registered for a library card remotely, and about 25 percent of e-Card recipients have visited the library to obtain the full-access card. More than 4,000 customers have used the online registration application in-house. Customer feedback has been positive.

We explore other issues relating to user service in most of the remaining chapters of this book.

CUSTOMER SERVICE TRAINING

Because frontline staff are so important in delivering customer service, public service staff today, especially circulation and reference staff, may expect to receive training in the fundamentals of customer service. Most of this training is typically done by circulation and reference supervisors, often including classroom instruction, role playing, computer-based instruction, and unsupervised instruction involving audio, written, or video materials.

One of the most common and important components of customer service training is how to handle "difficult" customers. People often come to the library with a specific need and try to find information unassisted. Some find what they want but many try unsuccessfully until their frustration and confusion builds up into the very real condition known as "library anxiety." Since the 1980s, a number of studies (see, for example, Mellon, 1986) have identified some of the causes of library anxiety including the size of the library, lack of knowledge about how to find information, where things are located, how to begin looking for information, and what to do to get help. Unfortunately, some people are reluctant to ask for help because that would reveal their inadequacy.

Library anxiety can affect the young or the elderly, the affluent as well as the poor, the college-educated and the marginally literate, and especially the recent immigrant or the person with limited proficiency in English. The ability to assist such clients by patient and sympathetic listening, giving helpful but not patronizing responses, and reformulating and modulating their questions as necessary is an important skill; it will almost always enable the staff person to help the anxious requester find what is needed.

There are, of course, customers who are impatient, confused, or angry for reasons other than simple anxiety. The physical and emotional makeup of individuals differs widely. Some people are on medication; others may have severe health problems. There are, sadly, people with substance abuse or emotional or mental health problems. Public libraries in some areas have been heavily impacted by a growing homeless population, or latchkey children who gather in libraries after school lets out. We explore these and other such issues in the chapter on security (Chapter 15).

From time to time all these people visit libraries, especially public libraries. If they act appropriately, everything can proceed as normal. Sometimes uncomfortable customers may express apprehension, perhaps for no reason other than a person's appearance, mumbling, or other relatively harmless reason. Especially in public libraries, there must be reluctance to take any punitive measures on two counts: first, because the person in question has a right to use the library as long as he or she does not infringe on another's rights; and second, because trying to evict the person may create more of a problem than just letting him or her be. Often, an unconventional customer will have a real interest in a particular library resource, such as browsing periodicals or trying to identify information about survival skills or coping. If help is asked for, it should be given with the same respect any person receives, whether or not the request is feasible. We explore the challenges handling "difficult" people in more detail in the chapter on security.

COMPLAINT PROCEDURES

One of the characteristics of good customer service is making it easy for the customer to register a complaint or suggestion. Public services staff should be aware that market research shows that the vast majority of dissatisfied customers tend not to complain, but take their business someplace else and share their frustrations with their friends. Therefore, every reported complaint probably represents the experiences of several other customers. Staff should be aware of the most frequent complaints made by users of their library and should pass these complaints on to their supervisors.

What types of problems are brought to the attention of a public services staff member? A review of the literature through the years reveals some common themes. In academic libraries, the principal problems reported by borrowers tend to be inability to find materials listed in the catalog on the shelves and lack of notification about overdue materials. Circulation limits on reserve items and restrictions on renewals were other problems, as well as dissatisfaction with strict application of circulation rules. The most frequent complaints of public library users tend to be insufficient numbers of desired titles and not being notified about their overdue materials. Borrowers were also unhappy about short loan periods, limited renewals, fines, and the use of collection agencies. The most frequent complaint of students using school libraries was that materials they wanted could not be found. Students also wanted to be notified about their overdue materials, and they disliked receiving overdue notices for materials they believed they had returned. Like other library users, students were annoyed at limited loan periods and restrictions on their library privileges.

Libraries should have complaint management policies in place to guide staff and managers in effectively handling complaints. Jackson (2002) recommends that such a policy include the following:

- *Offering opportunities to complain.* Many people do not know where to complain, or to whom. Opportunities like physical and online suggestion boxes, frequent customer surveys, and encouraging customers to let staff know about problems they encounter are important

- *Prepare library staff.* Frontline staff should be thoroughly oriented to the building and its services. They need to understand how important they are to the perceptions our customers have of the library. They also need to know how flexible they can be in resolving a customer's complaint

- *Plan for complaint management.* Written policies and procedures for speedy and fair complaint resolution are necessary

- *Respond to complaints.* Sometimes a thank you is sufficient. Complaints should be tracked so decisions can be made to improve customer satisfaction. A mechanism for public response to repeated complaints, like the library Web site or a bulletin board with written responses, will let your customers know that you have heard them

- *Follow up on complaints.* Acknowledge the effort a customer has made to complain rather than just leave the building. An e-mail thanking them for their interest and explaining how you are working on the problem is appropriate. You may not be able to solve every complaint, but customers may be happier to know that you care and are interested in their satisfaction (p. 212–215).

We will conclude this section with Weingand's (1997) suggested 10 "magic phrases" that should be a part of the customer service culture of any library:

1. *Of course w*
   effort will b
   quality se   people assurance that every
                       ts is a first step in delivering

2. *How ma*   . question encourages dialogue
   and fur

3. *Of cou*
   shou   . of the language of the policy
   spe   very courtesy to customers with
   ca   guidelines, not commandments that

4. *I*   to _____ *for you.* Go the extra mile
                  ; connected with the appropriate referral.

5   .ed? *How well does the information meet*
             ching else that I can find for you? These
             stions are most frequently asked by refer-

             ooking for, or shall I investigate further? This
             ed in combination with the previous question and
             member has been assisting the customer.

7. *There u.   . possible ways to address your question. Can you*
   give me a litt... nore background? This question probes a little deeper
   than the previous questions.

8. *I'm with another customer at the moment. May I call (or instant mes-*
   sage or text or chat) you back in a few minutes? Most people accept
   the "first come, first served" principle.

9. *Yes, that item is in and I'll be happy to hold it for you for 48 hours.*
   This statement demonstrates that you have made an effort to be
   responsive to the needs of the person and you have clearly stated the
   length of the hold so the customer understands the time parameters.

10. *Thanks for using the "XYZ" library.* This phrase acknowledges that
    the customer has choices and demonstrates gratitude for his or her
    patronage (p. 93–95).

These phrases cannot guarantee good customer service, but if used consistently by all public services staff demonstrate the service culture of the
library.

VOLUNTEER TRAINING

Volunteers are a part of the workforce of many libraries and often play a
variety of important roles. Whether they perform simple or the most advanced
and complicated work, volunteers are a part of the library staff and must be
trained, developed, and educated in customer service training.

Customer service training for volunteers involves certain challenges not
present for paid employees. Volunteers may enter the organization wishing to
perform particular, narrowly defined work responsibilities and not be interested in or expect, extensive training beyond their primary job responsibilities.

Another challenge is time. Volunteers typically work less than 40 hours per week, sometimes much less, and finding time for training may be difficult. Nevertheless, customer service should be addressed very early in the volunteer's orientation and training. Todaro and Smith (2006) recommend the following fundamentals for volunteer training:

- The vision and mission of the organization
- The values of the organization
- The organization's commitment to extraordinary customer service for external customers
- The organization's commitment to extraordinary customer service for internal customers
- The definitions of external customers
- The definitions of internal customers (other employees of the umbrella organization [city, county, school, company, college, and so forth], all library employees, all volunteers in the umbrella organization, all volunteers in the library)
- How volunteers interact with customers
- Any volunteer job descriptions
- Any management expectations for volunteers (staff may have to explain the reason for this customer service training requirement, since it might not be as clear to volunteers who "sign on to do a simple or little job" in the library)
- Any scripts appropriate to volunteer work responsibilities
- The volunteer evaluation form and how it addresses customer service expectations for volunteers (p. 41–42).

SUMMARY

With increasing demands on libraries for accountability, and competition from other information sources like Amazon and Google, libraries need to prove their worth to funding authorities. The customer service movement in libraries involves adopting certain concepts from the business marketing research in order to find out more about library users and improve customer satisfaction. Finding out more about our users' wants and needs allows library administrators to plan better, and satisfied customers tend to vote for library bond issues and become library supporters.

Having a customer service plan is an important part of providing consistent quality service. The plan should consist of a customer-focused mission statement, an assessment of customer wants and needs, an action plan for meeting the highest priority customer needs, and a regular assessment and analysis of how the plan is working so that continuous planning changes can be made to make it more effective.

Service quality is an important antecedent of customer service. While customer satisfaction is one measure of quality service, other types of assessments are necessary to get a true, comprehensive picture of a library's service quality. Each library will need to define quality service in terms of its own mission, goals, and objectives.

Technology offers new and challenging ways to improve quality and customer satisfaction. Making access to information and resources easier, faster, and more convenient should be a major goal; for example, implementing IM (instant messaging) and chat reference service, and access to library resources on portable technology platforms. Allowing customers to interact more personally with the library is the trend of Web 2.0 tools being adopted by libraries.

Chapter Review Material

1. Name at least two reasons for libraries to pay attention to customer service.
2. Why are some library staff uncomfortable with calling library users "customers?
3. What are some ways libraries ascertain customer needs and satisfaction?
4. What are some elements of a customer service plan?
5. Explain the relationship between customer service and service quality.
6. What are some ways of defining service quality?
7. What is Web 2.0, and how does it affect customer service?
8. What are some sources of customer dissatisfaction?
9. What are some ways staff can diffuse irate customers?

REFERENCES

American Library Association. 2007. *ALA Handbook of Organization 2007–2008.* Chicago: American Library Association.

Association of College and Research Libraries. 2008. *Environmental Scan 2007.* Chicago: American Library Association. http://www.acrl.org/ala/acrl/acrl pubs/whitepapers/Environmental_Scan_2.pdf.

Butler, Lorrie Ann, and Susan Kantor-Horning. 2007. "Online Library Card Registration Enables Free Passage to Digital Gems," *Computers in Libraries* 27, no.5: 13+.

Edgar, William B. 2006. "Questioning LibQUAL+™: Expanding Its Assessment of Academic Library Effectiveness," *Portal: Libraries and the Academy* 6, no. 4: 445–465.

Gordon, Rachel Singer, and Michael Stephens. 2007. "Tech Tips for Every Librarian," *Computers in Libraries* 27, no. 5: 30–31.

Hernon, Peter, and Ellen Altman. 1996. *Service Quality in Academic Libraries.* Norwood, NJ: Ablex Publishing Corp.

———. 1998. *Assessing Service Quality: Satisfying the Expectations of Library Customers.* Chicago: American Library Association.

Hernon, Peter, and Danuta Nitecki. 2001. "Service Quality: A Concept Not Fully Explored," *Library Trends* 49, no. 4: 687–708.

Hernon, Peter, Danuta A. Nitecki, and Ellen Altman. 1999. "Service Quality and Customer Satisfaction: An Assessment and Future Directions," *The Journal of Academic Librarianship* 25, no. 1: 9–17.

Hernon, Peter, and John R. Whitman. 2001. *Delivering Satisfaction and Service Quality: A Customer-Based Approach for Libraries*. Chicago: American Library Association.

Holt, Glen E. 2006. "Fitting Library Services into the Lives of the Poor," *The Bottom Line: Managing Library Finances* 19, no. 4: 179–186

Jackson, Rebecca. 2002. "The Customer Is Always Right: What the Business World Can Teach Us about Problem Patrons," *The Reference Librarian* no. 75/76: 205–216.

Joubert, Douglas J., and Tamara P. Lee. 2007. "Empowering Your Institution Through Assessment," *Journal of the Medical Library Association* 95, no.1: 46–53.

Jurewicz, Lynn, and Todd Cutler. 2003. *High Tech High Touch: Library Customer Service through Technology*. Chicago: American Library Association.

Maness, Jack M. 2006. "Library 2.0 Theory: Web 2.0 and Its Implications for Libraries," *Webology* 3, no. 2. http://www.webology.ir/2006/v3n2/a25.html.

McGuigan, Glenn S. 2002. "The Common Sense of Customer Service: Employing Advice from the Tread and Popular Literature of Business to Interactions with Irate Patrons in Libraries," *The Reference Librarian* no. 75/76: 197–204.

Mellon, Constance A. 1986. "Library Anxiety: A Grounded Theory and Its Development," *College and Research Libraries* 47, no. 2: 160–165.

Noruzi, Alireza. 2004. "Application of Ranganathan's Laws to the Web," *Webology* 1, no. 2. http://www.webology.ir/2004/v1n2/a8.html.

Omidsalar, Teresa Portilla, and Mahmoud Omidsalar. 1999. "Customer Service: A View from the Trenches," *American Libraries* 30, no. 2: 24–25.

Plummer, Elizabeth. 1996. "Customer Service Training in Academic Libraries." Unpublished master's thesis, Kent State University.

Ranganathan, S. R. 1931. *Five Laws of Library Science*. Madras: Madras Library Association.

Saunders, E. Stewart. 2007. "The LibQUAL+ Phenomenon: Who Judges Quality," *Reference & User Services Quarterly* 47, no. 1: 21–24.

Schachter, Debbie. 2006. "The True Value of Customer Service," *Information Outlook* 10, no. 8: 8–9.

Schroer, William J. 2003. "Too Much Customer Service?" *Library Journal* 128, no. 14: 54.

Stephens, Michael. 2006. "The Promise of Web 2.0," *American Libraries* 37, no. 9: 32.

Todaro, Julie, and Mark L. Smith. 2006. Training *Library Staff and Volunteers to Provide Extraordinary Customer Service*. New York: Neal-Schuman.

Walden, Graham R. 2006. "Focus Group Interviewing in the Library Literature," *Reference Services Review* 34, no. 2: 222–241.

Walters, Suzanne. 1994. *Customer Service: A How-To-Do-It Manual for Librarians*. New York: Neal-Schuman.

Wehmeyer, Susan, Dorothy Auchter, and Arnold Hirshon. 1996. "Saying What We Will Do, and Doing What We Say: Implementing a Customer Service Plan," *The Journal of Academic Librarianship* 22, no. 3: 173–80.

Weingand, Darlene E. 1997. *Customer Service Excellence: A Concise Guide for Librarians*. Chicago: American Library Association.

Zeithaml, Valarie A., A. Parasuraman, and Leonard L. Berry. 1990. *Delivering Quality Service: Balancing Customer Perceptions and Expectations*. New York: Free Press.

SUGGESTED READINGS

Brewer, Julie. 1995. "Service Management: How to Plan for it Rather Than Hope for It," *Library Administration & Management Association* 9, no. 4: 207–215.

Budd, John M. 1997. "A Critique of Customer and Commodity," *College & Research Libraries* 58, no. 4: 310–321.

Burkamp, Marlu, and Diane E. Virbick. 2002. "Through the Eyes of a Secret Shopper," *American Libraries* 33, no. 10: 56–57.

Chelton, Mary K. 2000. *Excellence in Library Services to Young Adults: The Nation's Top Programs.* Chicago: American Library Association.

Gupta, Dinesh, and Ashok Jambhekar. 2002. "Which Way Do You Want to Serve Your Customers?" *Information Outlook* 6, no. 7: 26–32.

Haynes, Abby. 2004. "Bridging the Gulf: Mixed Methods and Library Service Evaluation," *Australian Library Journal* 53, no. 3: 285–307.

Hernon, Peter. 2002. "First, Embracing Customer Service and, Second, Moving Beyond It: A Client Relationship," *The Journal of Academic Librarianship* 28, no. 4: 189–190.

Manjunatha, K., and D. Shivalingaiah. 2004. "Customer's Perception of Service Quality in Libraries," *Annals of Library & Information Studies* 51, no. 4: 145–151.

Melling, Maxine, and Joyce Little. 2002. *Building a Successful Customer-Service Culture: A Guide for Library and Information Managers.* London: Facet Publishing.

Ojala, Marydee. 2006. "Customer Service, Information Professionals, and Library 2.0," *Online* 30, no. 4: 5.

Todaro, Julie Beth. 1995. "Make 'Em Smile: 10 Essentials for Successful Customer Service," *School Library Journal* 41, no. 1: 24–27.

Whitlatch, Jo Bell. 1995. "Customer Service: Implications for Reference Practice," *Reference Librarian* no. 49–50: 5–25.

Chapter 4

Reference Services

The advent of the Internet has so decisively altered the user culture, and has so decisively changed the relative importance of different user types, that no effort to reassert a traditional reference . . . role can possibly succeed.

—M. C. Wilson, 2000

Chat reference, defined as the provision of human-assisted information services via synchronous communication applications on the Internet, is the most recent reference development in the library world.

—Lili Luo, 2008

Without question, the reference desk is one of the two most frequently visited public service points at the library. It therefore sets a standard that users consider when assessing their library service experiences.

Most people coming to the library expect good service and become disappointed when that does not materialize. A problem is that few people are willing to give a library a second chance if their last experience was unsatisfactory. They seldom assess or consider whether or not the problem was something the staff could control—that the information just does not exist in the desired form or that the ISP was having trouble maintaining Internet connectivity are but two such examples. Thus, there is a strong pressure on reference staff to do whatever they can to satisfy each information inquiry.

A reference desk in a library is a very sophisticated and complex form of the "information booth" people find in malls and large buildings. Therefore, many individuals when they come to a library assume the only assistance they can get at a reference desk is directions to where to find something. Sometimes that is all they do want, but assuming that all inquiries are such can lead to serious shortfalls in service.

As noted in Chapter 1, getting young people into the library is a challenge today. Sarah Houghton (2005) wrote, "I don't know a single public library that doesn't have a hard time bringing middle and high schoolers into the library. . . . Enter stage left: Instant Messaging Reference" (p. 192). Such changes make reference work an exciting and challenging career area. In this chapter, we explore the nature of the work and how to make the end-user's experience highly satisfactory, if not memorable.

THE ROLE OF REFERENCE SERVICES IN THE LIBRARY

The role of reference services, and of the reference staff, is to make information available to library users. Librarians and support staff do this most directly by delivering personal service in response to requests for information. This personal service takes three primary forms:

1. Finding information to answer specific questions.
2. Helping users find information for themselves.
3. Teaching people how to use library resources and how to do library research.

This chapter will introduce the reader to the traditional and innovative components of reference service common in libraries today.

Personalized reference service as we know it is a comparatively new addition to libraries (Rothstein, 1989). Only in the twentieth century did libraries become something other than storehouses for books, and librarians more than book collectors, catalogers, and custodians. In the latter part of the nineteenth century, public librarians began to realize that many users needed assistance to use the library effectively. Samuel Green, librarian of the Worcester Free Public Library in Massachusetts, published an article in *Library Journal* advocating personal assistance and service by librarians to library readers (Green, 1876). He conceived the relationship to be like that of a shopkeeper to a user, and held that the reader should be welcomed with the cordiality of an innkeeper. Green also realized that assistance of this sort would increase the popularity of the library and its support by library users.

Green's article became the basis for the development of reference service, although the service developed gradually. In addition to performing their other duties, librarians began to provide guidance in the use of the library and to suggest books to meet the information needs of their users. As this service became popular and generated more demand, reference came to be regarded as an important function and gradually became a central responsibility of the staff rather than a marginal duty. After 1890, the reference function had gained sufficient popularity to become formalized as a distinct department in the larger public libraries.

In university libraries, the rate of acceptance of this new service was slower. It began with the transformation of American higher education in the 1880s. It was then that American colleges, led by the foundation of Johns Hopkins University, began to adopt the German model of university education, with its increased emphasis on research and the use of books. Library use increased correspondingly, and librarians assisting students and faculty to find the books they wanted became a more obvious need.

In general, reference service in academic libraries followed the path blazed by the public libraries. Personal assistance first was provided on a part-time and occasional basis. Increased demand for the service resulted in reference work becoming a specialized function, with that function eventually gaining the status of a separate department in libraries.

However, the rate of advance was slower than in public libraries. The custodial nature of the academic library was more firmly established than in public libraries, and academic libraries did not depend as much for their support on the good will of satisfied users. By 1900, reference service had become a common feature in both public and university libraries. In the early years of the twentieth century, reference service was generally limited to teaching and guidance, implying a policy of minimal assistance and emphasis on the librarian as instructor. However, librarians soon found themselves increasingly drawn into "fact finding" and providing direct information service. The need for librarians to become more expert in diverse fields led eventually to a growing trend towards subject specialization in reference. These two trends, subject specialization and the expansion of reference techniques, resulted in a qualitative improvement in reference service, but at the cost of de-emphasizing the instructional function.

The growth in the number of special libraries after World War I radically affected the concept of reference service. Special libraries, while growing in importance to organizations, minimized guidance in favor of direct provision of information. Reference work was expanded to supply answers to specific questions and even to anticipate questions and furnish a reporting service on new developments.

This application of advanced reference service was uncommon in public and academic libraries before 1940. In addition, libraries generally did not have the resources or the time to support service at this level. This was a valid reason for busy public libraries not to provide reference service to this extent. However, the case for expanded reference to faculty and scholars in university libraries was strong and, when adopted, led to greater responsibilities for the reference librarian.

With the end of World War II and the tremendous growth in higher education that followed, the demand for information services in libraries grew exponentially. College and university enrollments swelled with thousands of ex-GIs, libraries expanded to accommodate the postwar information explosion, and reference staffs were called on to provide increased assistance in library use and in locating desired information.

The 1960s and 1970s saw two further developments that expanded the reference staff's ability to provide service, while placing greater demands on the librarian's professional expertise. As libraries became larger and more complex with the need to house increasing amounts of information, the need for assistance in using the library grew among all users. Many reference librarians recognized the need to reassert the traditional emphasis on instruction in library use. *Bibliographic instruction* (later, library instruction or information literacy instruction), defined as teaching students how to do library research for themselves in order to facilitate lifelong learning, became an important part of reference responsibility beginning in the 1970s (see the Information Literacy Instruction chapter).

Starting in the 1960s technology began to change reference service, a process that seems to increase in speed on a daily basis. Computerized reference services began with bibliographic databases (containing references to periodicals, books, and other documents). Services then expanded to include online catalogs, mediated searching of online databases, CD-ROM (compact disk-read only memory) sources, networking of libraries and library systems, end user searching of online databases, full text retrieval, and the Internet. These and other innovations have expanded the library's ability to provide diverse and complex information services. This trend has continued into the twenty-first century as the increasing user demand to access online information places a greater demand on libraries to provide more sophisticated reference service.

Wilson (2000), speaking about the increasing importance of the reference interview and instruction in serving the needs of today's technologically literate users, cautioned that "The advent of the Internet has so decisively altered the user culture, and has so decisively changed the relative importance of different user types, that no effort to reassert a traditional reference . . . role can possibly succeed" (p. 389). Today, reference departments in public, academic, and school libraries attempt to offer at least moderate levels of service in all three areas of reference service (finding information, helping others to find information, and teaching use of the library), while departmental, professional school, and research institute libraries offer reference service of a quality and depth approaching that of a special library.

PHILOSOPHY OF REFERENCE SERVICE

The purpose of reference service is to facilitate access to information. Reference work attempts to fully answer every individual's information needs. Realities of time, limitations on resources, and lack of universal subject expertise means no reference staff member can answer every inquiry. However, reference staff do use every resource at their disposal, physical and intellectual, to come as close to the ideal as possible. Expanding beyond the resources of an individual library to obtain information for users has become a standard reference strategy in libraries. Services and tools such as 24/7 reference networks, interlibrary loan and digital document delivery, electronic mail, chat and IM, online searching, Web-accessible integrated library systems, and sophisticated indexing tools are among the means employed to overcome the limitations of individual libraries in answering users' needs. As Lili Luo's opening quotation suggests, chat reference has become a very popular form of reference service, especially among young people.

The level of service delivered by a particular library depends on the nature of the institution. Special libraries, especially corporate libraries, often find and deliver information directly to the requester as quickly as possible. Corporate executives or research scientists generally are not interested in learning how to find information for themselves and employ library staff to do it for them. Public libraries emphasize finding information for users and, in some situations, helping users to locate information themselves. School libraries place a strong emphasis on teaching students about library use. Academic libraries probably deliver the most equal balance between these kinds of service: providing specific answers, assisting users to find information, and teaching library use.

According to the Reference and User Services Association (RUSA) of the ALA, "The library should develop and make available to the public a statement that describes the information services it strives to offer all members of its community" (RASD, 2000). This *service policy*, with clear objectives, should detail the circumstances under which services and resources are available, the extent to which they are provided, any limitation on their provision, and to whom and by whom such services are to be provided. Needless to say, the staff should review the policy regularly, and make it available to users. (See more on service policies in Chapter 3, Customer Service.)

EDUCATION AND TRAINING

Education and training for reference work in library technology programs has traditionally been utilitarian. Students memorize the characteristics of specific reference sources and perform exercises or case studies in the use of these sources to answer typical reference questions. General reference courses feature the most important reference tools in a variety of disciplines, while more specific sources are sometimes covered in specialized courses, for example, humanities bibliography or legal bibliography, commonly offered in master's level library science programs.

Bibliography courses like these are necessary to introduce the student to the tools needed to provide reference assistance. However, these courses do little to prepare the librarian or support staff member to provide personal service. Schools have given insufficient attention to the value of interpersonal relations in reference work and to the importance of negotiating the "reference interview" (see the section on reference interviews late in this chapter) in determining a user's information needs. Coursework on interpersonal relations, already offered by some institutions, should be mandatory for students planning on careers in public services.

Another aspect of interpersonal relations that is assuming increasing importance is serving multicultural populations. Sensitivity to the ways in which cultural differences affect information-seeking behavior is important for staff working in libraries that serve a multiethnic population. Some library technology programs offer internships or practicums where students are able to work for a time in the reference departments of nearby libraries. These programs offer the student valuable practical experience and should be taken advantage of wherever they are offered.

Library technicians will find that the most important part of training for reference work occurs on the job. The education gained through library technology programs serves as a necessary foundation for the more specific, comprehensive training in reference practices and resources provided by one's coworkers. New employees will typically be paired with other reference staff at the reference desk to learn about policies, procedures, and reference sources.

One of the most important areas of training for the new reference staff member is in the behavioral aspects of reference service. Every library has a cultural norm for providing reference services that addresses such positive behaviors as approachability, interest in the question, and good listening skills, as well as searching ability. Research has shown that how the library user views the behavior of the staff member is a significant factor in the perceived success or failure of the reference transaction, and libraries try to recruit and retain people who have these service orientations. RUSA adopted revised *Guidelines for Behavioral Performance of Reference and Information Providers* in 2004 (http://www.ala.org/ala/rusa/rusaprotools/referenceguide/guidelines behavioral.cfm) and new employees should attempt to model these behaviors while learning the policies and practices of their library. Additional information on how libraries have adapted user service practices and training for public service staff is covered in Chapter 3, Customer Service.

TYPES OF REFERENCE QUESTIONS

Reference questions come from every variety of human inquiry and curiosity, but most can be classified under the following categories:

1. *Directional questions* are informational or explanations of library policies and procedures. Examples are: "Where can I get a drink of water?" "Where do you keep your magazines?" "How do I log onto the computer?" "How do I get a library card?"

2. *Ready reference questions* are usually simple factual questions that ask for information, such as: "What is the population of China?" "Who is our state representative?" "How many pounds make a ton?"

3. *Reference questions* are more involved inquiries and usually require several steps to answer; for example, "I need all the information I can find on General Motors." "I need to write a term paper on whales."

4. *Research questions* are reference questions involving several categories of tools for a comprehensive look at what is available on a particular topic. Research questions are differentiated from reference questions by degree, rather than methodology. Preparing an extensive bibliography of sources both in the library and beyond; working with the user to develop one or a series of strategies to accomplish a research task; helping the requester search several databases; and locating hard-to-find specific references by extensive manual or online means are examples of research librarianship. Research questions often require extended time, referral, or follow-up contact with users.

5. *Technical and mechanical questions* primarily involve using the computing, printing, and copying technology now ubiquitous in libraries. These questions may involve how to use various applications like word processing programs, how to download a document to a flash drive, how send a print job to the local printing system, or how to purchase a copy card.

A person's information need might fall into several of these categories, sometimes in a steady progression as the individual's questions become more specific as the research progresses. For example, directional questions often evolve into reference questions as the librarian determines through the reference interview that a user needs information beyond the original request. Both reference and research questions might involve instruction, as the staff member shows the user the step-by-step procedure to acquire the desired information.

THE REFERENCE INTERVIEW

Requesters are often uncertain or unclear about what information they want. Sometimes it is because they have trouble expressing themselves. Often it is because they are not sure in their own minds what they want or need. For example, the individual who wants to search Google to find information on a corporation may really prefer a database like *Business Source Premier* or a corporate annual report to answer his or her question; the high school student asking for college catalogs might be better served with a directory of college majors. How does the reference staff member determine a person's true information need?

The *reference interview* is the process whereby the staff member communicates and interacts with the user to determine how best to answer an informational need. The interview is used to determine the true nature of a question before the staff member goes into action. It is an interactive process in which both staff and user ask questions and provide answers. The need may be a simple one, and the interview therefore short and sweet; for example, a group of children come up and one shyly asks, "Where's the bathroom?" "Boy's or girl's?" asks the staff member. "Both!" answers another child.

On the other hand, some questions are substantially incomplete, and the staff member must guide the user in a series of steps just to get the process going: choosing a topic, thinking about the topic, and making decisions about limiting the search to find what is really needed. For example, a young adult (YA) comes in and announces to a reference staff member (S):

YA: "I have to write a term paper."

S: "Oh, that sounds interesting. On what topic?"

YA: "Oh, I don't know. Anything, I guess."

S: "Did your teacher give you something that describes the assignment, like a handout?"

YA: "Yes, but I left it at home."

S: "Do you remember what it said?"

YA: "No, just to write a paper is all."

S: "What subject are you taking with this teacher?"

YA: "Well, history."

S: "History of what? The U.S.? European history? Asian history?"

YA: "European history."

S: "What are you interested in writing about"

YA: "Oh, I don't know. Anything, I guess."

S: "What are you studying in that class now?"

YA: "About the civil war."

S: "Which civil war?"

YA: "You know, the civil war."

S: "Do you mean the English civil war? Cromwell and all that?"

YA: "Yeah, I guess so."

S: "So would you like to write about the Roundheads or about the cavaliers?"

YA: "Who?"

S: "You know, the soldiers of Oliver Cromwell or the army of the king of England."

YA: "Well, how about Robert E. Lee?"

S: "Robert E. Lee? He fought in the *American* Civil War. Here, in the U.S.A."

YA: "That's what we're studying."

S: "You mean about Abe Lincoln and Jefferson Davis and Stonewall Jackson and Ulysses S. Grant?"

YA: "Yeah, that stuff."

S: "Oh, okay. Let's go over and look at a couple of good sources on Robert E. Lee to get you started. . . ."

The reference interview is a critical part of library service. Being given insufficient, incomplete, incorrect, or even too much information presents serious problems to library users. Identifying several sources with a variety of points of view, when appropriate, is usually good practice. For less complex needs, a good, balanced, and clear overview of a topic, such as may be found in general encyclopedias, may be all that is needed. In the example posed above, the "term paper" might be just that, with several sources beyond the encyclopedias required. It might also turn out to be a three-page handwritten essay on qualities the student admires in a historical personage, an "opinion" paper requiring little research.

Reading a user's nonverbal cues is also part of the reference interview. This is especially true when assisting someone with a limited command of English. As Pyati (2003) observes, "Communicating with LEP users is not only a question of language, but a question of culture as well" (p. 266). It is not always possible to have staff available who are fluent in the various language groups represented in a library's community. Sensitivity, patience, and a user-friendly approach are very important in these circumstances. Reading a user's body language, gestures, facial expressions, and so on may give clues to alert reference staff about whether he or she is effectively communicating with the individual or whether the person is satisfied with the information being given. Cultural values are a significant factor when it comes to "reading" nonverbals. It requires a sound understanding of the characteristics of the various constituencies of the service community. For example, eye contact alone may or may not be a sign of satisfaction, because in some cultures direct eye contact is considered rude.

Asking that one additional question may be the difference between reference "success" and confused failure. Confusion may be expected in the requester, but the reference staffer should not be the person confused. Quiet and patient persistence will usually enable a staff member to get to the heart of the matter by helping the requester define the true informational need.

READERS' ADVISORY SERVICE

Readers' advisory service, broadly defined, means helping readers find what they want by recommending specific titles. In this context, it is something that all reference staff occasionally do. Readers often ask for suggestions on what books to read on a particular topic, in a specific genre (for example, mysteries), or by a certain author. If we happen to know about the subject or writer requested, it is satisfying to be able to refer the user to a particular title we know is a "good" one.

However, readers' advisory also refers to a specialized service usually found in public libraries. The users of this service tend to be adult fiction readers, but range from children to housebound seniors. Underlying readers' advisory is the belief that reading has intrinsic value and that readers are well served by a good collection and knowledgeable staff who are able to guide them in pursuing their interests. The reading of fiction is very popular in public libraries and their collection development budgets reflect this interest. Given the high demand and resource commitment, libraries attempt to address the demands of readers in a structured way.

Readers' advisory service began during the first half of the twentieth century. In those days, libraries focused on the educational and therapeutic benefits of prescribed reading. Many librarians believed it was their role to improve the lot of the reader when they saw the need. Librarians presumed that they were able to identify certain personality types and could improve the lives of readers by persuading them to read a few judiciously selected titles. Today, "bibliotherapy" is closest to the old concept of "improving readers' lives" and is found primarily in the school library-media center environment.

Structured readers' advisory programs began in large urban libraries. The service covered both fiction and nonfiction reading. Advisors met with interested readers and outlined reading plans for them. Librarians directed readers towards the classics and other books of perceived educational value. The service grew during the late 1920s and 1930s because of the increased number of professionals working in public libraries, an increase in library use brought on by the Great Depression, and research on the problems of adult reading. With the decline in leisure time beginning in the 1940s, readers' advisory service declined as well.

Currently, the service enjoys renewed popularity in public libraries, although the focus has changed dramatically from its didactic origins. There are still readers who want to "better themselves" through reading and library staff assist these readers as they would any others. Today staff no longer prescribes readings to "improve" the reader. They advise borrowers primarily on recreational reading, and predominantly on fiction. Readers' advisors try to be familiar with popular literature and best sellers lists and respond with perception and insight to the reading interests of their users. Staff are now assisted in this endeavor by print and online references specifically designed to enhance readers' advisory service. Sources like *Genreflecting* (a guide to popular titles in genres like adventure, crime, horror, etc.), EBSCO's *NoveList* (a searchable database of over 155,000 popular titles—http://www.epnet.com/thisTopic.php?marketID=6&topicID=16), and *Fiction_L* (a listserv for readers advisory staff—http://www.webrary.org/rs/flmenu.html) help staff and readers alike identify titles.

A Web 2.0 innovation, adopted from business sites like Amazon and employed by an increasing number of libraries, allows readers to enter their own tags, reviews, ratings, and reading suggestions in the library OPAC and library blogs (Wyatt, 2007). Readers and staff may use these sources to begin with books they have read and discover like titles and authors. Some databases allow readers to enter words and phrases to describe a book they would like to read and search for books that contain the words or phrases in their subject headings. Readers may also explore titles in specific genres and examine lists of award-winning literature.

Readers' advisory is a popular and growing service in public libraries. Helping readers find stories they like and that are important to them help libraries build community support and increase circulation. Readers' advisors are not necessarily librarians, and trained paraprofessionals can be excellent advisors, especially with the aid of reference sources like the ones mentioned above (Saricks, 2005). We have included some readers' advisory resources in the Suggested Readings section of this chapter.

COMMUNITY INFORMATION AND REFERRAL SERVICES

A *community information and referral service* refers to a particular service offered in public libraries. Its goal is to provide a link between people and services, activities, information, or advice outside the library that can meet the user's needs. According to Durrance and Pettigrew (2000), the service "covers information about human services (health care, financial assistance, housing, etc.), as well as information on recreation programs, clubs, community events, and all levels of government, including participation in the political process" (p. 44). The service ordinarily involves using a paper or online directory of community resources and information about them, which supplements information in other sources like government or social services directories or the Web. Technology enhanced the ability of libraries to provide information and referral services. Libraries create collections or, increasingly, searchable databases of community information, which citizens may search from remote locations any time of the day or night to find the information they seek.

Community information and referral services generally fall into two main categories: online community directories and community calendars (Rogers et al., 2005). Many libraries use their integrated library systems (ILS) to manage their information and referral systems and the major vendors support software for this purpose. These databases are searchable by keyword and other search options. Other libraries have begun building their own customized information and referral databases to better meet the needs of their users.

This type of service is especially important for people or groups with special needs, such as the poor, recent immigrants, or individuals who speak limited English. In the underserved areas of communities, this service may be the only means people have for obtaining needed information. Community information and referral programs can help forge a stronger relationship between the library and local ethnic communities.

Another kind of information referral is to information in other libraries. Increased use of technology has made interlibrary referral very efficient and practical. Regional union lists of periodicals, which record the serial holdings of a number of libraries, have appeared in increasing numbers. These lists may be compiled for a particular location (for example, state, county, or city), or type of library. (For example, the University of California's *MELVYL* includes the periodical holdings of all the University of California libraries, the California State Library, as well as private academic libraries and the Center for Research Libraries.) Databases like OCLC's (Online Computer Library Center) *WorldCAT* and *Google Books* make it possible to identify which libraries across the nation hold a particular book or periodical.

Networks, consortia, and cooperative agreements to share resources among libraries, made more effective by technology, are increasing. Networks may be local or limited to libraries of the same type; for example, the public libraries in a city or rural area. They may also be expansive, multitype networks encompassing libraries of different kinds across counties or states or regions. Many networks are formed to allow libraries to take advantage of economies of scale in subscribing to or purchasing online services like periodical databases. Interlibrary loan is the most common evidence of resource sharing within a network, often enhanced by interlibrary courier service. Cooperative reference services are also established in many areas. These permit the referral of difficult queries or those submitted when the library is closed by Web form or e-mail, typically to a central location or directly to other consortium members, where answers are found and delivered later.

Some networks have formalized the referral process. Specific steps and protocols are agreed on and followed by each participating library. This avoids duplicating work since the second library is told what works were consulted, strategies tried, and so on by the referring library. Libraries share holdings information through a network, considerably improving access, guaranteeing better service, and minimizing delays and trouble for both users and staff.

E-mail, chat, and listservs allow staff in local or national networks to communicate almost instantaneously with colleagues in any location. Staff may consult with scores, even hundreds of reference staff at a time through these networks, holding the promise of greatly facilitating the referral process.

SERVICE TO OFF-SITE USERS

Part of the reference staff's duties may include service to off-site users. Libraries are available by telephone, letter, fax, Web form, e-mail, chat, text messages, and IM for both ready reference and research information, often on a 24/7 basis. The request might be for library hours, the date of the sinking of the *Titanic* or for a citation to an obscure article for which the requester has very little information. Some colleges and universities have sizable distance education programs and student populations who depend on the library's off-site services. Sometimes, a staff member from a distant library may contact the library with a question that cannot be answered with local resources. A library known for a particular subject strength, or the largest (or only) library in town, will receive a large number of these inquiries.

In general, staff should give an off-site requester, especially one who may be physically unable to visit the library (for example, homebound individuals or those who lack transportation) as full an answer as possible within the constraints of time and the reference policy. In most libraries, the users who are physically present have first priority. Staff should decline unreasonable requests (those that take an inordinate amount of staff time or effort to answer) in a professional manner, with patient explanation and an invitation to visit the library and obtain guidance in performing the necessary research.

The reference policy should address the issue of conflicting priorities regarding off-site versus in-person requests. For example, staff will look up no more than "X" number of books in the OPAC, or spend no more than "Y" number of minutes looking for an elusive statistic. During very hectic periods, such as term-paper season in an academic library, it may be necessary for staff to log the question or save it to be answered later. The staff person contacts the requester (or asks the requester to call back) at a specified time, by which the reference staff will have attempted to find the answer. Some libraries have a separate telephone line or e-mail reference address or an IM account, with a staff member dedicated to answering queries for directional and reference questions.

Electronic access to full-text resources, delivered via the Internet, makes much better service to students possible at distant satellite campuses or in the students' homes. In combination with intercampus delivery systems, such digital collections can help students who are physically remote from the main campus attain a good measure of library access. Nevertheless, with the increase in distance education offerings by universities around the country, many libraries find themselves called on to supply services to local students enrolled in programs offered at distant campuses. Some of these institutions contract with libraries to supply services to their students in particular areas, but this is not always the case. The library's reference service policy should address the level of service that is appropriate to deliver in support of distance education programs.

Like telephone, chat, text messaging, and IM reference, written, faxed, or e-mail correspondence needs the fastest feasible attention, and should be handled as thoroughly as other duties allow. Responding with a partial answer, with apologies and a notice that a fuller answer will take longer than one has time for at present, is an appropriate procedure when staff time is short. If it is known that the chances of answering soon are slim, a short reply politely stating this condition and an estimated date of reply would be welcomed by most researchers. Well-worded automated responses or form letters may be used if the backlog becomes a problem.

ADMINISTRATION

Organization of Reference Services

The organization of reference services can take several forms. The three most popular are *central* or general reference, *divisional* reference, and *departmental* reference. (See Figures 4.1, 4.2, and 4.3.) The organization of reference depends on many factors, the more important ones being philosophy of the library, physical layout of the building, size of the library's collection, abilities of the staff, type of library and type(s) of user, and financial resources.

Figure 4.1 Central or General Reference Organization

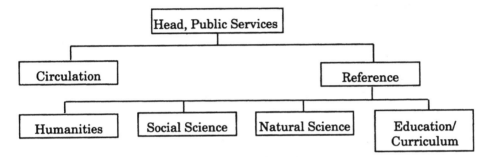

Figure 4.2 Divisional Reference Organization

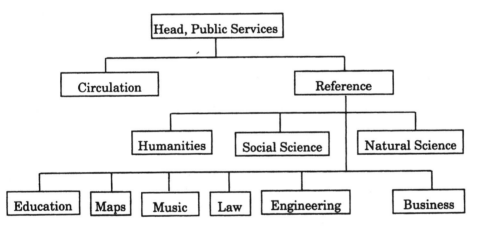

Figure 4.3 Departmental Reference Organization

A central or general reference department organization brings together all reference material in one physical location. Some arguments for this organization follow:

1. Reference materials are easier to locate because they are shelved together.
2. Because knowledge is interrelated and interdisciplinary, it is easier to do reference work if all the material is kept together.
3. It is not necessary to purchase duplicate materials or to duplicate services.
4. It is possible to make more economical use of staff at one service point rather than staffing several service points.

Nearly all small libraries and most medium-sized libraries use a central or general type of organization.

Divisional reference organization may be found in larger libraries and brings together the reference materials for a group of related subjects. A divisional reference organization may divide the collection into social sciences, humanities, and natural sciences, or any other arrangement best suited to the library. Some of the arguments in favor of divisional reference organization follow:

1. A smaller reference collection is easier to use.

2. The reference materials and the general collection on a particular subject are often closer together in a divisional arrangement, allowing easier access to both types of materials.

3. Reference staff who are subject specialists can utilize their talents and provide better service for specialized reference inquiries when they work in their area of expertise.

Departmental libraries may be found in larger libraries in addition to a central reference collection or divisional reference collections. The collection in a departmental library is usually restricted to one subject area, such as physics or philosophy, and different departments may have a reference collection and reference services of their own, often in different buildings. The advantages of this organization are the same as those stated for divisional reference organization.

Personnel Selection

Earlier in this chapter, and in Chapter 2, we mentioned the personal qualifications necessary for successful reference work and discussed the academic training one receives in preparation for a career in reference service. In selecting staff for reference positions, the reference administrator will be able to identify the academic and experiential qualifications of applicants by studying resumes, vitas, or applications and by contacting references. Preferably, this is done with the help of a search committee composed of other reference personnel. Once the top candidates for a position are identified, they should be invited to come to the library for on-site interviews.

It is a very good idea for the reference administrator to include other staff in the interview process. Interviewing is decidedly an art, not a science. It is much easier to get an accurate picture of an applicant's qualifications if the administrator considers the different observations of a number of people.

During the interview the search committee looks for the interpersonal qualities specified earlier in the chapter. Knowledge of reference sources is important but irrelevant if the individual is unable to communicate effectively with users. The committee looks for evidence of reticence or other personality characteristics that may inhibit the delivery of effective reference service.

Personality aside, the committee will try to select the candidate who best meets the requirements of the particular position through experience, knowledge, training, and the potential for success in reference service (see Chapter 2). The committee also asks questions designed to gauge the candidate's qualifications. Hypothetical questions or situations ("What would you do if . . .?) are useful in assessing the applicant's judgment, knowledge, and experience.

The cultural pluralism of the library's service community and of the library staff is also important to take into consideration. Policy guidelines in some libraries require that minority candidates be actively recruited. In addition, libraries should be sensitive to the ethnic composition of the populations they serve and endeavor to recruit a staff that reflects this diversity. A staff member may be better able to communicate and deliver service to members of an ethnic group if he or she is a member of that group. Outreach programs to underserved ethnic populations may be more effective if staffed by members of the populations targeted. This does not mean reference staff should fall into the habit of automatically referring all users of a particular ethnic group to a certain staff member just because he or she is a member of that group. If a library recruits a staff member to serve a particular population it should be for the right reason; that is, to provide better service for the library's users, not to relieve the rest of the staff from the responsibility to serve all the library's users. In addition, when a library recruits a staff member specifically to serve a particular ethnic population, the administrator should make this clear during the recruitment process. Some staff may resent being expected to serve the members of a particular population unless the requirement is made clear before the hiring process is completed.

Staff Training

The amount and kind of training given to the new reference employee will depend, of course, on his or her qualifications and on the specific duties of the position. The reference supervisor provides at least a general orientation to the department, the collection, departmental and library personnel, and policies and procedures of which the employee needs to be aware. The administrator often delegates specific training in such things as online searching, collection development, and library instruction to the staff who share responsibilities for these services. A significant portion of the new employee's time is spent getting acquainted with the reference collection and observing and assisting at the reference desk, preferably with different members of the staff. Not until the administrator is satisfied that the staff member can comfortably handle desk duty "solo" should the employee be scheduled alone, and then only with the assurance that, if needed for consultation, assistance is close at hand. Occasional meetings thereafter will reinforce new skills and help the supervisor gauge any need for further training.

Ongoing staff development is also important to maintain the reference staff's effectiveness. Acquisitions of new reference titles and databases, and regular changes to the interfaces of familiar databases, require that reference staff constantly keep up to date in order to be most effective. Regular staff meetings to review new and revised databases and other reference sources are an effective means of keeping current. Meetings of local, regional, and national professional associations often include programs on new reference sources and techniques. Regional organizations sometimes sponsor free webinars highlighting new reference services and resources. Vendors' representatives are sometimes invited to come to the library and describe a new database and the administrator routes or e-mails relevant articles to the staff. It is the administrator's responsibility to make sure that reference staff members have the opportunity to continually develop their reference skills. Additional information on the importance of training for good user service is addressed in Chapter 3.

Scheduling

The administrator must allow great flexibility in scheduling reference staff. This is because the hours of reference service are long and frequently include nights and weekends. Staff schedules often must vary from day to day and week to week in order to maintain reference service. Subject to the dictates of an institution's personnel policy or union contract, late arrivals, early departures, and long breaks are generally accepted to compensate for the occasional 10-hour day and working weekend. The administrator who is not flexible with staff scheduling will have difficulty obtaining the loyalty and cooperation necessary to maintain services in times of great activity or staff shortages.

The library administration establishes the amount of time that reference service is provided. At a minimum, management considers three variables: the number of hours the library is open, the number of staff available, and the information needs of the library's users. School and special libraries are open for the shortest periods and have assistance available the greatest proportion of hours. Public libraries usually have reference help available from opening to closing. Academic libraries are open the longest amount of time, often more than 100 hours per week, however, in-person reference service is seldom available all the time. Late-night and some weekend hours, especially, may not have scheduled reference service. Institutions that have a large population of resident students, or have active programs of evening and weekend classes, need to provide more hours of reference service than colleges or universities that are largely commuter campuses.

Smaller libraries schedule one person at a time at the reference desk, while larger libraries have multiple staffing. Some libraries, responding to decreased demand for face-to-face reference service, schedule " on-call" service some or all hours. When busy, it is a good idea to rotate desk coverage frequently to prevent fatigue. Hours "on the desk" vary, based on number of service hours offered, individuals skills and knowledge, and the number of available staff. A survey of reference desk staffing patterns in academic and public libraries showed considerable variations, both between the two kinds of libraries and within each type of library (Bunge, 1986). Although this survey was performed some time ago, the patterns of reference desk staffing remain largely the same. Common practices include weekday desk shifts of two hours, with longer shifts evenings and on weekends (usually three to four hours).

Typically a person in reference works between 7 and 21 hours per week on the desk. Public library reference personnel work a greater percentage of hours on the reference desk than their academic colleagues. Nearly three-quarters of public library staff surveyed worked over 18 hours per week on the desk, while almost two-thirds of academic library staff worked less than 16 hours on the desk. This difference can be explained by the aggregate quantity of off-desk duty performed by academic reference librarians, especially information literacy instruction and issues related to library and campus governance, or "academic citizenship," and service in professional organizations. In both public and academic libraries, evening and weekend hours often have to be covered. These "off hours" are rotated among the staff, assigned regularly to a few individuals, covered by part-time staff hired for the purpose, or some combination of the above.

Some libraries stretch their staffing and expand their service by joining library collaboratives established to provide 24/7 reference service to participating libraries. Typically, each participating library agrees to contribute a certain amount of time per week towards staffing the collaborative. Questions are usually submitted by users of any library in the consortium to the staff member(s) on duty via e-mail or chat software and answered in real time. Co-operating libraries advertise this service to their users, who may submit reference questions any time of the day or night.

Larger libraries have multiple staffing of reference desks, at least during busy periods. In this situation it is a good idea to schedule inexperienced staff with veterans. The less experienced staff can learn from their more practiced seniors, while the veterans may benefit from the enthusiasm of the younger staff. Another good idea is to schedule individuals with different academic backgrounds together. This will allow a cross-fertilization of knowledge and better service to users.

Staffing Issues

The profession has been debating about employing support staff on the reference desk since the 1970s. This was largely the result of the demand for more specialized reference service. Because there were often not enough librarians to meet the increasing demand, it was necessary in many libraries to delegate some reference functions to paraprofessional staff. Arguments both for and against the practice can be found in the library literature and there are valid arguments on both sides (Courtois, 1984; Emmick, 1985; Greiner, 1988; Jahoda, 1990; McKinzie, 2002).

Proponents of staffing the reference desk with nonlibrarians point to the well-established fact that the majority of questions asked at the typical reference desk are directional. Answering questions about library hours or policies and giving directions to various locations in the library does not, of course, require a graduate degree. The paraprofessional and, some say, even student workers should be used to screen these nonreference questions, freeing the librarian to use her or his expertise answering reference questions and doing other professional-level work (where library schools exist, employing the students in reference may be mutually beneficial). Some libraries that use multiple staffing on the reference desk include paraprofessionals with librarians. Other libraries assign paraprofessionals to the desk during less busy periods.

The traditional model of providing reference service involves direct staff–user interaction at some physical service point. Decreasing numbers of reference questions and increasing demands of providing digital reference services are prompting some libraries to consider alternative models. Some advocate a tiered service model, usually involving an information desk staffed by paraprofessional staff and students. The information desk personnel filter out simple directional questions and refer reference questions to librarians.

Rather than having librarians sit at the reference desk, some academic libraries use support staff at the desk with the librarians available in their offices to take referrals or have consultation appointments with users. This is the "research consultation model" pioneered by Brandeis University Libraries in 1990. Some libraries, responding to decreased demand for "face-to-face" reference service in many libraries and the increasing demands on reference staff, schedule "on-call" service some or all hours. Decreasing numbers of reference questions have even prompted some to call for the elimination of the reference desk entirely (for example, see Bell, 2007). Some libraries have merged the reference and circulation desks into one service point. Librarians spend their reference shifts working on other projects; for example, answering questions asked via IM, chat, or text messaging, designing Web sites, preparing instruction, and so forth until circulation staff call them to answer in-person reference questions.

Opponents of the practice of nonprofessional reference staffing, while conceding that many questions are directional and can be answered by nonlibrarians, nevertheless argue for the professional nature of reference work. Many reference questions, they assert, begin as apparent directional questions. "Where is the encyclopedia?" for example, often evolves into a research question. It takes a librarian's professional training and expertise, they say, to analyze a readers' request for information, ask the right questions, and answer a requester's true information need rather than contribute to the requester's ignorance of the library by giving him or her only what is asked for. The primary concern about using paraprofessionals to provide reference service has been their performance effectiveness. Several studies on the effectiveness of paraprofessionals at the reference desk, including both user satisfaction and accuracy of answers, indicate mixed results (Rieh, 1999, p. 180).

In practice, surveys show that it is common in many libraries for support staff to serve on the reference desk. Many libraries have both paraprofessional and professional assistance available. Given the increasing demands of implementing new technology to meet users' needs, pressures to document accountability and assess reference service effectiveness, and changing patterns of reference demand it is likely that support staff will continue to find their talents for providing reference services in demand. This allows reference departments to enjoy the benefits of employing nonlibrarians to answer nonresearch questions, while making better use of the knowledge and experience of the librarians.

Keeping and Using Records and Statistics

Like other public service departments, the reference section maintains records and statistics to measure the work accomplished by the section. The administrator uses this information for several purposes. The following are a few examples:

- To see if the demand for the various reference services is increasing or decreasing
- To guide departmental and library resource allocation
- To assess the degree of success in providing services
- To measure the daily and seasonal levels and demand for service
- To measure the impact of new programs and services
- To garner community support for the library and its services

More information on assessing the quality and effectiveness of reference service may be found in Chapters 3 and 16.

At a minimum the reference staff maintains the following types of statistics:

- The number of questions asked by time of day (usually categorized into directional, reference, and research)
- The mode of reference questions, for example, in-person, telephone, e-mail, chat, text, IM, or individual appointment
- The number of instruction sessions, orientations, and tours delivered, by subject or department and the number of attendees

As with other forms of record keeping, statistics and records of reference activity should be maintained only if useful or potentially useful. The categories of records should be studied occasionally to see whether they are still needed and worth the time and effort of continuing to compile them.

TECHNOLOGY'S IMPACT ON REFERENCE SERVICE

Technology is a blessing and a challenge for reference staff. It provides faster and more convenient access to more information. It also adds to the complexity of providing the information. Technology comes in a variety of "flavors" and each requires a different approach to the search process in order to produce a wealth of information.

The ability to use electronic resources increases the professional competence and abilities of reference staff. To provide quality service, reference staff must know both the existing printed sources and also know about the available networked resources, the different (and ever-changing) database interfaces, how to navigate the Web, and the intricacies of the online catalog. A by-product of this increased expertise and ability to answer questions may be greater esteem for library services and staff on the part of library users.

Technology presents challenges to the lives of the reference staff, especially in larger libraries with many resources. Staff who provide remote service via IM, chat, texting, or e-mail must work to establish and maintain effective behavioral aspects of reference service when the usual visual and verbal cues are not available. Reference staff must learn numerous databases and searching protocols in addition to the knowledge required for reference work with existing printed sources, while maintaining performance in other duties such as collection development, instruction, readers' advisory, and other tasks.

Conscientious staff members have to work harder, smarter, and longer to raise and maintain their level of expertise to take full advantage of the new and evolving resources available. It may be that the quality of performance and the ability to remain current with developments in the profession decline as the amount and sophistication of responsibilities increase.

Access to online sources in some cases changes the definition of quality reference service. Professional ethics require that reference staff give accurate information. Today, accurate (that is, the most up-to-date) information often is only available online. Using print sources to answer a question when online alternatives are available may mean giving the user less current data. In the last decade of the twentieth century, for example, an inquiry for current financial data on a corporation required reference staff to know about financial publications from publishers such as Moody's or Standard & Poor's, or perhaps have access to annual reports for the most recent available data. Now the staff member must know how to search one or more of the financial databases to retrieve the most up-to-the-minute—that is, most accurate—information. In addition, the staff member must know what information is available on the Web and must be able to gauge its reliability. The reference staff member who does not know how to use online databases effectively, or whose library does not provide sufficient resources to access this information, is in the frustrating position of not being able to provide the best information available.

Along with the advantages inherent in electronic reference sources, however, there are two dangers that are, paradoxically, in opposition to each other. The first is that the uncritical or unskilled user may inadvertently miss much available material. The speed, power, and ease of using OPACs, online databases, and the Web create the assumption in some users that assistance by the reference staff is no longer necessary. These users assume that they know how to search a database or Web site effectively enough to reveal its contents, and that the retrieved information accurately reflects the contents of the library or database.

In fact, to use digital reference sources effectively, one must know more than how to use a Web browser. One must at least understand the limits of the database or Web site searched. Users are often uncritical about which databases they search for information on a particular subject. Left alone, they will often choose an inappropriate resource (for example, search a business database for information on youth gangs) and retrieve far less information than they would using an appropriate source, including a printed one. And yet, research indicates that users seem to be satisfied no matter how much they retrieve from the Web. (Is this another instance of the medium being more important than the message?)

Many users are also not aware of the specialized searching procedures that enhance the effectiveness of electronic databases. The untutored user, for example, does not comprehend the technique of combining terms using Boolean logic (combining terms with the words "and," "or," and "not" to refine a search). The ability to limit searches (by date, language, scholarly journal, and so forth) for more precise retrieval is another characteristic often not understood. Even the most user-friendly systems do not provide enough instruction for some individuals to use the systems effectively, so they miss many of the advantages of digital reference sources.

This unsuspected complexity of automated reference sources makes it incumbent on reference staff in most situations to endeavor to instruct users about the systems. When referring a user to a database, staff should spend some time with the person at the terminal to make sure she/he knows how to operate the system effectively. Staff should approach other users who have not requested assistance and offer to answer any questions about their search. By teaching users to utilize electronic resources, the reference staff will be insuring that library users will be able to use the library's resources to their best advantage.

The other danger resulting from the revolution in digital reference sources is the opposite of the first: that the speed and power of electronic references will generate too much material and drown the user in information. Many library users do not need or want the scope and quantity of information that the Web gives them. These users may be better served by the traditional printed references available in all reference collections. Many people, too, lack the training to critically examine the mass of data presented and select the best quality information. Staff should use the reference interview to judge the user's need for information with these two considerations in mind, and give the user neither too much nor too little information.

Technostress is a popular term describing the frustration people feel in trying to cope with new technology (Kupersmith, 1992). Some staff members have a higher frustration level as a result of the challenges of learning new technologies and keeping up with changes in the old ones. Knowing about the advantages of automated reference sources and not being able to use them can also lead to frustration. Stress may be apparent in the following ways, among others: feelings of insecurity and inability to cope; resentment towards users or concern about not having enough time with them; and feelings of being overburdened, of lack of control, marginalization, and lack of administrative concern and support.

Digital reference is a permanent and increasingly important part of reference service and will become more important as libraries adapt to the changing needs of their users. Reference managers should recognize the demands of the technology on staff and reduce the demands in other areas so that people have the time to acquire and maintain the expertise necessary to perform digital reference. Identifying training opportunities and making the time and resources available so that staff can take advantage of them are incumbent on the manager. Individuals planning a career in reference services should take every opportunity to improve their computer literacy.

ETHICAL AND LEGAL CONSIDERATIONS

The question "What is the right thing to do?" challenges professionals in all fields. Written codes of ethics in librarianship, where they exist, tend to be vague and "toothless," with no provisions for investigation and punishment of malfeasance. RUSA has promulgated *Guidelines for Information Services* (2000) (http://www.ala.org/ala/rusa/rusaprotools/referenceguide/guideli nesinformation.cfm) which, combined with the ALA's *Code of Ethics* (1995) (http://www.ala.org/ala/oif/statementspols/codeofethics/codeethics.

htm), provides the best statement of the ethical standards for reference librarianship.

The performance of reference service has both affirmative and restrictive ethical and legal dimensions. The affirmative dimension includes the responsibilities and duties inherent in reference service regarding confidentiality, quality, and types of service provided. The restrictive dimension includes limitations in such matters as medical, tax, and legal advice or interpretation. The following paragraphs discuss some of the ethical and legal considerations of which the reference staff must be aware.

Information provided to the user should be the most accurate possible, regardless of the type of question or the status of the requester. There is a lot of pressure on reference staff to provide answers. At times, it may be tempting to guess at or speculate about an answer to a question rather than admit that one cannot be found. The proper procedure to follow if one cannot find an answer is to tell the requester that a number of sources (and their names, if asked) were consulted and to make a referral to another person or agency.

Community informational needs should be met locally as far as is possible and practical, within the local constraints of available informational and human resources (that is, library materials and staff time and expertise).

There should be no differentiation in service because of the person's individual characteristics. Age, ethnic or racial group, height, weight, religious or political affiliation, sexual orientation, personal appearance, or personality type have no bearing on the quality of service provided to eligible users. The role, scope, and mission of individual institutions should determine eligibility of users. In special libraries, for example, there frequently is differentiation in levels of service and access to information, but this is determined by the goals and objectives of the institution, not the whim of the staff member.

Library service should be given efficiently, openly, and amiably. Because most users will be unfamiliar and often uncomfortable with at least some aspects of library use, and because asking a question puts the person in a vulnerable position—admitting ignorance is not easy for many people—the reference staff should have a consistently positive attitude, without any hint of seeming patronizing or "superior." Belittling a user's question or ignorance either in front of the user or to others, even unintentionally, harms the user, the user–library relationship, and the library's reputation and standing in the community. As in any professional relationship, the user's right to privacy and to confidentiality should always be respected. The ALA's *Code of Ethics* (1995) includes the following relevant statement: "We protect each library user's right to privacy and confidentiality with respect to information sought or received and resources consulted, borrowed, acquired or transmitted" (http://www.ala. org/ala/oif/statementspols/codeofethics/codeethics.htm).

Digital reference services, such as IM, e-mail, and chat offer additional challenges to protecting user confidentiality. If the digital trails of reference transactions are preserved and if the requesters can be identified, for example by their e-mail addresses or user names, then maintaining user confidentiality is threatened. The USA PATRIOT Act permits government authorities to confiscate library records and computers without a court order, and if the reference desk computer contains an archive of reference transactions the user information could be revealed. Reference staff should make sure that digital records of reference questions are erased from hard drives and servers so confidentiality can be maintained. (We discuss the USA PATRIOT Act in more detail in Chapter 15.)

Sometimes, shy people have a hard time asking a question. At other times, a reader may not want to reveal the exact nature of the question, and only seek the most general kind of assistance. When a user asks a reference staff member a general question about medical dictionaries or self-help books, the staff member may encounter resistance when trying to help the user by defining the need more narrowly. Such resistance, or a perception that the user is uncomfortable or embarrassed, even a little angry, is a clue that the user may not want to identify the particular reason the information is desired. The reference person should be sensitive enough to recognize such clues about a desire for privacy, and not persist. Staff should show the user the reference area or collection or database and politely inform the user that further reference help is readily available if needed. "Sharing stories" about such users is, of course, a gross violation of professional ethics. Unless done for a constructive purpose, it works against both the individual library staff member and the professional role of reference staff members.

Because of legal and ethical complexities, there are limitations on the kinds of answers that can be given to users regarding medical, legal, and tax information. Staff should always help a user to find *information*, but should never give a user medical, legal, or tax *advice* or *interpretation*, even if the requester directly solicits it, unless the staff member is professionally qualified to give such information. For example, many law librarians have law degrees, which may qualify them to give legal advice or interpretations.

Staff can share personal opinions on social, political, religious, and other matters in a social situation, but *not* as part of a reference transaction. While "on the job," the librarian/staff member should try to keep an open perspective and promote awareness by giving users a variety of sources that address the information desired, especially on a controversial topic, from differing points of view. When the available sources are heavily opinionated or present a limited viewpoint, staff members ought to at least inform the user that other viewpoints exist, and may suggest additional materials which strive to be balanced, or, when these are not available, materials that present an opposite point of view. If information is dated, the reference person should so inform the user and suggest alternative sources with more current data to supplement or modify the older information. There should be no personal financial gain resulting from the role of the reference staff member as a representative of the library in dealing with the user.

The Children's Internet Protection Act (CIPA), enacted in 2000, requires libraries and schools to install filters on their Internet computers. The penalty for not doing so is loss of federal funding and discounts for computers and computer access. The intent of the law is to protect minors from pornography, however implementing the law challenges the principle of intellectual freedom and hampers the effectiveness of the Web as a reference source. Public and school libraries have developed various policies on implementing CIPA, from installing filters on all public stations, installing filters on some stations designated for children, and declining to install filters at all. Most public libraries have taken a middle ground, either designating certain stations without filters as "adults only" or disabling filters upon requests by adults (allowed by CIPA). (For additional information on CIPA, see Chapters 10 and 14).

Reference staff members are sometimes caught between their desire to provide information to users and the values of their professional associations, their personal values, and community standards. Internet access means that library users may read, view, or listen to information that may be considered pornographic or otherwise offensive to community standards. This is most likely to occur in public libraries. What should the reference staff member do if asked to help locate information on the Web that may be considered pornographic or otherwise offensive to one's personal or community values? If the staff member has a reason to believe the information may not be protected by the First Amendment, there is good reason for hesitancy. This circumstance would be very rare, however. As with any other request for information, the reference staff's responsibility is to assist the requester to locate the information as efficiently as possible, within the service standards of the particular library. This is true whether the desired information is the Web page for *Playboy* magazine or that for al-Qaeda.

Staff should be aware of and understand the ethical and legal limitations on reference service and be familiar with guidelines as presented in the reference policy of their institution. When questionable or "borderline" inquiries occur, staff should consult with appropriate colleagues for guidance.

SUMMARY

Reference librarianship, with its emphasis on personal service, potential for positive feedback from satisfied users, flexible hours, and wide variety of subjects, duties, and responsibilities is perhaps the most rewarding and most demanding area of library service. With the expansion of information technology and its effect on the delivery of reference services, it is also the most interesting and challenging. In the next chapter we will explore the different sources reference staff members use to answer questions.

Chapter Review Material

1. What are the three primary roles of reference services?
2. What is the philosophy behind reference service?
3. What duties do reference staff members commonly perform?
4. What is the most important quality to look for in reference personnel? Name some other desirable qualifications.
5. What are the types of questions asked at the reference desk and how do they illustrate the different levels of reference service?
6. Describe the "reference interview" and tell why it is important.
7. What are some of the potential problems reference staff must be prepared to deal with when working with the public?

8. Discuss the place of referrals in reference work. How has automation enhanced referral?
9. What are some of the advantages of digital reference services? Some of the challenges?
10. What is "readers' advisory service"?
11. What factors influence reference desk scheduling?
12. What are the pros and cons of staffing the reference desk with nonlibrarians?
13. What kinds of statistics are kept at the reference desk? How does the reference administrator use them?
14. Discuss some of the ethical and legal aspects of reference work.
15. While at the reference desk, you are asked by a foreign-looking individual with a heavy accent for information about building miniature atomic bombs. As you proceed toward the science and engineering indexes, you notice him giving quick, nervous glances in every direction. Should you call the FBI? CIA? Engineering librarian?

REFERENCES

Bell, Steven J. 2007. "Who Needs a Reference Desk?" *Library Issues* 27, no. 6: 1–4.

Bunge, Charles A. 1986. "Reference Desk Staffing Patterns: Report of a Survey," *RQ* 27, no. 2: 171–179.

Courtois, Martin.1984. "The Use of Nonprofessionals at Reference Desks," *College & Research Libraries* 45, no. 5: 385–391.

Durrance, Joan C., and Karen E. Pettigrew. 2000. "Community Information: The Technological Touch," *Library Journal* 125, no. 2: 44–46.

Emmick, Nancy. 1985. "Nonprofessionals on Reference Desks in Academic Libraries," *The Reference Librarian* 12, no. 12: 149–160.

Green, Samuel. 1876. "Personal Relations between Librarians and Readers," *Library Journal* 1: 74–81.

Greiner, J. M. 1988. "The Role of Nonprofessionals in Small Public Libraries," *Public Libraries* 27, no. 2: 76–78.

Houghton, Sarah. 2005. "Instant Messaging: Quick and Dirty Reference for Teens and Others," *Public Libraries* 44, no. 4:192–193.

Jahoda, Gerald, and Frank Bonney. 1990. "The Use of Paraprofessionals in Public Libraries for Answering Reference Questions," *RQ* 29, no. 3: 328–331.

Kupersmith, J. 1992. "Technostress and the Reference Librarian," *Reference Services Review* 20, no. 2: 7–14.

Luo, Lili. 2008. "Chat Reference Evaluation," *Reference Services Review* 36, no. 1: 71–85.

McKinzie, Steve. 2002. "For Ethical Reference, Pare the Paraprofessionals," *American Libraries* 33, no. 9: 42.

Pyati, Ajit. 2003. "Limited English Proficient Users and the Need for Improved Reference Services," *Reference Services Review* 31, no. 3: 264–271.

Reference and Adult Services Division. American Library Association. 2000. "Guidelines for Information Services." http://www.ala.org/ala/rusa/rusaprotools/referenceguide/guidelinesinformation.cfm.

Rieh, Soo Young. 1999. "Changing Reference Service Environment: A Review of Perspectives from Managers, Librarians, and Users," *The Journal of Academic Librarianship* 25, no. 3: 178–186.

Rogers, Tim, Atabong Fombon, and Erica Reynolds. 2005. "Community Information, Electrified," *Library Journal Netconnect*, Winter: 4–9.

Rothstein, Samuel. 1989. "The Development of Reference Services through Academic Traditions, Public Library Practice, and Special Librarianship," *The Reference Librarian* 25/26, no. 11: 33–156.

Saricks, Joyce G. 2005. *Reader's Advisory Service in the Public Library*, 3rd ed. Chicago: American Library Association.

Wilson, M. C. 2000. "Evolution or Entropy: Changing Reference/User Culture and the Future of Reference Librarians," *Reference & User Services Quarterly* 39, no. 4: 387–390.

Woodward, B.S. 1988. "The Effectiveness of an Information Desk Staffed by Graduate Students and Nonprofessionals," *Journal of Academic Librarianship* 50, no. 4: 455–467.

Wyatt, Neal. 2007. "2.0 for Readers," *Library Journal* 132, no. 18: 30–33.

SUGGESTED READINGS

Agosto, Denise, and Holly Anderton. 2007. "Whatever Happened to 'Always Cite the Source?" *Reference & Users Services Quarterly* 47, no. 1: 44–54.

Alfino, Mark, and Linda Pierce. 1997. *Information Ethics for Librarians.* Jefferson, NC: McFarland and Co.

Booth, Heather. 2007. *Serving Teens Through Readers' Advisory.* Chicago: American Library Association.

Bracke, Marianne Stowell, et al. 2007. "Finding Information in a New Landscape," *College & Research Libraries* 68, no. 3: 248–267.

Caputo, Janette S. 1991. *Stress and Burnout in Library Service.* Phoenix, AZ: Oryx Pr.

Cassell, Kay An, and Uma Hiremath. 2006. *Reference and Information Services in the 21st Century.* New York: Neal-Schuman.

Courtney, Nancy. 2001. "Evaluating the Use of Paraprofessionals at the Reference Desk," *College & Undergraduate Libraries* 8, no. 1: 31–40.

D'Aniello, C. A. 1989. "Cultural Literacy and Reference Service," *RQ* 28, no. 3: 370–380.

DeAngelis, P. 1987. "Pedro's Question: Learning Resource Centers and the Community," *Library Journal* 112, no. 12: 41–43.

De Souza, Yvonne. 1996. "Reference Work with International Students: Making the Most Use of the Neutral Question," *Reference Services Review* 24, no. 4: 41–48.

Dewdney, Patricia, and Gillian Mitchell. 1996. "Oranges and Peaches: Understanding Communication Accidents in the Reference Interview," *RQ* 35, no. 4: 520–535.

Gates, Jean Key. 1994. *Guide to the Use of Libraries and Information Sources,* 7th ed. New York: McGraw Hill.

Genz, Marcella D. 1998. "Working the Reference Desk," *Library Trends* 46, no. 3: 505–525.

Hirko, Buff, and Mary Bucher Ross. 2004. *Virtual Reference Training.* Chicago: American Library Association.

Hock, Randolph. 2007. *The Extreme Searcher's Internet Handbook: A Guide for the Serious Searcher.* 2nd ed. Medford, NJ: CyberAge Books.

Jennerich, Elaine Zaremba, and Edward J. Jennerich. 1997. *The Reference Interview as a Creative Art,* 2nd ed. Littleton, CO: Libraries Unlimited.

Katz, Bill, and Ruth Fraley, eds. 1986. *Personnel Issues in Reference Services.* Binghamton, NY: Haworth Press.

Katz, William A. 1996. *Introduction to Reference Work.* 7th ed. New York: McGraw-Hill.

Lam, R. Errol. 1988. "The Reference Interview: Some Intercultural Considerations." *RQ* 27, no. 2: 390–395.

Lanning, Scott, and John Bryner, J. 2004. *Essential Reference Services for Today's School Media Specialists.* Westport, CT: Libraries Unlimited.

Liu, Mengxiong. 1995. "Ethnicity and Information Seeking." *The Reference Librarian* no. 49–50: 123–134.

McKinzie, Steve. 2002. "For Ethical Reference, Pare the Paraprofessionals," *American Libraries* 33, no. 9: 42.

Mellon, Constance A. 1986. "Library Anxiety: A Grounded Theory and Its Development," *College & Research Libraries* 47, no. 2: 160–165.

Moyer, Jessica. 2008. *Research-Based Readers' Advisory.* Chicago: American Library Association.

Neuhaus, Paul, Connie Van Fleet, and Danny P. Wallace. 2003. "Privacy and Confidentiality in Digital Reference," *Reference & User Services Quarterly* 43, no. 1: 26–37.

Reed, Sally Gardner. 1992. "Breaking Through: Effective Reference Mediation for Non-traditional Public Library Users," *The Reference Librarian* 17, no. 37: 109–119.

Rieh, Sy. 1999. "Changing Reference Service Environment: A Review of Perspectives from Managers, Librarians, and Users," *The Journal of Academic Librarianship* 25, no. 3: 178–186.

Saxton, Matthew and John V. Richardson Jr. 2002. *Understanding Reference Transactions: Transforming an Art into a Science.* San Diego, CA: Academic Press.

Standerfer, Amanda E. 2006. "Reference Services in Rural Libraries," *The Reference Librarian* 45, no. 93: 137–149.

Stover, Kaite Mediatore. 2005. "Working Without a Net: Readers' Advisory in the Small Public Library," *Reference & User Services Quarterly* 45, no. 2: 122–125.

Strife, Mary L. 1994. "Special Libraries and Diversity: Ethical Considerations," *The Reference Librarian* no. 45–46: 213–219.

Sundin, Olof. 2005. "Negotiations on Information-Seeking Expertise," *Journal of Documentation* 64, no. 1: 24–44.

Thomas, Lucille C. 1989. "Multiculturalism: Challenges and Opportunities for School Libraries," *IFLA Journal* 15, no. 3: 203–209.

Tin, Koh Lay, and Suliman Al-Hawamdeh. 2002. "The Changing Role of Paraprofessionals in the Knowledge Economy," *Journal of Information Science* 28, no. 4: 331–343.

Whitlatch, Jo B. 2000. *Evaluating Reference Services: A Practical Guide.* Chicago: American Library Association.

Wyatt, Neal. 2007. *The Readers' Advisory Guide to Nonfiction.* Chicago: American Library Association.

Wyman, Andrea. 1988. "Working with Nontraditional Students in the Academic Library," *Journal of Academic Librarianship* 14, no. 1: 32–33.

Zanin-Yost, Alessia. 2004. "Digital Reference: What the Past has Taught Us and What the Future Will Hold," *Library Philosophy and Practice* 7, no. 1: http://www.webpages.uidaho.edu/~mbolin/lppv7n1.htm.

Chapter 5

Reference Sources

Knowledge is of two kinds. We know a subject ourselves or we know where we can find information upon it.
—Samuel Johnson, *Boswell's Life of Johnson*

Reference librarians are using online reference sources much more frequently than traditional print reference sources by a ratio of approximately 6–1.
—Jane T. Bradford et al., 2005

Access to collections and information, along with good customer service, is the key to successful reference service. Collections today come in a variety of formats and it requires time and effort to understand just which format and source will provide the best results. In an ever-increasing online world, it may surprise some people that a print source may have the best information on a topic even when there is an online version available. What the general user may not know is that some publishers of both print and electronic versions of a title hold back the release of the most current material from the e-version in the hope maintaining their print version income. (Journal publishers are the most likely to do this, often waiting six months to a year before releasing an issue for posting in a database.) Knowing which title format is most current can make the difference between a successful or disappointing reference experience for a user.

High-quality reference service also goes beyond knowing the local collections. This requires staff to have at least a general knowledge of other community resources. Today's online catalogs and a variety of resource-sharing projects make gaining such knowledge easier, but it still takes time and effort to explore what others have and that time may not be readily available. Given the wide assortment of daily reference duties, finding time to have a sound knowledge of one's home resources and some understanding of what others have is a significant challenge. However, those who do find the time and make the effort are the individuals who provide top quality rather than minimally good services.

REFERENCE COLLECTION: CHARACTERISTICS AND CATEGORIES

The reference collection is defined as the information resources selected by the reference staff to do reference work. These sources may be available in any format, especially in print and on the Internet. The resources may be housed in the library itself or accessed from remote locations via the library network. Every reference collection is unique, and the specific sources selected are based on the goals and objectives of the particular institution. Librarians build their reference collections to do three things:

1. To answer the information needs of a library's clientele.
2. To facilitate access to the library's collection.
3. To provide guidance to information resources beyond the local library collection.

Many standard reference works and databases list conventional reference materials, but there is little agreement as to which sources, if any, are *essential* to a collection. The bibliography at the end of this chapter cites some of the standard lists of reference materials and the selection tools that list and review or describe current reference sources.

The librarians and support staff responsible for developing and administering the reference collection establish guidelines for including sources in the collection. These guidelines, often codified into a reference collection development policy, consider such factors as:

1. *Usefulness in answering reference questions.* This factor is judged by the experience of the reference staff. The usefulness of an information source depends on a library's user needs.
2. *Depth of coverage.* A work the purpose of which is to introduce subjects with brief discussions rather than in great depth might reside in the reference collection. Examples of this would be encyclopedias or yearbooks, which cover a subject in a few pages or paragraphs.
3. *Local needs.* Libraries find that the recurrence of certain types of questions requires placing appropriate materials in the reference collection. The history of a city or a local environmental impact report, for example, if frequently consulted for reference inquiries, might be placed in reference rather than in the general collection.
4. *Format.* Some works are added to the reference collection because they are designed to answer questions of fact and not to be read in their entirety. This would include such materials as almanacs, atlases, books of mathematical tables, dictionaries, or telephone books.

5. *Frequency of use.* Some materials, like local road maps, are placed in a reference collection because they are consulted frequently. It saves time to keep them physically close to a reference or information desk, and noncirculating.

6. *Mission of the parent organization.* For example, the reference collection of a faith-based institution would collect materials relating to the institution's mission. It is especially crucial in the special library setting to understand the mission of the parent organization and to fine-tune the collection development policy accordingly.

7. *Expected user groups.* In addition to recognizing the mission of the parent organization, it is important to know the different user groups who expect to use the collection. These users may expect that certain materials be available in particular formats. They will certainly expect that material be as current as possible, especially in the corporate environment.

SELECTION OF REFERENCE SOURCES

Although the reference collection is of primary importance in providing good service, reference collection development has not enjoyed a primary focus in the professional literature. Reference librarians usually have the responsibility for selecting reference materials, with input from the support staff. When time is short, reference collection development is often subordinated to other responsibilities that are more people-oriented or otherwise compelling. In some libraries, staff members select new reference acquisitions in a haphazard fashion due to an uncoordinated collection development policy or even the lack of a policy. The emphasis in recent years has been on development of the digital reference collection.

Many factors play a part in determining what materials staff members select. In addition to the selection guidelines mentioned above, some of the more important considerations are the library budget, the resources of other libraries in the area, the evaluation of reference materials, and the format preference; that is, if the source is available in print and online, which format should be acquired? Both?

As new sources, in whatever format, are added or linked to the collection, staff members examine and evaluate them. When evaluating materials for purchase or use, staff members consider certain basic issues:

1. *Demand.* Will anyone ever use this item? Does the cost reflect its value to the library and its users?

2. *Aim and scope.* What is the purpose of the work? Does it meet its stated goals? Is it more suitable for a particular age group, for the layman, or for the expert? What are its chronological limitations? What kind of questions will it answer? Will this work do something different from material already in the collection, or do something similar, but better?

3. *Timeliness.* Is it necessary for a work in this subject field to have the latest information? If this source purports to have the latest information, does it? How is the work updated—for example, by supplements, regular revisions, or new editions, and how often is it updated? If available in multiple formats, which one is more up to date?

4. *Format.* Is the material arranged logically, whether alphabetically, topically, chronologically, or geographically? Is it easy to use? Are there sufficient cross-references and an index? Is the binding strong enough for heavy use? Is the database interface easy to navigate? Is computer response time acceptable? Is the typeface easy to read? Are there graphics of good quality? Are they in color?

5. *Authority.* What is the reputation and training of the author or editor? What are the sources of the data? Are they cited in the text? What is the publisher's reputation?

6. *Accuracy.* Is the information correct? Is it up to date?

7. *Alternatives.* When considering electronic reference sources, additional concerns must be considered, such as the stability of the site, hardware and software reliability and compatibility, and the availability and usefulness of help files.

One of the primary sources librarians use to select new reference sources is the book review journal. Professional publications like *Library Journal*, *Choice*, and *School Library Journal* include reviews of new reference sources in each issue, and have broadened their scope to include Internet sources. *The Charleston Advisor*, for example, specializes in reviewing Web sources. Journals in subject disciplines also include reference sources among the titles they review. The better reviews will use the selection criteria described above to evaluate a particular work, and compare the titles reviewed with similar works. These reviews, written by specialists in the field, are invaluable for assisting with selection decisions.

In order to help staff with the routine elements of collection development, many libraries make use of standing orders and approval plans. Standing orders are placed with publishers to assure that new volumes and editions of particular titles will be sent to the library as they are published. Libraries frequently acquire reference sources in this way, saving staff a great deal of time.

Approval plans automatically deliver new titles for the staff to review; staff may return unwanted items, unlike the standing order approach. The library staff develop profiles describing the collecting interests of their library, which publishers or "jobbers" (companies that act as middlemen between libraries and publishers) then use to determine which new titles to send. While this frees librarians from much routine ordering, staff may be misled into thinking that every appropriate reference title will always arrive, but this is not always the case. There is also a danger that staff will accept more "marginal" titles just because they are "in hand," thus reducing the funds available for more useful titles. Just because a publisher delivered appropriate materials in the past does not guarantee every new title will be appropriate. Publisher's goals sometimes change as do libraries; this means the staff ought to constantly monitor both its profile and what is arriving through the approval plan. The reference staff still need to review new arrivals and published reviews to assure the quality has not slipped.

Collection development criteria also change with changing user demands, and the profile for a particular subject may become inaccurate for this or for other reasons. In addition, many valuable alternative titles, published by small presses, are not included among the titles handled by the approval plan vendors. Clearly, being alert to changes in the environment of both the library and publishers as well as being aware of the total output of reference titles is a key element in having a quality reference collection.

Special libraries usually do not use approval plans. Staff must therefore be particularly vigilant in scanning catalogs, newspaper articles, press releases, and review materials. Many special librarians keep a "possible orders" file for use when funds become available. Such libraries also make the greatest effort to solicit input from their users to ensure that the collection is current and appropriate.

Librarians are generally responsible for selecting reference materials. However, support staff, especially those working at the reference desk, are in a good position to recommend materials for purchase. They can also keep the librarians informed about questions that have proven difficult or impossible to answer. The librarians use this information to help evaluate the reference collection and select new titles. New Internet sites or online databases, while evaluated in the literature, are often only discovered in the course of doing reference work. It is, therefore, important for all members of a reference department to share responsibility for updating colleagues about new, useful sites.

TYPES OF REFERENCE MATERIALS

There are several kinds of reference materials. In addition to the library catalog, there are bibliographies or bibliographic guides, dictionaries, directories, encyclopedias, handbooks and manuals, periodical indexes and abstracts, biographical sources, atlases and gazetteers, pamphlets, yearbooks and almanacs, and World Wide Web search engines. The following section includes definitions of the above categories and examples of each. For more comprehensive lists of individual reference works, the reader is directed to the bibliography at the end of this chapter.

Bibliographies are lists of books, periodical articles, and other materials. A bibliography may be a general list of books, like *Books in Print*, but is more often a list of materials relating to a specific subject, such as *The Hopi: A Bibliography* or *Bibliography of Bioethics*. Bibliographies do not necessarily provide information on a subject; rather, they are useful because they direct the reader to appropriate materials. Entries in a bibliography frequently include descriptive or evaluative annotations to help the reader better judge a work on the basis of its content or quality.

Dictionaries define words and give their spelling, pronunciation, syllabication, and origins. The dictionary may cover the words of a language in general, or it may be limited to a special subject. *The Oxford English Dictionary* is a dictionary of one language. *Harper's Bible Dictionary* and *The American Political Dictionary* are dictionaries limited to a specific subject area.

A *directory* lists names of persons or organizations and pertinent information about them. The directory may include addresses, telephone numbers, the officers of an organization, and a description of the organization. Examples are local directories, including telephone books and city directories; institutional directories, like *The College Bluebook*; and organizational directories, such as *The Encyclopedia of Associations* and the *United States Government Manual.*

Encyclopedias attempt to provide concise information on a wide variety of topics. The information is usually presented in short articles varying in length from a paragraph to several pages. There are general encyclopedias covering all fields of knowledge, for example, *Britannica Online* and *Wikipedia*, and subject encyclopedias containing more in-depth treatment of specific fields, like *The Encyclopedia of Religion* and the *Encyclopedia of Chemical Technology*. (See the suggested readings at the end of this chapter for Lucy Holman Rector's article comparing Wikipedia's accuracy with that of print encyclopedias.)

Gazetteers and *atlases* are important sources of geographical information. An atlas contains a collection of maps and related information; it may be general or limited to a country or region or focus on a particular topic. General atlases include the *Times Atlas of the World*, *The National Atlas* (http://nationalatlas.gov/) and *Mapquest*; specialized atlases include the digital files of the *TIGER Mapping Service* (http://tiger.census.gov), the *Rand McNally Commercial Atlas*, and *The California Water Atlas*. Because of changes in the landscape and, especially, in political divisions, it is important that atlases and maps be current.

A gazetteer identifies the names of towns, villages, rivers, mountains, lakes, and other geographic features. Supplemental information such as longitude and latitude or population statistics is usually part of the publication. An atlas may include a gazetteer as an index to its maps. Examples of stand-alone gazetteers are the *Columbia Lippincott Gazetteer of the World*, *Webster's Geographical Dictionary*, and the *U.S. Gazetteer* (http://www.census.gov/cgi-bin/gazetteer).

Handbooks and *manuals* serve as ready reference information sources in special or delimited areas of knowledge. The entries are usually concise and sometimes include selected bibliographies. Some examples of handbooks are the *Handbook of Chemistry and Physics* and *The Handbook of Western Philosophy*.

Biographical sources give information about people. The biographical reference may be general (*Biography Resource Center*), or limited to people of a particular profession (*Dictionary of Scientific Biography*), nationality (*Dictionary of American Biography*), ethnic group (*Who's Who among Black Americans*), or gender (*American Women Writers*), or to the living (*Who's Who*) or the dead (*Who Was Who*). The information presented about a person varies; it may consist only of brief factual data, or it may be an article several pages long with references to additional information.

Pamphlet collections contain ephemeral materials, which are not readily available elsewhere. Collections may include free or inexpensive booklets, brochures, leaflets, circulars, maps, newspaper clippings, posters, local government publications, and charts. The collections tend to feature items of local interest selected by the staff for their potential reference value. File arrangement varies with the needs of the library, sometimes by subject or format; for example, career files, AIDS information files, or picture files. Staff will often maintain a subject index of the collection to facilitate its use. The *Vertical File Index* is a bimonthly annotated pamphlet list useful in selecting pamphlets for a collection. Pamphlet collections are time-consuming to maintain and must be continually weeded of outdated material. If a library does not have sufficient resources to properly maintain a vertical file collection, it is probably better off not offering this resource (at least in a print form). Another and probably the most compelling reason for discarding or discontinuing vertical files is the increasing amount of local information found on the Web.

Yearbooks and *almanacs* contain miscellaneous facts and statistical information. These tools are useful in locating answers to a variety of ready reference questions. They contain recent statistical information and cover contemporary events. They are concise in their treatment of topics and may serve as supplements to encyclopedias. Examples of almanacs and yearbooks are the *World Almanac and Book of Facts*, *Statistical Abstract of the United States*, *The World in Figures*, and encyclopedia yearbooks like the *Britannica Book of the Year*.

Indexes systematically list the contents of specific works so that information in those works can be located. *Abstracts* have the added benefit of including summaries or descriptions of the works so indexed. Indexes and abstracts are particularly important as sources to locate information in periodicals, serials, and pamphlets. There are also special indexes for difficult-to-locate material like songs (*Song Index*) or poetry (*Granger's Index to Poetry*) or plays (*Play Index, Ottemiller's Index to Plays in Collections*).

Periodicals and Periodical Indexes

It would be difficult to overemphasize the importance of periodical literature as an information resource. (Periodicals are here defined as publications issued on a regular basis more than once a year). Periodical articles, whether from general interest magazines or scholarly journals, have unique characteristics that make them invaluable for the library collection.

1. Periodical articles generally contain the most current information available on a topic.
2. Periodicals contain information about almost every conceivable subject, often in greater detail than can be found elsewhere.
3. Periodicals are the primary means for communicating original scholarship in all fields of human inquiry.

See Chapter 10 for a detailed discussion of serials.

Each library develops its periodical collection using the same collection development criteria employed in building other collections, such as the circulating book or reference collections. Criteria include the mission of the library, the budget, user needs, collection balance, community standards, and so on. Also considered is whether the periodical is indexed in a periodical index accessible by the library's clientele, thus guaranteeing that the information in the periodical can be found by users. Libraries take greater care in purchasing periodical titles than with most other information sources, because subscribing to a periodical represents a long-term annual commitment of funds, usually on a steep inflationary ladder.

Another way libraries build their periodical collections is through subscribing to periodical aggregators; that is, collections of digital periodicals that cost far less than if subscribed to individually. Vendors like EBSCO and Gale put these collections together to appeal to different kinds of libraries; for example, collections of academic titles for colleges and universities, and collections of popular titles for public libraries. Subscribing to aggregate collections is often more cost-effective than subscribing to individual periodical titles. However, an unintended consequence of subscribing to aggregate collections is that they usually contain titles that do not meet the collection development criteria of individual libraries. There is not necessarily any harm in this, as long as the library has access to the titles that truly meet its users' needs.

Building an adequate periodical collection is only part of the challenge of providing access to this important resource. Indexing the collection so users may find specific articles on the subjects they are seeking has always been a problem. The availability of cataloging records from the Library of Congress and OCLC makes it possible for virtually every library to build a unique public catalog indexing every book, video, and sound recording in its collection. However, there is no similar indexing available for the millions of periodical articles published each year. It would be too expensive and time-consuming for all but the most specialized or smallest of libraries to individually index all the periodicals they receive.

Special libraries often go the extra mile to provide access to current periodicals through some sort of current awareness service. All materials cannot be routed. This would leave nothing on the periodical shelves and no one has time to read everything that interests them anyway. Awareness services can be provided via e-mail notification or by a product such as a "new arrivals" memo with tables of contents attached on an online update service.

Most libraries attempt to solve the problem of providing access to their periodical collections by subscribing to commercially produced periodical indexes. Printed periodical indexes are being replaced by their online counterparts, but print indexes are still being published and you may still encounter a few. If nothing else, the older volumes do index "historic" print serials that are not yet in digital form. They list the articles in a selected number of periodicals by subject and, often, by author. Digital versions improve access by generally including abstracts of the articles and indexing articles by words and phrases occurring in the title, subject headings, abstract, or the text of the articles, as well as by publication date(s), specific journal titles, and in other ways.

Indexing and abstracting tools generally encompass periodicals in a particular subject or field of knowledge. Subjects range from the specific (*PILOTS: Published International Literature on Traumatic Stress, Ethnic NewsWatch*) to the general (*Readers' Guide to Periodical Literature, Academic Search FullTEXT Elite*) and everything in between (*General Science Index, Social Sciences Citation Index*).

The currency of indexes and abstracts is a factor in their usefulness. Online indexes and abstracts, accessible via the Web or through a commercial vendor like Dialog, are generally much more current than printed or CD-ROM sources, and are generally updated within a few days of each title's publication. Printed sources are generally published monthly or quarterly, so the most current issue of a printed index or abstract is usually about three months out of date, and four to six months is not uncommon. Online sources tend to cumulate over a period of years, while printed indexes often cumulate in annual volumes. Some printed indexes and abstracts have coverage extending back more than 100 years. Readers often want the most current information available on a subject, and libraries expedite the processing of new print issues to make them available as soon as possible. Online indexes will almost always be more current than printed indexes.

Most print periodical indexes available in U.S. libraries tend to limit their coverage to a few hundred English-language periodicals. The typical format of a periodical index citation includes the following information: author, title of article, name of the periodical containing the article, volume and issue number, inclusive pages, and the date of issue. (See Figure 5.1.)

Abstracting services differ from indexes in important ways. As the word implies, an abstracting source will include a summary or description of each article, varying in length from a sentence or two to a full paragraph (see Figure 5.2). Abstracting services usually focus on the scholarly literature of a particular field, such as *PsycLit*, *Chemical Abstracts*, or *Sociofile*. They are more comprehensive than periodical indexes, often indexing as many as a few thousand periodicals from around the world. Because of their research value and expense, they are most usually accessible in academic and special libraries.

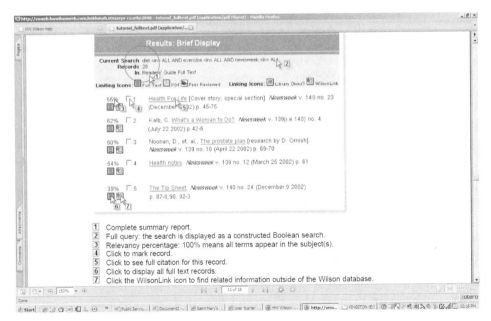

Figure 5.1 Online Index Screen

Reprinted with permission of the H. W. Wilson Company.

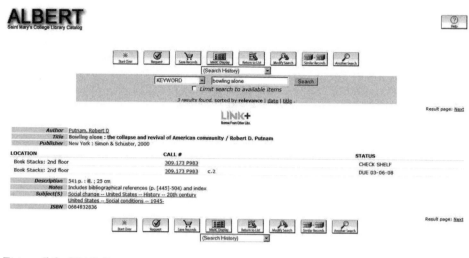

Figure 5.2 OPAC Screen

Virtually all indexes and abstracts now offer an electronic version, either via the Web or both the Web and CD-ROM (though the latter format is being phased out). While a few libraries may still collect the printed versions, the advantages of electronic access to these large databases are apparent.

A frequent and popular development among vendors of online indexing and abstracting services is the bundling of indexing with access to the full texts of the periodical articles. Vendors, including the aggregators we mentioned earlier, are leasing packages of indexing and articles geared to specific markets, like academic titles for colleges and universities, and general interest collections for public libraries. These packages generally consist of traditional indexing to a certain number of titles, from a few hundred to several thousand depending on the package, plus links to the full text of articles from a subset of the indexed titles. This allows the reader something like "one-stop shopping" for periodical articles. The reader can search the index for articles by author, title, subject, keyword, and so forth; retrieve a bibliography of articles; and then click on the references to obtain the full text of the articles themselves. Readers can then acquire the articles by printing, downloading to a disk or thumb drive, or e-mailing the texts to their own e-mail accounts. Of course, no package includes the indexing or the text of all the periodicals in a particular field, so reference staff must instruct customers to use other, more specialized sources if a particular database proves inadequate.

There are hundreds of indexes and abstracting services, many including the full text of at least some of the titles indexed, available for subscription or lease. Each library must choose those services that best meet the needs of its users. A school library media center or a small public library may find that offering access to one or a few periodical indexes will provide all the indexing required for its users. Large public and academic libraries and special libraries are committed to providing access to information beyond the boundaries of their own collections. They may subscribe to hundreds and sometimes thousands of titles in an attempt to provide for the research needs of their users (this is especially true in academic libraries, where more than two-thirds of the materials budget may go to periodical and database subscriptions). Even then, mediated searching of online databases may occasionally be necessary to compensate for the inevitable deficiencies of the indexes and abstracts affordable in-house.

Federated Searching

The proliferation of online databases described above, while greatly expanding the amount of available information, does present some problems for library users. Libraries often subscribe to databases from several different vendors, and each vendor's databases have their own look, feel, and functionality. It is often confusing for individuals to use two or more databases that look and act differently. It is also time consuming to search multiple databases one at a time. This is especially true for the person accustomed to the speed of Internet search engines. Another issue facing users is deciding which database, or databases, to search. When there are 100 or more databases to choose from, sometimes many more in large academic libraries, those people who are reluctant or unable to ask for reference assistance may feel overwhelmed and fail to select the most appropriate database, or databases, to answer their information need.

Libraries and automation vendors are working to solve these and other problems, and one of the more promising experiments of the past few years has been the idea of *federated searching* (sometimes known as *metasearching*). Attempting to do for subscription databases what Google does for the free Web, federated search engines allow the user to search across a range of commercial databases simultaneously. Several vendors, as of this writing, offer federated search products having the following characteristics:

- They allow users to search a range of databases at the same time
- They present a common search interface for the databases searched
- The results are "de-duped," that is, duplicate citations are identified and omitted
- The results allow for relevance ranking of search results according to the search engine's algorithm

Libraries that were early adopters of federated search engines hoped they would address some of the problems users experience when confronted with a multiplicity of databases. Unfortunately, as of this writing, the reality has not matched these expectations. Most federated search engines are able to search only a limited number of databases at a time, so in large libraries at least some databases are not searchable all at once. The number of databases searched simultaneously also affects the speed of the search results. Generally, the more databases searched, the longer the results take to display. Because different databases have different search functionality (for example, symbols used for truncation and implied or explicit Boolean connectors) the most powerful search capabilities of individual databases are lost and generally only simple keyword searches are effective in finding results. De-duping is not always successful because of the different ways database vendors display their citations. Successful federated searches may return a much larger amount of information than the user can successfully process. Finally, the systems are expensive and require a lot of staff time building and maintaining the connections from the search engine to the databases (Warren, 2007).

Nevertheless, assessments of the early versions of federated search engines show that people like the ability to search multiple databases at once. The authors expect to see improvement in federated search engines and that their employment in libraries will become more commonplace.

OPACs and Card Catalogs

The *library catalog*, also know as the OPAC (for online public access catalog) or WebPAC (for Web public access catalog) in the current vernacular, is the most important reference source in the library, other than the library staff. The catalog is the collection of data that attempts to list and index, in some consistent way, the resources of a library. Ideally, the catalog lists all the materials—of whatever format—the library owns or provides access to. In practice, the library catalog usually includes information about the library's collection of books; many catalogs also include media and/or periodical holdings, and in some instances holdings of government documents, archival, and other nonbook documents. OPACs often provide records and links to databases selected by a library as appropriate for the information needs of its clients. Publisher's collections of periodicals, for example, from the American Psychological Association, are usually cataloged and linked to in the OPAC. However, OPACs often do not contain records for the periodical titles available through aggregators due to the "here today, gone tomorrow" nature of the titles in the collections (the vendors sometimes lose the rights to particular titles and they suddenly disappear) and the cost to acquire and maintain the cataloging records.

Library catalogs have taken different forms over the years. The *book catalog* was a written or printed log of books owned, sometimes listed in the order of acquisition, sometimes alphabetized by author or subject. The explosion of literacy in the Industrial Age made the *card catalog* a much more desirable access tool, since many readers could search the catalog simultaneously. Today, OPACs have displaced nearly all card catalogs because of their speed, ease of use, superior indexing, ease of modification, and accessibility.

Although few libraries established after 1890 ever had a book catalog, published book catalogs of the special collections held by some exceptional libraries still exist. Examples include the published holdings of early manuscript materials at the Huntington Library; of the Newberry's Ayer Collection (Native American materials), John M. Wing Collection (History of Printing and Publishing), and Graff Collection (early history of the Trans-Mississippi West); and of the Folger Library's Shakespeareana. These catalogs are very useful for scholars researching the relevant fields. Especially when the collections they index are considered comprehensive collections (that is, everything of major importance, plus most related material of any importance), these published catalogs serve as bibliographic finding tools for other libraries, as well as listing the holdings in that subject area for loan or consultation. As libraries convert their holdings to machine-readable form, access to these special collections will be available online. The monumental *National Union Catalog: Pre-1956* (754 volumes), also called "Mansell," was perhaps the last attempt to manually compile a major printed catalog; this work endeavored to document all pre-1956 book holdings of sizeable libraries in the United States by reproducing library catalog cards.

Card catalogs are rare now, but are still found in some libraries, usually listing materials before the implementation of the online catalogs that supplanted them. Card catalogs offer a number of improvements over book catalogs. Besides permitting simultaneous access by multiple readers, the card catalog offers easy modification of individual records. Adding cards for newly acquired books, correcting or updating information, and entering additional access points (for example, cross-references), as well as withdrawing invalid cards, are functions easily accomplished but costly in staff time. Typically each cataloged item had an author card, title card, one or more subject cards, and shelflist card (A *shelflist* was a file of holdings in classification number order, and was considered the official, nonpublic list of what the library owned.) Other cards for an item might include added author, and series. Online catalogs came into their own during the 1980s. By the end of that decade several vendors offered "true" online catalogs, with author, title, subject, and keyword retrieval. A keyword is a distinguishing word that appears in the title, subjects, notes, or other parts of the cataloging record and provides access by various elements of the MARC cataloging record.

Boolean searching capability, in which a combination of terms is used to specify exact parameters for a specific topic, much like an online database search, links to resources on the Internet. (Boolean searching is built on a method of symbolic logic developed by George Boole, a nineteenth-century English mathematician.) An online catalog can provide remote access through the Web or telephone lines and thus be available to any approved or licensed user with a computer and network connection, or modem and a communications software package. OPACs are kept current far beyond the ability of earlier generations of library staff. Newly cataloged materials display on the catalog screen immediately. Library staff can modify both individual records and whole classes of materials either overnight or almost instantaneously. As subject headings or name authorities change, the library can update the catalog to near-total consistency. Antiquated or inappropriate subject headings are easily updated to their newer, more descriptive or less offensive forms. In addition, staff may add cross-references quickly and easily whenever user confusion dictates.

Online catalogs generally form one element in a library's integrated online system. Circulation, cataloging, acquisitions, serials, and reserve functions (Integrated Library Systems—ILS) are the typical systems. Such integrated systems provide the user a great deal of information about the library collection. If the library does not own an item, some systems allow the user to see if it is on order or recently received and is waiting processing. A user can see if a title is checked out and when it is due back or if the title is lost or missing. Some systems allow borrowers to place a hold for an item or permit borrowers to self–check out items. Most systems also display information about temporary unavailability, such as materials checked out for an exhibit, repairs, rebinding, or on reserve A staff member sitting at the reference desk can tell a caller that a particular item is likely to be on the shelf, or that it is out and due back by a certain date without ever leaving the desk. Staff can generate a myriad of reports, including library holdings, user success or failure rates in finding items in the catalog, acquisitions information, and the use rates for specific titles or categories of material. They can also provide users with bibliographies, recent acquisitions lists by subject, and other interesting or valuable data.

Card catalogs are still present in a few libraries. Some of the larger research libraries have a combination of both card and online catalogs. Library holdings to a certain year are in the card catalog, and materials acquired after that year are in the OPAC. Many school library media centers have OPACs.

In a different vein, many library systems provide online access to the catalogs of the other member institutions, or a combined union catalog of all holdings, searchable from any member's terminals. Individual titles have *tags* to identify the member library or libraries owning a particular title. In such situations, faster interlibrary loan among member libraries is an added benefit. Most libraries with online catalogs do not restrict access to their catalogs to outside users, and anyone may use the World Wide Web to access library catalogs around the world.

Internet Searching Tools

The *Internet* defies simple categorization but it is certainly one of the most important information sources in nearly all libraries. The primary use of the Internet by reference staff is to access local and remote databases and Web sites containing desired information. These databases and Web sites may include library catalogs, full-text journals and newspapers, video and audio files, government documents, consumer information, catalogs of other libraries, periodical indexes, encyclopedias, and just about any other kind of information one would care to name. The development of the Web, with its seamless linking of databases across networks, and easy-to-use point-and-click interface, has greatly improved the utility of the Internet as an information source. Different search tools have been developed to allow users to find the information they are looking for among the vast amount of information available on the Internet. All of these search tools have the potential for reference service and the most common types of tools are described below.

Web *search engines* like Google and Yahoo are the most popular and easiest way to search the Web. One can type a word or words into a search box and the search engine will scan publicly available Web pages, numbering in the billions, and list pages containing the requested terms. Search engines generally offer basic and advanced searching options and allow one to limit to a particular type of media, for example, videos or photographs. The more search terms entered in the search box, the narrower the search results and the more likely the pages retrieved will be relevant to a searchers request. Some search engines, like Ask.com, permit natural language searches in the form of a question or phrase. Search results are listed in order of relevancy, the definition of which differs according to the search algorithms used by each search engine. Generally, relevancy is based on such criteria as the number of times the term appears in the Web page, the location of the terms on the page, and the number of times the page is linked to or cited by other Web pages. *Meta search engines*, like Dogpile and Clusty, are a variation of this category which allows you the searching of several search engines at once. These are valuable because numerous studies have shown a surprising lack of overlap in search results among the major search engines. The user types a search statement and the meta engine sends the query to several engines, either combining the results into one list after removing duplicate records (called de-duping) or showing the results site by site. This has the advantage of searching more Web sites and obtaining more results than a search in only one search engine, although the process takes longer than searching an individual search engine and may result in information overload.

Subject directories take a different approach to searching the Web by categorizing Web sites by topic. This allows the searcher to drill down through the directory to progressively narrow the search and find pages containing the information they are looking for. Subject directories, like Librarians' Index to the Internet, and Infomine, have the advantage of selectivity, with sites selected by humans or machines based on certain criteria. Such vetted searches produce a more limited list, but generally the results are more pertinent than what you get using a search engine. However, the popularity of directories has declined in recent years. This is probably because search engine relevancy ranking formulas have improved and the quality of their "first page" results is now taking the place of the directories (Hock, 2007).

It is important to note that search engines search only the *visible Web*, that is, freely accessible Web pages that do not require a password, license, authentication, or some other kind of human intervention to view. The majority of the Web, however, consists of sites that are not accessible by search engines, sometimes called the *invisible Web* or the *dark Web* (Eggar-Sider and Devine, 2005). These include databases of library catalog data, commercial databases like digital journals and books, and bulletin boards. While the visible *Web* often contains sufficient information to answer most factual questions, the quality of some of the *Web* pages retrieved by a search engine is often open to question. From a reference perspective, the invisible *Web* has been shrinking. Once invisible sources like newspaper pages, encyclopedias, and audio, visual, and image files are now routinely accessed by search engines. While the majority of the Web is still concealed in invisible databases, we may expect the number of pages visible to the Web crawlers to increase and search results to continue to improve.

TECHNOLOGY AND REFERENCE SOURCES

Over the past generation, as one can see in our discussion of reference sources, advances in information technology have had a tremendous impact on reference services. Technology affects the speed of reference work, the amount of information provided, the quality of the information, the cost of obtaining information, and the skills necessary to do reference work. In this section, we will discuss recent developments in technology as they affect reference sources and reference staff. A more comprehensive discussion of the effects of technology on reference services may be found in Chapter 4.

The technological age of reference service began in the mid-1960s with the creation of online databases (a database here means a digital collection of data organized especially for rapid search and retrieval). The increasing sophistication and power of computers along with federal support of cultural and educational programs during the "Great Society" years made this development possible. The creation of computerized databases was necessary in order to control the vast amount of information resulting from the information explosion, which traditional printed sources were inadequate to keep up with. Public funding allowed the National Library of Medicine to create a database of medical literature called "Medlars" (Medical Literature Analysis and Retrieval System). A computerized educational database called ERIC (Educational Resources Information Center) soon followed. Both of these databases allowed searchers to connect by telephone modem to the host computer containing the database, to search the information in the database by subject and author, and to have the results printed out in the form of an annotated bibliography.

The advantages of online access to computerized databases quickly became apparent, as did their commercial viability. Since the 1960s, thousands of online databases have been created, from those containing only bibliographic data to numeric, full-text, audio, video, and graphical (that is, multimedia) retrieval systems. Searching protocols (procedures by which databases are searched and information retrieved) became more sophisticated, including provisions for Boolean searching, the ability to easily limit or expand search results, and other features designed to allow more precise information retrieval.

Advances in computer technology and the automation of library functions, including the development of bibliographic databases and electronic circulation systems, made the forerunner OPACs feasible in the 1970s. The next decade saw true online public access catalogs become relatively commonplace. Libraries at large institutions led the way as they had access to large mainframe computers. As computer hardware and software became more sophisticated and less expensive, smaller libraries were able to automate their catalogs.

The development of the microcomputer, or PC, occurred in the 1970s. This allowed libraries to apply the power of computing to everyday reference work. For example, they could digitize their ready reference files and record-keeping procedures. Libraries could also access the holdings records of national cataloging databases, like the OCLC, and transmit interlibrary loan requests instantly, cutting several days from the process. A very important use of the PC in reference services, however, awaited the next great technological breakthrough.

CD-ROM Resources

This innovation occurred in the mid-1980s, with the development of the "compact disc, read only memory," or CD-ROM. This hard disc of large storage capacity, coupled with a CD-ROM player and a microcomputer, permitted rapid access to large databases. Its searching power was equivalent to online searching of mediated databases, but at a much lower unit cost for high-use databases. The CD-ROM made it possible to provide library users with greatly expanded access to information databases: bibliographic, numerical, audio, visual, and full text. With all the advantages of online databases, CD-ROMs are not yet extinct. As of this writing there are over 6,800 titles on CD-ROM available for lease or purchase (Williams, 2006).

In special libraries, CD-ROMs often provide the full text of regulatory and legal information and analysis. For the small special library with limited shelf space, electronic formats such as CD-ROMs may be particularly appealing.

The most common use of CD-ROMs in academic, school, and public librar- ies was for periodical indexing. All the most popular periodical indexes and ab- stracts were available on both CD-ROM and online. This provided much better indexing of periodicals than the corresponding printed indexes. With a sub- scription to a CD-ROM service, libraries offered users the advantages of online searching without the online charges or connect time expenses of mediated on- line searching. Users could search by subject or by keywords from the author, title, abstract, year of publication, and more. Search results could be printed or copied to a portable storage device. Many libraries networked a CD-ROM drive to several PCs so that multiple users could search the database at the same time.

CD-ROMs had their disadvantages as well. Although a database could be networked for multiple simultaneous users, a maximum of about six users could use the database before degradations in response time were apparent. Also, CD-ROMs were strictly an in-house resource. They could not be net- worked so that users outside the library could use them. The CD-ROMs were normally updated monthly or quarterly, so they were generally no more cur- rent than their print counterparts.

The advent of end-user digital reference sources and indexes brought with it new responsibilities for reference staff, namely a more intense need to do one-on-one instruction for library users (see Chapter 6 for more on implica- tions for library instruction). For example, if they are to use CD-ROM or on- line databases, users must be taught *Boolean logic*: the use of specific words (called *Boolean operators*) to combine terms and/or fields to control a search and achieve the desired results.

Computer searches can result in hundreds or thousands of hits. Using the Boolean operator *and* between terms, sets, or fields will limit the number of hits to include only those containing both elements; using the operator *or* will broaden the search by gathering all hits having either element. Using the operator *not* will eliminate all hits containing a specified term. Although the wording may vary, some software packages will also allow *proximity opera- tors*; that is, ways to define how near two terms should be to each other to get picked up by the search.

With the development of online end-user searching in the late 1990s, CD- ROM technology was called a "dinosaur breed" as long ago as 2002 (Tenopir and Ennis, 2002). Nevertheless, full-text sources on CD-ROM are still numer- ous. Encyclopedias, corporate annual reports and financial information, sta- tistical data (for example, portions of the 1990 U.S. Census), archival runs of periodicals, and the Bible, among other sources, are now available (Williams, 2006). CD-ROM will probably remain a viable technology at least for the near future for specialized titles and niche products.

The Internet

During the 1990s libraries rushed to exploit the next great leap forward in information technology, the World Wide Web. Originally developed in the 1970s, the Internet's purpose was to help manage information for the U.S. Department of Defense. Academic libraries started using the technology in the 1980s. Since then it has become a staple element in the service offered by all types of libraries. Described as a network of networks, the Internet allows anyone, or any library, to access posted information anywhere in the world. The Internet improves reference service by allowing staff to locate and quickly retrieve information that would be unavailable, or at best difficult and time-consuming to obtain through conventional sources. Since its development in the early 1990s, the Web has improved the utility of the Internet by allowing users to link seamlessly from one database to another across networks and computers. Databases can include text, graphics, audio and video files, or any combination of the above, and commercial vendors have converted their traditional print and CD-ROM databases to the Web. Online access to reference sources generally means access to more current data than is available with printed or CD-ROM sources, plus the added advantage of access by any authorized customers regardless of their location or the time of day.

As the number of individuals, businesses, schools, and libraries with access to the Web increased, publishers saw the economic advantages of publishing electronically. Representatives of all of the kinds of reference sources discussed earlier in this chapter are available on the Internet and are popular with reference staff and library users. A 2001 study by Tenopir and Ennis found that research libraries have drastically shifted the emphasis in their reference collections to digital sources. These sources tend to be more current than their printed counterparts, far more accessible, and sometimes more expensive. As one of opening quotations stated (Bradford et al., 2005) the reference staff at one university was "using online reference sources much more frequently than traditional print sources by a ratio of approximately 6 to 1." This trend is likely to continue at other libraries.

Each library must weigh the advantages and disadvantages for its users in selecting the format of a particular reference source. It is easy for a person to believe that this trend towards computerization means our reference collections will soon become solely digital. This is not likely, however, at least not in the near future. While the technology is proven, the realities of library and publishing economics and diverse user needs suggest there will continue to be a market for the print versions of many traditional reference titles. For the near future, at least, print will remain a cost-effective way for libraries to acquire and provide access to many of the traditional reference sources.

KNOWING YOUR COLLECTIONS AND YOUR LIMITATIONS

In-House Sources

To provide reference service of good quality it is not necessary for all reference staff members to know every single reference source in the collection. In a small collection, for example in a branch library, special library, or school library, it may be possible for the staff to be familiar with every source as well as have an in-depth knowledge of the items. Many reference collections, however, contain thousands and even tens of thousands of physical and online sources. It is not likely that any one person will be familiar with all of them, nor should one try to be.

Online sources offer a particular challenge to reference staff in terms of "knowing" them. Not only are online databases among the most popular and useful reference sources in most libraries, they have the unsettling habit of frequently changing their look and feel. Database vendors are always trying to keep up with or stay ahead of the competition in terms of database appearance and functionality. This means that staying current with new interface designs and navigation schemes and changing functionality is a never-ending process.

Rather than trying to learn all the sources in the reference collection, it is more productive to concentrate first on learning the most frequently consulted sources, including the OPAC, based on the most frequently asked questions. With this knowledge reference staff will be able to answer many, if not most, of the reference questions. Intelligent use of the OPAC and library Web pages and consultation with colleagues will enable one to find the specific sources necessary to answer most of the rest of the questions.

It is also very helpful to understand enough about the classification system(s) used in a library to know where types of reference sources are classed together; for example, literary genre bibliographies or medical references. This allows staff members who do not remember a specific source to go to the shelves and browse among the titles for likely candidates to answer a question. Staff should also know how Web sites are organized on the library's Web pages and their use. As staff members examine new reference titles they should ponder the kinds of questions they will answer, and note where they are classed in the collection or located on the Web. Reference is a cooperative activity. No one is an expert in every area, and a staff member's best judgment may be to consult with a colleague who is more familiar with the informational territory to be covered. You are not expected to know everything, and reference staff members are generally more than willing to share their expertise with colleagues.

Every reference staff member eventually develops the skill of knowing his or her limitations (though these do shrink somewhat with experience). Developing a mental or physical file of which colleague best knows certain subject areas is another good tactic for improving the quality of service. Regular meetings of reference staff members should include discussions of difficult or unusual reference questions and new or recently discovered reference sources. Continuing education, regular reading of the professional literature and listservs (for example, RUSA-L), attending workshops and professional meetings, and other forms of ongoing education should be a part of every reference staff member's responsibility and receive appropriate administrative support.

References to Outside Sources
and Other Libraries

Every reference collection has its limitations. No library, after all, can be all things to all people. Even the largest library in the country, the Library of Congress, must occasionally call upon other agencies to answer the information needs of its clientele. Every reference staff member needs to be able to refer users to external sources of information when their local collection is inadequate to address a particular information need.

It is important for staff to know what kinds of questions are unlikely to be answered with their particular collection. However, this does not mean that staff should ever assume that an answer is not available without first searching for it. This is even more imperative with the growing number of information sources available on the Internet, plus the increasing sophistication of Web search engines. But with experience staff will know what questions are better answered by referring the user to other resources.

Requests for Outside Referral

The first requirement for outside referral is that the reference staff is aware of alternative information resources in the community and the information services they offer. Public agencies, community services, and other libraries are the most valuable sources to know. Public agencies such as the Veterans Administration, state and local health services departments, chambers of commerce, and employment development departments provide information in their areas of responsibility. Community services such as the Red Cross, legal aid foundations, and senior citizens groups disseminate information as part of the services they offer. Most libraries maintain a ready reference file or Web-accessible database of local information sources with addresses, phone numbers, and contact people to which staff can refer when the need arises. Public libraries provide a great deal of community and information referral, and we have included a section on this service in Chapter 4.

Knowledge of local libraries is also important. Helpful information includes the hours they are open, restrictions on use, and particular collection strengths. Gathering this kind of information is greatly facilitated by the increasing number of libraries accessible on the Web. Academic libraries generally have strong and eclectic collections based on the school's curriculum, and in-house access to materials is usually not denied to the public. Public libraries by their nature are open to all. They have general collections based on local community interests, and may have particular strengths that complement other libraries in the area. Special libraries often have very strong collections in a particular field but may restrict access to a specific clientele.

Some research libraries require letters of reference from supervising faculty or librarians before they will admit graduate students, or especially, undergraduates. These libraries expect the student to have pursued the topic in all available collections at their home institution. The reason for this is to limit the handling of "preservation copies" (often they are the last copies). The letter may be required to specify the particular materials or types of holdings that the student expects to use; the student may have to list such information on an application form before being admitted to the reading room.

Mediated Online Searching

Mediated online searching, that is, reference staff searching databases to retrieve information for users, is of diminishing importance in most libraries.

As databases proliferate on the Web and users learn to do their own searches, the need for mediated searches is declining. Nevertheless, the number of commercial online databases available, more than 17,000 in 2006, is increasing all the time, offering access to information sometimes not available in other formats (Williams, 2006). Some library users still require information not readily available through publicly available sources, and libraries have developed policies, procedures, and funding sources to provide their users with access to this information.

University and college faculty are sometimes unskilled in searching more sophisticated databases and reference staff do it for them. Public libraries, too, especially the larger ones, may offer mediated service to their users, particularly the business clientele who can afford and are willing to pay for the service. Mediated searching is still quite common in special libraries, particularly corporate, technical, and medical libraries, where library staff often perform searches to support the work of executives, scientists, or health professionals. The availability of unmediated online searching is common in school libraries, where learning to use this resource aids in developing students' critical thinking and research skills.

Libraries that provide mediated access to many databases often contract with one or more database vendors. The vendors (or *information brokers*), such as DIALOG, act as middlemen between a library and the creators of literally hundreds of databases. Vendors standardize database formats and searching protocols so clients may search any database offered by the vendor with the same basic commands and strategies. They also train searchers in effective searching techniques and publish documentation on how to search the various databases, thus greatly simplifying the searching process.

Mediated online searching procedures are seldom intuitive or "user-friendly." Specific commands and search strategies must be known or learned in order to retrieve information from a database effectively. The untutored user is often not able to use online databases well, although vendors are attempting to make online searching easier in order to expand their clientele. Libraries contribute professional expertise and equipment to provide the user with access to online databases. Library staff members receive training from the vendors or database creators in the various protocols and strategies necessary to search the databases and serve as resource people for users doing their own online searching.

The increasing variety and ease of use of Web-based databases, in combination with their widespread availability, are the main reasons user demand for mediated searches has declined in academic and public libraries.

LEGAL AND ETHICAL ISSUES

As we stated in Chapter 4, the availability of online sources in some cases changes the definition of quality reference service. Professional ethics require that reference staff give accurate information. Today, accurate (that is, up-to-date and correct) information sometimes is available only through online sources. Using print references to answer a question often means giving the requester less current data. A reference staff member who does not know how to use online resources as well as traditional print sources effectively is in the frustrating and ethically challenging position of not being able to provide the best quality information available.

When users are looking for information on a controversial topic, reference staff members should try to keep an open perspective, and they should promote awareness by giving individuals a variety of sources that address the information desired from differing points of view. Reference materials are often judged on their ability to present a balanced viewpoint, or materials are sometimes chosen to balance the viewpoints in existing sources. In the case of topics that may have more than one viewpoint, reference staff should be alert for gaps in their reference collections and purchase titles to provide alternative viewpoints. When the available materials are heavily opinionated or present a limited viewpoint, a reference staff member at least informs the user that other perspectives exist, and may suggest additional materials that strive to be balanced, or, when these are not available, materials that present an opposite point of view. If information is dated, the reference person should so inform the requester and suggest alternative sources with more current data to supplement or modify the older information.

The Internet provides reference staff with enormous potential for supplying library users with information. However, this virtually unlimited ability to access information also results in one of the greatest challenges to librarianship's traditional adherence to the principal of intellectual freedom. Typically, libraries build their collections by selecting specific books, periodicals, media, reference sources, government documents, online databases, and so on, for use by the library's users. These selection decisions have been made by library staff, based on collection development policies that reflect the information needs, and standards, of the library's users. In school and academic libraries, the institution's curriculum tends to guide selection decisions. In special libraries, the information needs of the library's sponsoring organization determine collection-building decisions.

The connectivity of the Web allows library users the freedom to do their own selection of what they wish to read or view, unfettered by library policies or community standards. This means people may select material to read or view or listen to that would not be selected under the library's collection development policy. This may include pornography, hate speech, and other material that is offensive to other library users. This potential for offense or, in the case of minors, exposure to material the individual is not emotionally or psychologically prepared to experience, has resulted in challenges to this new freedom of access. The most obvious challenges thus far are legislative, for example the Child Internet Protection Act (CIPA), largely aimed at protecting children from exposure to pornography or other materials judged harmful to minors.

A common aspect of many of these challenges is the idea of "filtering," or censoring, the information obtained on the Web to eliminate, or reduce, objectionable material. Filtering involves installing computer software that blocks access to specific search terms or Web sites deemed objectionable. For example, sites that feature the words *sex* or *nude* may be blocked, preventing access to those sites by library users. Filtering advocates point to the protection such software offers minors using the Internet and the preservation of traditional community standards. Opponents maintain that filtering software is imperfect and blocks access to many non-offensive sites, for example, those dealing with breast cancer or sex education. Further, many librarians reaffirm the tenant of intellectual freedom, described in the *Library Bill of Rights*, and the reader's right to access any constitutionally protected information they desire. They also maintain the position that it is the parents' responsibility, and not the library's, to guide and protect their children regarding their access to information. Needless to say, filtering Web sites limits their utility as reference sources. We discuss some of the filtering software packages in the security chapter.

The ALA and many regional organizations take a firm stance on the intellectual freedom side of this issue, holding to the reader's unrestricted right to select what they want within the limits of the Constitution (See the ALA's *Resolution on the Use of Filtering Software in Libraries*, http://www.ala.org/ ala/oif/statementspols/ifresolutions/filteringresolution.pdf). Other library professionals, however, see the desire to limit access to the Web as legitimate, both to protect children and to uphold community standards for appropriate material (Hyman, 1997).

As of this writing, libraries are handling this issue in a variety of ways, from open access/use "at your own risk," to minimal or no public Internet use, and every option in between. Some public libraries are filtering children's terminals but not adult terminals. Some are using privacy screens. Some school districts only allow children to search a list of district-approved sites, or even prohibit Internet use altogether (Bell, 2007). Nearly all school libraries filter their Web content. Many libraries require specific parental permission for children to use the Internet.

"To charge or not to charge" became an ethical debate among librarians during the 1970s and 1980s, when the number of libraries offering mediated online searching increased dramatically. Opponents of charging for online information pointed out that it violates two of the most sacred principles of library service: free and equal access to information. To charge users for online information, foes argued, restricts information to those who can afford it. The consequence would be to create an "information elite" and intensify social and economic inequality.

Some proponents of charging reply that information costs money to produce and is a commodity like any other. As a product it is subject to the law of supply and demand and should cost whatever the market will bear. Others argue that some libraries could not afford to provide the service at all without some form of cost recovery. The service is expensive and library budgets would not be augmented to cover it, nor could most libraries absorb the cost, therefore, it is better to provide the service to those who can pay for it than not to provide the service at all. (You can find examples of the early arguments in works such as Myers, 1993; Smith, 1989; and Vidmar et al., 1997.)

With the development of the Web and the ease and popularity of end-user searching, charging for online searching today is seldom an issue. Even charges for printing are mitigated by the capability of e-mailing search results to one's home computer or downloading to a portable storage device and printing outside of the library.

SECURITY MATTERS AND PRESERVATION

Security matters, as well as preservation, if reference service is to be of consistent quality. Access to information is denied if the information is not available for any reason. A disregard of potential or discovered theft, concealment, mishandling, or mutilation of library materials may lead progressively to a deterioration of reference service. User after user (and staff member after staff member) is frustrated by not being able to find what was once available.

Most reference departments have a policy of not circulating reference materials. Most also try to keep reference sources within a particular area, so that staff and readers can find the more heavily used items easily. Many departments house their highest use items close to the service desk(s)—"ready reference." Some libraries have surrendered the principle of "open access" to particular materials because of theft, and keep certain titles in areas with limited or staff access, given out only at borrower request in exchange for identification. Certainly, this situation is not ideal, but constant replacing of vandalized or stolen materials prevents purchase of, and therefore, access to other materials for other users.

One of the advantages of the gradual migration from paper to digital reference sources is protection from theft and vandalization of reference sources. Digital sources may be temporarily unavailable for other reasons, but theft and vandalism will not be among them. However, at least a portion of most libraries' collections will remain paper for the foreseeable future, so attention to preservation and security will continue to be important.

The reference staff's major contribution to preservation is in the day-to-day education of library users in the handling of materials. Reference staff set the example for user behavior, both within the library and after checkout. Rough handling, dog-earing, or ticking off information with pencil or pen by library staff tells readers it is fine to trash library materials. Thus, reference loses and has to replace or rebind materials more often, again preventing the purchase of additional reference tools and narrowing the ability of the library to help its clientele.

Practicing proper and consistent shelving habits in reference, as elsewhere in the library, keeps materials available longer and teaches users good practice. Straightening leaning volumes, using bookends, and shelving materials properly does not take any extra time, but lengthens shelf life and gives the library a neat and usable look.

Reference staff, like other public service personnel, need to be on the lookout for telltale signs of wear and needed repair or replacement. Often, catching and repairing a volume at, for example, a state of slightly loosened hinges will prevent later costs of total rebinding or replacement. Anticipating repair and replacement needs leads to a continuous availability of information, rather than long periods without the tools necessary to supply information to users.

SUMMARY

A necessary prerequisite for reference service is the reference collection. Although such collections were once limited to the materials housed within a particular library, online networks have expanded the reference staff's ability to access sources located anywhere in the world. Staff members purchase, lease, or create Web links to sources with the information needs of a library's clientele in mind, and they are usually guided by a collection development policy that specifies the criteria used to select sources.

The traditional types of reference sources typically consist of bibliographies, dictionaries, directories, encyclopedias, atlases and gazetteers, handbooks and manuals, biographical sources, pamphlets, yearbooks and almanacs, indexes (including periodical indexes and abstracts), OPACs, and Web search engines. Technology has greatly improved the utility of reference sources for staff and users by making them more easily searchable and more widely available.

The Internet defies categorization as a traditional kind of reference source, but it is used to gain access to digital versions of each of the traditional types of reference sources listed above, and to index a virtually unlimited amount of networked information around the world. The increasing sophistication of database and Web search engines makes finding information on the Internet easier all the time, and navigating the Net may be the most important reference skill for staff to master.

In some public and many school libraries the reference utility of the Internet is compromised by filtering software. This software, usually in response to concerns about pornography or hate speech on the Web, blocks specific sites or sites containing certain words. Unfortunately, entirely appropriate and useful Web sites may also be blocked. Reference staff must be aware of their library's policy on Internet use and the limitations this may place on their work.

While staff members need to be aware of the sources available in their library, they must also know about the most important external sources of information available to their users, especially community and public agencies and other libraries. Networks, or consortia, of libraries have developed cooperative agreements to make resources available to each other. Mediated online searching is a means reference staff members employ to extend reference service beyond the information the library commonly makes available to requesters. While readers are becoming more experienced in using online databases, and the searching software is becoming more user-friendly, there are still occasions when specialized databases need to be consulted or sophisticated search strategies need to be employed in order to find the information desired. Libraries pay for access to databases for this purpose, and establish policies and procedures to guide the service.

Chapter Review Material

1. What are the purposes of the reference collection?
2. Name several kinds of reference sources and the characteristics of each.
3. What criteria are considered when selecting reference items?
5. What are some characteristics of OPACs?
6. Why are periodicals important for library collections?
7. What are some of the characteristics of periodical indexes?
8. Why is mediated online searching decreasing in most libraries?
9. From an ethical standpoint, why is it important for reference staff to be proficient with the Internet?
10. What are the implications of filtering software on reference service?
11. What is the best contribution reference staff can make to the library's preservation efforts?

REFERENCES

Bradford, Jane T., Barbara Costello, and Robert Lenholt. 2005. "Reference Service in the Digital Age: An Analysis of Sources Used to Answer Reference Questions," *The Journal of Academic Librarianship* 31, no. 3: 263–272.

Egger-Sider, Francine, and Jane Devine. 2005. "Google, the Invisible Web, and Librarians: Slaying the Research Goliath," *Internet Reference Services Quarterly* 10, nos. 3/4: 89–101.

Hock, Ran. 2007. "Search Engines: From Web 0.0 to Web 2.0 and Beyond," *Online* 31, no. 3: 26–30.

Hyman, Karen. 1997. "Internet Policies: Managing in the Real World," *American Libraries* 28, no.10: 60+.

Myers, Troy Gordon. 1993. *User Fees for Information Services: An Exploration in North American Publicly Funded Libraries.* Master's thesis, Dalhousie University.

Smith, Barbara. 1989. "A Strategic Approach to Online User Fees in Public Libraries," *Library Journal* 114, no. 2: 33–36.

Tenopir, Carol, and Lisa Ennis. 2001. "Reference Services in the New Millennium: University Reference Services from 1991 to 2001," *Online* 25, no. 4: 40–45.

———. 2002. "A Decade of Digital Reference: 1991–2001," *Reference & User Services Quarterly* 41, no. 3: 264–274.

Vidmar, Dale J., Marshall A. Berger, and Connie J. Anderson. 1997. "Implementing a Cost Recovery System for Printing," *Reference Services Review* 25, no. 3–4: 97–101.

Warren, Dennis. 2007. "Lost in Translation: The Reality of Federated Searching," *Australian Academic & Research Libraries* 38, no. 4: 258–269.

Williams, Martha E. 2006. "The State of Databases Today: 2006," *Gale Directory of Databases 2006*, Vol. 1: xv–xxv.

SUGGESTED READINGS

Cassell, Kay Ann, and Uma Hiremath. 2006. *Reference and Information Services in the 21st Century.* New York: Neal-Schuman.

Dickstein, Ruth, Louise Greenfield, and Jeff Rosen. 1997. "Using the World Wide Web at the Reference Desk," *Computers in Libraries* 17, no. 8: 61–65.

Hattendorf, Lynn C. 1989. "The Art of Reference Collection Development," *RQ* 29, no. 2: 219–229.

Jaeger. Paul T., John Carlo Bertot, and Charles R. McClure. 2004. "The Effects of the Children's Internet Protection Act (CIPA) in Public Libraries and its Implications for Research: A Statistical, Policy, and Legal Analysis," *Journal of the American Society for Information Science and Technology* 55, no. 13: 1131–1140.

Rector, Lucy Holman. 2008. "Comparison of Wikipedia and other Encyclopedias for Accuracy, Breath, and Depth in Historical Articles," *Reference Services Review* 36, no. 1: 7–22.

Robbins, Sarah, Cheryl McCain, and Laurie Scrivener. 2006. "The Changing Format of Reference Collections: Are Research Libraries Favoring Electronic Access over Print?" *The Acquisitions Librarian* 18, no. 35/36: 75–95.

Wrubel, Laura, and Kari Schmidt. 2007. "Usability Testing of a Metasearch Interface: A Case Study," *College & Research Libraries* 68, no. 4: 292–311.

SELECTED BIBLIOGRAPHIES OF REFERENCE SOURCES

American Reference Books Annual. Westport, CT: Libraries Unlimited.

Balay, Robert, ed. 1996. *Guide to Reference Books.* 11th ed. Chicago: American Library Association.

Blazek, Ron, and Elizabeth Aversa. 2000. *The Humanities: A Selective Guide to Information Sources.* 5th ed. Englewood, CO: Libraries Unlimited.

The Booklist. 1969. v.66, September. Chicago: American Library Association. (Continues as *Booklist and Subscription Books Bulletin*).

Choice. 1961. v.1, March. Middletown, CT: Association of College and Research Libraries

Fisher, David, ed. 2002. *Information Sources in the Social Sciences.* Munich: K.G. Saur.

Herron, Nancy L., ed. 2002. *The Social Sciences: A Cross-Disciplinary Guide to Selected Sources.* 3rd ed. Englewood, CO: Libraries Unlimited.

Hurt, C. D. 1998. *Information Sources in Science and Technology.* 3rd ed. Englewood, CO: Libraries Unlimited.

Hysell, Shannon Graff, ed. 2007. *Recommended Reference Books for Small and Medium-Sized Libraries and Media Centers.* 27th ed. Westport, CT: Libraries Unlimited.

Internet Public Library. http://www.ipl.org/

Librarians Internet Index. http://lii.org/

Walford, Albert John. 1999. *Walford's Guide to Reference Material, Vol. 1: Science & Technology.* 8th ed. London: Library Association.

———. 2000. *Walford's Guide to Reference Material, Vol. 2: Social and Historical Sciences, Philosophy & Religion.* 8th ed. London: Library Association.

———. 1998. *Walford's Guide to Reference Material, Vol. 3: Generalia, Language & Literature, the Arts.* 7th ed. London: Library Association.

Chapter 6

Information Literacy Instruction

Freedom to learn is the first necessity of guaranteeing that man himself shall be self-reliant enough to be free . . . The ultimate victory of tomorrow is through democracy with education.
—Franklin Delano Roosevelt, 1938

In the 19th and early 20th century, a person who had acquired enough knowledge was considered learned and educated . . . Today's graduates must be learners as well.
—Joan Denham, 2007

People are not born knowing how to use a library. *Information literacy* instruction is the term most generally used today to describe the ways in which library staff teach users how to identify, access, evaluate, and use information. Previously termed *bibliographic instruction, library instruction,* and *user instruction,* information literacy can be one-on-one teaching or group instruction. In the first instance, often termed *informal* (or point-of-use) *instruction,* it typically occurs while answering someone's question, as in a normal reference transaction, but it goes beyond merely answering the question. Rather, while answering a question, the library staff member teaches the requester how to obtain the answer using library and other resources. The other major mode of library instruction is the planned teaching of library and information knowledge and skills to groups, usually in a classroom or workshop setting. This is often called *formal instruction.*

Instruction is an important service component in many libraries. It promotes lifelong learning by enabling people not only to get the information they are currently seeking, but also to learn to find information for themselves in the future. Today, the amount of accessible information continues to grow exponentially. The ability to identify, access, evaluate, and ethically use today's wide variety of informational formats efficiently and effectively is vital. These information literacy skills are steadily becoming as important as literacy itself was to earlier generations.

ROLE AND PHILOSOPHY OF LIBRARY INSTRUCTION

Information Literacy

Information literacy is not just the ability to find information. It consists of knowing the following:

- The fact that information is needed
- What information is needed
- How to describe it
- What resources to use to retrieve it
- How to use those resources
- How to judge the value and validity of what has been found ("critical thinking")
- How to organize and integrate the selected information (Association of College and Research Libraries, 2000)

The definition of *literacy* is largely stable (the ability to read and understand), but the definition of information literacy has evolved beyond that basic meaning. Until the development of the Web in a library environment, if people knew how to use the subject, author, and title cards in a catalog, the indexes of encyclopedias and other reference books, and printed periodical and newspaper indexes, they would be considered information literate. Today, people with only these skills would be completely at sea in today's technology-filled library (although perhaps better off than many because they at least know the fundamentals).

Information literacy includes an understanding about what information is, and what it is not. Information is not knowledge, per se, and certainly not wisdom. Information is created, collected, organized, disseminated and interpreted by human beings, with all their limitations, biases, and inexactitudes. Information is important, but, as opposed to facts, it is also changeable and often not 100 percent reliable, especially in a wiki environment where anyone can claim authority. The ability to make good judgments about information quality raises one's literacy quotient, and makes information-gathering more fruitful. A senior researcher initially daunted by numerous databases and changing interfaces can become comfortable with their technology with a little bit of help. On the other hand, a technical wizard who can surf the Web, create dazzling Web pages, and rescue lost information from a crashed hard drive, but who accepts all the information found as being equally valid, is not really information literate.

The Need for Information Literacy Instruction

The information explosion and new forms of technology make a solid case for the importance of information literacy. New databases and upgrades are regularly added to reference computers and campus or workplace networks.

Administrators, like students, face the confusing torrent of information on the Web. These new challenges have made the need for information literacy even more evident. The nature of what has to be taught changes with time and technology. Unmediated self-instruction, especially with online tools, is beginning to take hold, but total software standardization, library and nonlibrary, has not yet arrived. Even though commercial information providers have begun to move toward more standardization, someone still has to show people, including those who know how to use computers, how to use the technology *effectively.*

Few things make the need for critical thinking more obvious than the unevenness of quality in what is found on the Web. Nowadays, any 12-year-old can learn how to create an impressively graphic Web page. So can anyone promoting a personal agenda. There are organizations and people who contribute a lot of time and expense to put objective information, or clearly labeled opinion, where the world can reach it. However, the Web also contains a lot of inaccurate information, disguised personal opinion, pseudo-research, promotional, one-sided advocacy material, and even straight-out deception. We have seen more than one bogus site that masquerades as a real organization's "official" home page via wording, design, language and/or similar Web address. There are "free" offers that invite you to browse a site, only to have a piece of "malware," like a virus or worm, invade and damage or disrupt your system. Aside from commercial interests, people with personal agendas, both harmless and socially harmful, create impressive-looking Web sites. As with media advertising, people will eventually learn not to believe everything they see as being accurate. At this point, however, many people think any information that is important is online and that all online information is accurate information. Teaching users how to judge a reliable source and how to recognize questionable sites may be as much help as teaching them how to select the best database for a particular task.

The accrediting agencies of both schools and colleges and universities recognize the importance of information literacy instruction by including it in their accreditation standards. Regional accrediting agencies (like the Western Association of Schools and Colleges [WASC]), states, and counties have incorporated information literacy as a required learning outcome, and this has gone far to assist libraries in persuading administrators and teachers about the importance of information literacy instruction.

TYPES OF INFORMATION LITERACY INSTRUCTION

A library provides its users with a variety of aids to access library resources, including explanatory signage, printed handouts, audio-visual and online aids, and reference help in general. While all these may have information literacy components, the areas we focus on here are those most specifically identified with the discipline of library instruction, namely *informal* (or *point-of-use) instruction* and *formal instruction.*

Informal Instruction

Informal, or point-of-use instruction, sometimes called one-on-one instruction, is the kind of instruction most often provided by support staff, usually while providing reference service. Informal instruction, including homework support, Internet access, and other point-of-use instruction is the kind of instruction most often provided in public libraries. A 2004 study (Julien and Breu) of Canadian public libraries revealed that 70 percent of the libraries provided informal training. It is sometimes quite detailed and is often considered the most effective form of information literacy instruction. It usually occurs on demand at the point at which the user wants or needs to find information. Typically, the reference staff member helps a reader with specific resources useful for the information the user is actively seeking. Staff members also supply point-of-use instructional materials, such as Web pages, signs, or handouts, that point out and/or explain the purpose and use of particular library materials. Libraries typically locate such materials physically next to the paper resources or linked to the digital resources on the Web pages. However, we use point-of-use instruction here in a more active and personal sense, particularly to mean the learning that occurs in the course of regular reference service. A person comes to the reference desk with a question. The staff member, while answering that question, shows the individual how she or he could answer a similar question in the future. This can be instruction by demonstration, as the person observes the staff member using library resources to answer the question. Better, the staff member can also explain what he or she is doing to give the user better insight into the procedure of obtaining the answer. ("First, let's check the index to see where your topic might be covered in this book.")

A further example: Asked if the library has any books by Amiri Baraka, the reference staff member accompanies the person to an OPAC terminal and demonstrates the search process. Seemingly casual remarks, such as "You'll notice that there are older materials here by him published under his former name, Leroi Jones," may lead to further questions about how the catalog works. If the individual has been frustrated by a catalog that hasn't exactly "worked" when they have tried to use it for their question, staff might explain further. The follow-up, "Are you also interested in books *about* Baraka?" might lead to an explanation of what subject headings are, and how to use them or the advantages of keyword searching. With more experienced users, instruction may be a matter of initiating the research process, by first sufficiently explaining and/or demonstrating the components of the process for that particular user, and then leaving the individual to work independently.

Point-of-use instruction includes such things as explaining how to use an encyclopedia's index, or the gazetteer of an atlas, or the scale of a map, or how to find the online thesaurus of a periodical database, or a certain statistic in a particular reference book or Web site. Of course, not every reference question calls for library instruction, but reference staff should be ready and able to "do" informal information literacy instruction at the drop of a hat—especially in school and academic libraries.

Formal Instruction

Formal instruction is the other main form of user education. Formal instruction includes library tours and orientations for groups, formal classroom instruction within a school or academic institution, and workshops or tutorials for groups or individuals. Formal instruction can range from teaching children how to check out a book, to teaching an advanced graduate-level research seminar, and everything in between. The simplest way to distinguish between formal and point-of-use instruction is to look at two factors, taken together:

1. The component of advance preparation by the instructor; and
2. The nature of the encounter with the audience.

In many school libraries and special libraries, support staff may be responsible for at least some formal instruction. Indeed, there are many school and special libraries in which the library technician is the sole library staff and must do everything. On the other hand, in most academic institutions librarians typically conduct the formal library instruction activities, although support staff may provide general library orientations.

TYPES OF LIBRARIES AND FORMAL INSTRUCTION

Academic

A review of the literature (Rader, 2002) reveals that the concept of information literacy instruction was developed by academic and school librarians during the twentieth and early twenty-first centuries. It began as library orientation and evolved to library instruction, course-integrated user instruction, and now to information skills or information literacy instruction.

Historically, information literacy instruction has been most prominently the domain of academic libraries. Because of their focus on teaching and learning, academic libraries have long embraced their role in teaching students about library use and information retrieval. Starting in the late 1960s, academic librarians began to promote library instruction to administrators, faculty, and students alike. This engendered gradual success, as library and institutional administrators and faculty began to embrace library instruction as an important component of a student's competency.

Originally adopted by the ALA in 1989, the *Information Literacy Competency Standards for Higher Education* (http://www.acrl.org/ala/acrl/acrlstandards/informationliteracycompetency.htm) have since been adopted by the American Association of Higher Education and the Council of Independent Colleges. The *Standards* include the following general competencies:

- Determine the extent of information needed
- Access the needed information effectively and efficiently
- Evaluate information and its sources critically
- Incorporate selected information into one's knowledge base
- Use information effectively to accomplish a specific purpose
- Understand the economic, legal, and social issues surrounding the use of information, and access and use information ethically and legally

Public

Typically, user instruction at public libraries consists of one-on-one informal library instruction provided at the reference desk—point-of-use instruction. Many public library users just want to have their questions answered or informational needs addressed without having to do the searching themselves. They have no interest in learning library skills. While some public libraries have successfully offered talks on doing library research to groups for many years, most have not. The exception has been those public libraries that have provided regularly scheduled sessions for homework help for local school children (see Chapter 15 for a further discussion of this topic).

The Internet, especially its World Wide Web component, has brought about a change in public libraries. An increasing number of public library users expect to do their own online searching. As nearly all public libraries are "wired," the demand for individual and group instruction on using technology continues to grow. The current Public Library Association planning model, *The New Planning for Results* (Nelson, 2001), offers public libraries information literacy as a choice for a service response for their communities. Some public libraries offer computer classes on topics such as e-mail, using the online catalog, how to place holds and manage their own circulation record, and access library resources both inside and outside the library. Senior citizens are often drawn to computer basics classes, and job seekers are another important audience (Jehlik, 2004). A 2007 study (Davis) found that 76 percent of public libraries reported they offer some form of instructional technology training.

Another factor is new demands for information support related to distance education and K–12 homework support. This translates into a lot more one-on-one instruction, and, new for most public libraries, group sessions on online resources. Julien and Breu (2004) found that one-third of Canadian public libraries deliver formal instruction for their users. Some public libraries' handouts now cover territory quite similar to those of academic information literacy programs.

School

The concept of librarian as teacher in school libraries is not new, and may be traced back to the 1960s. The *Standards for School Library Programs* was a milestone, as 20 national educational associations collaborated with the American Association of School Librarians to approve descriptions of an enhanced teaching role for the school librarian. The school media center was identified as a primary instructional center supporting, complementing, and expanding the work of the classroom (Callison, 2006, p.18).

The International Society for Technology in Education lists "research and information fluency" as one of the subjects "students should know and be able to do to learn effectively and live productively in an increasingly digital world" (International Society for Technology in Education, 2007). Both Canada and the United States (http://www.ala.org/ala/aasl/aaslproftools/informa tionpower/InformationLiteracyStandards_final.pdf) have adopted information literacy standards for schools, based on *Information Power* (http://www.ala.org/ala/aasl/aaslproftools/informationpower/informationpower.cfm), outlining information literacy needs and corresponding instruction for children in grades K through 12. and adopted by the American School Library Association in 1998. Many states and school districts have adopted the information literacy goals for grades K through 12 presented in the document. A study (Islam and Murno, 2006) of instruction in U.S. school libraries revealed the most common instruction involves how to avoid plagiarism and documenting sources, critical evaluation and analysis of information, and determining when, how much, and what type of information is needed to address a particular problem or task. Topics least likely to be covered are developing a thesis statement, conducting comparative analysis of information retrieved, and using truncation characters or wild cards in different information retrieval systems.

Special

Special libraries, especially those in the business environment, are generally the least likely to provide instruction. However, law, medical, and other professional libraries have become more involved with instruction. As shown in the literature they sometimes provide specific and detailed information literacy instruction to their users (Rader, 2002). In many traditional corporate libraries, little or no library instruction takes place. Library staff members often do much or all of the research, and even prepare draft reports; the corporate employee initiating the research only provides the research topic and its parameters. However, with cutbacks becoming a part of corporate life, many employees are now expected to do their own research. New employees are expected to have good computer skills. Corporations have long conducted employee training, and some, recognizing the importance of information skills, have begun to offer training for information searching to their employees.

Many professional people like doing part of or even most of their own research themselves. Institutional library staff may need to instruct and/or guide such individuals in the initial or advanced use of a database, such as Medline in a hospital library, or Lexis/Nexis in a corporate library. Often, a particular research need will lead to follow-up consultations.

TYPES OF FORMAL INSTRUCTION

The most basic types of "formal" instruction are orientations and tours. *Orientations* consist of presenting information regarding the library's layout and location of basic services and types of library materials. They also usually include procedural information about such things as obtaining borrowing privileges, checking out types of material, loan periods, fines, connecting to the network, and so forth. *Tours* add the dimension of actually walking around the service areas, book stacks, and other parts of the library. Tours and orientations provide a good opportunity to introduce people to the usefulness of public services personnel, and are the most likely kind of formal instruction that support staff engage in. An upbeat presentation stressing the availability of help is often the first step toward relieving or preventing *library anxiety*.

Library anxiety is a real psychological phenomenon; articles by Van Kampen (2004) and Mech and Brooks (1997) provide an insight into this concept. Some people get very confused trying to find information in a library. The cause may be as simple as being under a deadline or the sheer size of the collections; but it may be more psychologically complex. Feelings of inadequacy, fear of being looked down on by library staff, a bad childhood experience with a school or library, confusion from sensory overload, claustrophobia, even hunger, or all of these in various combinations, may be factors in creating internal tension and emotional upset, sometimes severe.

Public service staff members may notice a kind of technophobia in some older or returning users, who may not be comfortable with technology. A major component of any library instruction is to help prevent or alleviate library anxiety. By emphasizing the availability of help at any stage in the research process and by presenting a warm and friendly attitude toward the group or individual, the library staff helps new users learn to be more relaxed in the library setting. If potential users realize that for the library staff answering the most basic questions is normal, and that for staff members there is no such thing as a "stupid question," they will experience less or little library anxiety.

It may be appropriate for library orientations and tours to include some subtle tips on library etiquette. Besides general library rules, this might include remarks on loud talking, cell phones, guidelines on food and drink or placing liquids near electronic equipment, and so forth. Rather than a list of "thou shalt nots," presenting rules as benefiting everyone is most effective (see, for example, Tweedy and Valdez, 1997).

A cursory look at the OPAC is a good idea, but an orientation tour may not be the best time to explain all the issues of cataloging, authority file practices, and the correct procedures for transliterating Urdu. In other words, keep the session relatively focused, short, and sweet—and keep it moving.

Some libraries have computer-based or audio tours of the library available, similar to those found in museums. Some of these tours have stopping points, perhaps shown on a map of the library. These are dependent on users' willingness to take in the entire presentation, which is often a problem. Self-paced printed orientation guides are also a viable method for giving people an orientation to the library and its services.

Classroom Presentations

Classroom presentations, generally delivered by librarians, go into more depth about library procedures and the research process than orientations and tours. Presentations can be course-integrated or stand alone.

Course-Integrated Instruction

The teaching of information literacy skills over a school term, where the instructor works up a series of individual class units and programmatically interweaves these into the curriculum of a particular class, is known as *course-integrated instruction*. There may be separate units on different aspects of information literacy and/or on information-gathering activities in general.

Each unit may have a pretest followed by a posttest to determine the effectiveness of the learning and how to improve the program. In this kind of programmatic teaching, the library instructor gets to know a group of students, resulting in better interaction with them and more effective assistance.

A library instructor, who collaborates closely with the regular class instructor, especially over a period of weeks, may share or take responsibility for creating assignments and/or quizzes involving information literacy. An interesting article related to collaboration is Russell Hall's (2008) "The Embedded Librarian in a Freshman Speech Class." Over a semester or school term, there are more chances to help faculty further students' ability to engage in critical thinking regarding print materials, media, and the Internet. The library instructor collaborates with the classroom teacher by reinforcing mutually set instructional goals. In such an atmosphere of cooperation, the classroom teacher and library staff member can use their combined gifts of imagination, creativity, and pedagogical excellence to create an effective and exciting program for their students. The experience can be quite enriching for the staff member because, unlike some duties, you can see the results of your efforts as the students grow in knowledge.

On the other hand, it is the lot of most academic library instructors (and, sadly, many school library staff) to have to "do it all" in the space of one class session. This has come to be known as the *one-shot lecture* or "the 50-minute stand."

One-Shot Lectures

A "one-shot" presentation can be grueling, especially if you really try to "do it all." But an overabundance of detail can be detrimental to audience attention and to retention of the material. Those brought up under the tutelage of Internet gaming and multiple simultaneous text messaging may have short attention spans, and an abundance of detail might overwhelm them. Making sure that students know the basic library orientation material (that is, location of services, availability of help at reference and other service points, circulation policies, location of main shelving areas, and so forth); plus how to develop a search strategy plan; plus how to use encyclopedias, other reference sources, the public catalog, periodical indexes, and Boolean logic; plus how to read a call number, do proper citations, avoid plagiarism, *and* satisfy the need for sources for the current range of class topics as delineated by the faculty member is a lot to squeeze into 50 minutes (or one sentence). It has been done, but it's never very satisfying, either to the instructor or the students. When you only have one session, and the faculty member wants you to "do it all," you attempt to do what you can—but with very careful planning and a great deal of selectivity.

Good planning includes deciding exactly what *basic messages* you want to get across, and then being sure to focus on those messages. When possible, collaboration with the teacher can help assure mutual agreement on these basic goals. Observing your colleagues doing instruction can suggest various ways to structure information for an audience. Using these structures to shape a talk can help give it form, and make the main points more memorable.

CLASSROOM PEDAGOGY

Some say that the best advice on teaching technique is to follow the old tried-and-true dictum: first, explain what you're going to tell them; then tell them; then tell them what you told them. Repetition may still be the mother of learning. However, today's students dislike being patronized. The instructor must repeat without seeming to repeat, to make the information easily digestible without making it appear to be baby food. Involving the students in the session is the key to reaching them. Younger students have short attention spans—and that goes for entering college students as well. The formal lecture format used by college faculty for generations just doesn't work as well as it used to. A "sage on the stage" is being replaced by the "guide on the side" who plans active learning experiences to allow the students to discover the material as they work with other students to understand the curriculum. Younger students have come to expect visually exciting material, participative learning activities, and up-to-date technology. As with other educators, library instructors have been bringing active learning techniques to the classroom. These techniques include role playing, hands-on projects, audience response systems (for example, clickers), group activities and discussion (such as small group feedback), and teacher-driven questioning (Lorenzen, 2001).

Active learning techniques have been shown to be very effective in student learning and retention of what is learned. The activity should be something meaningful in the context of the class; instructors have had students create key words or subject headings for a topic under discussion, create a set of search terms using Boolean logic for a computer search, decide which databases would best serve a particular topic, and so forth. Follow-up discussion and a demonstration using the results presented by the students will help keep their interest.

Although this may be somewhat difficult in a one-shot situation, knowing your audience is an important part of reaching them. Certainly the approach to the young and inexperienced will be different from the approach to a class of returning adults or graduate students. In general, the younger audience may need less general explanation about technology, and more explanation about basic library and information resources, as well as basic definitions. The more mature audience is usually less reluctant to ask questions, while you may have to read the expression on the faces of a younger audience for clues about what they don't understand. However, even in a group of like-aged people, you will find a wide variety of library experience. Most academic classes will be a mixed bag of students with high, low, and no library experience. Communicating with the regular instructor—even sitting in on a class or two if there is time—is a good start for getting to know a class. For other audiences, some kind of quick survey, whether written, online, or done orally at the start or during the session may help gauge their needs.

A positive outlook, respect for your audience, the use of good analogies that your audience relates to and understands, and some good graphical material is almost essential for a successful library session. Personal energy, good voice projection and eye contact, and the other things one learns in speech class are just as necessary with a class of five students as they are for a large auditorium audience.

However, in the one-shot/50-minute stand, you must control the length of digressions, discussion, and student activity in order to complete your task. This may go against the pedagogy of active learning, but sometimes you are given a less than ideal situation and must make the most of it.

Factors outside the instructor's control can have an effect on the relative success or failure of a particular session. The day of the week, time of day, room temperature, lighting, day of the week, presence/absence of the regular teacher, quality of visuals or network connection, and the prevailing psychology of the individual class are some of these. The presenter should be well prepared so that whatever the obstacle, at least the main points of the session "come across" to the audience, using whatever good examples, analogies, diagrams, graphics, and explanations are necessary to make things clearer.

OFF-SITE INSTRUCTION AND DISTANCE EDUCATION

Technology, especially the Internet and its Web offshoots, have made it possible for many underserved populations to learn online. The geographically or economically isolated, or those with full or erratic work or family schedules, can take credit courses at both the undergraduate and graduate levels. Termed *distance education*, this can mean anything from a student obtaining textual material via a PDF link in an e-mail message to geographically remote students participating in "live" class discussions via video and audio hookups. Some institutions grant credentials and academic degrees for online coursework. Most academic libraries cooperate with other institutions' distance education programs by making these students welcome—to a point—at their libraries. Some libraries issue borrowers cards to distance education students at a nominal fee. While public libraries also welcome distance education students, only the larger ones have the depth of collections to support a regular undergraduate curriculum.

Providing effective instruction for an institution's distance learners presents certain challenges. In order to prepare the appropriate instruction techniques and materials, it is especially important to assess the distance population, especially their academic skill levels, computer connectivity, and technology literacy. The "digital divide" presents some real barriers to distance instruction and must be taken into consideration when preparing instruction.

Some institutions provide instruction to distance learners by arranging visits by instruction staff to the remote site. At one of the author's institutions, a distance education program with a cohort in New York paid to fly a librarian across the country and back to provide a day of instruction. More typical are one or two day visits to satellite campuses within a few hundred miles of the home institution.

Increasingly, technology is providing an alternative to in-person instruction with commercial Web-based meeting tools, learning modules and tutorials, and Web-based course management chat and discussion tools (Adams and Evans, 2006). There are occasional (and real) technological barriers to this kind of instruction. For example, at one of the authors' institutions, it is common for graduate students not to receive their campus ID cards (which contain their library bar code number) until well after they register. Without the bar code number, these students (who make up a large portion of the institution's distant students) are unable to access library databases from off campus. Nevertheless, as problems like this are gradually solved we may expect to see more information literacy delivered to distant populations in this way as library staff become more expert and experienced in designing and using digital learning tools.

Good distance learning institutions (and satellite campuses) provide the best possible library service they can to their students, using various combinations of the Internet, ILL, cooperative agreements with local libraries, and document delivery of needed research materials. In these situations, an attempt is usually made to provide reference service—which opens the opportunity for information literacy education. For some students, remote reference service is the only library contact they have, and the only information literacy they may receive.

Policy should specify parameters to address the needs of outside groups who ask for instruction, which can range from a 15-minute tour to a formal classroom instruction session. Local schools should be made aware of these policies; an unannounced walk-around tour of your library by 200 tiny voices during quiet study for final exams is not the ideal. On the other hand, college libraries often have formal cooperative arrangements with local high schools regarding use of the library. Good communication will facilitate coordination, meaning that the high school students' need for at least point-of-use instruction, and possibly classroom instruction, can be met.

INSTRUCTION: THEORY AND PRACTICE

Learning to Teach

In the case of library instruction, at least some familiarity with learning theory can be very useful. You do not have to earn a second master's degree or even take formal coursework in education. You can learn through teaching experience, continuing education classes or seminars, personal reading in the literature, and/or discussion with and observation of practitioners. Staff members frequently encounter individuals or groups with special needs—slow learners, seniors, people with reading or learning disabilities, nonnative speakers of English, underprepared entering students—who need a slightly different approach in explanations. Work in learning styles by teachers and librarians has shown that a good percentage of students in every class, even when students have very similar backgrounds, will have variant styles of hearing, seeing, and absorbing information, whether spoken or from a diagram, computer screen, or printed page. Reading a few articles on this subject will allow you to take advantage of the differing modalities of presentation and to more consciously design both what is said and what is shown to classes to reach all major types of learners (see, for example, Stripling and Hughes-Hassell, 2003, and Grassian and Kaplowitz, 2001).

Electronic Classrooms

There is no doubt that students who do hands-on practice with one or more databases during or immediately after a session will learn more and remember what they've learned better. For this reason, many libraries that do a lot of instruction and can afford it have installed electronic classrooms. Usually, there will be a workstation for the instructor, plus software and equipment to permit all learners to see live demonstrations done for their benefit via a projected screen, or on the individual workstation monitors, or both. One feature that most instructors like is using what is termed "control software"; this gives the instructor the ability to control or disable individual or all student screens, or to display any screen while demonstrations are going on. The lure of e-mail, games, and Web entertainment has been known to be a significant temptation for students with network-connected computers (McDermott, 1998).

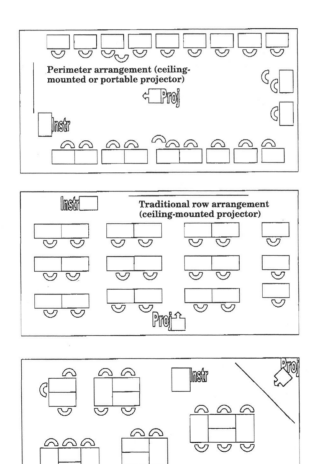

Figure 6.1 Electronic Classroom Configurations

In many cases, instructional staff have input into the design of electronic classrooms. This will range from the kind of projector to the type and arrangement of computer seating. Classroom configurations include perimeter seating (that is, computer stations backed against the walls), scattered clusters, and traditional rows (see Figure 6.1). Although different instructors may prefer different seating arrangements, what is important is that the instructor or assistant has the capability to move easily throughout the room, and to stand close enough to each computer to see the screen and provide help for individual or partnered students. The traditional row configuration is the most problematic in this regard. The perimeter arrangement gives a clear view of both monitors and projected screens for both instructor and student.

With mobile work stations, that is, tables and chairs on wheels, the room can be configured initially like a traditional classroom, quickly reconfigured to allow small group interaction, and then reconvened to allow a summing up and conclusion.

INFORMATION LITERACY TEACHING AIDS: HANDOUTS, COMPUTER-ASSISTED INSTRUCTION, AND MEDIA

Printed Handouts and Web Pages

Handouts and Web pages can play an important part in instructing the user. They can serve as an aid in the instruction process, as a reminder of things taught, or as a more detailed supplement to the information presented in a session. They also can be designed to be a self-instruction tool for those readers who, for one reason or another, do not seek help from library staff or who need assistance when reference help is not available. Many libraries have translated handout information into Web pages, which people can consult at a point of need in their searching. Some instructors use printouts of their Web pages as handouts.

Handouts and Web pages might include some of the following:

- General information introducing the reader to library services. This might include such information as library hours, service points, circulation policy, and special services. When needed, some add a map or diagram of the library, information on the scope of the collections, and possibilities for research consultation

- A basic introduction to library research, listing categories and examples of tools and aids (including, of course, the reference librarian as a facilitator)

- Forms encouraging user input, such as suggestions for new titles, for user evaluation of new library resources, for satisfaction or dissatisfaction with services or a particular reference resource, and for other suggestions in general

In teaching institutions or libraries having students as a major user group, the following additional handouts might be helpful:

- A survey form or pretest given out to students some days before an upcoming instruction session, the results of which will help determine what topics need to be covered or given focused attention

- *Pathfinders*, that is, structured guides to library research, usually including lists of sources, to be used for a specific classroom assignment or term project. A pathfinder might feature or embody a sample research strategy for a particular topic, similar to those being assigned in the class (see Figure 6.2)

- A point-of-use guide explaining particular resources or procedures, step by step. With some sophistication, these can be integrated on-screen with the display of an online resource

- Information about documenting sources. Tailored to local practice, this might include how to construct footnotes, parenthetical citations, or endnotes, works-cited lists, and guidelines for avoiding plagiarism

- Evaluation forms or post-tests to determine what skills or concepts students learn from a session, as well as what was missed, covered inadequately, or inadvertently omitted

Workbooks

As mentioned above, a number of school and academic institutions use a student workbook as a means of instruction. In combination with classroom lectures and on-site workshops, workbooks can be an effective learning tool for teaching information literacy objectives (Trail et al., 2006). They are often self-paced, so that the brighter students neither intimidate the slower ones nor get bored with the lesson. Even when friends work in "teams" and become each other's teachers, the material is covered and learning occurs. Practical, well-written step-by-step exercises will help users overcome library anxiety.

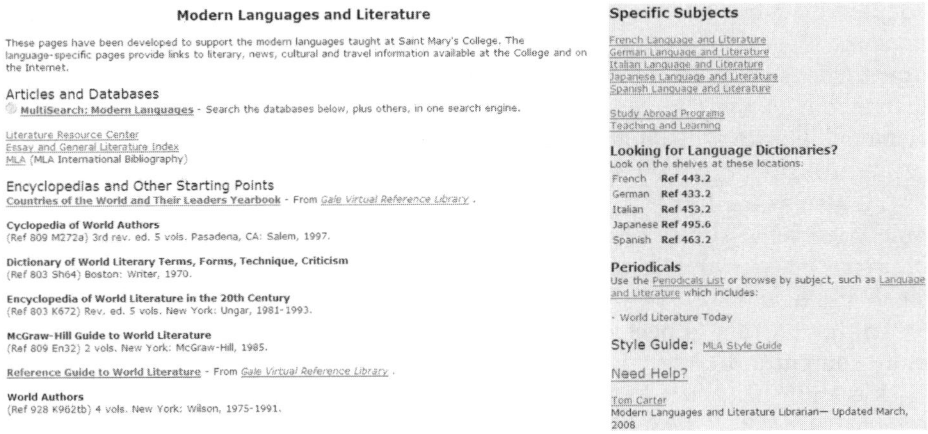

Figure 6.2 Pathfinder

Assuring students that seeking help at the reference desk is appropriate—in fact, encouraged—should be a part of any workbook, as well as in handouts, Web sites and presentations. We expect to see most of the remaining paper workbooks translated to the Web in the next few years to better accommodate today's technology-literate library staff and users.

Computer-Assisted Instruction

Somewhat less "formal" from the user's point of view, but certainly involving as much if not more preparation and effort from a staffing point of view, is computer-assisted instruction, or CAI. CAI was defined by Salisbury (1971) as "a man-machine interaction in which the teaching function is accomplished by a computer system without intervention by a human instructor." With advances in technology and positive research on the effectiveness of CAI, a growing number of libraries are using CAI to deliver information literacy instruction.

Online tutorials are the most prominent form of CAI in information literacy instruction, and usually focus on various aspects of the research process (for example, topic selection, Boolean search operators, evaluating information, or citing sources), how to use specific indexes or the OPAC, or general orientation to the library. In order to promote user engagement, the best CAI programs are interactive, easy to use, and responsive to learners' experiences. (See the tutorial links maintained by the Library Instruction Round Table at http://www3. baylor.edu/LIRT/lirtproj.html).

CAI has both advantages and disadvantages. Evan Ira Farber (1995), one of information literacy's pioneers, outlined some of the advantages of using CAI for repetitive forms of instruction: "A computer has infinite patience, no time constraints, does not take coffee breaks or fails to show up on weekends, and can adapt to individual needs and requests" (p. 435). CAI programs can also be self-paced, allowing users to work at their own rate and repeat or skip sections according to their own needs. They are consistent in providing the same information to each user and are easily updated, especially those on the Web, to include different information or reflect a new database interface. CAI programs can be linked to the course management systems (for example, Blackboard) adopted by many schools and colleges, making course integration easier. Perhaps the biggest advantage to the library is that the technology allows the staff time to focus on more complex instruction by leaving some of the more routine instruction to the CAI. As demand for instruction increases, particularly in academic libraries, CAI allows the staff to stretch its resources and provide a greater range of instruction to more users than would otherwise be possible.

CAI also as its disadvantages. The programs are expensive, at least in staff time, to develop and update. CAI does not provide an opportunity for contact between the user and library staff, reducing the opportunity for questions and feedback. Also, CAI may exclude users who are not comfortable with computers, although this is becoming less of a problem as the population becomes more computer literate.

One thing that would argue against greater adoption of CAI would be evidence that it is less effective than face-to-face instruction. Since about 1990, numerous studies have assessed the effectiveness of CAI in delivering

information literacy skills. An analysis of the studies done in academic libraries reveals that face-to-face instruction and CAI appear to be equally effective
in teaching basic information literacy skills (Zhang et al., 2007). In addition,
at least some students show a more positive attitude towards the interactivity
and game-like nature of CAI than they do towards in-person instruction sessions (Armstrong and Georgas, 2006).

Besides the CAI programs for basic information we mentioned earlier, there
are now more in-depth programs that go well beyond orientation information.
Podcasts and vodcasts have been developed to introduce voice and video into
the instruction modules. Good interactive programs can produce real learning
experiences, including grappling with various aspects of research methodology and critical thinking. CAI thus can extend some aspects of both reference
help and instruction, however limited, to being available 24 hours a day.

Media

There are a variety of media that are used to deliver information literacy
instruction. Besides text, they include analog audio and video, digital multimedia, Webcasting, audio and video streaming, multimedia clips, blogs, chat,
voice over IP, e-mail, and discussion forums (Smith, 2005).

Audio and/or visual materials can greatly enhance an orientation or instructional session, both providing a change of pace and accommodating different styles of learning. Using audiovisual materials in class helps to bypass
the need for long group sessions out in the reading areas, where interrupting
or disturbing the work of other readers should be avoided. Larger tour groups
lead to visibility problems for some participants, and those around the fringes
will start paying attention to each other instead of the information. A classroom presentation with audiovisual can be followed by a quick, focused walk
around for physical orientation, if necessary.

A simple chalkboard or whiteboard can be used as a dynamic tool, especially if writing and diagrams are clear and well-thought-out beforehand.
Digital slides, when designed to be legible and give a clear message, can be
an effective tool for instruction; these can serve the neophyte and experienced
lecturer alike as a good substitute for written notes. Scanned images, document cameras, and screen shots also make it possible for students to "get" the
actual look, if not the feel, of individual resources; this method avoids the distraction and, often, damage resulting from passing bound volumes around.

Instructors today can project real-time demonstrations of online catalogs
and Web-based databases using a networked computer and a video projector.
Some projectors can even store prepared demonstrations for later display.
More complex (and expensive) projectors can display a very large, bright image
for auditorium-like classrooms. Videos are another option for changing the
pace and feel of an instruction session. Producing a professional-looking video
in-house can be expensive and time-consuming. Both commercial firms and
academic institutions have produced generic instruction videos for sale. Even
better, Web video sharing sites such as YouTube offer short instructional videos produced by libraries and available for sharing with a class. These can be
used as a class assignment, or shown as part of an instruction session.

Do-It-Yourself

Sometimes local conditions or the specificity of the topic will dictate the use of localized materials, including digital slide shows, podcasts, online tutorials, or videos produced in-house. Digital slides have been used in schools and libraries for years. The technology is ubiquitous and most have been produced locally (that is, by the instructor). Some have proven effective, others not. Certainly the youth of today are used to more sophisticated technology, which leads to hesitancy regarding this form of teaching aid unaccompanied by more active teaching pedagogy. As the capabilities of equipment for playing them have improved, digital videos and tutorials are becoming more popular as a means of varying pedagogy. These latter two have the advantages of localized flexibility, the ability to be updated continuously, and a level of specificity that no generic material can provide. A combination of local and general media can probably provide the variety and flexibility required to address the different needs of the variety of audiences libraries serve.

Design of Instruction Materials

Handouts, other printed materials, and Web pages should be as professional looking as possible. Desktop publishing software and more user-friendly Web editors have enabled many staff members to produce thoroughly professional-looking materials; those who don't have the skills usually know someone who does. But special effects aren't a substitute for clear presentation. Attention should always be given to accepted design principles, for example providing adequate "white space" (that is, empty space around and between text, avoiding crowding or clutter) and a minimum number of different type fonts. Well-thought-out and well-written text, embellished by a few well-chosen and well-placed illustrations, and duplicated on a decent photocopier, works well. A badly designed handout or Web page, no matter how colorful the illustrations, or how clever the special effects, probably will not.

Designing handouts or Web pages requires time and an eye for basic layout principles and practices. Being held to a minimum budget and having little technology is a common limitation for instructors; so word-processed text, with a couple of carefully placed photocopied or screen-printed illustrations will often suffice. Some instructors maintain a file of copyright-free visual material, sorted by general type and collected over time, to be used as illustrations. Web sites, book sale catalogues, commercial flyers, and other published and online treasuries of public domain illustrations and clipart are good sources.

Overall, the quality of library handouts and digital resources is largely the product of staff members' efforts, limited only by their resourcefulness and imagination. Time is one important factor that may rein in creativity. For handouts, keeping an online file of masters and bookmarks to online illustration Web sites is a good time-saving strategy. Updating a good but slightly outdated handout is easier and quicker than having to do the whole thing from scratch. One can easily update an older word-processed or Web document; deleting and importing titles, call numbers, and Web site URLs from various files and databases is relatively easy. Today, printing huge numbers of any hand-out is probably not a good idea, since Web sites, and even certain periodicals held "virtually" via a commercial database vendor, can be changed, added, or dropped unexpectedly. (Keep this in mind as you view the Web references in this book!)

Web pages should be reviewed on a variety of browsers in order to spot problem areas with specific browsers. The choice of screen backgrounds and text colors can be particularly critical for legibility. What looks great on your browser may be illegible on others. You should also have any friends or ac-quaintances with vision problems (such as poor eyesight or color blindness) view your pages to be sure you are not creating problems for your readers ("Bobby" is a program that checks your Web site for possible problems for the disabled, available via the Web at the time of writing at http://www.bobby.com/). Also see the home page of the "Web Accessibility Initiative" (available at http://www.w3.org/WAI/).

Pages should also be reviewed regularly to update information and URLs/hypertext links, especially links to outside resources, which can change or die without warning. That dreaded "404—File Not Found" message a reader gets from one of your external links does not inspire confidence in your site.

SECURITY MATTERS AND PRESERVATION

Vulnerability to Theft

Instruction staff typically use or supervise the use of at least some mon-etarily valuable equipment. At least temporarily, they are in possession of ev-erything from laser pointers to computer equipment (some of it portable), to LCD panels and video projectors. Although it is rare for students in a class to steal equipment, even a short transition time between classes can be a time of great vulnerability. When we lost an inexpensive laser pen, we figuratively just shook our heads. But we woke up when, during a very quick post-session tour, someone made off with the laptop computer we used for demonstrations. Cabling vulnerable equipment to its table or cart helps, as well as placing a theft detection strip on the equipment. However, a locked door during walk-about and whenever the room is vacant is now standard procedure. Valuable equipment should be, as ours was, indelibly marked or engraved with trace-able identification in case of police recovery.

Preservation Component

Instructors have a clear obligation to address library preservation. Of all library staff, the instructor has the best opportunity to directly influence those individuals who might damage resources through ignorance. Of course, modi-fying the behavior of the uncaring or willfully destructive is more difficult.

If time and circumstances permit, presenting information in an orientation or other formal library session is perhaps the most direct way to inform a sub-stantial number of readers about library preservation. This should be done by emphasizing the positive benefits to the audience of careful, responsible use of library materials; for example, the importance to everyone of maintaining complete information in the library (Amodeo, 1988). The instructor should avoid actually explaining methods of theft or mutilation, or showing heartbreaking examples; both of these practices have been shown to encourage destructive imitation. The instructing library staff can make the learner aware of the seriousness of the loss of library information in any format (see Chapter 15 regarding library damage).

ADMINISTRATION OF THE INSTRUCTIONAL PROGRAM

Typically, formal instruction is a function of the reference department. In larger institutions, there may be an entire subdepartment devoted to instructional activities, managed by an administrator at the level of a department head. But most library instructors are reference staff, who may or may not have had training in pedagogy.

Personnel Selection

Instructing on information literacy is like doing reference work, only more so. An instructor should have the ability to relate to people and have a broad educational background. The ability to hold an audience's attention is vital; a speaker should know if he or she has distracting personal idiosyncrasies and eliminate them. In a way, you have to be like good motion picture music: carry the message well without distracting the audience by calling attention to yourself. At the same time, you need a personality presence or the material will come across as boring. You need to be able to "think on your feet" because the audiences will have questions, some of them unexpected, even a bit bizarre. A sense of humor is important. Intelligent planning of lectures/sessions, competent designing of visuals and handouts, and the mental agility to switch gears and improvise to meet unexpected circumstances (for example, balky technology) are also important.

Education for Information Literacy

Most support staff educational programs do not offer separate units or classes on information literacy, although some do (Burke, 2000). Instead it is treated, if at all, as a part of a reference or public services course. This is the reason we present the level of detail that we do in this chapter.

In smaller institutions, where library staff must do a little—or rather, a lot—of everything, the rule may be "you learn by doing." A session is called for, the newly graduated staff member is assigned, and that's that. This may be disadvantageous to the students, who may be subjected to a carefully written 10-page script read by a nervous first-timer who makes little eye contact with the audience. Better results will come from a little reading and a little practice ahead of time, as well as whatever experience coursework, seminars, or other pertinent practical information can be garnered. Because the instructor will likely work with colleagues who graduated from library programs without a formal class in library instruction, they also will have had to learn at least some new skills on the job, and no doubt will lend you some sympathetic guidance.

Where an instruction program already exists, there is usually a "break-in" period. The new staff member attends several classroom sessions given by one or more colleagues. Later, that person is assigned some basic orientations, and perhaps later will give one or two components of a team-taught library session. Eventually, exposure and practice give the newcomer the confidence of good experience. There are many useful texts and articles about library instruction, and reading them can be of great help (see the Suggested Readings at the end of this chapter).

Information Literacy Group Support

The California Clearinghouse on Library Instruction (now split into CCLI-North and its Southern California sister group, SCIL), mentioned above, is one of the oldest of a growing number of library organizations, chapters, and local networking groups devoted to improving the level of library education while making life a little easier for practitioners. In the United States, the Institute for Information Literacy (IIL) offers intensive training seminars for both the initiated and the uninitiated. (See "Suggested Resources for Keeping Up to Date" for the URLs of groups mentioned here). Local groups, like the Chicago Area Instruction Librarians Group, and regional groups, like the New England Library Instruction Group (NELIG), have joined larger associations like LOEX (the U.S. national IL clearinghouse); the Library Instruction Round Table (LIRT) of the ALA; the Instruction Section (IS) of ACRL; Canada's Information Literacy Conference (WILU); and the Australian Library and Information Association (ALIA) in presenting programs and exchanging information, handouts, methods, problems, and solutions—and a lot of funny stories. Subscribing to ILI-L, the Information Literacy Instruction Discussion List, is a must for instructors.

Individual contact with experienced professionals will make the most insecure beginner a better instructor. In our years of library instruction, we have never met a "library instruction person" who wasn't willing to share every trick of the trade with a newcomer. So if you find yourself doing information literacy "solo," don't be afraid to reach out.

Scheduling

Library instruction requires time and energy. Giving general library tours and orientation talks becomes second nature after a while; it often can be done by the experienced with minimal preparation. However, almost every subject session or workshop requires additional time for preparation. Lists of appropriate resources plus subject-related exercises and other handouts take time and care to produce. Even when the same faculty member asks for the same library session year after year, handouts and visuals must be updated with the newest reference sources, indexes, Web sites, and database interfaces, strategies reviewed, and often a new set of slides or tutorial pages made. A change in the nature of the research assignment may necessitate additional preparation, or even a completely different approach. Instructors are constantly updating their knowledge because technological products and interfaces are always in flux.

The information literacy coordinator or administrator needs to regularize the process of scheduling lectures, lest room conflicts, media or equipment shortages, or even inadequate preparation undermine the effectiveness of both the individual session and the information literacy program at large. A paper or online scheduling form with a fairly complete checklist, used by all who schedule information literacy sessions, will help prevent scheduling conflicts and oversights (see Figure 6.3 for a sample). A shared online calendar is also an effective way of avoiding room conflicts and inviting volunteers to teach individual sessions. Such forms are also useful for record-keeping. Including the staff member's evaluation of what went right or wrong may help the administrator make productive changes in scheduling, approach or program strategy—or help convince the maintenance people to change the thermostat.

Preventing Burnout

Instructors, like all other employees, are subject to becoming tired or even to burn out. Peak periods can be exhausting for an overburdened reference staff. In academic libraries, peaks may occur during freshman orientation, or when the majority of college writing instructors ask for a basic research session, or during the term paper rush late in the semester. There is always some faculty member who calls for an impromptu lecture right in the middle of the maelstrom, because he or she forgot to schedule a lecture, or is going out of town, or has laryngitis. Often, an ill-prepared presentation may do more harm than good for the students, as they may become disenchanted with the library. This is a situation the library tries to avoid.

Preparation Time

A well-publicized policy of requiring teachers and faculty to give a certain amount of advance notice for lectures (say, 10 days or 2 weeks) is a good way to maintain some control, protect the staff, and make sure the sessions are "up to snuff." On the other hand, as public service people interested in promoting information literacy, staff members who teach try to take any opportunity offered to promote better information use; with the lecturer's approval, the supervisor may allow exceptions. A good supervisor will try to negotiate the best "deal" for all parties, remaining as flexible as befits the situation and the people involved. A good supervisor will also recognize that some information literacy instructors won't know how to say "no" to lecture requests, and will intervene to prevent potential burnout of staff.

Timing the Session

Scheduling has another aspect. Staff giving an information literacy session or workshop often face the problem of disinterest in the case of younger students and underclassmen. If the instruction students receive is not of immediate

Classroom instructors may schedule a library instruction session for their undergraduate and graduate students, tailored to the course and the students' research topics. Library sessions can cover a range of print and electronic resources, as well as general research strategies. We recommend course instructors submit requests *at least three weeks in advance* of preferred dates to ensure the availability of library staff, access to an instruction room, and preparation of materials.

INSTRUCTOR and COURSE INFORMATION

Instructor Name:

Phone:

E-mail:

Department & Course Number:

Course Theme and Readings:

Course Meeting Times:

Number of Students:

INFORMATION FOR LIBRARY SESSION

Preferred Dates and Times:

First choice:

Second choice:

Third choice:

Brief Description of Assignment:
(subject, length, criteria, etc.)

Types of Resources Desired:
(requirements and restrictions)

Goals for the Session:
(what you would like students to know, or be able to do, by the end of the library session)

Submit this Form   Erase this Form

Figure 6.3 Library Instruction Request Form

use, or if they have no context for the use of such information, interest may be quite low. The best research lecture ever given will be forgotten at the lunch bell, unless it is put to use by these students in the very near future.

Timing sessions to coincide with the beginnings of a research assignment is important. Students who know they will soon need to apply the lessons of a information literacy session are likely to retain more of the information. An exercise that flows from the presentation and reinforces each of the skills presented will insure better retention and future application. Thus, getting the teacher to schedule instruction sessions at the appropriate time or times during the school term is important. Perhaps the best solution for entering students is a short general orientation/tour at the beginning of the semester, focusing on the library's service points where students can find help, with the longer introduction to research scheduled in conjunction with an assignment. One advantage of having instruction pages or CAI on a Web site is that students can indeed seek out help when they most need it—which may be at 2 A.M. when no one is available.

Publicity

Until information literacy becomes imbedded in the conscience and consciousness of teachers as a normal and integral part of any course of study, library staff must engage in sustained efforts to promote it. In some institutions, there are so few instruction staff and such a high demand for lectures and workshops that additional publicity would threaten the physical and emotional survival of the beleaguered staff, but this not the rule. In a few institutions, library instruction still has to be presented to some faculty or department heads as a new way to benefit all concerned. There are some model situations, such as Ohio's Earlham College, King's College in Pennsylvania, and the California State College and University system, in which library instructors and faculty have cooperated to create a program of library instruction integrated into the curriculum. Faculty and librarians work closely and sometimes team-teach the classes. At other institutions, there is a program of required student library course work, or there are independent classes taught by librarians for academic credit. Regional higher education accrediting agencies, like the Western Association of Schools and Colleges (WASC), have included information literacy as one of the learning outcomes institutions of higher education are expected to teach their students. But in many institutions (at least for now), it is an uphill battle to get faculty attention focused on information literacy. Older faculty who had no personal experience with information literacy may be less than receptive, but they are often surprisingly interested. Younger faculty who have personally had library instruction as a part of their education are much less reluctant to participate in library instruction programs, and often do so enthusiastically. This is one more reason we have to thank the pioneers of library instruction, who have given us a jump on the future.

Assessment, Records, and Statistics

As with other services, keeping statistics is useful for evaluating, improving, and promoting an information literacy program. The number of tours and orientations, subject sessions, term paper clinics delivered, tutorials accessed, the number of attendees, and even the number of new handouts designed are raw material for the departmental annual report. These data will also allow better planning for future years, and enable better targeting of groups and more effective use of time and resources. Taking this information into account, instructional goals and objectives can be defined more realistically, and the program made more effective. If good statistics are maintained at the reference desk, changes in the number or quality of inquiries can reflect well on the information literacy program. For example, if a sharp rise in the number of reference questions follows a new high in orientation attendees, a correlation might be drawn. If the proportion of reference or research questions to merely directional questions increases dramatically after a hard-fought campaign to reach all entering students, this may well be an indication of a success story. Of course, things may not always progress smoothly, but evidence is important in planning and gaining administrative support.

An important development in the purpose of assessment has been to document evidence of student learning. This reflects a new assessment emphasis in educational institutions as government agencies, funding authorities, accrediting institutions, parents, and students look for evidence that students are really learning what schools and colleges teach them. Assessment of the effectiveness of an information literacy program in improving student learning is important to demonstrate its value in the school's or college's curriculum. Assessment is also important to determine the strengths and weaknesses of the program in order to improve its effectiveness. Assessment criteria might include raw statistics like those described above, such as the number of students reached, or given a particular kind of session. More qualitative criteria are usually necessary to assess learning and the successful application of those skills in later tasks. While useful, they are also harder to measure. Staff members have developed many ways of doing this, from pre- and post-tests to studies of the quality of bibliographic citations.

In academic programs, written student survey forms and faculty survey forms, pre- and post-tests, portfolio assessment, citation analysis, and even formal focus groups are among the tools used to evaluate student learning in an information literacy program. More information on assessment of information literacy activities is presented in the Chapter 16, Assessment. Records of evaluative activities should be kept for several years, since they are often requested during regional accreditations.

SUMMARY

Information literacy may be defined as knowing when information is necessary, how to identify and access it, how to evaluate its quality, and how to use it ethically and legally. Information literacy has evolved from library instruction, the understanding and use of resources contained in a library. Information literacy instruction includes a variety of processes and materials through which staff members convey to users the ways and methods by which they may acquire and use needed information. Information literacy instruction includes such things as informative signage and Web tutorials. Primarily, however, it includes the instruction of a user or groups of users by staff.

Staff members instruct readers in several ways. At the reference desk, one-on-one contact allows the reference staff to explain the use of individual library tools as they become relevant to the client's needs (informal or point-of-use instruction). In library introductory talks and tours, staff members introduce users to both the physical layout of the library and the variety of services and materials available (library orientation). Using a more formal setting (class-rooms), staff present information about search strategies, the use of specific tools or classes of tools pertinent to the group's needs, and the evaluation and ethical use of information.

School and academic libraries have a most specific mission regarding in-struction. Their librarians and support staff use a variety of means to in-struct students. Both general and assignment-specific publications, including workbooks and digital slide programs, video and audio programs, and Web programs including tutorials, can be used to help convey knowledge of both specific library tools and the thinking processes whereby students may become library, and information, literate. Other types of libraries may do less or no formal instruction, but library public service staff in any type of library should know about library anxiety, work to prevent or reduce it if possible, and be able to recognize and deal with the customer struggling under its influence.

A successful instruction program is based on the actual needs of library users. Good planning, solid, well-articulated, and achievable goals, and a co-ordinated effort to publicize information literacy services and programs are necessary components. Appropriate scheduling, gathering of statistics, and ongoing evaluation of the program, its success in aiding readers, and its prac-titioners and materials are necessary activities for the person coordinating the information literacy effort. Finally, assessing the effectiveness of a library's information literacy program is important to establishing quality service.

Chapter Review Material

1. How does library instruction relate to access to information?
2. What are the basic elements of information literacy?
3. Name four kinds of formal library instruction, and give an example of each.
4. Name five kinds of library-produced materials that can be used in an information literacy program.
5. What are some things to watch out for when creating a Web site for library instruction?
6. What are the instructing library staff's responsibilities regarding pres-ervation of library information?
7. How might statistics be used to support a library instruction program?
8. Give a best-case and a worst-case scenario for information literacy at an academic library or a school library. In the worst case, what might one do to generate interest and progress?
9. You are asked to set up an instruction program at a school/college li-brary where you have just begun working.

    a. What are some of the questions you should ask—and answer—as you begin thinking about how to set up a program?

b. What are some of the options you may have to consider? What may limit your choices?

c. What are the foremost steps you should take before publicizing a new program?

d. Where might you seek advice and counsel, presuming no one at your institution has done any programmatic library instruction before?

e. What classes might you take (or wish you had taken) to improve your performance as a library instructor?

SUGGESTED RESOURCES FOR KEEPING UP-TO-DATE

The newsletters of LOEX, LIRT, and other national and regional information literacy organizations and clearinghouses are good sources of continuing information in library instruction. Each of these publications also lists suggested current literature in the field, as do annual reviews in *Reference Services Review* and the *LIRT Newsletter*. The journal *Research Strategies* is specifically focused on library instruction. Of course, *Library Literature* and *LISTA*, as well as *ERIC* and *Education FT*, index individual articles, books, and book reviews. Those without academic work in library instruction, as well as the rest of us, can benefit from the programs of the Institute for Information Literacy. Most of the annual library instruction conferences focus on an important information literacy issue, and, happily, some of these are published (e.g., the annual LOEX conferences) or put on a Web site. Many information literacy organizations maintain a Web presence, and often include an excellent selection of standards, issues, and good links. The following are URLs for some of these sites, all current at the time of this writing.

Instruction Section of ACRL: http://www.ala.org/ala/acrl/aboutacrl/acrlsections/instruction/homepage.cfm

LIRT (Library Instruction Round Table) of ALA: http://www3.baylor.edu/LIRT/ (See also the links there to the annual "Top Twenty" list of instruction articles, and to the list of links for "Library Instruction Tutorials.")

ACRL Information Literacy: http://www.ala.org/ala/acrl/acrlissues/acrlinfolit/informationliteracy.cfm

LOEX (Library Orientation Exchange): http://www.emich.edu/public/loex/loex.html

WILU (Workshop on Instruction in Library Use): http://www.yorku.ca/wilu2007/about/#wilu2008 (Note: Site of annual conference and pertinent Web site change each year.)

IIL (Institute for Information Literacy): http://www.ala.org/ala/acrl/acrlissues/acrlinfolit/professactivity/iil/welcome.cfm. (Check this site for intensive training workshops on information literacy, as well as standards, statements and informational updates.)

ALIA Information Literacy Forum (ALIA's Australian literacy group, with its own listserv): aliaINFOLIT http://www.alia.org.au/groups/infolit/

One of the best ways of keeping up with the field is by subscribing to ILI-L (formerly BI-L), the major listserv dedicated to library instruction. Messages include announcements, inquiries, and answers from members about all manner of relevant instruction issues, from philosophy to equipment. You can subscribe, unsubscribe, or access the ILI-L archive (May 2002–present), by going to http://lists.ala.org/wws/info/ili-l.

REFERENCES

Association of College and Research Libraries. 2000. *Information Literacy Competency Standards for Higher Education.* http://www.ala.org/ala/acrl/acrl standards/standards.pdf.

Adams, Tina M., and R. Sean Evans, 2006. "Tailoring Instruction for Students in Distance Learning Environments," In *Information Literacy that Works: A Guide to Teaching by Discipline and Student Population*, ed. Patrick Ragains. New York: Neal-Schuman.

Amodeo, Anthony. 1988. "A Debt Unpaid: The Bibliographic Instruction Librarian and Library Conservation," *College & Research Libraries News* 49, no. 9: 601, 603.

Armstrong, Annie, and Helen Georgas. 2006. "Using Interactive Technology to Teach Information Literacy Concepts to Undergraduate Students," *Reference Services Review* 34, no. 4: 491–497.

Burke, John J. 2000. "Library Technical Assistant Programs: Library Education for Support Staff," *Community & Junior College Libraries* 9, no. 3: 23–31.

Callison, Daniel. 2006. *The Blue Book on Information Age Inquiry, Instruction and Literacy.* Westport, CT: Libraries Unlimited.

Davis, Denise M. 2007. *Libraries Connect Communities: Public Library Funding & Technology Access Study, 2006–2007.* Chicago: American Library Association.

Farber, Evan Ira. 1995. "Plus Ca Change. . . ," *Library Trends* 44, no. 2: 430–439.

Grassian, Esther S., and Joan Kaplowitz. 2001. *Information Literacy Instruction: Theory and Practice.* New York: Neal-Schuman.

Hall, Russell. 2008. "The Embedded Librarian in a Freshman Speech Class," *College & Research Library News* 69, no. 1: 28–30.

International Society for Technology in Education. 2007. *National Education Technology Standards for Students: The Next Generation.* 2nd ed. Washington, DC: ISTE.

Islam, Ramona L., and Lisa Anne Murno. 2006. "From Perceptions to Connections: Informing Information Literacy Program Planning in Academic Libraries through Examination of High School Library Media Center Curricula," *College & Research Libraries* 67, no. 6: 492–514.

Jehlik, Theresa. 2004. "Information Literacy in the Public Library," *Nebraska Library Association Quarterly* 35, no. 4: 7–13.

Julien, Heidi, and Reegan Breu. 2005. "Instructional Practices in Canadian Public Libraries," *Library & Information Science Research* 27, no. 3: 281–301.

Lorenzen, Michael. 2001. "Active Learning and Library Instruction," *Illinois Libraries* 83, no. 2: 19–24.

McDermott, Irene E. 1998. "Solitaire Confinement: The Impact of the Physical Environment on Computer Training," *Computers in Libraries* 18, no. 1: 22–27.

Mech, Terrence F., and Charles I. Brooks. 1997 "Anxiety and Confidence in Using a Library by College Freshmen and Seniors," *Psychological Reports* 81, no. 3: 929–930.

Nelson, Sandra. 2001. The *New Planning for Results: A Streamlined Approach*. Chicago: American Library Association.

Rader, Hannelore B. 2002. "Information Literacy 1973–2002: A Selected Literature Review," *Library Trends* 51, no. 2: 242–259.

Salisbury, Alan B. 1971. "An Overview of CAI," *Educational Technology* 11, no. 10: 48–50.

Smith, Susan Sharpless. 2005. *Web-Based Instruction: A Guide for Libraries*. 2nd ed. Chicago: American Library Association.

Stripling, B. K., and S. Hughes-Hassell, eds. 2003. *Curriculum Connections through the Library*. Westport, CT: Libraries Unlimited.

Trail, Mary Ann, Carolyn Gutierrez, and David Lechner. 2006. "Reconsidering a Traditional Instruction Technique: Reassessing the Print Workbook," *Journal of Academic Librarianship* 32, no. 6: 632–640.

Tweedy, Duffy, and Esteban Valdez. 1997. "Preservation to the People! Mainstreaming Preservation into Instructional Sessions at an Undergraduate Library," in *Promoting Preservation Awareness in Libraries: A Sourcebook for Academic, Public, School, and Special Collections*, ed. Jeanne M. Drewes and Julie A. Page. Westport CT: Greenwood Press, 240–245.

Van Kampen, Doris Judy. 2004. *Library Anxiety, the Information Search Process and Doctoral Use of the Library*. Unpublished doctoral dissertation. University of Central Florida, Orlando.

Zhang, Li, Erin M. Watson, and Laura Banfield. 2007. "The Efficacy of Computer-Assisted Instruction versus Face-to-Face Instruction in Academic Libraries: A Systematic Review," *Journal of Academic Librarianship* 33, no. 4: 478–484.

SUGGESTED READINGS

Association of College and Research Libraries Instruction Section Task Force. 2003. *Guidelines for Instruction Programs in Academic Libraries*. http://www.ala.org/ala/acrl/acrlstandards/guidelinesinstruction.cfm.

American Association of School Libraries. 1997. *Information Literacy Standards for Student Learning: Linking the Library Media Program to the Content Areas*. Chicago: American Library Association. http://www.ala.org/ala/aasl/aaslproftools/informationpower/informationliteracy.htm.

American Library Association and the Association for Educational Communications and Technology. 1998. *Information Power: Building Partnerships for Learning*. Chicago: American Library Association.

Association for Teacher-Librarianship in Canada and the Canadian School Library Association. 2003. *Achieving Information Literacy: Standards for School Library Programs in Canada*. Chicago: American Library Association.

Behrens, Shirley J. 1994. "A Conceptual Analysis and Historical Overview of Information Literacy," *College & Research Libraries* 55, no. 4: 309–322.

Bruce, Christine, and P. Candy. 2000. *Information Literacy around the World: Advances in Programs and Research*. Wagga Wagga, New South Wales: Charles Stuart University.

Byerly, Greg, and Carolyn S. Brodie. 2006. "Some Lesser Known Websites For, By, and About Library Media Specialists," *School Library Media Activities Monthly* 23, no. 3: 40–42.

Canadian Association for School Libraries. 1997. *Students' Information Literacy Needs in the 21st Century: Competencies for Teacher-Librarians*. http://www.cla.ca/casl/literacyneeds.html.

Collins, Linda J. 2007. "Livening Up the Classroom: Using Audience Response Systems to Promote Active Learning," *Medical Reference Services Quarterly* 26, no. 1: 81–88.

Durando, Paola, and Patricia Oakley. 2005. "Developing Information Literacy Skills in Nursing and Rehabilitation Therapy Students," *Journal of the Canadian Health Libraries Association* 26: 7–11.

Grassian, Easter S., and Joan R. Kaplowitz. 2005. *Learning to Lead and Manage Information Literacy Instruction.* New York: Neal-Schuman.

Kiron, Jennifer, and Lyn Barham. 2005. "Added Information Literacy in the Workplace," *Australian Library Journal* 54 no. 4: 365–376.

Kuhlthau, Carol Collier. 2002. *Teaching the Library Research Process: A Step-by-Step Program for Secondary School Students.* 2nd ed. Metuchen, NJ: Scarecrow Press.

Mediavella, Cindy. 2003. "Homework Helpers," *School Library Journal* 49, no. 3: 56–59.

Michel, Stephanie. 2001. "What Do They Really Think? Assessing Student and Faculty Perspectives on a Web-Based Tutorial to Library Research," *College & Research Libraries* 62, no. 4: 317–332.

Moore, Penny. 2005. "An Analysis of Information Literacy Education Worldwide," *School Libraries Worldwide* 11, no. 2: 1–23.

———. 2006. "Information Literacy in the New Zealand Education Sector," *School Libraries Worldwide* 12, no 1: 1–21.

Ragains, Patrick, ed. 2006. *Information Literacy that Works: A Guide to Teaching by Discipline and Student Population.* New York: Neal-Schuman.

Riedling, Ann Marlow. 2004. *Information Literacy: What Does It Look Like in the School Library Media Center?* Westport, CT: Libraries Unlimited.

Rockman, Ilene. 2004. *Integrating Information Literacy in the Higher Education Curriculum.* San Francisco: Jossey-Bass.

Thomas, Nancy Pickering. 2004. *Information Literacy and Information Skills Instruction: Applying Research to Practice in the School Library Media Center.* Westport, CT: Libraries Unlimited.

Chapter 7

Interlibrary Loan and Document Delivery

We forbid those who belong to a religious order to formulate any vow against lending their books to those who are in need of them, seeing that to lend is enumerated among the principal works of mercy.

—Decree of the Church Council
Paris, 1212 c.e.

In most cases, user-initiated services have lower unit costs, higher fill rates, and faster turnaround times than mediated services.

—Mary Jackson, 2004

With the tremendous increase in the amount of information available on the open Web, and with the licensed databases available to public, academic, and special library users, you may be surprised to learn that there is still a significant demand for interlibrary loans. In fact, the vast majority of the information people want is not free on the Web. Finding tools like Google and WorldCat reveal the availability of information around the United States and the world, and individuals continue to utilize interlibrary loan services to obtain the information they wish to read or view. The amount of interlibrary lending continues to increase (see OCLC annual reports for interlibrary loan data) and obtaining information not available locally is an important library service.

ROLE AND PHILOSOPHY OF INTERLIBRARY LOAN

Interlibrary loan (ILL) goes by many names, including interlibrary borrowing, interlibrary lending, interlibrary services, document delivery, and resource sharing. It is the process by which a library borrows an item from another library for one of its users. With today's technologies the lending library may be half the world away and yet service is fast. At its simplest, a branch library user requests a book or video from the central library. A more complex transaction might be a researcher requesting a filmed or paper copy of a medieval manuscript from an overseas library. In either case, aside from the number of steps in each procedure and the needed expertise of the parties involved, the philosophy as well as the procedure is basically the same.

Loans to libraries may have occurred in ancient Egypt and Greece, but the evidence is sketchy. There was a famous "loan" of the Athenian state copies of the works of Aeschylus, Sophocles, and Euripides to the library of the Egyptian Pharaoh Ptolemaios III Evergetes (who ruled 247–222 B.C.E.). However, Ptolemaios kept the valuable originals and returned only copies to Athens. Cooperative loaning of materials from library to library in Western Europe goes back at least as far as early medieval times, if not the so-called Dark Ages (Jackson, 1974).

Monasteries often loaned out books for copying to the scriptoria of other monasteries, sometimes hundreds of miles distant. These libraries sometimes never recovered the loaned materials, due to the exigencies of medieval travel, warfare, fire, barbarian raids, and the occasional thief (good evidence for book thievery in medieval and later times are the various forms of anathemas against such profaners of libraries, found as inscriptions on book covers, on posted parchment, and even carved at the entrance to the library scriptorium). On the whole, libraries fare much better today regarding materials loaned to other libraries (barring the occasional barbarian raid, of course).

According to the annals of U.S. library history, ILL began in the early 1900s, and was first codified in 1917. Borrowing activity remained low until the 1950s when a standardized request form was adopted by the ALA. The development of union catalogs and serials lists in the 1960s containing the holdings of multiple libraries greatly aided the ability to locate wanted materials, and the introduction of the OCLC ILL subsystem in the 1970s allowed the electronic transmission of requests. ILL continues to evolve today through the medium of the Internet, resulting in speedier fulfillment of requests and more user control over the process as well as generating greater satisfaction.

Document delivery is a supplemental ILL service, especially for special libraries. Document delivery has several different meanings in the context of ILL. One definition involves purchasing information (especially periodical articles) from commercial document suppliers when access from other libraries is either unavailable or too slow. People sometimes prefer document delivery over traditional ILL because of its speed. Some commercial suppliers can deliver requested items within 24 hours or less; needless to say there is a higher cost for such service. This turnaround time is more rapid than most traditional ILL systems can achieve. However, a number of studies have shown that turnaround time for most document suppliers is no faster than the average ILL turnaround time (for example see Kurosman and Duriak, 1994, and Pedersen and Gregory, 1994). In addition, document suppliers' fees are often between $10 and $25 per item as well as a copyright fee that ranges from $8 to $10, thus making the service very expensive for many libraries. Some libraries, on the other hand, use document delivery to stretch their materials budgets by purchasing information for their service community in lieu of subscribing to low-use or expensive periodicals.

Another version of document delivery is delivering library-owned materials, via mail or the Internet, directly to library clientele. Staff members frequently do this to assist users who live at a distance or are otherwise unable to come to the library. It may also be offered as a service enhancement, for example, by academic libraries for faculty (See, for example, Yang, 2004).

A third definition is when libraries offer fee-based document delivery, and sometimes research service, to the general public or businesses (for example, see Luzius and King, 2006). Libraries sometimes charge for this kind of document delivery to be able to extend access to library services and resources to people outside the official service community, and sometimes to generate revenue. If a library offers document delivery, in many cases the ILL department handles the service.

Philosophically, ILL stems from the premise that no library can be completely self-sufficient in meeting the needs of its users. It is a dictate of modern librarianship that improving access to information enhances the library's mission. There will always be overworked staff and underfunded libraries, but staff make the effort to meet the community's needs whenever possible. The economic status of the person should be irrelevant to the level of library service. Generally, libraries limit their services only on the financial and workload realities of the library. There are exceptions, especially for special libraries, when the parent organization's mission and goals limit who may access what service. For example, one of the authors works for a museum with a noncirculating collection. While open to the public, the library does not borrow materials for anyone except research/curator staff members.

An active ILL program is a significant commitment of library resources. A 2002 study of mediated ILL costs revealed average borrowing costs of $17.50 for research libraries and lending costs of $9.27. Approximately two-thirds of the cost of ILL is staff time (Jackson, 2004). This same study revealed that user-initiated ILLs (also known as unmediated loans) have lower unit costs, primarily due to the lack of staff participation.

Each library must make decisions about which services to emphasize based on its mission and priorities. There are some libraries that do little ILL work because it might cripple their basic services. A few get around the problem by borrowing from others but limiting the amount of their lending. As good faith cooperation between libraries is the basis of ILL, this is acceptable only in the case of true financial distress. ILL requires staff time with users, verification, searching, communicating, expediting, record-keeping, retrieval, and returning materials. There are also costs involving forms, shipping, automation hardware and software, database licensing, packaging, furniture and space, and postage.

At the same time, interlibrary cooperation and document delivery may save the library money. Libraries can borrow rarely used items rather than buying them, or acquire the information "just in time" to answer a specific information need rather than purchasing it "just in case." Many libraries belong to networks formed for the purpose of facilitating interlibrary borrowing. These networks sometimes employ union catalogs and courier services to expedite the process. Access to information becomes a matter of not only what one library can purchase, but what subject strengths all participating libraries can provide. Rarely used expensive volumes, sets, or specialized periodical subscriptions may be bought only by the most appropriate library, but access is maintained for the patrons of all cooperating libraries. Indeed, there are specific institutions that have as their mission the lending of materials to other libraries, just as others have as their mission the preservation of last or only copies. Examples of each of these are the British Lending Library and the Center for Research Libraries, respectively.

Such schemes might lead you to believe that large university research libraries or large public libraries might be drained by many smaller libraries nibbling away at their collections. In fact, when the lending versus borrowing transactions are tallied, many of the smaller college and public libraries are net lenders, rather than borrowers, from larger libraries. People often need to borrow from the specialized materials and collections in smaller libraries, and smaller institutions often have a faster turnaround time, making them preferred lenders.

ILL removes the limitations of borrower location and is thus inherently democratic. It provides rural borrowers access to knowledge despite their physical distance from research centers. Scholars do not have to drive or fly hundreds of miles just to see a particular book. Foreign-born or non-English-speaking users may gain access to books in their native language no matter where they live. Immobilized citizens may read wherever their interests lead them despite their inability to travel across town. ILL solves many more problems than it creates, removing barriers to information and knowledge across all levels of borrower.

BORROWING

Borrowers initiate the typical ILL request at the circulation or reference desk, or via a Web form when a person cannot satisfy her/his particular informational need. The requester typically completes a form, digital or paper, which the ILL staff reviews for completeness. Today, user-initiated systems send the request directly to the lending library, bypassing the borrowing library. Web forms for ILL requests allow borrowers to request materials any time, day or night, from any location, and represent the majority of ILL requests. (Figure 7.1 is an example of an ILL form.) The more information the borrower supplies, the more accurate and more timely the loan will be. (See Figure 7.2 for a summary diagram of these and the following steps.)

Securing the borrower's e-mail or telephone number at the outset is a useful policy. The ability to clarify verification problems by contacting the borrower before transmitting the loan request saves time and trouble for all concerned.

Before initiating an ILL or document delivery, the borrowing library must be certain that it does not already own or have electronic access to the material sought. If a book or video is desired, staff members check the library OPAC to see if the item is on order or is awaiting cataloging and processing. When the request is for a journal article, a staff member also checks local journal holdings, including electronic collections, to avoid unnecessary borrowing. Some unmediated systems automatically check to determine if the requested item is available locally. If so, they notify the requester and cancel the request. If the library owns the desired issue or volume but it seems to be missing, a staff

ILLiad

Search
◉ Active ○ All

• Logoff tom carter
* Main Menu
* New Request
  → Article
  → Book
  → Book Chapter
  → Thesis
  → Other

* View
  → Outstanding Requests
  → Electronically Received Articles
  → Checked Out Items
  → Cancelled Requests
  → History Requests
  → All Requests
  → Notifications

* Tools
  → Change User Information
  → Change Password

* About ILLiad

Photocopy Request

*Indicates required field

Enter information below and press the Submit Information button to send.

Describe the item you want

*Title (Journal, Conference Proceedings, Anthology)
Please do not abbreviate unless your citation is abbreviated

Volume

Issue Number or Designation

Month

*Year

*Inclusive Pages

ISSN/ISBN (International Standard Serial/Book Number)
If given will speed request processing

OCLC or Docline UI Number

Article Author

*Article Title

*Not Wanted After Date
(MM/DD/YYYY)   04/17/2008

Will you accept the item in a language other than English?
If yes, specify acceptable languages in the notes field.   No

Notes
Put any information here that may help us find the item, as well as any other pertinent information.

Where did you learn about this item?

Where did you find this item cited?
Examples are Dissertation Abstracts, Dialog (specify which database), or a specific journal or book.

Date of the work that cited the item.

Volume number of the work that cited the item.

Pages where the item is cited.

STOP! PLEASE READ! Did you remember to check the Catalog first? If you need an article, check the Periodicals List and search for the journal title. If you need a book or book chapter, check in Albert FIRST, then LINK +. If you're requesting document delivery, please state so in the "Notes" section above. Thanks!

Submit Request   Clear Form   Cancel - Return to Main Menu

Figure 7.1 Web ILL Form

member conducts a search before placing the request. Occasionally a desired item is part of the local collection, but is mutilated or defaced in some manner; the library may initiate an order for replacement pages or a new copy (when available and desirable) in addition to carrying out the ILL transaction.

With nonlocal items, ILL staff members verify the actual existence of the item, a process known as bibliographic verification. Frequently what looks like a complete citation contains incorrect data; sending the request off in that state will only delay the delivery of the actually desired material. Issues may be as minor as a missing edition statement on a thriller or as important

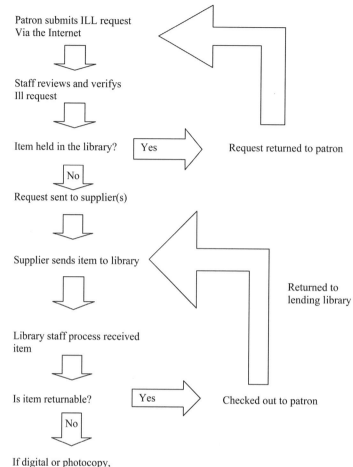

Figure 7.2 ILL Procedures

as a missing edition statement on a request for a microfilmed rare book. It may be a misspelled or mistaken author or title. Sometimes the fault is with an uninformed or careless requester, but at other times it lies with the source of the citation. Typographical errors do exist in databases and Web sites, and researchers' tired eyes can blur when looking at long lists of citations. There are even spurious references by a pseudo scholar.

Typically, one verifies the information by consulting an online bibliographic utility such as OCLC, WorldCat, or DOCLINE (for medical libraries), or an index or abstracting source. Whether checking for item records in OCLC, in a system-wide catalog such as the University of California's MELVYL, or checking a periodical index or abstract for a published article, verification work is an integral part of the preparation for ILL.

Once the staff confirms the existence of the item the borrowing process then begins, usually through electronic transmission of requests to a potential lending library or document supplier. Knowing who owns the desired material (holdings information) is, of course, of primary interest in ILL. Using a large bibliographic database like OCLC, for instance, verification of location is usually quick and easy. However, OCLC data also identify libraries that do or do not loan materials (noncirculating collections). Staff typically search by author and title, title alone, author alone, International Standard Book Number (ISBN) or International Standard Serials Number (ISSN).

After identifying a list of libraries holding the item, the searcher selects which libraries to contact and then prioritizes them (for example, by geographical proximity, best service, or lowest fee). Alternatively, some user-initiated systems automatically select potential lenders based on preprogrammed selection parameters. The system contacts the first library, which either accepts or refuses the loan. If refused, the request moves on to the next target library on the list, then the next, and so on until the loan is achieved or the list of potential lenders is exhausted. This happens automatically, without the staff member reentering the request or continually monitoring the loan, saving much valuable time. Such an arrangement also multiplies the probability that the needed material will be available to the borrower within a reasonable waiting period when compared with the traditional waiting game of mail out, mail in, mail out, mail in, which is the lot of the manual method. A missing copy here, mutilated issue there can cost weeks, not days, of waiting. If the initial list of potential lenders is unsuccessful the staff member will submit the request to a second list after notifying the requester of the delay.

ILL management systems (IMS), like OCLC's ILLiad, are central to high-performing operations. Automated procedures are crucial to improving performance measures like fill rate, turnaround time, and user satisfaction. Of course, to the small public or special library without an IMS, the thought of spending a considerable amount of money to maintain a time-consuming service for the benefit of a limited number of individuals may appear wasteful; this is especially true in times of rising materials costs and lowered governmental support. Some libraries have to charge for some ILL expenses, such as photocopy charges. Some small communities, however, have an educated, motivated, demanding clientele willing to support good library service with their votes and taxes or donated dollars. Some are willing to pay total service charges, direct and indirect, to maintain highly desired services. In such situations, libraries might find it in their interest to make the possibilities evident to the community, and let their public decide whether or not such service can be supported.

Many smaller libraries belong to regional networks, which perform the automated part of the loan process as part of shared services. In some states, a regional headquarters will not only support smaller libraries through coordination of shared access, but will also actually buy and maintain a collection of the more expensive materials that only a few readers at any small library will want to borrow.

Some libraries still have occasion to use nonautomated ILL procedures, either because they lack an IMS or because the system was unsuccessful in obtaining the desired item. Because there are different kinds of ILL, nonautomated procedures will vary in complexity according to type and size of both borrowing and lending institutions, as well as the nature of the materials lent. In smaller systems, a simple phone call to another branch or the public library in the next community might be all that is required. Larger institutions and longer distances require more formal procedures. The ILL form developed by the ALA continues to be the standard and is used by many hundreds of libraries around the United States (see figure 7.3).

There are specific advantages to using the standardized, multicopy form. The form includes consistent requirements for documentation, verification, and citation. The size is constant for ease of filing and the familiarity of

ALA Interlibrary Loan Request Form 2002

Request date _____
Need before _____
Request number _____
Client information _____

Borrowing library name and address

Citation Information
Book author _____
Book title
Publisher _____ Place _____ Date _____
Series _____
This edition only _____ ISBN _____

Serial title _____
Volume / issue _____ Date _____ Pages _____
Author of article _____
Title of article _____
ISSN _____

Audiovisual title _____
Date of publication _____

Verified in and / or cited in _____
Other bibliographic number _____
Lending library name and address

Lending library phone _____
Lending library fax _____
Lending library email _____
Lending library electronic delivery address _____

Notes _____

Request complies with
[ ] 108(g) (2) Guidelines (CCG)
[ ] other provision of copyright law (CCL)

Authorization _____
Phone _____
Fax _____
Email _____
Electronic delivery address _____

Type of request:
[ ] Loan
[ ] Photocopy
[ ] Estimate
[ ] Locations
Charge information
Account number _____
Maximum willing to pay _____
Have reciprocal agreement _____
Payment provided _____
Lending library report
Date of response _____
Date shipped _____
Shipped via _____
Insured for _____
Return Insured [ ]
Packing Requirements _____
Charge _____
Date due _____
Use restrictions
[ ] Library Use Only
[ ] Copying not permitted
[ ] No Renewals
[ ] _____
Not sent because
[ ] At bindery
[ ] Charge exceeds limit
[ ] Hold placed
[ ] In process
[ ] In use
[ ] Lacking
[ ] Lacks copyright compliance
[ ] Locations not found
[ ] Lost
[ ] Non-circulating
[ ] Not found as cited
[ ] Not on shelf
[ ] Not owned
[ ] On order
[ ] On reserve
[ ] Poor condition
[ ] Prepayment required
[ ] Request on _____
[ ] Volume / issue not yet available
[ ] _____
Estimate for
Loan _____
Copy _____
Microfilm _____
Microfiche _____
Borrowing library report
Date Received _____
Date Returned _____
Returned via _____
Insured for _____
Payment Enclosed [ ]
Renewals
Date Requested _____
New Due Date _____
Renewal Denied [ ]

Figure 7.3 ALA ILL Request Form

Used with permission of the Reference and User Services Association (RUSA), American Library Association.

handling identical forms saves confusion. The standard form also contains check-off boxes to indicate compliance with fair-use copyright guidelines and restrictions. By completing the form as fully as possible with accurate information, the requesting library helps to assure a timely response. On the other hand, inaccurate or incomplete information may lead to slower or even less service. The busy ILL staff may put such "problem requests," no matter how they are submitted, at the bottom of the pile, if only to get the largest number of orders filled in the quickest time. Indeed, some libraries have a policy of not filling requests that do not include complete information. Another possible consequence of incomplete or inaccurate information is actually receiving the wrong information desired.

Mini-Case Study 1: At the local public library, an individual requests a periodical article in an obscure journal. The person indicates that the source of the reference to the article is the bibliography in a particular book. After verifying that the library does not own the journal, the staff member confirms the reference by looking in the stated bibliography, and then processes the ILL request. The Freedonia Library receives the request, and the ILL staff member confirms holding the journal. However, upon examination the page numbers prove to be in the middle of an unrelated article. The staff member then checks the table of contents, but doesn't find the article. The volume number and issue match the information given. At that point, it is time to check the stated source bibliography; the information in that source is identical to what the requester submitted. The request is now a challenge. An ILL staffer starts reviewing periodical indexes and identifies a likely resource for checking the citation. Often the next step is slow, going both forward and backward from the date given. Usually the article turns up, but the citation is to a different volume of the journal, with different page numbers. Although this situation does not occur very often, it does occur frequently enough that knowing the process will help assure the requester receives quality service. The process also is helpful in handling less complex requests.

With either automated or nonautomated ILL you will use a mix of both standardized procedures, or protocols, and local rules and policies in initiating the loan process. This insures efficiency and consistency with the practices of other libraries. The *ILL Code for the United States* (American Library Association, 2001) provides a good summary of the responsibilities of both borrowing and lending institutions. ILL staff should be familiar with this code and with the state and local practices that may govern ILL locally, regionally, or within networks. Most other countries have their own ILL codes, and the International Federation of Library Associations and Institutions (IFLA) has developed guidelines for best practices for ILL and document delivery (International Federation of Library Associations, 2007) to assist ILL staff in all countries. (http://www.ifla.org/VI/2/p3/Guidelines_ILDD-en.htm).

User-Initiated Requests

Technology spurred tremendous changes in ILL in the decade of the 1990s. As is typical with computer-related advances, computerization simplified some aspects of ILL while making other parts more complex. It has certainly raised user expectations. People are use to downloading entire articles (full-text retrieval) from various commercial databases, assuming they have Web access. To them, even automated ILL seems cumbersome.

In order to improve service by speeding up the borrowing process, libraries and vendors developed systems that permit borrowers to request books and articles directly from lending institutions. User-initiated requests are a recent enhancement to the ILL process, dating from the 1990s, and are an effective and popular way to handle many routine requests. The systems enable borrowers to initiate their own requests for items, and even receive materials directly from document suppliers. Systems track the progress of the loan requests and the users are able to log on to their account and check on the progress of their request. This adaptation is available in networks such as Link+ in California, OhioLINK, and ILLINET, which allow borrowers to order directly from libraries. Document delivery suppliers like Infotrieve and Ingenta also accept requests directly from customers, and some libraries permit borrowers to order articles directly from commercial document suppliers for journals not owned. Larger institutions may assume the fees for their users. However, many libraries do not pay for user-initiated requests from commercial suppliers for fear of encouraging "too many" requests, even though some libraries spend less on the articles than on the staff time spent to process traditional requests. A list of some document delivery suppliers appears, as of this writing, on the Virginia Commonwealth University Library's Web site (http://www.library.vcu.edu/tml/docsupp/).

User-initiated ILL and document delivery services are proving very popular and efficient. A 2002 study revels that "In most cases, user initiated services have lower unit costs, higher fill rates, and faster turnaround time than mediated services" (Jackson, 2004). In addition, by largely bypassing borrowing library staff, user-initiated ILL allows libraries to accommodate increased ILL volume without adding personnel.

LENDING

The other side of the ILL coin is lending. Once the potential lending institution receives a request via IMS, e-mail, fax, or paper ILL form, the staff verifies that the library owns the requested item and that it is available for lending. Occasionally a request will be incomplete, and you will have to do bibliographic checking (unless your library's policy forbids the processing of incomplete requests). Staff members at the majority of borrowing institutions do everything possible to avoid sending incomplete requests; but, as in every human situation, there will be those few who do not. There are always some new and untrained personnel in any network, and you should forgive the occasional mistake. And remember, the requester might have provided misinformation that could not be checked. (To be sure, this will happen to all ILL staff at some point.)

Occasionally an item will be unavailable for lending for one of a number of reasons, such as being checked out, on class reserve, or located in a remote storage facility. In these cases, the library will have to deny the request. Computer-based systems automatically route the request to another potential lender. With a paper request, the lending library returns the request to the requesting institution, which then identifies another potential lender and sends on the request. Having agreed to lend an item, the loaning institution has an obligation to follow through in a timely fashion

If the requested item is available in paper, a staff member pulls the book or journal from the collection or from storage. If there are branch libraries, staff members may forward the request to the appropriate branch. ILL staff check out those items that must be returned through the circulation system, then label them with the due date and send them to the borrowing institution. Electronic books, if allowed by the license agreement, arrive as a link to the digital copy. Staff may digitize periodical articles or book chapters according to the fair use provisions of copyright law and deliver them via an online utility like ARIEL. They may also fax or photocopy them and send by mail. Once the borrowing library receives the item, the requester receives notification that the material is available for pickup, typically via e-mail notification. In the case of a digitized article, ILL personnel typically check for transmission errors or illegible pages before notifying the requester. The e-mail notice may contain a URL linking to the digitized document, usually in a PDF format, or the document may be attached to the e-mail.

When libraries return borrowed items, ILL staff inspect the material(s) for damage, the status is updated to "completed" in the IMS or bibliographic utility, and the material is reshelved.

DELIVERY SYSTEMS

Document delivery systems for ILL materials exist in a variety of forms. Today's ILL department uses a combination of traditional and technology-based systems to deliver requested items. The Internet, U.S. Postal Service, private companies such as United Parcel Service, and cooperative network-operated vehicles have all been used for years as modes of delivery. Networks and consortia often include interlibrary delivery among their services. Delivery can be institutional, such as the inter-campus bus used by the multiple campuses of larger universities (for example, the University of California), a large city public library with many branches, or a corporation with multiple locations. It can be private and interinstitutional, such as the delivery service that connects the Link+ consortium of over 40 colleges, universities, and public libraries located in California and Nevada. It can also be regional or statewide; for example, Minnesota has a network of 83 academic and private libraries serving over 200,000 customers. MnSCU/PALS (Minnesota State Colleges and Universities/Project for Automated Library Systems) combines an online system and a document delivery service called MINITEX. MINITEX is supplemented in MnSCU/PALS with local delivery services between nearby libraries, faxing of articles, and commercial couriers.

Traditionally, libraries loaned periodical articles by mailing photocopies and occasionally by faxing. With the advent of digital scanning the technology of ILL entered a new stage. Access can be achieved in a matter of hours, even minutes rather than weeks, for those libraries able to afford (or willing to charge for) the equipment, staff time, and software and network costs. Users are becoming more sophisticated in their use of technology and in their expectations for improved service. Increasingly, traditional postal service is proving too slow for customers accustomed to almost instantaneous retrieval of information. People expect to be able to download journal articles and even e-books from a library's IMS. Utilities like ARIEL and DOCLINE allow for the secure Internet delivery of materials to and from libraries and their users. The current high-quality reproduction of periodical articles and other information in digital formats results in less dependence on the mail for ILL and document delivery, speedier delivery of requested items, and greater user satisfaction. (But see "Ethical and Legal Considerations" later in this chapter about copyright-based restrictions that complicate such information transfers.)

MONEY MATTERS: FEES, COLLECTION, AND INSURANCE

Most libraries have an aversion to charging for services rendered in the line of duty—at least many still do. If, to some people, staff members seem avid about collecting fines, it is usually a matter of keeping the library's collections and levels of service from deteriorating because of a few irresponsible or dishonest users. Replacement of lost materials (when they are available, and many are not) is a costly but necessary activity. Libraries don't usually come out ahead by collecting fines, and the profit motive is not what libraries are about.

In the real world, many libraries do charge for some services. Photocopying and video rentals are two examples. Libraries sometimes pass on to the user the direct charges involved in ILL and document delivery, such as database charges, postage, insurance, photocopy charges, royalty fees, or service charges. The point is not for either the borrowing library or lending library to make a profit, but to cover at least the extra costs involved beyond ordinary library service. On the other hand, most libraries will attempt to avoid charging fees by borrowing from institutions with which cooperative lending agreements have been arranged. There are libraries with noncirculating collections that will make photocopies of specialized materials, if the borrowing institution is willing to absorb the costs.

Policies on collection of fees will be determined locally. Questions to address include: Does the customer pay a fee? If yes, is it a standard fee, or is it dependent on the actual charges? Does the library accept cash, personal checks, credit cards, or travelers' checks? Does the user pay before or after the loan has been completed? If before, the user may be more likely to show up and collect the requested material—but how is the money banked, held, refunded? All these are local decisions implemented in a convenient and workable way for the local library.

PRESERVATION AND ILL

Library materials sent on ILL are subject not only to the usual handling problems at either end of the transaction, but also to mishandling and rough handling in transit. Whether sent through the rain, sleet, snow, and heat of the mail or through a network vehicle, damage is a very real possibility. The packing of library materials is therefore of great importance.

Good judgment is essential for ILL. You can pack most books in a padded paper mailing envelope and mail them without great worry. Other items should be carefully wrapped in layers, including extra protection from such threats as water and the bumping of corners. Some materials should be not only wrapped but also boxed or even crated. A few items should not be loaned at all and while lending policies will usually specify classes of such items you may encounter an item in poor condition that is covered by the policy. It is best to ask the supervisor before proceeding with the loan. Similarly, photocopying or digitizing items may be restricted due to the condition of the paper or binding. Magnetic media such as audio and video tapes must be conspicuously labeled as such on the outside of packaging, lest they be accidentally erased. General criteria and guidelines can be set by the supervising librarian, but the judgment and good sense of staff members is often the difference between a successful transaction and damage or loss of library materials.

Some books are *artifactually valuable*: that is, the book itself in its present physical form is important. This may be because of bibliographic details of the particular printing or edition, the binding or its decoration, an autograph or inscription, or other physical features that are significant to scholars. Some libraries loan artifactually valuable materials for exhibits. If so, there should be a thoroughly documented procedure, from the receipt of request to the final physical examination of returned materials by the appropriate staff member. This might be the special collections librarian or conservator or the chief administrator. In cases of truly unique items of scholarly or historical importance, a library might consider digitization or other reproduction before lending the item, to prevent the item's damage or loss.

Every library that lends artifactually valuable materials should include special instructions as part of the loan agreement. Such things as financial responsibility and insurance, as well as acceptable levels of heat, lighting, length of loan, exhibition mounting procedures, security, and repackaging for transport should all be part of an agreement reached and signed by both sides before the loan is approved or begun. The ALA *Guidelines for the Interlibrary Loan of Rare and Unique Materials* (http://www.ala.org/ala/acrl/acrlstandards/rareguidelines.cfm) cited in the Suggested Readings provides useful guidelines.

Consult with the appropriate librarian if there is even the suspicion that any material is of artifactual or historic value, or too fragile for loan. The loan may be offered conditionally, with explanation and explicit use limitations; for example, to be used only in the library, or in the presence of a librarian, or with photocopying disallowed. Loans of microform often have "in-house use only" as a condition of loan. Unless there are duplicate copies, original, unique bound paper copies of masters' theses and doctoral dissertations are often unavailable for ILL.

Mini-Case Study 2: The conservation department of a great metropolitan research library prepares and sends a valuable book for an exhibit at the P. T. Barnum Library at a distant college. The book is covered with waterproof wrapping in a special hard case, along with explicit directions on rewrapping and returning. Both a label on the box and a sheet of instructions request the reuse of the original packaging. However, after the exhibit, the book is returned via book rate in a padded mailing bag. After sending a letter pointing out the gaffe, the lending library receives a reply in the form of the original packing material, without explanation or comment. Some years later, the research library refuses to honor another request from this college.

The above case, though based on a real occurrence, is a clear exception to the rule and the norm of interlibrary cooperation. Countering every such negative event, there are literally thousands of positive transactions that occur daily, immeasurably improving public access to information.

Many ILLs and most document deliveries are in the form of photocopies or digitized copies, which become the property of the requesting user. The handling of materials during scanning or photocopying has much to do with the shelf life of any bound volume. If the margins are too small, the binding too tight, the paper or binding too fragile, the volume too large or thick, or if the item is of artifactual value and would suffer a loss of bibliographic information, the loaning library staff member has an obligation to inform the borrowing library to look elsewhere first. Again, good judgment comes into play, as does a willingness to ask the appropriate librarian for advice or approval.

ADMINISTRATION

ILL is usually supervised by a librarian. Library support staff, often supplemented by student assistants in academic institutions, usually perform most if not all of the verification, solicitation, communication, scanning, faxing, packing, forwarding, filing, and record keeping. In some institutions, ILL will be one person's added responsibility and usually be administered within the circulation, access, or reference department. In larger libraries it will be an entire department unto itself, with several full- and part-time staff. As in every organization, good and open communication among colleagues is essential to a successful venture.

Personnel Selection and Training

As with any library staff member, qualities of accuracy, good judgment, honesty, openness, patience, good humor, and basic computer literacy are important preconditions of employment. ILL can be a relatively solitary activity at times, so the ability to work independently is important. ILL work can also be quite hectic, with occasional flurries of intense activity during certain times. Examples in school and academic libraries are term-paper time, academic year endings, and faculty preparations for vacations or sabbaticals. Special libraries go full tilt during project planning or product development. Sometimes that one voracious reader, who has finished off your entire collection, seems to keep the department busy single-handedly.

Occasionally the user's demand for speed is unreasonable, or even unattainable. In such cases, a written policy and patient good will are very useful things to have. Good interpersonal skills are a great help in negotiating with the requester who needs the information yesterday, or in obtaining correct information from a confused borrower or a flustered staff member at a co-operating library on the other side of the telephone line, or from the local information technology technician. Good manual skills and eye-hand coordination impact everything from wrapping rare books to accurate typing of bibliographic information at the terminal.

Scheduling

Staffing of ILL activities can vary from the occasional extra duty of one staff member to a full-time department. This depends on the volume of requests received from both local users and other libraries. In a high-volume situation an ILL department may split into two groups, one to fill requests from other libraries and another to handle user requests for outside loans. Scheduling of staff time, therefore, varies from institution to institution.

Setting staff priorities requires at least some concession to dealing with ILL on a timely basis, whether for local borrowers or distant libraries. Shunting loan requests into a pile for attention later in the month is not something that will enhance a library's reputation for service. Many requests are made by serious researchers, whether for personal business success, to meet a dissertation, term paper, or grant application deadline, or to satisfy the urgent need to know before interest flags—or when that opportunity to appear on *Jeopardy* appears.

Scheduling the return of materials borrowed from another library is important. Due dates are more than suggested guidelines; they are due dates set by the lending library that both library staff and borrowing users must know and honor. A due date that allows time for the paperwork, packing, and delivery of materials is prudent. A little margin may be included to allow enough time to solicit a renewal from the loaning library, if requested. Many computer-based systems automatically send a reminder to users a few days before an item's due date. In the case of overdue materials, particularly bad cases, a short e-mail to the lending library explaining and apologizing for the delay might be appropriate. Providing timely billing and forwarding of overdue fines is also necessary.

In understaffed libraries (and they are legion), ILL may have to take second or third or fourth place to the pressing needs of other library services. Staff may delineate categories of off-site borrowers so that, for example, the borrowing requests of the library that always promptly honors the home institution's requests receive priority over requests from distant libraries to borrow materials that are widely available elsewhere. Patience and good sense can help maintain the balance of fairness and reasonable service limits needed to deal with the radically different examples of information needs that pass through library portals every day.

Workspace Considerations

ILL is by no means a laptop operation. Besides adequate filing space for both incoming and outgoing requests, statistics, customer billing files, and rubber stamps for copyright statements, usage restrictions, postal class, dates, magnetic media warnings, and so forth, there must be adequate space for the storage of packaging materials. This will include various sizes of mailing envelopes, padded mailing bags, boxes for book and microform loans, rolls of wrapping paper and cushioning materials, various kinds of tape, and string. The requirements also include an adequate packing and wrapping surface at an ergonomically comfortable height. There must be space for both incoming and outgoing materials, both in the ILL area and at the point of loan, usually at or near the circulation desk.

Online database services, such as OCLC and ILLiad, require sufficient space for terminal and printer, software manuals, and an adequate power supply and network connections. It may be vital to communicate by e-mail or telephone with a borrower in case clarification or more information is needed. A scanner and fax machine are also important for digitizing requested documents, contacting cooperating (or those few not-so-cooperating) institutions, canceling unneeded loans, and so forth.

Keeping and Using Records and Statistics

As in any transaction between disparate institutions, a paper trail is useful in solving problems. This can be an actual "trail" of paper forms, e-mails, checklists, document delivery requests, and schedules. The standard paper ALA ILL form is quadruplicate for precisely this reason: records can be kept at both libraries. More often today the trail is some form of automated record keeping. Libraries with an IMS have their statistics tracked automatically, and should avoid the time and expense of maintaining duplicate record systems. Copyright legislation can be interpreted as *requiring* that records be kept regarding photocopies made and received. (Although this is not as yet totally clear, it is better to play it safe; see "Ethical and Legal Considerations" in the next section.)

In any modern institution, records and statistics are useful in determining appropriate staffing levels for the operation, its share of the overall budget, formation of goals and objectives, and other administrative decisions. Libraries use statistics the same way, as well as to measure the level of service to the community of which it is a part. Keeping records can help administrators plan a library's goals and assess whether or not a library is meeting its goals or needs to make changes in order to meet them.

In these days of decreasing financial support and cuts in actual buying power for many libraries, statistics documenting outcomes can be very useful in garnering support for any of the library's functions. ILL is no exception. The money spent on ILL is usually well spent, but, in a cost-conscious world, it may be necessary to prove the obvious on paper. Keeping track of items borrowed and loaned, the number of users and institutions served, moneys saved and spent, and projections of future demand based on carefully kept records will be of great assistance to any administrator.

Maintaining data on titles borrowed can also be useful in collection development decisions. Some libraries are experimenting with models of collaboration between the ILL, circulation, collection development, and acquisitions departments to improve service and increase user satisfaction. The libraries set aside funds to purchase selected materials requested through ILL instead of borrowing them. The criteria include how closely the requested item meets the library's collection development policy and how likely it is to circulate again. The items are rush ordered and processed and circulated to the requester. Studies show that the cost and turnaround time are reasonable and users are satisfied with the service (see Campbell, 2006, and Allen et al., 2003). Records of periodical titles borrowed from can also be helpful in database selection decisions. As libraries consider different publisher packages or aggregators' collections of periodicals for purchase or lease, those containing high-demand titles identified through ILL data may be likely candidates for selection.

ETHICAL AND LEGAL CONSIDERATIONS

As in all areas of library service, confidentiality of user records is a basic tenet of ILL. Nearly all states have laws protecting citizens' library records. Most libraries have a written policy protecting each user's right to privacy and confidentiality, especially with respect to information and resources sought and received, including those requested through ILL. Just as with circulation records, staff members should delete ILL borrower records upon completion of the transaction(s). Only in the face of a legally obtained court order, process, or subpoena should library staff surrender user records, and then only after consulting legal counsel.

Today one of the most difficult areas to understand is copyright law. ILL and document delivery is one of the services most affected by this legislation, since much of what is reproduced for loan from books, journals, Web sites, microform, software, magnetic tape, and other materials is protected by copyright.

Copyright is a form of protection provided by title 17 of the U.S. Code to the authors of "original works of scholarship." Copyright holders have the exclusive right to do and authorize others to, among other things:

- *Reproduce* and *distribute* the copyrighted work
- *Sell* copies of the copyrighted work
- *Perform* or *display* the copyrighted work publicly (Hilyer, 2006)

These rights are not unlimited, however. Section 108 of Title 17 of the *Copyright Revision Act of 1976* (17USC§108) and the interpretive guidelines provided by the National Commission on New Technological Uses of Copyrighted Works (CONTU) provide for "fair use" duplication of copyrighted material for ILL use provided two conditions are met: the requested copy becomes the property of the user; and a copyright notice is displayed where requests are made and on the order form and the copy itself (National Commission on New Technological Uses of Copyrighted Works, 1979).

Section 108 also prohibits reproduction of "aggregate quantities" of a work that might affect sales. Because the law is vague as to just what aggregate quantities means, the CONTU guidelines also address this issue. The Commission developed the "Guideline of Five": during one calendar year, no more than five copies may be received from any one work whose publication date is within five years of the date of the user's request without obtaining copyright permission (Hilyer, 2006). This requires borrowing libraries to maintain detailed records of copies requested from specific periodical titles. Libraries with an IMS have this information automatically tracked. When a library receives a request that would exceed fair use or CONTU guidelines there are several possible options: refusing the request; requesting permission from the copyright holder; sending the user to another library that holds the title; or paying the appropriate royalty for permission to copy. There exists, in fact, a Copyright Clearance Center, established by the American Association of Publishers at the suggestion of the U.S. Congress. It serves as a publisher-supported collector and distributor of fees payable to copyright holders. Libraries, especially for-profit corporate libraries and large academic libraries, participate by paying fees to the Center to cover royalty charges for reproducing copyrighted material. Although contacting the individual publishers may seem burdensome, it is often worthwhile. It is the author's experience that most requests to publishers to reproduce without cost are either granted or go unanswered.

While libraries may make copies of paper items (within limits), some lease agreements with e-journal and e-book vendors often prohibit making copies for those not affiliated with the contracting institution. This practice prohibits libraries from offering their electronic holdings for ILL. As more libraries subscribe to electronic journals and books, librarians are insisting that license agreements specifically permit the use of digital articles and books for ILL. Libraries must be careful not to voluntarily sign away their fair use rights to duplicate material for educational purposes when negotiating contracts for electronic products.

The question of copyright royalties is simplified concerning document delivery. The fee charged by commercial vendors includes the royalty fee paid to the copyright holder for the reproduction.

Many libraries base their ILL photocopying and digitizing policies on fair use, the CONTU guidelines, and the ALA's *Interlibrary Loan Code for the United States* (http://www.ala.org/ala/rusa/rusaprotools/referenceguide/interlibrary.htm). Every library needs to establish ILL guidelines with the best workable interpretation possible for the local situation.

While the courts and Congress will continue to modify copyright legislation that deals with reproduction of digital documents, every library should arm itself with a policy that is within the current tenets of copyright law. Where the law is murky or inconsistent, libraries should at least conform to authoritative published guidelines. The resources listed in the Suggested Readings for this chapter are helpful in this regard.

SUMMARY

Despite the amount of information available on the Web, ILL and document delivery remain important adjuncts to the library collection. An increasingly technology-savvy population and advances in user-initiated ILL and document delivery have greatly increased the speed of delivery and user satisfaction.

Though local procedures differ, established protocols for ILL transactions help provide the necessary qualities of consistency, accountability, and efficiency that make ILL practicable. The typical borrowing process for the physical loan of materials includes the following steps:

- User request, confirmation of non-ownership, verification of the item's existence, identification of institutions holding the item, transmission of request by borrowing library, usually by an electronic system. OCLC is the most commonly used ILL system in the United States

- Loaning library's reception of request, verification of ownership, confirmation of availability, any necessary clearances for loan, checkout, proper packaging and labeling and shipment, and possible notification of borrowing library regarding overdue materials

- Borrowing library's reception of material, notification of customer, and communication to customer of any special conditions including due date, possible follow-up notification of customer if return is late, possible collection of fee and/or fine, repackaging, and shipment with insurance

- Loaning library's reception of material, examination of condition, check-in, and return to shelves

- Both sides file and retain appropriate paperwork and records

Obtaining digital copies or photocopies of articles or other reproduction generally follows the same lines, except for billing and collection of fees, closer examination of the item before copying to prevent damage, and procedures necessary to guarantee that fair use limits are not exceeded. Although fair use may be a somewhat nebulous concept, individual library guidelines should be established in accordance with some authoritative published guide, for example, the *CONTU Guidelines on Photocopying under Interlibrary Loan Arrangements* (http://www.cni.org/docs/infopols/CONTU.html). Scanned image technology, which allows for almost instantaneous, high-quality document transmission, enhances ILL and document delivery functions for those libraries with the resources to employ it.

Some libraries utilize commercial document delivery suppliers to supplement ILL because of their speed of response. Despite the popularity of digital resources, there are thousands of nondigitized titles from which articles are still available only through traditional means.

Trends we may expect to see in the future include increasing use of the Internet to transmit ILLs as the amount of scanned material increases, and greater use of user-initiated ILL. While still comprising a minority of requests, user-initiated ILL is less expensive than traditional mediated ILL and offers better service through typically higher fill rates and faster turnaround time.

Chapter Review Material

1. How are ILL and access to information interconnected as library issues?
2. What differences might there be in borrowing a book from . . .

   a. a small public library?
   b. a large academic library?
   c. a corporate library?
   d. a small, private research library?

   Would you prefer to borrow from one type over another? Why or why not?
3. What are the advantages of direct electronic transfer of textual and/or graphic information between libraries? Is there anything that might offset these advantages?
4. What are the advantages of user-initiated ILL over mediated ILL? Are there any disadvantages?
5. If you were to hire a new person to perform the day-to-day chores of ILL, what kind of person would you look for? What kind of skills or experience? What kind of testing might you employ to help you choose?
6. Having delivered a requested ILL item to a user, you notice her photocopying page after page, evidently intending to copy the entire item cover-to-cover. What should you do?

REFERENCES

Allen, Megan, Suzanne M. Ward, Tanner Wray, and Karl E. Debus-Lopez. 2003. "Patron-Focused Services in Three US Libraries: Collaborative Interlibrary Loan, Collection Development and Acquisitions," *Interlibrary Lending & Document Supply* 31, no. 2: 138–141.

American Library Association. 2001. *Interlibrary Loan Code for the United States.* Chicago: ALA. http://www.ala.org/ala/rusa/protools/referenceguide/inter library.cfm.

Campbell, Sharon A. 2006. "To Buy or to Borrow, That is the Question." *Journal of Interlibrary Loan, Document Supply & Electronic Reserves* 16, no. 3: 35–39.

Hilyer, Lee Andrew. 2006. *Interlibrary Loan and Document Delivery: Best Practices for Operating and Managing Interlibrary Loan Services in All Libraries.* Binghamton, NY: Haworth Pr.

International Federation of Library Associations and Institutions. 2007. *Guidelines for Best Practice in Interlibrary Loan and Document Delivery.* http://www.ifla.org/VI/2/p3/Guidelines_ILDD-en.htm.

Jackson, Mary E., with Bruce Kingma and Tom Delaney. 2004. *Assessing ILL/DD Services: New Cost-Effective Alternatives.* Washington, DC: Association of Research Libraries.

Jackson, Sidney L. 1974. *Libraries and Librarianship in the West: A Brief History.* New York: McGraw-Hill.

Kurosman, Katheen, and Barbara Duriak. 1994. "Document Delivery: A Comparison of Commercial Document Suppliers and Interlibrary Loan Services," *College and Research Libraries* 55, no. 2: 129–139.

Luzius, Jeff, and Pambanisha King. 2006. "Fee-Based Document Delivery: Who's Buying?" *Journal of ILL, Document Delivery & Electronic Reserve* 16, no. 3: 67–73.

National Commission on New Technological Uses of Copyright Works (CONTU). 1979. *CONTU Guidelines for Photocopying Under Interlibrary Loan Arrangements.* Washington, DC: Library of Congress.

Online Computer Library Center. *Annual Reports.* Dublin, OH: OCLC.

Pedersen, Wayne, and David Gregory. 1994. "Interlibrary Loan and Commercial Document Delivery," *Journal of Academic Librarianship* 20, no. 5/6: 263–272.

Yang, Zheng Ye. 2004. "Customer Satisfaction with Interlibrary Loan Service-deliverEdocs: A Case Study." *Journal of Interlibrary Loan, Document Delivery & Information Supply* 14, no. 4: 79–94.

SUGGESTED READINGS

American Library Association. 2004. *Guidelines for the Interlibrary Loan of Rare and Unique Materials.* Chicago: American Library Association. http://www.ala.org/ala/acrl/acrlstandards/rareguidelines.htm.

———. 2004. *Interlibrary Loan Packaging and Wrapping Guidelines.* Chicago: American Library Association. http://www.ala.org/ala/rusa/rusaprotools/referenceguide/interlibraryloan.htm.

Amodeo, Anthony J. 1983. "Photocopying without (Much) Damage," *College & Research Libraries News.* 44, no. 10: 368–70.

Boucher, Virginia. 1997. *Interlibrary Loan Practices Handbook.* 2nd ed. Chicago: American Library Association.

Croft, Janet Brennan. 2004. *Legal Solutions in Electronic Reserves and the Electronic Delivery of Interlibrary Loan.* Binghamton, NY: Haworth Press.

Harper, Georgia K. 2008. *Crash Course in Copyright.* University of Texas System. http://www.utsystem.edu/ogc/Intellectualproperty/cprtindx.htm.

Hollerich, Mary. 2007. *ILLWeb.* http://www.law.northwestern.edu/lawlibrary/illweb/index.htm.

Jackson, Mary E. 1998. "Loan Stars: ILL Comes of Age," *Library Journal* 123, no. 2: 44–47.

———. 1998. *Measuring the Performance of Interlibrary Loan Operations in North American Research and College Libraries.* Washington, DC: Association of Research Libraries.

Liller, Connie, and Patricia Tegler. 1988. "An Analysis of ILL and Commercial Document Supply Performance," *Library Quarterly* 58, no. 4: 352–366.

Morris, Leslie R. 2002. *Interlibrary Loan Policies Directory.* 7th ed. New York: Neal-Schuman.

Stanford University Libraries. 2008. *Copyright & Fair Use.* http://fairuse.stanford.edu/.

Chapter 8

Circulation Services

We protect each library user's right to privacy and confidentiality with respect to information sought or received, and resources consulted, borrowed, acquired or transmitted.
—American Library Association (ALA), 1939, *Code of Ethics*

Beyond basic skills, directional reference, and specialized training in customer interactions dealing with money, circulation staff need training in handling difficult customers as well as advanced conflict resolution.
—Julie Todaro and Mark Smith, 2006

John Moorman (2006) defined library circulation as "the process by which items in a collection are taken out of the library by a user and returned to the library" (p. 263). That relatively straightforward definition, while accurate, does belie the complexity of the activities encompassed in "circulation." There are issues of what materials people may borrow, who may do so, for how long items may be out on loan, and what happens when they are not returned on time, as well as many other concerns. As suggested in the opening quotation from Todaro and Smith, when staff members must collect money, especially fines or special fees, public relations become critical.

Circulation department staff members are the true "front line" of the library, as they are the staff members most likely to be contacted by users to deliver services or answer questions. Indeed, they are often the only staff members with which the public interacts. The circulation desk is also the point at which the service philosophy is most apparent, and where a person's first and most important impressions are formed.

It has been the authors' experience that circulation personnel believe they are unappreciated and misunderstood by both the public and their work colleagues. Many of the circulation unit staff members are unaware of the valuable information their work provides, when properly performed, for planning

171

library services and activities. Often understanding the value of their activities makes all the difference between quality and lackluster service as well as making for good morale. Circulation data has value in other units of the library; first, data about what topics and authors are receiving heavy circulation aid collection development personnel in selecting items that are most likely to receive use and perhaps require additional copies. Second, demographic data about registered borrowers assists in planning marketing and promotional activities and perhaps new service locations. When it comes to thinking through circulation policies, data about overdues/fines that may indicate loan periods for a class of material ought to be evaluated. Knowing their work is not just a basic service, but also one that generates valuable planning operational data for the entire library, can boost morale for circulation personnel as well as generate greater care in work performance.

We explore all the above issues in the following pages. We also believe that circulation activities, other than collection/stack maintenance, are not suitable for volunteers due to the critical importance of these activities to the library's reputation/image.

ROLE OF CIRCULATION SERVICES

The circulation unit fills two important roles. The first and perhaps most obvious role is that of circulation control (checking collection materials out and in). Throughout history, people have desired access to books and other forms of information. The primary reason for the existence of the library, as noted in Chapter 1, is its specialized service, which makes available to readers, viewers, and listeners a wider variety of information and ideas than they could otherwise obtain. This service is the foundation upon which the whole structure of the modern library rests. The use of modern reference tools and instruction and guidance in the use of the library are unimportant if users cannot obtain the materials they want. Circulation routines are established, records maintained, and personnel employed and trained in order to make information efficiently available to borrowers or to explain why requested items cannot be immediately supplied.

A second and equally important role of circulation services is that of public relations. Often the first contact people make with a library is at the circulation desk, the center of library activity for most users. Public opinion of the value and usefulness of a library results from the many personal contacts between individual users and the library staff. In many cases, circulation practices determine whether users continue to use the library or whether they become discouraged at failures to obtain desired items promptly. Whole library systems may be judged by the work of a single part-time circulation assistant.

Proper training of circulation staff is a must; it is the best way to assure they will be able to provide effective and efficient service. Staff members must internalize the service ideals of the library as well as understand the philosophy behind the routines they perform. When this occurs they will treat each user as an individual whose request is important and is entitled to the full measure of service consistent with library policy. We provide information on the importance of quality service in Chapter 3 (Customer Service).

PHILOSOPHY OF CIRCULATION SERVICES

The circulation philosophy of a particular library springs from its mission and goals and governing body. Commonly, this philosophy involves guaranteeing to a library's users equal and fair access to the library's collection. Libraries express the desire to provide equal access to the collection and services through the actions of staff members and having appropriate policies and procedures.

Such democratic ideals were not always the norm. For centuries libraries were more the preservers and guardians of knowledge than the purveyors of it. Until the invention of moveable type in the fifteenth century, books were both scarce and valuable, and few people were literate. Libraries, whether government collections, religious collections attached to temples, churches, or monasteries, private collections, or academic collections, had very restrictive circulation policies. The generous circulation privileges we know today are of recent vintage. Indeed, the whole notion of a publicly supported lending library, whose purpose is to make books available to all, is a relatively new idea.

In the United States, public libraries, as we know them today, date from the mid-nineteenth century. Initially, public libraries performed an educational function. During the early 1800s, librarians argued over the question of open access to the bookshelves. Free access to the books first was conceived as a privilege for the scholarly searcher. Later, people advocated access to the collections as a basis of service to the needs of working people. Supporters of closed stacks maintained that unfettered access would lead to disorder on the shelves and decimation of the collection through theft. They also argued that the masses would be unable to use the library effectively and that the presence of intelligent desk attendants would be more helpful than stack access.

Recreational reading began to take on importance in the late nineteenth and early twentieth centuries. Emphasis on the use of books gradually increased and library workers understood, even in the nineteenth century, that the card catalog did not provide sufficient access to the collection for most users. In response, library staff developed annotated book lists, subject lists, and bulletins of recent acquisitions, and printed daily lists on subjects of current interest. They lowered the minimum age of borrowers, and even established children's rooms as well as extending service hours to cover nights and weekends.

Academic libraries lagged behind public libraries in emphasizing use. "In the old days at Columbia College, freshmen and sophomores were allowed to visit the library only once a month to gaze at the backs of books; the juniors were taken there once a week by a tutor who gave verbal information about the contents of the books, but only seniors were permitted to open the precious volumes, which they could draw from the library during one hour on Wednesday afternoons" (Koch, 1912). In 1893 Lodilla Ambrose wrote: "Several large institutions limit students to a reference use of the library. . . . In a certain college a student may have only two books a week; one of these must be from the religious department, and these will only be given to him on presentation of a ticket signed by one of his professors."

One does find exceptions to these limitations on student use of the library. However, before the first generation of the twentieth century, the traditions and the literature of college libraries emphasized preservation rather than use.

Today, circulation staff members find themselves handling a variety of formats aside from books, such as microforms, audio and video cassettes, CDs, DVDs, and other forms of digital media. Libraries determine circulation policies and routines with the goal of providing maximum access to these materials. The circulation staff member sees his or her work through this ideal as expressed in library policies and individual attitudes. As the staff member becomes familiar with the rules and regulations, the policy of the library with regard to their role will be better understood. Although personnel generally enforce rules with impartial fairness, some circumstances require a literal interpretation while others call for a more liberal rendering; for example, staff at a library that requires a valid library card may overlook the occasional forgetfulness of a well-known borrower and allow the user to check out books without a card. The more fully circulation staff understand the underlying philosophy of the institution, the more accurately they can determine which circumstances might call for exceptions to the rules.

PUBLIC RELATIONS

Almost everything done in a library is an act of public relations. Anything that affects the user's attitude toward the library, negatively or positively, is part of public relations (PR). How long it takes to process items for use, how employees answer the telephone, the accuracy of the reshelving process, the inflection in one's voice in answering a question, the presence and quality of signage, and the "warmth" or atmosphere of a library are only a few examples of things that have an impact on PR.

There are philosophical and practical reasons to be concerned about PR. Good PR stems from the delivery of quality service. Conversely, bad PR is a sign that the service philosophy of the library is defective in vision, execution, or both. Many libraries make formal attempts to assess user satisfaction in order to determine how well they are meeting and exceeding the needs of their users (See Chapter 3, Customer Service, for more information on this).

From a practical standpoint, good user relations are vital for the stability of a library's financial base. Whether public, academic, special, or school, a library must depend on a parent agency for funding. Libraries are expensive yet low-profile institutions and in times of financial exigency (that is, most of the time) they are easy targets for budget slashing unless they can rally supporters. Good PR is essential in building this corps of advocates and thus helps to guarantee that a library will continue to have the resources it needs to fulfill its mission and goals.

Because of their central role in providing service to library users, a large share of the responsibility for good PR rests on the circulation staff. Increasingly in some libraries, working with culturally diverse groups presents a challenge. There is a growing need to understand cultural differences and the needs of non-English speakers in order to provide good quality service. Earlier in this chapter we wrote of the service philosophy that should underlie the actions of each member of the circulation department. If staff members apply rules and regulations with fairness and flexibility, if each user receives individualized treatment in the sense that the person's needs are important, and if routines aimed at providing efficient service are accurately performed, positive user feelings about the library will almost surely follow.

There are, however, a small number of library users who do not respond to courteous treatment and efficient service. These users are sometimes categorized as "*problem users.*" The largest category of problem users is those individuals with contentious personalities or chronically bad attitudes. Such individuals ignore attempts at fair treatment and reasonable library service is never sufficient. Nevertheless, library staff must make reasonable attempts to satisfy every user's library needs, even those of problem users.

Urban libraries, especially public libraries, are sometimes visited by individuals who are, for instance, intoxicated, or by homeless people seeking shelter. Latchkey children gather in many libraries after schools let out. Although these and other users may cause occasional problems for the staff, no *class* of users should be singled out for special treatment. The same policies should govern treatment of everyone. If certain behavior problems are common at a particular library, a policy for handling *individuals* exhibiting this behavior should be in writing and known to all library staff. Posting such a policy to make users aware of it may also be helpful.

It is important that circulation staff members do not get into the habit of considering all library users with problems as problem users. Users often have valid criticisms and to treat them all as problem users is to reflect a negative service attitude on the part of staff. (See Chapters 3 and 14 for a more thorough discussion of dealing with problem users.)

What sorts of problems are brought to the attention of a circulation staff member? A review of the literature through the years reveals some common themes. Inability to find cataloged materials on the shelves and insufficient numbers of desired titles are common complaints. Circulation limits on reserve items and restrictions on renewals were other problems, as well as dissatisfaction with strict application of circulation rules. Short loan periods and not being notified about their overdue materials, or about materials they believed they had returned, are also common user problems.

Circulation staff should be aware of the most frequent complaints made by users of their library and should pass complaints on to their supervisors. Many libraries have manual or online suggestion boxes or complaint forms to document problem areas. Appropriate responses to complaints should be taught to all circulation desk workers and the responses should be made with courtesy and tact. Some libraries post responses, in writing or online, to user questions or complaints.

CHARACTERISTICS OF CIRCULATION CONTROL SYSTEMS

In theory, a circulation control system allows staff to determine, at a minimum, the location of each book in the collection and to fairly administer the circulation policy. Each system has unique characteristics that determine its value to a library. The traits discussed below occur, in varying degrees, in all circulation systems. When considering a new or replacement system, the importance of each characteristic for a particular library's operation is paramount.

First, the system must be easy for borrowers to use and for library personnel to operate. A complex or cumbersome system often results in poor service and poor user relations, especially if borrowers view it as an obstacle to their needs rather than an aid. Simplicity and ease of use might be the most important qualities of any circulation control system.

Second, it must be reliable. The system must accurately record transactions with little opportunity for user or staff error.

Third, the system should allow library staff and the borrower to identify the material borrowed, any fines owed or other restrictions on borrowing, and the date items are due back. All integrated library systems (ILSs) provide this information instantaneously upon checkout and it may be retrieved when needed. Many ILSs include a "my account" feature that allows borrowers to check their records over the Web at any time.

Fourth, the system must provide a record of overdue materials. Staff members or the system uses this information to send overdue notices, provide a record for fines, and develop a list of materials for possible replacement. Some libraries identify overdue material daily, while other libraries do it less often.

Fifth, the system should provide easy and accurate retrieval of requested materials when they are returned. Borrowers often request materials already on loan. The system should notify the requester when material is again available for further use. This process is called reserving a book, or a *hold* request. The system should check returned materials against hold requests so that items can be held for the next borrower.

Sixth, the system should automatically delete the link between item and borrower on return of the item.

Seventh, the system should allow easy retrieval of statistics tracking circulation activity. Modern online systems provide sophisticated records on reading patterns and collection use.

Eighth, the system must be cost-effective. The system must not make an undue claim upon the staff, material, or financial resources of a library in proportion to the benefits received from the system and the rest of the library budget.

And finally, computerized circulation systems should integrate with the other modules in the ILS; for example, the online catalog and acquisitions systems, so the information is widely available to all who need it.

CIRCULATION CONTROL SYSTEMS

Except in the case of very small or specialized libraries, nearly all the circulation control systems support personnel are apt to encounter are ILSs. The vast majority of public, academic, and school libraries possess some type of computerized systems for handling basic operations. A 2000 study of school libraries revealed 9 out of 10 had an automated circulation system (Prestebak and Wightman, 2000). You should also know there are hundreds, if not thousands of schools that have *no* library. A 2002 survey found that 99 percent of public libraries and 100 percent of academic libraries enjoyed some level of ILS operations (Institute of Museum and Library Services, 2002). These numbers have increased even further at the time of this writing.

Today all of the most popular ILSs offer circulation modules, and a number of PC-based systems are also available for smaller libraries. Systems vary from a single-PC-based system in a small library to centralized Web-based systems in larger libraries with many public and staff terminals. Each system operates in the same general manner but with certain unique features. The description that follows covers only the basic characteristics common to most computer-based systems.

Automated circulation systems generally require little or no user participation. Each authorized borrower has a unique identification number that appears as a barcode (also called a zebra number or optical character recognition [OCR] label). The borrower's card contains that bar code number and staff scan (or "read") it with a light pen or optical scanner (see Figure 8.1). Anyone who shops in a grocery store will recognize the bar codes, which are similar to those that appear on most food packaging. A recent alternative to bar codes is radio frequency identification (RFID) tags. Staff members also apply a unique bar code or coded RFID tag to each item in the library's collection. The item's bar code or tag number is linked to the item's record in the online catalog.

To check out an item, borrowers present their bar-coded or tagged identification card to the circulation attendant together with the material they are checking out. The attendant scans the bar code or tag on the identification card or may enter user and item data via a keyboard, if a borrower has forgotten his or her ID card. The system automatically retrieves the person's record and checks borrowing eligibility (for example, no current excessive overdue fines, enrollment in the school, and so on). If the user's status report is satisfactory, the attendant scans in the bar code on each item or passes the RFID-tagged item by a reader to be checked out. Each item checked out is automatically linked to the user's record in the system memory. The attendant returns the identification card and completes the transaction, usually by placing a preprinted date due notice in the book or stamping the date due slip in the book to remind the borrower of the items' due dates. Finally, the staff member desensitizes items so they will pass through the theft detection system without setting off the alarm.

When items come back, the staff member places the circulation system into the discharge, or check-in, mode. The system reads the bar code or tag on the item and clears the record from the circulation database unless the item is overdue, in which case the system automatically generates a fine notice. The borrower's record is either cleared or attached to the overdue information. If another borrower has a reservation (hold) on the item, the system displays this on the monitor and the staff member takes appropriate action to notify the requesting borrower.

Some systems offer a portable device containing the basic circulation software as well as an independent power source. This allows staff to check material out at remote locations, such as on a bookmobile, or use it as a backup system during a power failure. The unit is also used to scan items used within the library to compile records of in-house use of reference and other materials and to assist in inventorying the collection.

Figure 8.1 Library ID Card with Bar Code

In most cases, computer-based circulation systems directly link into the OPAC. This allows users to determine the circulation status of materials when searching the OPAC. That feature reduces users' frustrations from going to stacks, not finding the desired item, and then going to the circulation desk to learn that the item is already checked out. It also allows users to determine the circulation status of materials in the collections of other libraries with integrated systems. This is especially useful information for ILLs and interlibrary referral.

Some systems also allow self-charging by users. Permitting borrowers to check out their own items frees circulation staff to perform other service functions. Borrowers like these systems as they often allow them to bypass a line at the circulation desk, thus speeding their transactions. It may also improve productivity and efficiency, reduce expenses, and allow libraries to handle increasing circulation activity without increasing staff while affording users an option for self-service resulting in increased user satisfaction. The technology is similar to that used in automatic teller machines and grocery stores. The borrower places a library card in the system, if the card is approved, instructions appear on how to position the item and scan the bar code or read the tag. The system then verifies the circulation status of the item, checks it out, and desensitizes the item. Date due slips are sometimes printed, and if there is a problem the system prompts the user to inquire at the circulation desk.

Below is a list of tasks most automated circulation systems automatically perform:

1. Identifying delinquent borrowers who have overdue materials and/or owe fines
2. Displaying the reason for the delinquency
3. Alerting staff to lost or stolen identification cards when one is presented
4. Displaying all items currently checked out to a borrower, and eliminating any record of past circulation activity upon check in, thereby preserving borrowers' confidentiality
5. Allowing placement and notification of reserves (holds) and indicates when a reserve has been placed on an item
6. Calculating fines and fees for overdue items
7. Printing and sending recall, hold, and fine notices
8. Automatically printing overdue and fee statements
9. Indicating whether a particular item is already checked out or is temporarily unavailable; for example, at the bindery or lost
10. Recording and printing a variety of statistical information concerning collection use and circulation activities

Automated systems are flexible and a library may tailor the functions cited above to meet its specific needs. The only way to understand an automated circulation system is to see one in operation or, better yet, use one in person. A visit to a successful operational system is far more useful than reading a description. (See Figures 8.2 and 8.3, which provide a summary of major circulation operations).

Circulation of Nonbook Materials

Although the ILS circulation control systems described above are capable of handling all types of materials, many libraries choose to handle certain nonbook materials separately. The cost of controlling these special materials is often lower using a separate system because the circulation frequency of special materials is often too low to justify anything but the simplest and least costly system available. Also, the loan periods for these materials may be different from those for books. Many libraries develop their own special forms for charging out nonbook material. To check out such materials manually, the borrower usually fills out a special charge card for the item.

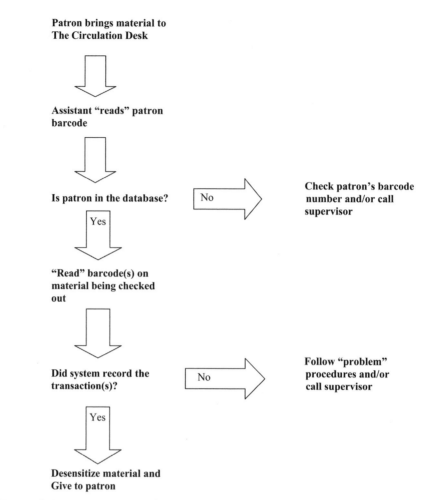

Figure 8.2 Basic Automated Checkout Procedures

BORROWER REGISTRATION

Most libraries require borrowers to register and to obtain a special identification card to check materials out of the library. Applying for this card is often the user's first contact with a library. This is especially true in a public library. In academic and special libraries a general identification card used for many purposes may also serve as a library card. When a library does require the borrower to register, the procedure should be simple and trouble-free.

There are several important reasons for requiring borrowers to register:

1. To identify persons who have the right to borrow materials, or in some cases the right to use a library;
2. To give a borrower some special form of identification necessary to check out material or use a library;

Patron returns material

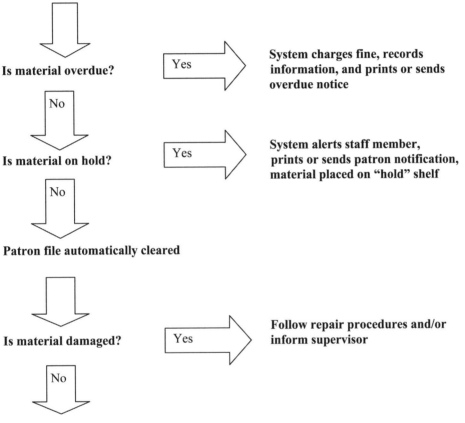

**Assistant "reads" patron barcode
with system in "checkin" mode**

Is material overdue?   Yes →   **System charges fine, records
information, and prints or sends
overdue notice**

No

Is material on hold?   Yes →   **System alerts staff member,
prints or sends patron notification,
material placed on "hold" shelf**

No

Patron file automatically cleared

Is material damaged?   Yes →   **Follow repair procedures and/or
inform supervisor**

No

Resensitize and shelve material

Figure 8.3 Basic Automated Check-in Procedures

3. To obtain communication information so library staff can communicate with users regarding holds, overdues, and so forth;

4. To obtain information on the demographics of a library's clientele in order to help plan for services and acquisition of materials. This last reason applies especially to public libraries. It is important for a library to know who it is serving and, equally importantly, who it is not serving, and;

5. The application form may include reminders about borrowers' responsibilities to return materials on time, fees for lost or damaged items, and any other fees associated with the lending services.

Circulation staff usually handles borrower registration; in academic libraries, it is often handled by student workers, with overall supervision by a paraprofessional. The levels of personnel employed for registration in a particular library vary depending on its size, type, and policies. The rest of this section is an overview of user registration procedures. Because daily work details vary greatly among libraries we will not discuss them here but leave them to when they are best learned—that is, while working in a library.

Registration in Public Libraries

Public libraries have a prescribed registration procedure. Most public libraries include local residents and taxpayers among their primary clientele. Many public libraries also grant borrowing privileges to nonresident users. Sometimes these nonresident circulation privileges are granted on a temporary basis, generally for a small fee or deposit. The privileges may be valid for only a limited time, commonly between one and six months.

Registration usually requires the prospective borrower to show proof of identity and eligibility (often an ID card and proof of residency) and to fill out an application (see Figure 8.4). Applications are often available in languages other than English, especially in libraries serving multicultural populations. Children and young adults often must have the sponsorship of an adult to obtain a card, and often have their application co-signed by their parent or guardian, especially if the child is to have full access to the library's collection, including the Internet terminals. This is also to assure that parents understand they have the responsibility of paying the child's fine/fees if incurred.

Many libraries are members of consortia or networks or entered into cooperative agreements with other libraries to allow all registered borrowers to have equal access and check-out privileges in all member libraries. Some libraries extend borrowing privileges to cardholders from any public library in that state (called universal borrowing). Others have contractual arrangements with other jurisdictions to serve their users without charge. Some libraries charge fees to nonresidents, but typically the amounts are relatively low.

A public library branch may keep its own database of registered borrowers or there may be a centralized database for an entire system. In either case, an important task is to keep these records current, deleting inactive names and obsolete addresses. Most library cards expire at regular intervals so borrowers are required to register again. The system automatically removes the records of those borrowers who do not renew their registration. Some public libraries use cards with no expiration date, and purge their user database of inactive registrants at regular intervals. Many public libraries also grant borrowing privileges to nonresidents, including immigrants.

Registration in Academic Libraries

The primary responsibility of the academic library is to provide service to the institution's students, faculty, and staff. Faculty and staff receive identification cards when hired and have library privileges because they work for the

Figure 8.4 e-Card Application

Printed with permission of the Contra Costa County Library.

institution. Students usually need one of three forms of identification in order to check materials out of the library:

1. An institutional identification card issued or validated when the student registers for the academic term;
2. An identification card issued by the library; or
3. Absent either of the above, a receipt for fees paid for the academic term.

The registrar's office usually supplies the student records for loading into the library's circulation database and a staff member works with the registrar's staff to be sure that regular updates get uploaded. Sometimes the library will have access to the registrar's database as a backup.

Academic libraries often make provisions for circulation service to certain classes of noninstitutional borrowers. Alumni sometimes have borrowing privileges. Publicly supported institutions usually allow members of the public to purchase a library card for a nominal fee while admitting them to the library free of charge. Even private institutions may make borrowing privileges available to visiting scholars and sell library cards to members of the local community in the interest of good public relations. Unaffiliated borrowers usually must fill out an application form with their name, address, telephone number, and social security number, and present valid identification, after which they receive a temporary library card.

Registration in Special Libraries

Registration of borrowers for special libraries can take a variety of forms. An identification card indicating employment with a company or government agency may give a person library privileges. Registration as a general library user in a public or academic library may also include privileges to use a special library that is part of the institution. Occasionally a special borrower's card is available for a limited time to persons needing to use a special library. Special libraries often issue temporary cards to scholars and specialists in a particular field. There are thousands of special libraries and, of course, many variations in the manner of user registration. Frequently, there is no special registration since the staff is small and the library staff is familiar with everyone on sight.

Registration in School Libraries

School libraries have the most homogeneous clientele of the libraries we are examining. Eligible borrowers are generally the students enrolled in the school, although there are schools and districts that serve parents, students from other schools, or members of the community at large. This is especially true in the cases of school and public library partnerships, where schools or school districts share resources with public libraries.

Because of the limited clientele, few school libraries issue library cards. Proof of eligibility is less problematic than in other types of libraries. It can be easily established by personal recognition, school identification cards, and class registers. For those libraries that grant privileges to nonstudents, forms of identification other than library cards are the norm. Where partnerships or alliances exist with public libraries, students often have library cards so they can use the public library resources.

CHECKOUT AND CHECK-IN

Libraries establish limits on the length of time a borrower may keep library materials. The limits insure that borrowers will return items within a reasonable time, making them available to others. The length of the loan period depends on the size of the collection, amount of circulation, purpose of lending materials, the clientele served, and sometimes the nature of the material loaned. For most items, loan periods are typically from one to four weeks. Certain materials (such as periodicals, CDs, or DVDs) are usually lent for shorter periods of one to seven days. In some libraries certain categories of borrowers are permitted longer loan periods than others. Academic libraries, for example, usually permit faculty and graduate students, because of their more scholarly research needs, to check out materials for longer periods than undergraduates. In this case, items with extended loan periods usually are subject to "recall" after the standard loan period is over. This process allows undergraduates and others to gain access to items that may have loan periods of a year in the case of faculty. These periods vary depending on the library. With larger collections there is less need for such limits.

Libraries with smaller collections or high circulation rates tend to have shorter loan periods in order to make material available to as many users as possible. Libraries with larger collections may allow longer loan periods. Library staff will take all of these factors into consideration when establishing loan policies.

Some libraries limit the number of items a borrower may check out at one time or the number of items that one may borrow on a particular topic. This is common in smaller libraries where one borrower could deplete an entire subject area. With larger collections there is less need for such limits.

Some libraries, often the larger ones, have equipment that allows borrowers to check out their own materials (self-checkout). The equipment reads the item's bar codes and the borrower's bar code number, and automatically records the transaction.

We covered the various ways to discharge (check in) borrowed materials earlier in the section on circulation systems. Regardless of the system employed, the result of discharging is the same—the loan is canceled and the borrower's responsibility ends.

As staff members discharge material, they inspect it for wear or damage. This is the time to identify damage that will require repair and for which the borrower will have to pay for the work. Repairing torn pages or loose bindings is a must before the material circulates again, or the item may be damaged beyond repair and perhaps the wrong person will be charged for the damage. This is a serious problem because many items are out of print (i.e., the publisher has no copies available for purchase) and replacements are only available at great cost. It is rare for the circulation staff to make repairs. Usually they send the damaged material to the bindery unit, which decides how to handle the repair—in-house or using the services of a commercial bindery or restoration service. When the item goes to the bindery/repair unit the circulation department updates the item's location in the OPAC.

Search and Hold Procedures

Circulation systems are, essentially, inventory control systems. The goal of an inventory control system is to be able to locate any item in the system at any time. Users often ask circulation staff to find material that the library owns but that is not on the shelf. One of the measures of a good circulation control system is how well it allows staff to locate materials when they are not filed in their proper location or checked out. Procedures for locating requested materials and notifying the requester that materials are available are often called "search and hold" procedures.

To initiate the procedure, the user or staff member usually fills out a search request form (see Figure 8.5), either manually or online. (Circulation staff employs the same search procedure when a borrower claims she/he has returned an item that the system indicates is still on loan.) Sometimes, most often in public libraries, there is a small fee for placing a hold. The requester or staff member fills out the call number, author, and title on the search form, as well as the requester's name and address, so a notification can go out when the item is again available. Staff members begin the search by checking the circulation records and the shelves. (It is the authors' experience that approximately 50 percent of the "searched" items are actually in their proper location.) If the material is not on the shelf, an extended and standard search procedure follows. The search expands to all possible locations—book carts, sorting shelves, missing files, mending areas, the tops of dust canopies in the stacks (some tall individuals or someone using a step stool may forget they laid an item up there), and other locations materials might be found. Many academic libraries maintain remote storage facilities for seldom-used material, and if the item is found there it is retrieved for the requester, typically within a few days. Because of the library's emphasis on providing access to information, this is an important service, and libraries make every effort to locate missing items for their users.

Another characteristic of a good circulation system is its ability to identify holds, also known as reserve requests, when material is returned. Many on-line systems allow the public to place holds in the OPAC. The system links the requestors' data with the desired item and notifies staff when a requested item is checked in and a notice of availability goes to the requestor. The library holds the material for only a limited time, usually a few days. If the person does not check out the item, a staff member notifies the next person in the hold queue or it goes to the reshelving area. Some libraries mail the material directly to the borrower who requested it instead of requiring the individual to come to the library.

OVERDUES, FINES, AND BILLING

Overdue materials present some service issues for both the public and staff because they are not available to others who may wish to consult them and most libraries charge fines for past due items. Both of these facts create potential PR concerns. The latter especially can cause tension and require conflict resolution as suggested in one of our opening quotations. Libraries levy fines in the hope that economic incentives/penalties will encourage borrowers to return materials on time. Overdue and fine procedures vary by type of library and collection size/service considerations.

Through the years there have been trends to lower or eliminate fines in some libraries, while others raised fines in the hope increased costs would improve the timely return of materials. Some have tried alternate methods of collecting

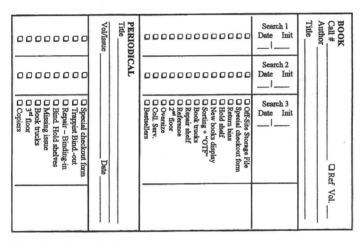

Figure 8.5 Search Request Form

fines to make the process less onerous; for example, accepting credit card payments. A few accept food donations for the needy in lieu of cash, especially around holidays. While there is a lack of confirming evidence in the literature, most libraries believe some form of a fines and billing system is an effective means for convincing borrowers to return books on time. Some library parent organizations even assume a certain level of fine/fee income from the library when establishing the annual budget.

As part of the registration process, the new borrower should receive a copy of the basic loan policies and information about fines and fees. Some libraries print the fine schedule on the transaction card inserted in the book pocket, on the pocket itself, and on their Web page. A few post a sign at the circulation desk listing rates and fees.

Few libraries have complete freedom to set the fine policy; instead, they must conform to the desires of their governing bodies. In a public library, the director may make recommendations on a fine policy, but the library board of trustees has legal authority to establish the policy. In a college or university, the director makes recommendations first to the advisory board (usually made of faculty and students) and then to the senior campus administrators that oversee the library.

Fine rates vary for different types of loans; for example, fines for short-term loans are often higher than for long-term loans. Fine amounts may also vary according to type of item, for example, higher fines for high-demand items like popular videos or books on CD. There may be a different fine schedule for children or juvenile borrowers (usually lower than the rate used for adults). Some libraries do not charge children overdue fines at all, believing it is more important to encourage reading as a positive experience. The Columbus Metropolitan Library in Ohio allows children to write off fines by reading with staff members or volunteers. (Futty, 2003). Colleges and universities often do not fine faculty or staff, although they often bill for lost items. Most libraries have a maximum fine amount per item.

Some libraries have a policy of rescinding fines for borrowers who are unable to pay, encouraged by the ALA's *Policy Manual* section on services to the poor (http://www.ala.org/ala/ourassociation/governingdocs/policymanual/servicespoor.htm). Many libraries have tried moratoriums to encourage the return of overdue material. If a borrower returns the overdue material within the specified period, the staff cancels the fine. The rationale for such amnesty programs is that the purpose of fines is not to punish borrowers or to make money for the library; rather fines are levied as an incentive to encourage the timely return of material.

Most systems automatically produce overdue notices for the circulation unit to send to the delinquent borrowers (by either snail or e-mail). See Figure 8.6 for an example of a system-generated notice. Some systems place phone call reminders in place of written notices. If the borrower does not respond to the first notice, the system may generate second, third, or more notices at predetermined intervals. The number of notices is a matter of library policy. Staff or the circulation system keep manual or online records of the notices sent and on the eventual resolution of the matter. A library usually bills a delinquent borrower for the amount of the fine, plus a service charge to cover the cost of processing.

If the fine remains unpaid or the material unreturned, libraries generally suspend further borrowing privileges until the individual resolves the outstanding loans/fines. This is an easy process to handle with an ILS.

Libraries may resort to the employment of collection agencies, which sometimes report delinquent users to companies that are sources of credit checks, affecting users' credit ratings. In some extreme instances, libraries may take legal action in small claims court. The decision to initiate legal proceedings generally rests with the chief librarian. Public libraries may work with the city or county legal department to act against borrowers who fail to respond to overdue notices. Implementing such action against borrowers guilty of flagrant violations is never undertaken lightly due to potential bad PR; however, it is done in the hope that it will deter others from committing similar transgressions. Academic libraries work with the university registrar or business office to withhold transcripts or degrees from students with unpaid library fines. School libraries usually contact parents to take care of rule violations.

```
25151000675130
Thomas L Carter
310 Sutton Circle
Danville CA 94506
```

```
1ST OVERDUE NOTICE
The following library materials are now overdue.
Please return them promptly to avoid replacement charges or,
if you need them longer, please call to inquire about renewing.
Thank you for your immediate response to this notice.
CIRCULATION DESK: (925) 631-4229
     <PLEASE DO NOT REPLY TO THIS EMAIL>
```

```
AUTHOR:  Putnam, Robert D
Bowling alone : the collapse and re
CALL NO: 309.173 P983 c.2
BARCODE: 35151002120111
Book Stacks: 2nd floor DUE: 03-06-08
DATE CHECKED OUT: 03-06-08 08:43AM
```

Figure 8.6 Automated Overdue Notice

Collecting Fines and Fees

Collection of fines and fees is an important responsibility because it usually involves accountability in handling money. Often, fine and fee collection takes place at the loan desk. This requires a cash register or cash box for making change, a ledger of some sort for recording transactions, and accurate accounting procedures. Fines must be computed carefully; a fine is a poor PR device in any case, and miscalculating the fine only aggravates the situation. Automated systems automatically calculate fines.

Circulation personnel often encounter borrowers who contest their fines. The most common contention is that the items were, in fact, returned on time and library records are in error. If the material is, in fact, found, the library policy is to give the borrower the benefit of the doubt and cancel the fine. Flexibility in collecting fines does much to preserve good PR while obtaining the return of overdue materials.

Some libraries, usually academic, do not collect the fine, but issue a bill and the borrower pays the fee at the business office or other campus agency. Often fine money does not go into a library-accessible account, but rather goes into a general fund for use by the governing body of the institution.

Libraries also collect fees for damaged or lost books. Often the library is allowed to retain a large percentage of these funds in order to pay for the repairs or replacement copy. Generally libraries charge the cost to replace or repair the material plus a service charge to cover the expenses of staff time in processing the item. The amount of the service charge varies from library to library. For example, a lost book that costs $29.95 to replace might be billed at $34.95, the cost of the book plus a replacement fee of $5.00. Some libraries permit borrowers to purchase a replacement copy in return for reducing or eliminating the fee.

Some academic libraries have rental reserve collections and some public libraries have rental collections of popular materials. Rental money collected is usually available for purchasing additional copies of popular titles. If multiple copies of particular works are needed and funds limited, the library might purchase several copies for rental and thereby recover the cost of the material.

The circulation staff member may not do the actual collecting of fines and fees but will probably supervise the operation and must be aware of library policy and be able to solve problems that may arise. One of these is negotiating fines and fees with borrowers. When bargaining, it is important for the staff to remember the philosophy behind the charges. Staff should be willing, and authorized, to negotiate a reduction in fines for returned overdue materials if they perceive a legitimate reason to do so. Such a willingness to consider the special circumstances of individual borrowers does much to ease the negative situation. It enhances the library's public reputation and achieves the basic aim of getting material back on the shelves.

ETHICAL AND LEGAL CONSIDERATIONS

Circulation personnel are ethically bound not to reveal the reading habits of borrowers. This is consistent with the ALA's *Library Bill of Rights* (http://www.ala.org/ala/oif/statementspols/statementsif/librarybillrights.htm) and the principle of intellectual freedom (the right to read and think whatever one wishes). The ALA *Code of Ethics* (http://www.ala.org/ala/oif/statementspols/codeofethics/codeethics.htm) states "we protect each library user's right to privacy and confidentiality with respect to information sought or received, and resources consulted, borrowed, acquired or transmitted." Only the reader and the circulation staff, in the legitimate performance of their duties, have a right to know what information sources the user consulted or checked out, and circulation staff have an obligation to prevent others from obtaining this information.

Probably for as long as libraries have existed, police, government officials, ministers, parents, spouses, and others have asked library staff about the reading habits of borrowers. Only during the past 70 years, however, has the library profession expressed a desire to keep circulation records confidential. In 1938, the ALA's *Code of Ethics* specified the confidentiality of library records, the first formal acknowledgment of this issue in the United States (ALA, 1939). Since 1970, the profession's stand on confidentiality has become stronger. There is currently, for example, a movement to keep users' records confidential from warrantless searches by government officials pursuant to the USA PATRIOT Act.

The following discussion of this issue is necessarily brief. The authors of this book do not intend that anything in the following paragraphs be construed as legal advice.

From a strictly legal standpoint, government officials sometimes have legitimate reasons to view library records. Public safety is the strongest justification for disclosure of library records; for example, requests relating to investigations of specific crimes. Legitimate national security concerns may also justify legally obtained government access to library records.

Citizen access to library records is much less defensible. Although the records of libraries that are government agencies (publicly funded in some way) may be categorized as public records, access to these records serves no public function. Citizens have few legitimate uses for library records. Most requests for circulation records infringe on the privacy of the borrower. Privacy may be considered an intrinsic and a prophylactic right that secures and safeguards other rights. A person has the right "to be left alone," according to Justice Brandeis, and the right to be free from the harassment, intimidation, and persecution that might result from free access to circulation records.

In 1970 the ALA adopted a *Policy on the Confidentiality of Library Records*, the current version of which was published in 1986 (http://www.ala.org/ ala/oif/statementspols/otherpolicies/confidentialitylibraryrecords.pdf). This policy attempts to constrain unlimited police access to library records by requiring an order from a judicial, legislative, or administrative body. The 1995 revised ALA *Code of Ethics* reaffirms the library's duty to protect each user's right to privacy with respect to library records. Many libraries and library associations responded to these documents by adopting confidentiality policies of their own.

Although there are no federal laws protecting the confidentiality of library records, as of this writing 48 states and the District of Columbia have passed confidentiality legislation, and a summary of state laws and practices may be viewed at http://www.library.cmu.edu/People/neuhaus/state_laws.html. These statutes attempt to strike a balance between access and privacy. Each law permits some access, especially in response to court orders or subpoenas. Thirty-five states provide that libraries need not disclose circulation records under the state open-records law. Common exceptions include that records may be disclosed to permit the performance of library routines, if the user consents, and pursuant to a subpoena, court order, or otherwise required by law (Bowers, 2006).

The current status of confidentiality laws leaves several issues unclear. Under current legislation, library staff may be liable for civil or criminal liability for wrongful disclosure of records. There is no federal law regarding confidentiality of library records, and federal legislation like the USA PATRIOT Act overrides state statutes.

Many libraries have a confidentiality policy, and the ALA's *Policy on Confidentiality of Library Records* offers guidance here. Policy in most libraries requires that staff attempt to eradicate past circulation records and preserve the confidentiality of users. Libraries with automated systems are in a good position to act in defense of confidentiality by insuring that the system eliminates any link between the borrower's name and the specific material borrowed once the item has been returned and any fees paid. If the circulation system used in a library requires that the name of a borrower appear on a book card or some other record traceable to the book involved, staff should render the name illegible as part of the discharging process.

All library staff must be familiar with library policy on disclosure of library records because someday a citizen or government authority may approach any library employee with the request that the library disclose information on the reading habits or other library use of particular users. Staff who receive such a request of this kind should refuse to comply and immediately report the request to their supervisor or otherwise follow their library's policy.

STACK MAINTENANCE

Maintaining an orderly arrangement of library materials is an important function generally assigned to circulation. A library must have an accurate and efficient shelving operation or quality library service is impossible. Backlogs of unshelved materials cause delays in service and require staff time to locate material. Misshelved items are essentially lost until they are noticed and reshelved correctly. When closed stacks were the rule with only library staff having access, maintaining an accurate arrangement was at least possible. When the profession came to realize that allowing readers unrestricted access to the collections resulted in greater usage ("open stacks"), maintaining orderly collections of materials became a constant battle for the circulation staff.

The most common way in which libraries first sort their collections is by format. Books, periodicals, audiovisual media, government documents, pamphlets, and so on are usually grouped together by format. This is done for two reasons. First, different formats are often arranged differently. For example, books are filed by classification number, periodicals are often organized by title, government documents may be arranged by special federal or state classification systems, and pamphlets are grouped by subject.

Another factor is that some formats, due to shape or size, require special storage units. Books and periodicals are housed on "standard shelving," pamphlets in file cabinets, microfilm in specially designed cabinets, and maps generally laid flat in map cases. Some libraries shelve CDs and videos (or their empty cases) in the stacks along with books and periodicals, but this is the exception. More commonly, audio and video recordings are stored separately. Because books and periodicals are the most common items in libraries, we will limit our discussion here of stack maintenance procedures to these formats. (See Chapter 11 for information on media shelving).

Books are the most traditional item in most collections and are housed on shelves in bookstacks and arranged by classification number. Some titles, such as rare or antiquarian books, special collections materials, and oversized volumes, require special handling, but these, too, will have a classification or accession number to allow orderly shelving. Although support staff (full- or part-time) usually do little shelving, they must know enough to train volunteers and student assistants to handle all phases of the shelving operation.

In some cases, library collections are growing faster than the library's ability to house them. Building space is expensive and funding authorities are sometimes slow to respond to the need for space to house the increasing size of library collections. Then too, some authorities have fallen victim to the hype that "everything is on the Web," and believe building additional space for physical collections is no longer necessary.

Many libraries respond to the lack of collection space by building or renting high-volume storage spaces and filling them with the lesser used portions of their collections. This is particularly true in academic libraries. A number of newer academic library facilities include automated storage and retrieval systems (ASRS). These allow for high-density storage of items in close proximity, often adjacent to the library. Generally the storage area is a return to the "closed stack" concept with only library personnel having access. Borrowers wanting an item in storage request it via the catalog terminal. The request activates the automated retrieval system and the item is delivered via conveyer belt to the circulation desk, usually in just a few minutes.

Remote storage facilities usually involve the shipping of items to a warehouse-like facility that the library contracts with to house the items. The facility may be close by or many miles away. Items in off-site storage are indicated in the OPAC and generally are retrievable via a request to the storage facility staff, and delivery usually takes a few days.

CLASSIFICATION SYSTEMS

There are two popular classification systems in use in the United States. The older Dewey decimal classification (DDC) is found primarily in school and public libraries, and the more recent Library of Congress system (LC) is used in most academic libraries. Special libraries frequently use their own classification system rather than DDC or LC. Often these libraries contain materials on a single topic and a chronological numbering system may be more useful.

The conceptual basis behind the DDC and LC systems is similar: to group books together by subject, and within each subject by author. The DDC uses decimal numbers to classify knowledge, while the LC system employs a combination of letters and whole numbers. The DDC system may present more problems in shelving because of the numbers to the right of the decimal point. It is important for shelvers to remember that, because these numbers are decimal fractions, a number like .16 is smaller than .9 and will file before the latter. As an example, the DDC numbers below are given in the order in which they would appear on the shelves:

| 581.21 | 581.21 | 581.31 | 581.4 | 581.498 | 581.5 |
| D4 | E73 | A4 | A47 | R3 | J6 |

Notice that .498 files before .5 because it is the smaller decimal. The second line is a combination letter and number, also a decimal, used to group items by the same author together (and sometimes called the author number). For example:

| 512 | 512 | 512 |
| A37 | A4 | D26 |

The LC classification is arranged first by letters and then by numbers. The third line is the number that, like the second line of the DDC, serves to keep material in alphabetical order by author. Notice that the author number in the examples below is treated like a decimal:

L	L	LA	LB	LC	LC
7	7	96	3063	4701	4701
D47	D5	G5	R71	R19	R2

Circulation staff must train shelvers to understand the classification system used and its relation to shelving materials. Those who do the shelving must also understand the importance of correct shelving and how it relates to good library service.

SHELVING

Materials to be shelved come from several sources:

1. New acquisitions;

2. Circulated materials that have been returned; and

3. Materials used in the library and not reshelved by the users (most libraries, to prevent misshelving, discourage users from reshelving materials).

The details of shelving operations vary among libraries. Shelvers may bring materials to a central location where they first rough-sort them and then place them in precise order. Larger libraries commonly have sorting areas on each floor. Prior to shelving, books may be sorted on shelves and then filed in exact order on book trucks, or sorted and placed in exact order on the shelves before being loaded onto book trucks. Shelving is a tiring and uninteresting job if performed for lengthy periods. The supervisor must establish schedules so no one shelves for too long (one or two hours at a time is common) and becomes careless.

Shelf-reading

To maintain the library collection in good order staff must regularly check the order of materials on the shelves. This is called *shelf-reading*. You engage in self-reading by scanning the shelves and reading the call numbers on the material to see that each item stands on the shelf in proper order. A collection with material out of order is difficult to use; trying to locate misshelved items costs a lot of user and staff time.

As the clerk or student assistant reads the shelves, they place misshelved items in correct order and straighten the items on the shelves. The shelf reader also sometimes shifts books from one shelf to another to alleviate overcrowding. The employee also looks for damaged material and loose or defaced labels and removes this material for repair.

Full-time circulation staff generally do little shelf-reading, except during special projects or to check or revise the work of new personnel. The supervisor will establish schedules to ensure that the collection is shelf-read at regular intervals. Some of the more heavily used parts of the collection require frequent shelf-reading, while other parts of the collection may need to be checked only occasionally. Staff must be familiar with circulation patterns and shelf-reading statistics in order to identify the more heavily used parts of the collection.

As may be surmised, shelf-reading is tedious work. Shelf readers can maintain the concentration needed for accuracy for only about one or two hours at a time. When scheduling personnel for this work, the supervisor should consider these limitations.

Collection Growth and Shifting

Collection arrangement is anything but random; it requires considerable planning. In formulating such plans circulation staff may consider some of the following:

1. Placing frequently used materials in easily accessible places;
2. Keeping related materials together;
3. Placing little-used materials where they do not occupy the most valuable floor space; and
4. Arranging materials logically on each floor so users are able to find them with as easily as possible.

As the library adds materials to its collection the shelves in some areas become full. When this happens staff must shift materials to permit further growth. A section of shelving is considered full, for practical purposes, at about 75 percent capacity. At this point, shelvers will frequently have to move books from shelf to shelf to create needed space. When shelves become full, the shelvers should report this to the person responsible for stack maintenance. Also, staff members who are responsible for stack maintenance should check the shelves regularly for crowded areas. Books should never be shelved tightly as damage often results.

A book shift may involve moving only a few shelves of books or it may require the movement of several stack ranges or even the entire collection. The less space for growth a library has, the more shifting is necessary to move the existing space to where it is needed. Libraries running out of shelf space may need to shift substantial portions of their collection every year, at considerable cost, and/or resort to remote storage of a portion of their collections.

Shifting requires a great deal of planning. When planning a shift, staff must consider collection growth rates, understand the nuances of shelving patterns, make sure that the workers performing the shift have received adequate training in shifting and handling techniques, and perform accurate measurements on the portion of the collection to be shifted in order to guarantee that the shift is successful. Although it is the librarian who makes shelving decisions, support staff generally assists in the planning, carries out the plan, and must be aware of the rationale behind the decisions. Circulation staff should be alert for shelving problems and report these problems to the librarian with recommendations for their solution.

PRESERVATION

Of all library departments, circulation personnel probably have the greatest impact on the condition, and often the survival, of library materials. Proper procedures for check-in and checkout as well as shelving, selection for repair, and other circulation work will prevent much damage. Good handling practice among circulation staff prevents damage by those who most often handle library materials; that is, those same staff members.

Staff members also model the handling of books and materials for library users. If the staff member checking out a book treats it roughly, borrowers will, consciously or unconsciously, learn to devalue the book and treat it in a similar manner. If the borrower returning a book notices that books have been allowed to accumulate like so much trash in the library book drop, books may become so much trash in the borrower's mind. If shelving is sloppy, with materials stuffed in helter-skelter, with books leaning so loosely they warp, with volumes falling off shelves or off overloaded and unbalanced book carts, the user's attitude toward library materials will deteriorate.

Staff training and the foundation of good book handling habits are the best way to begin to improve handling practice by both staff and library users. All new employees need specific instruction in preventive preservation. Instruction should be continuous over a period of time, including supervision, checking, and reinforcement. Occurrences of spine-up shelving, shelving too tightly, shelving too loosely, and rough handling in general must be corrected quickly, lest bad habits develop. People have a tendency to become sloppy with any repetitive task; setting a good example, good training, and follow-up supervision are the best ways to overcome this tendency. If circulation staff stamp books with due dates and dates returned, a list of procedural guidelines and training is necessary. Attachment of date due slips or pockets over useful information is to be avoided; for example, if there are charts, lists, keys, maps or other unrepeated information on the inside covers or end papers, slips should be attached somewhere else. Bound books with date due slips on the inside cover instead of the flyleaf should be held with the cover flat, and the text block at a 90-degree angle, so that the pressure of stamping is not conveyed to the unsupported hinge area. Over-inking stamps, bad aim with stamps, and piling and stamping open books one upon the other should be avoided.

User education is another means to avoid damage to library materials. Besides library staff setting a good example, such things as providing thin, non-harmful bookmarks, signage that informs users of situations dangerous to library materials, and well-publicized information about library problems may all be of help. A CD-ROM or DVD melted in the sun is often used in public libraries for this purpose, sometimes with a lot of creativity. Some libraries, for example, have turned the melted DVD into a nice-looking sunflower, with a cautionary message and statement concerning user responsibility for such damage. Exhibiting examples of willful mutilation, however, has been shown to be counterproductive. Staff should convey a positive message whenever possible (Drews and Page, 1997).

SECURITY MATTERS

Circulation staff members are often responsible for much of the security of the library building and its collections. This is so for a number of reasons:

1. The circulation area is often located near entrance and exit doors, and circulation staff are likely to be the first to become aware of security problems.
2. Circulation staff are, by the nature of their work, often more familiar with the building than other library personnel.
3. Circulation departments are typically staffed all the hours the library is open.

Responsibility for library security generally falls into two categories: (1) notifying the proper authorities about crimes or transgressions, or facility problems; and (2) assuming responsibility for the security of the building and its contents, especially at opening and closing times.

Later in this section we will discuss theft detection systems and the role of circulation personnel. Circulation personnel usually have the responsibility of notifying appropriate authorities in the event of thefts or other problems, including inappropriate behavior by users. Staff may also contact medical personnel in the event of emergencies. In cases such as these, employees at school or academic libraries will probably inform campus authorities, while public library workers contact city or county authorities. All libraries should have written procedures for dealing with security and medical emergencies and all staff should be thoroughly familiar with them.

Responsibility for building security includes opening the library in the morning and preparing it for use (turning on the lights, the computer terminals, and the copy machines, opening doors, unlocking the cash box, etc). Emptying the bookdrop(s), if present, is important to make sure they do not overflow, which threatens the security of the books as well as their preservation. Security also involves making sure the building is empty of people at closing time, turning things off, and locking the doors. This is an extremely important operation and evening and weekend personnel must be well versed in closing procedures to ensure that uninvited guests do not remain and that the building is secure against unauthorized entry. Both opening and closing procedures should be in writing and personnel performing these functions should be thoroughly trained in the routines.

To perform these security chores, and to enable staff to provide building access to authorized workmen when necessary, the circulation department is often assigned a full set of building keys. These keys are carefully controlled by the circulation staff and stored in a secure area accessible only to authorized personnel. See Chapter 15 for a fuller discussion of security issues.

Theft Detection Systems

Electronic theft detection systems have been available since the mid-1960s. Today they are in general use in all types of libraries. The purpose of these systems is to reduce theft and other types of unauthorized removal of library materials, such as the user or library director who innocently forgets to check out material. These systems, which operate on the principles of magnetism, electromagnetism, or radio frequency, are generally effective, and they are the single best deterrent to library material loss. To determine whether a library has a theft problem, one can use inventorying and sampling techniques. Studies have shown that book and DVD loss is a common problem. These studies also show, based on before and after loss data at the time of system installation, that the presence of the equipment alone may reduce theft by 50 percent, and a fully protected library may see a 70 percent to 90 percent reduction in loss (Witt, 1996). Theft detection systems are available from several commercial vendors.

The systems operate by placing a sensitized element, called a *trigger*, *tag*, or *target*, in library items. When staff check materials out they deactivate the target with a special piece of equipment or pass the item around the detection system and the borrower exits through the detection system normally. When a user does not properly check out material, a sensing unit installed near the exit doors detects the sensitized target and an alarm sounds (or a light flashes). The sensing unit can detect sensitized targets even in concealed material.

Libraries with a theft detection system will have a policy outlining the procedures to follow when the system activates. Because the person detected is in a sensitive situation and because of possible legal consequences, circulation staff must be careful not to accuse someone of theft and must strictly follow library policy and routine.

Several problems may result from the presence of a theft detection system. In large collections, there are often not enough human or financial resources to target all materials, so it must be done selectively. Generally, this means the more expensive, hard to replace, or most used titles. Even items that are targeted or tagged may not always activate the system, and savvy thieves may remove targets from items. There are some materials that should not be placed in or near a desensitizing or sensitizing unit. Some magnetic detection systems, for example, can damage audiotapes and videotapes if they are placed in or very near the sensitizing unit. To prevent these accidents, staff must be aware of the dangers inherent in the system used by the library. Some libraries report that mutilation of materials increases after the theft detection unit is installed. Mutilation is impossible to completely prevent, but staff can increase their vigilance if they are alert to the problem.

Libraries with theft detection systems must not fall into a false sense of security. The system is meant to stop the occasional dishonest user and the forgetful borrower. The person determined to steal or the professional thief can find a way to defeat most security precautions. (For more information on library security, see Chapter 15.)

ADMINISTRATION

Despite the differences in size of operations and type of library, in most libraries the duties of administering circulation functions are basically the same. The librarian or paraprofessional in charge selects and organizes the staff; is responsible for the details of supervision, instruction, and development; and assigns responsibility for the work. The choice of equipment and supplies is also that of the administrator.

In small libraries, the librarian often combines the administrative duties of the circulation function with those of the rest of the library. In larger libraries, a department head, sometimes a paraprofessional, usually discharges these administrative duties. This administrator is an intermediary between the librarian and the staff and often between the library and the public. In large libraries this individual may be accountable to an assistant librarian or a division chief.

Whatever the administrative relationship with those exercising greater authority, the head of the circulation department is the representative of the circulation staff. This person should be a leader with training, experience, and an understanding of his or her relations to the library staff as a whole, to the circulation staff in particular, and to the public. Due to the interpretive functions of the position, a good administrator has mature judgment and wisdom in dealing with people young and old. In the eyes of the users, the administrator represents the library and the service that makes materials available. As a member of the general staff, the administrator must keep in close touch with all activities in any way related to the department and must see that rivalry with the other library departments does not exist. The administrator must introduce into actual practice the policies and procedures determined by the chief librarian, the school board, the board of trustees, or by other authorities.

Personnel Selection and Training

In keeping with the service nature of circulation work, and the amount of detail necessary to maintain accurate records, the following characteristics are desirable when selecting circulation assistants:

- A pleasing personality (including courtesy and patience)
- Accuracy
- Adaptability to different tasks and levels of service demand
- Punctuality
- Intelligence

Of these traits, personality is the most important. Circulation assistants must be able to relate well to library users. They must display courtesy and patience in all circumstances, especially those problem situations described earlier. Brusque or otherwise disagreeable behavior by a staff member at a service desk is contrary to the service ideal. Supervisors should consider personality the first priority when interviewing candidates for circulation positions.

Accuracy, too, is important in circulation work. This is especially so in the tasks of shelving books and other items, inputting data, and communicating library rules and regulations. Accuracy requires an attention to detail that not all people possess.

Adaptability, or flexibility, is another essential characteristic of the circulation assistant. The amount of user activity at the circulation desk is subject to great variation, depending on the time of day, season, level of staffing, and other considerations. The circulation attendant must be able to switch gears quickly to handle a sudden swell of users at the loan desk and, conversely, switch back again to other duties when the tide has subsided. These fluctuations in activity are particularly apparent in academic and school libraries, where they tend to coincide with the release of classes.

The need for dependability is a given. Service at the circulation desk depends on the presence of staff. Attendants must arrive punctually so adequate staffing is always available. Supervisors must also be able to rely on the circulation staff to follow through on instructions and to complete assigned tasks.

A sufficient level of intelligence is required to learn the circulation system, circulation policy and routines, classification systems, and the philosophy behind the service. Most libraries try to insure sufficient aptitude in applicants by specifying certain educational requirements in the position description.

In addition to the above essential characteristics, other traits are important to a greater or lesser degree depending on the library or the nature of the position's responsibilities: the ability to work without close supervision, good health, imagination, initiative, judgment, memory, neatness, and speed. Supervisors should use the probationary period common in libraries to judge the fitness of newly hired personnel, and winnow out those who do not have the required qualifications for work at a busy service desk.

A few words are appropriate here about part-time assistants. Most libraries depend, to a greater or lesser degree, on the employment of lower-paid, part-time employees. These assistants perform basic labor-intensive jobs, allowing full-time staff to perform the more technical and service-oriented functions for which they are trained. Academic libraries depend absolutely on part-time student workers, while school and public libraries count on them to a lesser degree. No library department is likely to hire more part-time assistants than the circulation section. While part-time assistants have the advantage of being inexpensive and usually available, their presence creates certain administrative problems for the circulation supervisor.

Part-time employees are generally not as committed to or as interested in library work as full-time staff. This is especially true regarding student workers whose main concern, rightly enough, is their education. Punctuality is often a problem and is difficult to solve. Unwillingness to work is a problem with a few people, and the supervisor should discharge these individuals as soon as they discover them. Most part-timers are willing enough workers, but their level of interest in the often unchallenging work assigned them is low. The result is often poor-quality work, apparent in misshelved books and periodicals, mishandling of materials, and other mistakes. Thorough initial training, follow-up testing and observation, retraining if indicated, and friendly but careful supervision are required to get the most from part-time employees.

Before training in specific circulation functions, new employees should receive a tour of the entire library and an orientation to the library's mission and goals. This allows the employee to put the mission of the circulation department in its proper perspective. A detailed orientation to the circulation department generally follows, with introductions to all available circulation personnel.

Training of circulation assistants is generally based on written procedure manuals. Manuals should exist for all frequently performed and complex circulation routines. New employees are trained by experienced staff members to perform one task at a time, then checked and observed in the accurate performance of that task before moving to another job. The employee's supervisor should be available at all times to answer questions and reassure the new staff member when problems arise.

Scheduling

An important administrative function in circulation is personnel scheduling. The circulation department, as previously noted, typically offers service all hours the library is open. In some cases, especially in academic libraries, this can mean staffing the circulation desk more than 100 hours per week.

Both full-time and part-time employees are scheduled to cover these hours. The importance of having an experienced full-time staff member on duty, especially nights and weekends, is critical. Part-time assistants need training and supervision, and it is important that a knowledgeable staff member be available to interpret policies. Full-time personnel are often assigned one night a week or a weekend day as part of their regular schedule, or staff may rotate to cover these hours, or staff are hired specifically to work nights and weekends. Part-time assistants are especially important in working night and weekend hours, when full-time staffing is at a minimum. Only the most reliable part-time assistants should be scheduled at these times, and the administrator should always try to assign one or two more assistants than are necessary, to account for illness, vacations, and other absences. All staff who work nights and weekends should be especially well versed in emergency policies and procedures.

Records and Statistics

The use and abuse of statistics have long been the subject of debate among librarians. The old saying, that statistics can be manipulated to prove anything, may have more than a little basis in fact. Nevertheless, statistics are often the only objective measure available of library use and performance. Among the most definite and tangible statistics of library use are those recording the various aspects of circulation work. All libraries maintain statistical records, although the degree to which libraries record statistics varies widely. Automated systems are a great help in keeping and analyzing statistical records. Statistics measuring certain aspects of library work are necessary to satisfy governing boards, city, state, and federal authorities, academic administrators, and school boards that annual appropriations are being wisely spent and library services efficiently delivered. Some of the questions, which require regular compilation of statistics to answer, are:

- To what extent are people using the library, and is use increasing or decreasing?
- What portions of the collection receive the greatest use, and is this changing?
- What is the level of in-house use of library materials?
- What amount of money in fines and fees is collected?

In order to answer these and other questions, the following kinds of statistics are generally calculated by automated circulation systems, or recorded by circulation staff:

1. The number of items circulated, recorded by type of material (book, video, government document, etc.) and by status of user (adult, juvenile, student, faculty, and so forth), and by time of day.
2. The number of items circulated by subject (usually determined by classification number).
3. The amount of fine money received.
4. The number of questions answered at the circulation desk.
5. The number of items used within the library.
6. The number of items requested and either supplied or not supplied.
7. The number of ILL and document delivery requests filled and not filled.
8. The number of people who come into the library.
9. The number of materials lost or missing.

These traditional indicators of circulation and library activity have come under increasing criticism as underrepresenting the true use of the library. A report from the ALA (2007), *The State of America's Libraries*, reports that use of electronic resources is increasing much faster than use of the traditional print and physical resources libraries are used to counting. As electronic provision of library resources and services continues to increase, library staff must measure and represent this usage to library administrators, users, and funding authorities.

In addition to providing information for governing authorities, the analysis of statistics can provide the circulation manager and/or librarian with information that can be employed for a number of planning and management uses. These include assessing current levels of performance and comparing them with past and desired levels; diagnosing problem areas; monitoring progress towards the library's goals and objectives; planning for the future; justifying, internally and externally, resource allocations; and documenting service improvements.

Statistics collected serve as the basis of reports required at regular intervals by the library administration. The monthly or annual report of the circulation section forms a unit in the report of all library activities, showing the relation of circulation work to that of the library as a whole.

Special circumstances occasionally arise that require information not contained in the regular reports. This will necessitate additional reports for a specific period or purpose. For example, when requests arise to open the library for longer periods of time, a record of the hour-by-hour use of the library may enable the librarian to decide and justify policy one way or the other. The records of a circulation department should be arranged so that, within the limits of the statistics collected, any reasonable question may be answered. Staff must record each day's work completely and accurately. The extent to which this is accomplished will depend on the amount and quality of training provided to circulation personnel. More information on the importance of evaluating library services and effective ways of doing so may be found in Chapter 16, Assessment.

SUMMARY

The circulation section is the front line of the library. The work of circulation staff members will define, to a great extent, user satisfaction with the entire library and its program. Circulation staff members work a greater variety of hours and do a wider assortment of jobs than other library employees. The circulation staff member must be a jack- or jane-of-all trades (and master of many) to meet the demands of circulation work. Staff providing circulation services find themselves in greater direct user contact in a wider variety of situations than staff in any other library department. Library media technical assistants who work in circulation will find the work challenging, diversified, interpersonal, and rarely dull.

Chapter Review Material

1. What are two important roles of circulation services?
2. What is the basic philosophy underlying circulation operations?
3. Name some characteristics of successful circulation control systems.
4. What factors are considered when a library selects a circulation system?
5. Why is borrower registration important?
6. Other than checking out materials and checking them in, what are some other functions performed by circulation staff?
7. What is the primary purpose of charging fines? Are there other purposes?
8. What can staff do to lessen the negative impact of fines?
9. How do circulation staff attempt to locate materials when the system fails to provide location information?
10 Why is user relations an important concern?
11. What should govern the manner in which staff respond to problem users?
12. Discuss the issue of confidentiality of circulation records.
13. What two general principles govern the arrangement of materials in most libraries?
14. What is the conceptual basis of both the Dewey decimal and Library of Congress classification systems?
15. What three operations are most commonly identified with stack maintenance?
16. How can circulation staff contribute to the preservation of library materials?
17. What responsibilities for library security do circulation sections commonly share?
18. What is the most effective deterrent to unauthorized removal of library materials?
19. What is the most important characteristic to look for in recruiting circulation personnel? Name some other desirable traits.
20. What are the pros and cons of relying on part-time assistants?
21. What sorts of statistics are commonly maintained by circulation staff? How are they used?

REFERENCES

Ambrose, Lodilla. 1893. "A Study of College Libraries," *Library Journal* 18: 116.

American Library Association (ALA). 1939. "Code of Ethics for Librarians." *A.L.A. Bulletin* 33: 128–130.

———. 2007. *The State of America's Libraries.* Chicago: ALA. http://www.ala.org/ala/pressreleases2007/march2007/SAL_AnnualReport-FINAL.pdf.

Bowers, Stacey L. 2006. "Privacy and Library Records," *The Journal of Academic Librarianship* 32, no. 4: 377–383.

Drews, Jeanne M., and Julie A. Page, eds. 1997. *Promoting Preservation Awareness in Libraries: A Sourcebook for Academic, Public, School and Special Collections.* Westport, CT: Greenwood Press.

Futty, John. 2003. "An Incentive to Read: Library System Lets Children Pay off Fines by Hitting the Books," *The Columbus Dispatch*, July 14, 2003: 1C.

Institute of Museum and Library Services (IMLS). 2002. *Status of Technology and Digitization in the Nation's Libraries, 2002 Report.* Washington, DC: IMLS.

Koch, T. W. 1912. "Some Phases of the Administrative History of College and University Libraries," *ALA Bulletin* 6: 274.

Moorman, John A. 2006. *Running a Small Library.* New York: Neal-Schuman.

Prestebak, Jane, and Konnie Wightman. 2000. "Losing Our Drawers," *School Library Journal.* 46, no. 10: 66–73.

Todaro, Julie, and Mark Smith. 2006. *Training Library Staff and Volunteers to Provide Extraordinary Customer Service.* New York: Neal-Schuman.

Witt, Thomas A. 1996. "The Use of Electronic Book Theft Detection Systems in Libraries," *Journal of Interlibrary Loan, Document Delivery & Information Supply* 6, no. 4: 45–60.

SUGGESTED READINGS

Ditizen, Sidney. 1947. *Arsenals of a Democratic Culture: A Social History of the American Public Library.* Chicago: American Library Association.

Futty, John. 2003. "An Incentive to Read: Library System Lets Children Pay off Fines by Hitting the Books," *The Columbus Dispatch*, July 14, 2003: 1C.

Greiner, Joy M. 1989. "Professional Views: The Philosophy and Practice of Fines and Fees," *Public Libraries* 28, no. 6: 257–261.

Leung, Yau Ching. 2005. "User Education on Circulation Policies," *Journal of Access Services.* 3, no. 1: 37–46.

Martin, M. S. 1998. *Charging and Collecting Fees and Fines: A Handbook for Libraries.* New York: Neal-Schuman.

Prestebak, Jane, and Konnie Wightman. 2000. "Losing Our Drawers," *School Library Journal* 46, no. 10: 67–73.

Ristau, Holly. 1988. "Keeping Your Shelves in Order: Techniques for Training Pages," *School Library Journal* 35, no. 5: 39–43.

Shahid, Syed Md. 2005. "Use of RFID Technology in Libraries: A New Approach to Circulation, Tracking, Inventorying, and Security of Library Materials," *Library Philosophy and Practice* 8, no. 1: 1–9.

Shuman, Bruce A. 1999. *Library Security and Safety Handbook: Prevention, Policies, and Procedures.* Chicago: American Library Association.

Stephens, Claire, and Pat Franklin. 2005. "Management Matters: To Circulate or Not to Circulate: That Is the Question," *School Library Media Activities Monthly* 22, no. 1: 43–44.

Chapter 9

Reserve Services

But a new vice developed itself. Sum of the students in their zeal for lerning wanted it all; and, as these books wer on open shelves where each helpt himself, we soon found that the books most wanted often disappeard.
—Melvil Dewey, 1887 (in his unique spelling style)

For now, in today's world, managing e-reserves is about managing risk.
—Andrew Richard Albanese, 2007

Reserve services are a particular characteristic of libraries serving educational institutions, especially colleges and universities. Instructors sometimes wish to supplement the library collection in order to support their teaching. Instructors assign various types of material, for example, copies of journal articles, teachers' personal copies of books or other instructional materials, videos, copies of quizzes and answers, and so on. Libraries support this instructional endeavor by establishing policies and procedures to make these "reserved" materials available to students.

Reserve service guarantees that assigned material will be available, on a first come, first served basis, for students to use as needed. The service also allows instructors and library staff to place on reserve or make available electronically, within limits, digitized copies of copyrighted materials. This assures their availability in sufficient quantity to meet demand.

ROLE AND PHILOSOPHY OF RESERVE SERVICES

The philosophy of a reserve service is to enhance the teaching and learning process by enabling instructors to temporarily supplement library collections in support of their courses. Electronic reserve systems permit the scanning of document images into a database and their retrieval by students at their convenience, day or night. These systems are becoming popular as a more effective and labor saving means of distributing reserve readings than manual systems.

Reserve services are also used to protect high risk items, that is, material that is likely to be mutilated or stolen if placed on the open shelves. In developing countries, where libraries have few resources, reserve services are more widely used than in affluent countries, primarily to guarantee the availability of scarce items.

Reserve, or assigned, reading is a fairly recent addition to the academic library and appeared towards the end of the nineteenth century. The professional literature contains little about reserve readings before 1900. In 1878, Harvard College, under the heading "Special Reserves," reported the following:

> It is the custom of the professors at Harvard to hand in at the library lists of books to which they intend to refer their classes during the term. These books are reserved from circulation, are covered, and a colored label is pasted on the backs, each professor having a distinctive color. The books are then arranged in an alcove, to which the students have free access . . . Other libraries might adopt this plan for books in which there chanced to be some special interest, so that many people desired to consult them, (Dewey, 1878)

Melvil Dewey reported in the same article that books recommended by professors were placed behind the loan desk at Columbia University: "Each professor is invited to send in lists of books which he wishes withdrawn for a time from circulation and kept in the reading room, so that each student may be sure of the opportunity of consulting them." Dewey goes on to describe "a long slip, (7.5 x 25 cm) five times the size" of the ordinary book card, which was used for charging "restricted reference books" (Dewey, 1887). This long card originated by Dewey is still used in some libraries.

Today's reserve room operates like a mini-library within the larger institution. Staff members accept reserve requests from teachers and faculty, remove books and periodicals from the stacks, and make photocopies of or scan requested items. Reserve personnel bind loose materials so they will withstand heavy use, purchase necessary supplies, and process and house the material in a restricted area. Digitized documents are placed in files created for each instructor and course. Staff also make sure there is copyright compliance, prepare online and print bibliographic aids to facilitate access to the collection, create links to requested articles if they are contained in licensed databases, create links to digitized reserve items in the institution's course management system, check items in and out, administer fines and billing for overdue and lost items, remove material from reserve or disable electronic access when it is no longer needed, and troubleshoot the equipment. In large libraries, the reserve collection may contain thousands of items for hundreds of courses. The items are usually divided between library-owned and teachers' personal materials. The composition of the collection changes each term, and the maintenance of this service requires a significant library commitment of staff, time, and space, although e-reserve is reducing the need for extensive study/reading space for its service.

It is important to note in this discussion that some question the value of reserve services. Writers have commented on the low use of some reserve items, along with the high cost of administration (see, for example, Bradley, 2007; De Jager, 2001; and Self, 1987). Students, faculty, and staff are sometimes critical about various aspects of traditional reserve service. Students complain that material is not put on reserve fast enough, that service is poor and waiting times too long. Teachers sometimes also protest about the time it takes to process assigned material, about the amount of work they must do before material goes on reserve, and about copyright limitations. Library staff complain about the amount of time it takes to process materials, that faculty do not give them sufficient time to process reserve items before assigning them, do not appreciate or adhere to copyright restrictions, place excess quantities of material on reserve that students never look at, and are slow to remove items when they are no longer assigned.

In addition to these complaints, there are pedagogic arguments against reserve services. There is evidence that using assigned reserve materials has no significant influence on academic performance. A study at the University of Virginia measured the correlation between over 8,000 students' use of reserve materials and the grades they received in their courses. The study revealed only a weak connection between reserve use and grades. The study also revealed that depending on reserve readings may even obstruct the educational process. Relying on reserve services to provide library materials may discourage students from using the rest of the library and learning necessary library use skills. It also prevents the serendipitous discovery of information that occurs through normal library use (Self, 1987).

These arguments notwithstanding, reserve operations are present and very popular in many libraries. Third-world libraries rely on reserve readings more than libraries in affluent countries because of the lack of available books and periodicals. In developed countries, students' preference for digital information and the spread of electronic reserve services have increased the popularity of reserve systems. Recent studies of electronic reserve systems reveal that students tend to prefer digital reserves to traditional reserve services. Freedom from the restrictions of limited numbers of copies and short circulation periods result in greater use of digital reserves than their print counterparts and greater satisfaction with the service (Isenberg, 2006; Jacoby and Laskowski, 2004; Pilston and Hart, 2002).

ARRANGEMENT AND STORAGE

Generally, traditional reserve materials like books and videos are removed from the circulating collection by library staff or teachers. In the case of materials owned by the instructors, they are delivered to the library and, along with the library materials, placed in a special room or area within the library with controlled access. Although reserve readings were originally housed in open stacks, most libraries now have a closed stack system for reserves or a combination of open and closed stacks. The argument for closed stacks was stated convincingly by Dewey (in his inimitable simplified spelling system) in our opening quotation.

Activity around the reserve area is heavy, and the location of the service should be carefully planned. The room or service point must be easy to find and traffic to and from the area should not interfere with other library operations. In smaller libraries, the reserve collection is often part of the circulation desk activities. Locating the reserve room outside of the library building has been tried and found wanting due to the inconvenience for users and staff. The only reasonable rationale for doing so is the temporary alleviation of space problems. As most reserve material may not be taken out of the library, it is a good idea to have photocopy machines located nearby.

The primary criterion for arranging material in the reserve area is to enable staff to locate and easily retrieve the items requested by students. Staff generally house unclassified materials and professors' personal copies on bookshelves arranged by course number or the instructor's name. Sometimes unclassified materials receive an accession number and are arranged numerically. Classified materials may be grouped with other material for a course or filed separately by call number. Housing for photocopies and other loose materials is problematic. Some libraries place photocopied materials in binders; some staple the pages together and place them in cardboard boxes or manila folders; and others arrange them in file cabinets. Media, too, can be housed with the rest of the material for a course or remain in special media housing. Scanned documents are indexed in the reserve database or the reserve module of the ILS so files for particular professors or courses can be easily retrieved, generally by department, professor's name, title and author of the document, course name, course number, and section number.

ACCESS

Making reserve readings accessible requires several different steps. The first step is to persuade instructors to submit their reserve lists or materials in a timely manner. The greatest amount of processing work, which is time consuming, comes at the beginning of the semester or academic term. To help guarantee that staff will have enough time to prepare materials for circulation or scan them into a database and index them, nearly all libraries request that faculty place material on reserve at least two weeks before classes begin. Nevertheless, many teachers do not submit materials until just before or even after they have assigned them.

Once staff process reserve materials, access depends on students knowing what items are on reserve. All students and instructors must be able to tell which materials are removed from public access to the reserve room, and students need to know what materials are placed on reserve by their instructors.

Libraries with ILSs have an answer to many of these problems. A message can be attached to any record in the online catalog indicating that the item is "on reserve." The most popular ILSs have reserve modules integrated with the library's OPAC, and there are commercial stand-alone alternatives as well, which can be integrated into the library Web site. Reserve modules permit staff to list all items, including nonlibrary and scanned materials kept on reserve.

Students typically access reserve holdings by searching for the teacher's or faculty member's name, the course name or number, the author, or the title (see Figure 9.1). Digital items, scanned by library staff or linked to licensed databases, may be retrieved with a click and downloaded or printed, while physical items may be checked out at the reserve desk. Faculty and teachers using course management systems, like Blackboard, often include links to scanned images in the reserve system from their course pages.

Printed lists of items on reserve may be located at the reserve desk itself for public consultation. These lists may take the form of card files, or typed or handwritten lists filed in three-ring binders with entries arranged by instructor's name or course number. There are two essential characteristics of these lists in whatever form they take: they must be user-friendly so both customers and staff may easily identify wanted items, and they must be flexible enough to permit easy updating as items are added and withdrawn throughout the term.

The policy of restricting access to reserve materials begs the question of who is and is not permitted to borrow the material. As we have seen, the reserve room's reason for being is to guarantee access to materials for students in particular classes; this is the rationale for closed stacks and limited circulation periods. Access to a professor's personal copies or to scanned documents is generally denied to all but those students authorized by the instructor to use the material. For personal copies this is to protect the materials. For scanned images, it is to attempt to stay within the "fair use" provisions of copyright law. However, access to library-owned materials on reserve is given to other authorized library users, although they must abide by the same use restrictions specified by the instructor. This practice is consistent with the philosophy of equitable access to information.

Access to traditional materials is obtained by readers coming to the reserve desk and requesting the items. Digital reserve collections, accessed via the Web, are available to authorized students anywhere the student has a computer, network connection, and password (see Figure 9.2). This makes digital reserve items much more accessible than traditional collections and extremely important for students taking classes through distance education. These students are not readily able to come to the library, and a database of scanned images allows them to get the readings they need for their coursework. As a result of their potential for anytime/anywhere access, digital reserves have

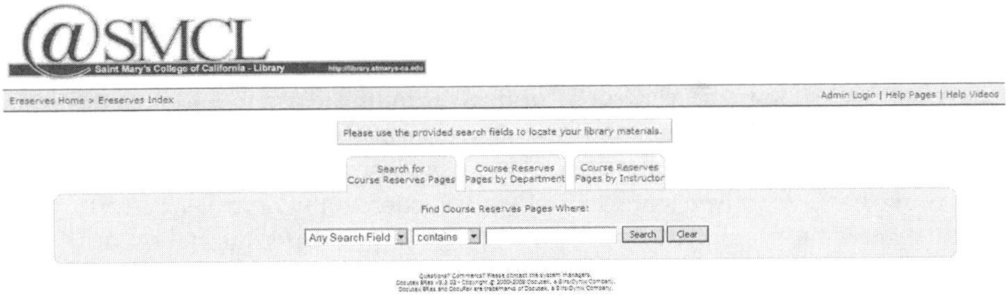

Figure 9.1 Reserves Search Page. Courtesy SirsiDynix. All rights reserved.

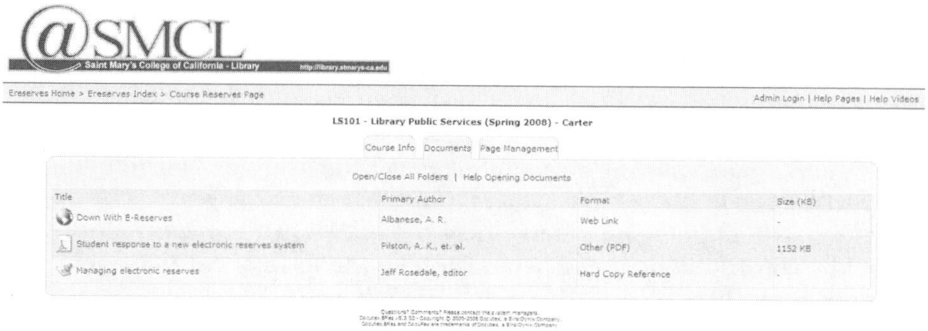

Figure 9.2 Reserves List. Courtesy SirsiDynix. All rights reserved.

great utility for facilitating distance education courses and should become more common as distance education offerings increase.

It is the reserve supervisor's responsibility to monitor the demand for traditional library materials placed on reserve. Because of their reference value or popularity, access to some books should not be restricted by placing them on reserve. If the value of placing a particular book or library item on reserve is overshadowed by the inconvenience it causes other library customers, an alternative to restricting access to the material should be found.

TEACHER AND FACULTY RELATIONS

Diplomacy with regard to teacher and faculty relations is important in all aspects of public services, but especially so in the reserve room. Teachers and faculty probably take a greater personal interest in the reserve room than in any other service, except perhaps ILL. This is because they believe reserve services play an important role in supporting their day-to-day classroom instruction. Teachers and faculty will often have the majority of their contact with library personnel at the reserve desk. Consequently, they will form their opinion of the importance and value of the library from the quality of these interactions and the service they receive.

The nature of many of these encounters between reserve staff and instructors, however, is sensitive. They sometimes involve requests to change policy or procedures to meet the desires of a particular instructor. The exceptions teachers typically request include processing their items ahead of others, placing more items on reserve than normally allowed, substituting different loan periods than those offered, leaving items on reserve for extended periods (sometimes called "permanent reserve"), and overlooking copyright restrictions on photocopying (see "Ethical and Legal Considerations" in this chapter). Communicating with faculty on these and other points requires finesse and reserve staff must have good interpersonal skills in order to negotiate effectively.

Staff must be both sympathetic to a teacher's particular needs and able to make exceptions to policy when appropriate. There may be nothing wrong with placing materials on reserve after the normal deadline or accepting more material than policy allows if doing so will benefit the students in a particular course, and if the decision does not create problems for others. Some requests, however, would compromise the efficient operations of the service or perhaps be illegal under copyright law. Staff must be able to refuse courteously and explain the reason for the denial and, if possible, offer alternative solutions. Administrators responsible for reserve services should carefully select personnel who possess good interpersonal skills and train them to negotiate effectively with faculty and other users.

CIRCULATION OF RESERVE ITEMS

Whether a library uses a manual or automated system, or both, the process of circulating physical reserve items is more complex than that performed at the circulation desk. There are several characteristics of reserve collections that make this so: the processing required to prepare items for circulation, numerous loan periods and fine schedules, the number of nonlibrary and nonbook materials circulated, and the ever-changing composition of the collection.

Automated Circulation

Effective automated reserve systems present greater challenges than automated circulation systems. This is because it is more complex to program the system to handle the large number of different loan periods and item types. Nevertheless, effective reserve modules do exist and they greatly simplify reserve operations. Scanned items in online reserve systems are retrieved directly by students without intervention by library staff. The following pertains to the automated circulation of physical items.

As personnel add items to the reserve collection, they identify them by course, instructor, and circulation period. They enter this information into the reserve system and link it to the item's existing bar code, or to a new dumb bar code, which they attach to the item itself or to a book card created for the item. As items circulate, reserve personnel employ a bar code reader to read or wand the item bar code and the borrower's ID into the system. The time due is stamped on the date due slip and the transaction is complete.

Discharging the items is equally simple. The system is placed in the discharge mode and a staff member scans each item's bar code to remove the link between the patron and item, and the material is ready for reshelving. The system automatically records overdue information, calculates fines, and generates overdue and fine notices.

Manual Circulation

When instructors deliver items to the reserve area, staff must first process them for reserve circulation. Each item, whether book, photocopy, teacher's personal copy, or other type of material, must be identified with the following information: instructor's name, course number, circulation period, and any use limitations applicable, such as "Reserve Book Room use only" or "Library use only."

A common way to identify materials is to type or print the information for each item on two book cards, including a special long book card like that described by Dewey earlier in the chapter. Staff either insert the cards into the book pocket of library books or paper-clip them to the item. Often, libraries use color-coded cards to indicate different circulation periods. Borrowers write their name and/or identification numbers on the long card, which serves as the circulation record, while the other card remains with the item and identifies it when the item returns. An additional preparation step required for photocopies is to affix a copyright notice on them if one does not already appear (see "Ethical and Legal Considerations").

Once processed and housed as described earlier, the item is ready for circulation. One distinguishing feature of reserve circulation is the number of different loan periods. Most reserve materials circulate for very brief periods; for example, one hour, two hours, or overnight. This is enough time to allow students to read or view a short document or film or to photocopy an item.

As each item circulates, staff records the time it is due. A time clock is sometimes used to stamp the time due on the book cards, or the attendant uses a date stamp to record the date or simply write the date and the time due on the cards. For items with longer circulation periods, for example, one, two, or seven days, date-stamping the two cards is sufficient for circulation control. Staff file the checkout cards together according to circulation period (one-hour cards together, one-day cards together, and so on) for easy retrieval when items return. It is usual to require students to return reserve materials directly to the reserve desk to avoid any delay in their being available to other students.

When items return to the reserve desk, someone pulls the checkout cards, matches the cards with the items, and checks for delinquency. Borrowers' names and the times due are blocked or canceled in some way for timely returns and they are returned to the shelves for further use. Overdue items are marked with the return time and processed for fines and billing.

With hourly circulation periods and high use, the potential for many overdue items in traditional reserve collections is great. Reserve departments, like circulation, dislike spending the time and effort required to process overdue fines (especially if, as in many cases, the library does not get to keep the money collected). Most reserve services try to discourage overdues by publicizing heavy fine schedules, for example, $1.00 per hour, $10.00 per day, and so on. Nevertheless, borrowers return many hourly checkouts late. As long as other users are not inconvenienced, reserve personnel often allow generous grace periods to avoid a massive billing operation. Exceptions to these grace periods occur when the overdues are flagrant or, especially, when other students are denied access to the information. Libraries also levy fines for damaged or lost materials.

ADMINISTRATION

On most library organization charts the reserve room appears under the authority of the circulation section. Most commonly, the circulation supervisor or a paraprofessional reporting to the head of circulation supervises the service. The individual in charge of reserve must be experienced, as many problems arise requiring mature judgment, tact, and well-developed interpersonal skills.

The supervisor of reserve services does more than merely oversee an inventory control operation. Service at a reserve desk housing many physical materials is at times the most frenetic and mechanical in the library. More than in any other public service, reserve staff are subject to periods of stress resulting from waves of heavy user demand. The first wave rises like a tsunami at the beginning of each academic term when instructors flood the area with their reserve lists. These requests and the items to be processed often pile up faster than staff can handle, and there is pressure to prepare the material for circulation as soon as possible before the readings are assigned. Once the term begins, several waves of students break against the reserve desk each day as class periods end and borrowers arrive to get their assigned readings. These waves may increase to tsunami proportions again at examination times, especially towards the end of the term. The administrator selects, trains, and schedules staff to accommodate the fluctuations in activity inherent in reserve service.

The supervisor is also responsible for removing unused permanent reserve materials from the collection, and removing materials, or the link to the virtual equivalent, which may be in violation of copyright. Since unused physical items unnecessarily increase the size of the collection, they may delay service. In addition, they are not available for regular library use. The supervisor may also be responsible for maintaining satisfactory study conditions in the reserve reading area, as noisy students make it difficult to study.

Personnel Selection and Training

The reserve supervisor selects, trains, and supervises the work of the reserve staff, most of whom are students. The supervisor must make sure employees have work to do during slack periods, but that other duties do not interfere with service delivery.

In selecting personnel for the reserve book room, administrators consider the unique characteristics of the service. As a first criterion, reserve staff must have good interpersonal skills. This includes the ability to always interact courteously and politely with customers. Situations arise requiring patient explanation of procedures and policies to frustrated teachers and students. Other occasions require tactful clarification of the restrictions placed on availability of materials including copyright restrictions on digital and physical materials.

As in all circulation work, the ability to perform detailed work accurately is required in reserve. Also important is the ability to work under pressure. As described above, the volume of business at the reserve desk can seem quite frantic at times. Employees must be able to stand the pace until the demand eventually slackens.

Punctuality is a necessity. Students must arrive on time to replace others leaving for class. Service will suffer if there are not enough personnel to staff the desk when help is needed. The ability to work nights and weekends is also necessary as the reserve book room is normally open for service whenever the library is open.

Scheduling

To schedule staff effectively, the administrator must be familiar with the use patterns of reserve materials. The busiest periods at the reserve desk occur several times each day when classes are dismissed and students arrive en masse to check out the readings just assigned. Another busy time is at the beginning and end of each term, when additional help is sometimes needed to handle the processing required to add and remove items from reserve. The supervisor, sometimes in coordination with the circulation head, must schedule adequate staffing at these times to prevent queuing problems.

Inexperienced employees are usually scheduled with experienced personnel who can assist in their training. The reserve schedule must also make provision for nights and weekends, when full-time staff may not be available to assist with busy periods. Staffing schedules must provide enough backup to guarantee service during the inevitable illnesses, vacations, and other absences. In some libraries the reserve room serves as a study hall when the library is closed, and staffing is scheduled to meet these hours.

Keeping and Using Statistics

Planning for good service requires the analysis of information from accurate statistical records of reserve book room activity. Statistics can track circulation volume by time of day and season and user population to allow an accurate picture of use patterns and facilitate effective scheduling. Statistics can also measure how many times the different kinds of material circulate so the supervisor can project space and supply needs. Finally, a record of how often each individual item is used should be maintained. A heavily used personal item may be a candidate for purchase by the library, while library-owned books may be considered for duplicate copies. Library materials receiving little or no use are candidates for weeding from reserve.

In an automated reserve operation, the system tabulates these statistics automatically. With a manual system, staff members maintain hourly records of circulation activity. Along with the individual item data, the reserve supervisor analyzes these data in order to provide the appropriate planning information.

ETHICAL AND LEGAL CONSIDERATIONS

The principle guaranteeing the confidentiality of circulation records is the same in reserve as in circulation. Even though the reading is required and assigned by a teacher, no one has a right to know what anyone else reads without that person's permission. Faculty wishing to find out which students have done the required reading for their class may find it difficult to understand this principle. To reveal the circulation records, however, violates the library's responsibility to guard the intellectual freedom of the students. The question may arise whether teachers have the right to see the circulation records for personally owned items placed on reserve: the answer is that they do not.

While the materials are in the custody of the library, the principle of confidentiality applies to all materials issued and controlled by the library, even if only temporarily held.

The library may, however, furnish the instructor with information that does not violate borrower confidentiality. Statistics may, for example, be provided on the number of times an item circulated for a particular course. Information can also be furnished on the number of individual students who checked out reserve material. Any information that does not violate individual borrower confidentiality may be provided as a service to teachers.

The most vexing legal consideration in reserve operations is adherence to copyright law. Copyright law permits the copyright holder exclusive rights to reproduce, distribute, adapt, perform, and display their creations. However, federal law recognizes that the public should also have some access to copyrighted information without having to ask permission or pay royalties. The "fair use" exemption is the most applicable provision for libraries: "Fair use of a copyrighted work, including such use by reproduction in copies . . . for purposes such as criticism, comment, news reporting, teaching (including multiple copies for classroom use) scholarship, or research, is not an infringement of copyright . . ." (17 USC § 107).

With traditional reserve collections, only original book or journal volumes were on reserve so there were no copyright concerns. But instructors sometimes ask the library to make copies of various materials and place them on reserve, or they will bring in already-made copies for placement on reserve. With requests to reproduce items for reserve, especially journal articles and book chapters, copyright law entered the picture.

The criteria libraries use to determine whether use or reproduction of a copyrighted work qualifies as fair use includes four factors:

1. *The purpose and character of the use.* Is the use for a commercial or educational purpose?
2. *The nature of the work.* Is the copyrighted item a work of fiction or a factual work?
3. *The amount and substantiality of the portion copied.* Copying a limited portion points more toward fair use.
4. *The effect on the market value.* Will use affect the publisher's sales?

Each of these factors carries the same weight, and library policies attempt to balance the factors so they are weighted in favor of fair use.

To help guide libraries with respect to requests for photocopies, the ALA adopted the *Model Policy Concerning College and University Photocopying for Classroom, Research and Library Reserve.* (American Library Association, 1982). Among the restrictions recommended for materials photocopied for reserve are the following:

1. The distribution of the same material should not occur every semester.
2. Only one copy per student.

3. The material should include a copyright notice.

4. The students are not assessed any fee beyond photocopying costs (Gasaway, 2002).

For multiple copies placed on reserve the *Model Policy* specifies that the amount and number of copies should be "reasonable," given the nature of the course and the assignments, that the copies should contain a copyright notice, and that the photocopying should not be detrimental to the market for the work.

Although it has no legal standing, many libraries used the *Model Policy* as a basis for their photocopying guidelines. Interpretations of "reasonable" numbers of copies ranged from one to several to a number equaling the number of students in a particular course. The ALA's 1982 policy is vague in a number of areas. If the reserve staff decides a reserves request does not meet fair use criteria, the safest course for a library is to request permission from the copyright holder or ask the faculty member to request permission from the copyright holder, or request that the faculty member do so before photocopying material for reserve.

However difficult and confusing copyright is with relationship to traditional items, it is even more so when considering digital sources. Growing up in a Google world, students today expect rapid and seamless access to digital information resources. Digitizing copyrighted works involves copying and distribution, so it must conform to copyright law. Libraries are in the difficult position of trying to provide access to digital resources while remaining in copyright compliance regarding digitizing requests. While copyright law offers no clear and direct answers about the scope of fair use for electronic reserves, a number of different interpretations of the law may be found in the literature.

Questions about the applicability of fair use standards to digitized images generally revolve around the number of potential viewers of an image, the transmission of the images beyond the educational setting of the library or classroom, and the potential for printing, downloading, or copying the images to undermine restricted access. In 1994, the Conference on Fair Use—CONFU—(Lehman, 1998) was convened to try and address the meaning of fair use in a digital world. Librarians, educators, and publishers struggled for two years to but were unable to reach consensus on electronic reserves. However, the draft e-reserve guidelines, the *Fair Use Guidelines for Electronic Reserve Systems* (http://www.utsystem.edu/ogc/intellectualProperty/rsrvguid.htm), have been adopted by some libraries as a basis for their digital reserve copying policies. Essentially, the *Guidelines* recommend that libraries follow the same fair use guidelines that pertain to paper copies of copyrighted material. Images should be limited to single articles or chapters or several graphs, charts, or illustrations, or other small parts of a work, and they should be copies of legally obtained materials. Included with the images should be a copyright notice, and permission should be obtained for materials used repeatedly by the same instructor for the same class. Finally, access should be limited to students enrolled in the class and to library staff as needed, and access should be terminated at the end of the class term.

Library and higher education associations did not endorse the CONFU guidelines because they were seen as too restrictive (while publishers felt they were not restrictive enough). A more recent development is the Association of Research Libraries' 2003 statement, *Applying Fair Use in the Development of Electronic Reserves Systems* (http://www.arl.org/pp/ppcopyright/copyright resources/applying.shtml). This statement stresses the importance of relying on the four fair use factors as the basis for an electronic reserves policy.

Some libraries' approaches to the copyright question have been conservative, including seeking permission to digitize any copyrighted work. Most libraries take a middle ground, relying on fair use guidelines developed at their institution. Typically articles, book chapters, and other documents are scanned and posted for students in a particular class, with access discontinued at the end of the school term. Increasingly, libraries make sure that license agreements for full text journal collections allow linking to the articles for reserve use, a practice that eliminates the need for scanning and worries about copyright. Audiovisual works are generally added sparingly to reserve systems. Images are sometimes scanned and posted, but in many cases an image is a complete work so the amount factor in the fair use test weighs against use (Ferullo, 2002, p. 35). As Albanese (2007) notes, "For now, in today's world, managing e-reserves is about managing risk." A library's policy on copying will generally reflect the institution's risk tolerance for litigation and libraries should seek legal counsel before adopting an electronic reserve policy.

SECURITY AND PRESERVATION

Because of their high use, physical reserve materials suffer a great deal of wear and tear. It is important for staff to handle reserve items carefully to help prolong their life and value as instructional aids. When withdrawn from reserve, books especially should have all extra inserts, paper clips and other added materials removed. (If paper clips have rusted in place, they should be pried away from the paper, which will prevent tearing.)

Training staff in the proper techniques of handling the various materials placed on reserve will help prevent damage. The physical process of digitizing is quite similar to photocopying, so the same care must be taken to ensure book and bound journal bindings are not damaged. Media should be stored in appropriate housing. Binders or folders help protect photocopied or other loose materials from the damage that accompanies high use. If there is time, staff may educate borrowers about ways to avoid damage while photocopying, or posters or other materials may be used to caution them. Staff should also identify materials needing preventive minor repair. Repairs should be done promptly so materials will last, both during and after their stint in reserve.

Administrators train staff to pay special attention to security and preservation of teacher-owned materials in the reserve collection. Personal materials such as books, videos, and other items may be easily stolen, so care must be taken to verify and record borrower identification information before the materials circulate. As the practice of digitizing reserve materials becomes more common, the concerns of reserve staff for the preservation and security of physical items will necessarily decrease.

SUMMARY

Reserve services are viewed by many faculty and teachers as a valuable adjunct to their teaching. They provide a way to supplement the library collections in direct support of their classes. They also help guarantee students' access to materials that are either required reading or pertinent to their classes. The volume of business at a reserve desk tends to be cyclic throughout the day, corresponding to class periods, and during the school term, with busy periods at the beginning and end of the term.

Photocopying of copyrighted items is generally permitted under the fair use provisions of copyright law, although subject to restrictions such as the quantity of material copied and the number of copies made. Because of the issues of duplication and distribution inherent in digital copies available through the Web, offering digital reserves is a particular challenge to libraries in educational settings. However, the fair use exemption in copyright law is interpreted by many institutions as allowing access to digitized information, restricted to students in a particular course and for limited time periods. Electronic reserves greatly increase access to reserve readings, once a library adopts a policy that conforms to its interpretation of copyright law, and an increase in electronic reserves is a trend we expect to see continue.

However, reserve service is costly to maintain and often underutilized. These arguments suggest that libraries facing personnel shortages or space limitations should consider carefully the value of continuing full reserve service before cutting more essential services and resources.

Chapter Review Material

1. What is the role of reserve services?
2. Why do some question the value of reserve services?
3. How is reserve material usually arranged? Why?
4. How do library staff provide access to physical materials placed on reserve?
5. How is access provided to digital materials?
6. Who is permitted to use reserve materials?
7. Why is attention to teacher/faculty relations especially important for reserve staff?
8. Describe the processing necessary to prepare physical and digital reserve items for circulation.
9. What is the major identifying characteristic of reserve circulation?
10. Name the most important criterion for selecting reserve personnel.
11. Discuss the importance of confidentiality of records in reserve.
12. What is the most important legal consideration for reserve staff?
13. How do reserve staff participate in library preservation? How are materials protected from wear and tear?
14. What are some advantages of electronic reserve systems? Disadvantages?

REFERENCES

Albanese, Andrew Richard. 2007. "Down with E-Reserves," *Library Journal* 32, no. 16: 36–38.

American Library Association. 1982. "Model Policy Concerning College and University Photocopying for Classroom, Research and Library Reserve Use," *College & Research Libraries News* 43: 127.

Association of Research Libraries. 2003. *Applying Fair Use in the Development of Electronic Reserves Systems.* Chicago: American Library Association. http://www.arl.org/pp/ppcopyright/copyrightresources/applying.shtml.

Bradley, Karen. 2007. "Reading Noncompliance: A Case Study and Reflection," *Mountainrise: The International Journal of the Scholarship of Teaching and Learning* 4, no. 1: 1–16.

De Jager, Karin. 2001. "Impacts and Outcomes: Searching for the Most Elusive Indicators of Academic Library Performance," In *Meaningful Measures for Emerging Realities, Proceedings of the 4th Northumbria International Conference on Performance Measurement in Libraries and Information Services.* Washington, DC: Association of Research Libraries, pp. 291–297.

Dewey, Melvil. 1878. "Special Reserves," *Library Journal* 3: 271.

Dewey, Melvil. 1887. "Restricted Reference Books," *Library Notes* 2: 216.

Ferullo, Donna L. 2002. "The Challenge of E-Reserves." *School Library Journal Net Connect.* Summer: 33–35.

Gasaway, Laura N. 2002. "Copyright Considerations for Electronic Reserves." In *Managing Electronic Reserves*, Jeff Rosedale, ed. Chicago: American Library Association.

Isenberg, Laurie. 2006. "Online Course Reserves and Graduate Student Satisfaction," *Journal of Academic Librarianship* 32, no.2: 166–172.

Jacoby, JoAnn, and Mary S. Laskowski. 2004. "Measurement and Analysis of Electronic Reserve Usage," *Libraries and the Academy* 4, no. 2: 219–232.

Lehman, Bruce A. 1998. *The Conference on Fair Use: Final Report to the Commissioner on the Conclusion of the Conference on Fair Use.* Washington, DC: U.S. Patent and Trademark Office. http://uspto.gov/web/offices/dcom/olia/confu/confurep.pdf.

Pilston, Anna Klump, and Richard L. Hart. 2002. "Student Response to a New Electronic Reserves System," *Journal of Academic Librarianship* 28, no. 3: 147–151.

Self, James. 1987. "Reserve Readings and Student Grades: Analysis of a Case Study," *Library and Information Science Reports* 9, no. 1: 29–40.

SUGGESTED READINGS

Association of College and Research Libraries. 2003. *Statement on Fair Use and Electronic Reserves.* Chicago: American Library Association. http://www.ala.org/ala/acrl/acrlpubs/whitepapers/statementfair.cfm.

Austin, Bruce. (2004). *Reserves, Electronic Reserves, and Copyright: The Past and the Future.* Binghamton, NY: Haworth Press.

Gasaway, Laura N. 2002. "Copyright Considerations for Electronic Reserves." In *Managing Electronic Reserves*, Jeff Rosedale, ed. Chicago: American Library Association.

Neyer, Linda, and Thomas W. Leonhardt. 2006. "Copyright and Fair Use: Electronic Reserves," *Handbook of Electronic & Digital Acquisitions*. Binghamton, NY: Haworth Press, pp. 21–40.

Rosedale, Jeff, ed. 2002. *Managing Electronic Reserves.* Chicago: American Library Association.

Smith, Donny. 2003. "A Copyright Primer for Electronic Reserve: Copyright for Harried Electronic Reserve Staff," *Journal of Interlibrary Loan, Document Delivery & Information Supply* 13, no. 4: 79–90.

Stevens, Norman D. 1978. "A Hard Look at Reserve," *The Journal of Academic Librarianship* 4, no. 2: 86–87.

Warner, David. 2006. "Electronic Reserves: A Changed Landscape," *Journal of Interlibrary Loan, Document Delivery & Electronic Reserves* 16, no. 4: 125–133.

Chapter 10

Serial Services

More is demanded to produce one wise man today, than seven formerly; and more is needed to deal with a single individual in our times, than with a whole people in the past.
—Baltasar Gracian, *A Truthtelling Manual and the Art of Worldly Wisdom*, 1653

Love e-journals or hate them, one thing a library cannot do is ignore them.
—Margaret Sylvia, 2005

Much has changed over the 30-plus years that this title has been in print. One of the areas of public service that probably has evolved more than others is serials work.

Certainly technology has modified almost every aspect of library operations, but its impact on many activities, if not most, has been in how we do something—via computer operations—rather than what we do. With serials, at least for the electronic versions (or e-serials), the what is done is very different now (a few examples being the elimination of activities such as check-in, labeling issues, inserting security strips, shelving and reshelving, searching for missing issues, gathering up issues to go to the bindery, or shifting of bound copies [well, at least not for the e-only titles] to make room for new volumes). Obviously, while these advances are major changes in the way serials work is done—all those steps do still apply to paper-based serials in the vast majority of libraries.

A shift to e-serials is an ongoing process in most libraries, as they secure the necessary funding or are able to leverage the price advantages of consortial pricing of publishers' or aggregators' packages. Some academic libraries have established a policy that electronic versions of serials are the first choice rather than paper. However, there are some reasons beyond cost that many libraries are and will continue to retain paper titles, perhaps in addition to an e-version. Any library that offers "recreational" reading materials is likely keep subscriptions to paper versions of the most popular serials—magazines and newspapers. There are still people who enjoy sitting and reading the entire issue of a magazine or newspaper. Although it is possible to do this with electronic publications, the process is cumbersome, time consuming, and not all that pleasant. There are also individuals who enjoy looking at the advertisements; something that is generally omitted in the e-version. From a library point of view, having a user tie up a computer for an hour or more while reading all of the articles in a journal is rarely practical, as few libraries have sufficient machines to allow more than a limited time per user. Another factor is many people don't have home access to high-speed broadband network connections. Downloading even a relatively small PDF containing modest graphics with a dial-up connection takes a very long time. Another factor is the escalating cost of subscriptions, even for individuals, which translates into people depending on libraries for access to some of their lower interest journals/magazines.

From a public service point of view, currency is the most important factor for individuals who use serials, except for those engaged in historical research. Related to currency is the frequency with which information is updated. For books that do go into new editions, and only a small percentage do so, the updating interval is a number of years. However, for serials, the update interval can be very short, daily in the case of many newspapers. Articles in a serial are usually short and focus on a fairly narrow subject. Readers with very specific information needs frequently find that serials provide the desired data more quickly than books. Finally, serials are often the first printed source of information about a new subject or development. People use serials as a source for learning about new things while using books to gain a broader or deeper knowledge of a subject they may have first encountered in a serial. Also, the sheer volume of "new" information appearing in serials far exceeds that of books.

In some disciplines, especially the sciences, serial publications are *the* basis for research and other scholarly activities. Corporate library collections also contain a high percentage of serial publications. Given the diversity of topics covered in serials and the number of titles on a topic, few if any individuals can afford to subscribe to all the titles of interest. They therefore depend on libraries to supplement their personal subscription lists. (Something that the Internet enthusiasts often fail to mention is that significant serials, from a scholarly point of view, are *not* available on the Web free of charge. They may be available to you, if you have a paid subscription and a password—but even then, issues are frequently embargoed—or issued online only after a specified time period has passed, presumably so individuals will seek out print versions.) As subscription prices rise, individuals often drop their subscriptions and plan to use the library's title in paper or electronic form. Perhaps the only type of library not facing the problem of high demand, in part due to individuals canceling their subscriptions, is the school library. Certainly the science and engineering libraries in government, business, and academic settings face heavy user demand and escalating prices for serials. Public libraries serving businesses as well as individuals are experiencing similar problems.

Given the foregoing, for some time to come libraries will have a mix of both paper-based and e-serials as a part of their service programs. The mix increases the complexity of providing users with quality serial services. Serials, print and electronic, produce thousand of pages of new material every day. What might Baltasar Gracian (the author of our opening quotation) have to say about what it takes to produce a "wise person" in today's flood of information? Just the output of serials in less than a year far outstrips all the information available in 1653. Keeping up to date is a challenge for most of us and serials play a major role in our efforts to stay reasonably current. E-versions make the information available more quickly, but one of the challenges is to find the time to get to it.

For many people, there is a belief that the Internet is the ready answer. They, like Laurence Hawker (a character in a novel by Simon Brett), have a somewhat inaccurate view of the e-environment: "There's the whole Internet out there . . . Brilliant for my sort of work. Researching articles, going through newspapers for references. The amount you can download is wonderful. University libraries hardly get used these days" (Brett, 2003, pp.168–169). Perhaps, if Brett's character had used some university's Web site to access his information, the opinion stated might have some limited merit—you can often have access to library databases through the Internet. What is overlooked by the general public and many of the cheerleaders for the Internet is most of the serial information that one can place a high degree of trust in and that is available through the Internet requires a payment for access (paid for by someone or some institution) and a password—it is not free.

Serials (magazines, journals, newspapers, etc.) are one of the high-interest collection areas for many people. Serials are generally the first place where new ideas, news, and developments in subjects appear. Currency is the goal of most serial publications. For the library staff, helping users gain access to the material is a constant challenge. "Where is today's copy of the *New York Times*? I've looked for it for more than 30 minutes," or, "I can't seem to access the *New York Times* online, what's the problem?" Variations of the preceding are heard every day at public service desks.

WHAT IS A SERIAL?

Just what is a "serial"? Librarianship has its share of jargon and the topic of this chapter contributes more than its share to that pool. The public may use the term *magazines* or *periodicals*. A few people will ask for *journals*. In the library world, all three terms are labels for publications that fall into the broad class of materials called *serials* and each has a slightly different meaning.

Serials are a little like breakfast cereals: They come in a variety of forms, with something to suit almost anyone's taste and interests. "Serial" is an all-inclusive term encompassing many publication variations in form, content, and purpose. The *ALA Glossary of Library and Information Science* (American Library Association, 1983) provides the following definitions:

> *Serial*—A publication issued in successive parts, usually at regular intervals, and, as a rule, intended to be continued indefinitely.

Serials include periodicals, annuals (reports, yearbooks, etc.) and memoirs, proceedings, and transactions of societies.

Periodical—A publication with a distinctive title intended to appear in successive (usually unbound) numbers of parts at stated or regular intervals and, as a rule, for an indefinite time. Each part generally contains articles by several contributors. Newspapers, whose chief function it is to disseminate news, and the memoirs, proceedings, journals, etc. of societies are not considered periodicals.

There is overlap in the ALA definitions. General dictionaries, however, have even greater overlap and frequently use phrases such as "a journal is a magazine" or "a magazine is a periodical." Thus, it is not surprising that users, and sometimes library staff, use these terms interchangeably.

A number of years ago, Fritz Machlup (1978) developed an 18-part serial classification system covering all types of serials, including one for serials "not elsewhere classified." We have yet to encounter a serial that does not fit into one of the other 17 categories. Because it is a comprehensive system, we use it as the basis for this section and we will cover eight of the most common categories found in many libraries.

Institutional Reports

This category covers annuals, semi-annuals, quarterlies, and occasional reports of organizations. Within this group are the financial reports of corporations and financial institutions, a form widely collected by academic and corporate libraries as well as larger public libraries. Two characteristics of all the publications in this class are important for public service staff. First, most of these publications are relatively short (15–30 pages) and second, they are often smaller than the 8-by-11-inch format. Generally, libraries do not classify such items, and house them in file boxes or filing cabinets. If your library collects these items, keeping the files in order is an area of concern for public services. Typically the reports are filed in alphabetical order by the name of the issuing organization. When the name of the issuing body is not prominently displayed on the cover, some type of label or marking system is necessary to highlight the proper filing name. Online finding aids can be useful in helping point users to these resources.

Yearbooks and Proceedings

Annuals, biennials, and occasional publications of societies and associations constitute another common serial found in libraries. These yearbooks, almanacs, proceedings, transactions, memoirs, directories, and reports are usually already bound or stapled. Most of the publications in this category are substantial in length and size, and many libraries normally treat them as books. The only problem this group may give to public service staff occurs with those titles for which the current year volume is in the reference area and older volumes are in the stacks. Knowing what the *current year* is for a title and where to find it can cause frustration for both the staff and users. Delays of months and, all too often, years can occur between the issues of society or professional association yearbooks, annuals, or directories, which can cause confusion for everyone. This delay makes it perfectly possible that even though the calendar year may be 2008, the *current year* for a society annual may be 2004.

Superseding Serials

In the past, the most problematic serial category was the superseding serial service. This was and occasionally still is a publication in which each new issue or part supersedes the previous issue/part and the library discards the older material. Included in this category are telephone directories, airline and other travel-related schedules, catalogs, as well as loose-leaf data services. It is the latter group, loose-leaf services, which created the most challenges; today most such services are available online and thus present no maintenance problems. Legal, accounting, and tax information publishers use this system: two examples are the *Labor Relations Reporter* (Bureau of National Affairs) and *Standard Federal Tax Reporter* (Commerce Clearing House). Some services still offer a print version, in which case a volume consists of a loose-leaf notebook capable of holding hundreds of pages. The pages carry a code number designed to show which section they belong in, as well as a date of issue. It is the library's responsibility to remove the superseded sections and insert the new material, which may be individual pages, sections within chapters, or entire chapters. Given the type of information published in this format, it is imperative to maintain these serials properly; the consequences for failing to do so can be significant. Errors can arise from misfiling, failing to remove superseded information or, worst of all, both of these. If several people in an organization use a loose-leaf service while working on similar issues and arrive at different answers, the organizations and their clients may face serious legal or financial trouble.

Newspapers

This category can cause some problems for public service personnel. Keeping the newspapers in good order, with all the sections for a given date in place, can be a frustrating activity. Especially frustrating is keeping track, whenever possible, of who has or had today's copy of the *Times* or where they left it. "Where is today's newspaper?" is a very common question for staff members to respond to and having a good answer can be challenging. Sometimes staff finds an issue has "walked out the front door," as it is rare for a library to property-mark, much less "target" every page or even every section of each newspaper. This means that pages and sections get misplaced or lost, especially if users bring in personal copies of the same newspaper.

Access to and storage of newspapers is another problem for libraries. Indexing of local smaller newspapers, up to now, has been rare. Today, even relatively small newspapers have a Web presence and at least some search capabilities. Only research libraries make major attempts to retain hard copy backfiles of newspapers—they are too large and are printed on poor-quality paper—so microfilm or digitized files have taken over long-term storage and access.

Newsletters

One serial category that a surprising number of libraries collect is newsletters, leaflets, and news releases. For many special/business libraries, they are the primary collecting area. Due to their small size and assumptions about the worth of small-sized, short-length formats, they present some challenges for staff. Numbered items in this class are easy to keep in order. Unfortunately, for many items in this class, the only clue to their proper order is a date appearing somewhere in the publication. The good news is that long-term retention is not usually necessary for many items in this class. Depending on the library's goals, most of these items may be truly ephemeral in nature. However, there are some very expensive (tens of thousands of dollars per year, especially for energy-related topics) newsletters that supply critical data for organizations and receive treatment similar to other items intended for long-term storage. As was the case for institutional reports, creating online finding aids can be useful in helping point users to these resources.

Nonsuperseding Serials

Most of the remaining types that we cover present similar issues for the staff—what has arrived, where is it, and how to preserve it long-term, for example. Often, statistical information is disseminated in this nonsuperseding manner. While the new material is current and may, in one sense, supersede older data, there is historical value to the older sheets. Again, common questions such as, "How did this month/quarter/year of whatever compare with the same period in 20XX?" may make it necessary to maintain old files. From a public service point of view, however, they are no more trouble than other more common serials.

Magazines

What are the most common serials? Eleven of Machlup's categories cover the variations in the common serials. Machlup created two broad divisions, magazines (popular publications) and journals (scholarly publications), and then subdivided these into 11 categories. His magazine grouping includes:

- Mass market serials, weekly or monthly newsmagazines (such as *Time*)
- Popular magazines dealing with fiction, pictures, sports, travel, fashion, sex, humor, and comics (such as *ESPN: The Magazine*)
- Magazines that popularize science, social, political, and cultural affairs (such as *National Geographic*)
- Magazines focusing on opinion and criticism, especially social, political, literary, artistic, aesthetic, or religious (such as *National Review*)
- "Other magazines not elsewhere classified" category. An example of an item in this category is an organization publication (governmental or private) that is really a public relations vehicle, sometimes called a

house organ. These publications often contain general interest material, but there is usually some clearly stated or implied relationship between the subject covered and the issuing organization (for example, *Plain Truth*)

Journals

Within the journals category Machlup identified four subcategories. "Nonspecialized journals for the intelligentsia" are for persons well informed on topics such as literature, art, social affairs, science, or politics (*Science* would be an example). "Learned journals for specialists," both primary and secondary, are major components in academic and large public libraries' serials collections—*American Indian Culture and Research Journal* for example. "Practical professional journals" in fields such as medicine, law, agriculture, management, and librarianship (*Library Mosaics* was such a title) are also common in all libraries. Finally, there are the "parochial journals" that are of interest to a local or regional audience (*Rock Art* is an example). Local history groups often publish a small journal for members. While most issues are only of local interest, some large research libraries collect such publications in support of their mission of collecting and preserving research and potential research materials.

The above variations help make it clear why there is confusion about terms relating to these publications. Each type fills a niche in the information dissemination system. While they did (in paper) and sometimes still do (when online) create special handling procedures and problems, they are a necessary part of any library's collection, and the public service staff must deal with them.

ACCESS TO SERIALS

Serials normally contain the most current information about a topic, although some professional society/association publications are slow to appear, even in digital form. There are some people today, perhaps many, who believe that the paper-based serial is ready to become a museum object at best. As we noted earlier in this chapter, paper serials are still with us and likely to remain so for some time to come. If you are doubtful, take look in your local grocery or drugstore and you will see a large number of paper serials. Keep in mind that no commercial operation will devote much if any space to items that do not sell, so someone must be buying, if not reading, magazines. We agree with view expressed by Childers and Martin (2006), "In this age of electronic publications, Web sites, and 24-hour cable news, it may seem that the day of the popular magazine is over and an examination of the paper based serial is a worthless exercise. This absolutely is far from true. Magazines are still a way of preserving and spreading the culture of the moment to the masses" (p. 34). That said, there is no doubt that the e-serial is the growing format of choice for many libraries. This is particularly true for those libraries with a high percentage of users who need and use scholarly titles. One of the major advantages of the e-format is the ability to have access whenever the user desires.

However, even libraries that are going e-first with serials still have substantial runs of backfiles of serials and most are still getting some titles in paper. Thus, we devote some space to paper-based serials and their "care and maintenance."

In the past, one of the major challenges for public service personnel was assisting people in locating desired articles in serials. An entire industry existed to index and/or abstract articles in a variety of publications. Even with a service that indexed hundreds of potentially useful titles, the search process was slow, tedious, and, more often than not, left you with the very strong sense you probably missed something significant. Today's online search capabilities that allow for keyword and Boolean searches—even cross-database searches—generate many more useful "hits" than hours and hours of searching in the paper indexes ever could. Old standby indexing services, such as H. W. Wilson, may still make available a print version of their indexes; however, when you visit their Web site you will see the electronic products are featured. (Wilson now produces full-text databases such as Wilson Omni File, which has over 4,000 full-text titles.) The issue that results from the use of such online indexes is that you may have backfiles of paper journals that are not covered by online resources or—a real possibility—your library cannot afford to have access to all of the journals indexed. In cases where print indexes are available you may find yourself still having to help users with the paper indexes, if you can get them to take the time to do so. Generally today, only those with a historical interest have some familiarity with print indexes.

Decisions regarding the organization, access, and circulation of paper-based serials will cause public service staff to have more or less work. The decisions involve several factors: storage, preservation, copyright, staffing, type of users, users' needs, security, and prior history (how serials were handled in the past in the library). The factors are interrelated; a change in one may, and usually does, influence one or more other factors. Thus, the decision to change some aspect of handling serials will have an influence in many areas.

There are three basic ways to organize paper journals and magazines for the public: alphabetically by title, alphabetically by title within broad topical groupings—also know as reader's interest (gardening, travel, or homemaking, for example), and in classified order, using the same classification system as used for the books in the collection. When using a classified approach, a decision to integrate the serials into the book collection may result in the public service staff regularly shifting thousands of feet of shelved books to make room for the constant growth of the serials titles. Figure 10.1 illustrates the variations within each of the three broad categories. Another variation is that current issues may be maintained in a different order than the bound volumes.

What are the implications of these options? From a user's perspective, the fewer places a person has to look to locate materials, the better. Thus, the classified approach, with the current issues shelved next to the backfiles and books with the same classification number, is ideal for users. Unfortunately, from the staff's point of view this option generates the greatest amount of work as they have to shift a high volume of material as both new books and serials arrive. It is possible to make this less onerous, if you have ample empty shelf space and lots of data about the growth rates for serials and books by call number. There would probably be weeks of shifting materials to start with as

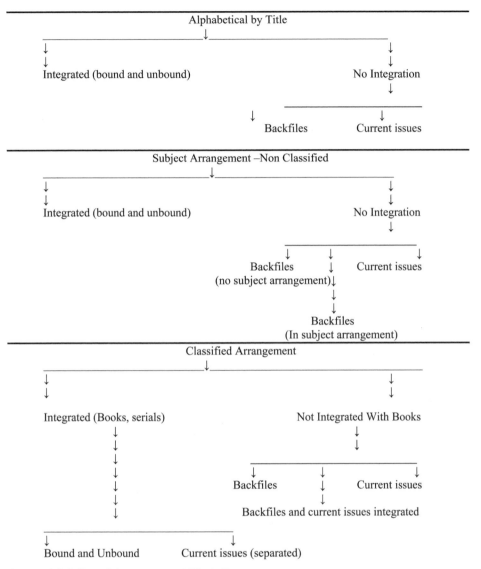

Figure 10.1 Serial Arrangement Variations

you opened up shelves in the right amount in the right area, but then there should only be minor shifts for some time. (One given for print serials is their constant growth; this necessitates shifting them to make room for new materials, at some point in time no matter what approach the library takes to housing them. Shifting serials is an ongoing challenge for the public service staff.)

Users approve of the classified approach only as long as *all* of their most frequently used titles are together. In any large collection (100,000 titles or more) there will be questions from users such as, "Why did the library class this item here? It obviously belongs there!" The "why" and "obviously" are clear to that person, but, to someone else, that rationale may be "obviously wrong."

Very few publications truly have a single focus; almost all can and do have multiple subject headings. Classification schemes only provide one location for a single item. What is to be done with a serial about criminal sociology? When the library receives only one copy of the journal, the staff must select a single location, whether it is the sociology, law, criminology, or perhaps the criminal sociology section, and some users may be unhappy with the choice. All you can do is base the decision on a judgment about the content of the work *and* the most frequent potential user of the title in question. In an academic environment, using the above example, if there is either a sociology or a criminology department, the choice would be simple. If both units are present, however, the journal's overall orientation would dictate the final choice.

Serials, and especially periodicals, have a nasty habit of changing their names. This causes confusion for users and staff when the library employs the alphabetical-by-title arrangement. For reasons beyond most people's understanding (both the public and library staff), a publication changes it name from *American Association of Title Changers' Journal* to *Journal of the American Association of Title Changers.* (In the classified approach, this type of change is no problem, unless the title change signals a major change in content.) How to handle such changes in the alphabetical arrangement can be the topic of heated debate among public service staff. Those staff members responsible for maintaining stack areas and shelving would prefer to keep shifting to a minimum; they therefore often advocate leaving copies or volumes of the old title under the old name and only making room for the "new" title in its proper place. Using that approach will require less staff effort because there is no need to move the backfiles. Very often title changes are like our fictional example, shifting the word *Journal* from one end of the title to the other, or a similar small shift. Unfortunately these "small" changes have major implications for where the title falls in the alphabet. Regular users of the title may continue to think of it and look for the item under its former name for some time.

The topical or subject arrangement is a compromise between full classification and alphabetical by title. It provides some grouping by periodical content, and some users have less trouble finding what they want. The debates about the groupings will be less frequent because the groupings are very broad in character. However, this arrangement seldom diminishes the amount of shifting required when titles and content change.

No system, increased use of signs, or added bibliographic instruction will eliminate all the problems for the users. The way a library decides to organize its serials depends on the type of titles in the collection, collection size, and the users. Popular magazines seem to change names less often than their scholarly cousins, the journals. If most of the users are individuals who use the library regularly and over time, the most efficient system from a library staffing perspective is the most reasonable approach. If the user population has a significant turnover rate or consists of infrequent users, the system used needs to be simple, even if it does require more staff effort. The library must also decide if it wants integrated or separate backfiles and current issues. Often the deciding factors are the budget and availability of staff.

When space is a problem, keeping all the current issues together, regardless of the system used to organize the issues on the shelf, provides maximum space utilization. Keeping all the current issues in one area allows for more shelves per shelving section. Improved preservation and security also result from keeping all the current issues in one location. Preservation is better because the tighter shelf spacing reduces the chances of issues falling behind shelves and becoming "lost" or damaged. Security is also better for the loose issues, because staff can walk through the unbound periodical area more frequently than covering the entire stack area.

While the arrangement helps keep mutilation and theft of periodical material under some degree of control, other factors are also important. Having photocopy machines helps, but does not eliminate the loss of articles and entire issues. Serial circulation policies also relate to the mutilation problem. Because serials' primary purpose is to quickly disseminate new information, current issues often have more usage than do the backfiles. Therefore, very few libraries allow the current issues to circulate. An unwanted outcome of such a policy is that current issues also experience more mutilation. By keeping the current issues in one area, the staff can provide more constant supervision and reduce the damage. Having both an online and paper version of heavily used titles does reduce the mutilation rate, but again, journal embargoes of e-titles may result in some gap between availability of the print and e-version of the title.

Although only a few studies of the mutilation of library materials exist, their results are instructive. One study (Birney and Williams, 1985) had a person sit down at a table near other library users and in full view of the individuals tear or cut out some pages from a periodical or book. The experimenter continued damaging the material until all the people in the area knew what was going on. The experimenter then left the area and a second experimenter interviewed the users in the area about what they saw. Most of the people claimed they saw nothing. Those admitting they saw the pages being ripped out said they thought the item belonged to the person doing the damage. Less than 10 percent made any attempt to question the person tearing out the pages or to report the incident to the library staff. What this means for the public service staff is that they can expect little or no help from the public in controlling this type of damage. Frequent library staff "patrols" of areas where such behavior is likely to occur is the best deterrent.

In educational libraries, there is a heavy reliance on part-time student help in public services. To expect library student assistants to function as effective monitors of their peers' behavior is probably naive. It is not fair to the student assistants, nor is it reasonable to expect them to be effective if you try to impose this responsibility on them. This is true with regard not only to periodical mutilation, but also to employing students as exit monitors or just as general enforcers of library rules. Certainly some student assistants will see the significance of the rules, if they have an understanding of the issues involved, and will help enforce most of the library rules and regulations. Nevertheless, enforcement is a responsibility of the full-time staff.

Some libraries, where staffing and space allow, house current periodicals together and out of the public areas. A user submits a request to use a specific issue and a staff member brings the issue to the user. The user signs for the issue and may have a fixed time to return the issue, in essence a closed reserve system. Using this system provides better control of the current serials. Not only are people less likely to damage the issues, much less steal them, but the staff knows where the issues are, in use or on the shelf. In the open stack self-service system a user often leaves the issue on the table or desk or in the photocopy room when finished with the material. Depending on the staffing pattern and work load, that issue may not be back in its proper location for several hours, or perhaps a day or two. Worse yet, some readers shelve their own "private collections" of various items in an out-of-the-way corner for their own personal future use. Neither users nor staff like to spend time searching for "missing" items, and public-access current periodical issues are among the most common "temporarily missing" items.

For all of the above reasons, keeping current issues separate from the back-files is a common practice. If current issues do not circulate, mixing them in with circulating materials can cause confusion for the public and new staff about what does and does not circulate. Backfiles, because they have less use, often do circulate, but only for a short period; three-day loans for bound periodicals are fairly common. The loan period should and can be shorter because, unlike with books, few users read every page of a bound periodical. Also, other users may want access to the same volume, making a short loan period appropriate.

DIGITAL OR PAPER?

As Margaret Sylvia stated (in one of our opening quotations), libraries cannot ignore e-journals; if they do they will fail to provide quality service. Today, assuming the library has funds available, the serial collection can be in the tens of thousands when in the past it may have only been in the hundreds thanks to online "bundles." As mentioned earlier, old line indexing services, such as H. W. Wilson, offer packages of full-text journals; serial jobbers (firms that handle library serial subscriptions)—for example EBSCO—also have packages of full-text serials. Some serial publishers, such as Elsevier and Emerald, provide access, for a fee, to full-text packages of their publications. There is no question about the popularity of such materials with the public. They often prefer the electronic version, especially for its strong search capabilities. Another advantage is the ease of printing or downloading the search results. Something to keep in mind about e-journals is they do not all reflect the full content of their print versions; one common exception is "letters to the editor," another may be book reviews or the "comments" section, and very few in online "full-text" include advertisements.

There is some debate whether or not bundles, which include a variety of titles that the library never subscribed to in paper, are useful and worth the cost. Two studies that explored some of these questions were those of Karla Hahn (2006) and Brady and colleagues (2006). Both articles were positive about the concept; however, there is significant concern about long-term archiving of backfiles as well as access to files for years when the library paid for access but has had to drop the package.

There are a number of issues to consider in the interplay between digitized and paper-based serials. One issue is how to provide access. Digital serials, in theory, are accessible anywhere, anytime as long as there is a reliable connection between a computer and the full-text database. Many users and technology supporters believe that has been achieved—they are right most of the time: anywhere, anytime. There are still problems especially in terms of remote access and also in end-user computer capabilities in handling large files with graphics.

Long-term access is another library consideration that is often viewed as an ownership-versus-access issue. When a library subscribes to a paper journal, the library owns the paper copies for which it has paid the appropriate fee(s). Electronic formats are often a different matter, in that the provider considers the arrangement as a lease rather than a purchase. E-producers usually include a license agreement that limits the library's ability to use the material and, not infrequently, states that the library has access rights only so long as the annual fee is current—a lease. If a library has any responsibility for long-term retention of information, leasing is a problematic policy. These licenses also frequently contain language that imposes on the library, and its staff, the responsibility to monitor the end user's use of the material she/he downloads and prints. (Something that is impossible for the staff to do.)

Another aspect of serials is the issue of the concepts of "just in case" and "just in time"; this applies, or should, equally to electronic and print titles. Long-term preservation is, in a sense, "just-in-case." That is, someone will require the information some time. "Just in time" is locating the desired material at the time the user needs it, most often from somewhere other than the home library. Digitizing data makes just-in-time delivery a realistic option. One reality is that fewer and fewer libraries, for financial and space reasons, can continue to subscribe to thousands of paper serial titles "just in case." Needless to say, "just in time" carries with a significant cost. There are services that will provide a single article for a fee, a variety of document delivery services; more than 60 are listed on the Virginia Commonwealth University library's Document Deliver Suppliers Web page (http://www.library.vcu.edu/tml/docsupp/) that provide such services. Although the cost per item is high, the overall cost may be substantially lower than having a just-in-case subscription and some libraries subsidize document delivery for their primary service population (see the chapter on ILL/document delivery for a detailed discussion).

One important element about serials, as we noted earlier, is their currency. Digitized articles from print-based serials may or may not be as current as the print volume. If the publisher of the print volume has the material already in a digital form it may be accessible as soon as paper edition appears. Such is not always the case, and the supplier of the digital version must sometimes convert the paper version. That process takes some time and it must include a verification step to assure the two versions are identical. Some suppliers, to keep costs as low as possible, have the work done "off shore," which adds still more time to the process. Also, as noted earlier, some publishers place an "embargo" on the e-version, not making it available until following the release of the next paper version. The length of the embargo varies from a few weeks to several months. Thus, the e-version *may not* contain the most current information. Public service staff can provide a real service when they know which titles have an embargo and how long that lasts.

The library where both of the authors once worked found that dropping the paper version in favor of an electronic one did not work as well as desired; certainly there have been *no* cost savings. (There was, however, a substantial increase in the number of titles available to users. And many libraries benefit from having such an increase.) We decided to acquire annual microform versions of the electronic volumes in case the publisher or vendor ceased providing access. If there is adequate funding available, a library can assure long-term "ownership" through programs such as JSTOR (Journal Storage), LOCKSS (Lots of Copies Keep Stuff Safe), and Portico. Further, we found time delays between the paper and digital versions too great for some users, so we reestablished subscriptions to the paper versions along with the digital.

Just as users want photocopying machines available to copy paper articles, they also want printers to generate paper copies of the electronic materials. Not surprisingly, more and more libraries are charging for this service. Costs of paper, ink cartridges, maintenance service agreements on the printers, and replacement printers, not to mention staffing for such tasks as loading paper and clearing paper jams, are too high for libraries to absorb. Efforts to get users to download files onto a disk or flash drive have not been too successful; asking them to e-mail the files to themselves appears to work better. Fast printing of material is important because few if any libraries can afford to have enough computers available to satisfy all user needs, if the person must read everything from the computer screen. Many libraries find it necessary to limit customer use to 20 to 30 minutes during high demand periods.

As mentioned earlier, recently some academic libraries have implemented a policy of e-only (perhaps better stated, an e-preference). Essentially, it means making the e-version the first and often the only choice. Three major factors are driving this trend—user preference, lack of space to continue to house paper versions, and inability to afford duplicate subscriptions. Laura McElfresh (2006, 2007) outlined the pros and cons of such a policy. Some of the concerns she raised were: Does one retain archival rights even if the library drops it subscription? What are the printing/document delivery rights? Is reserve usage allowed? If the concerns are appropriately addressed, the e-only policy is likely to be effective in the long run.

Digitized serials are a mixed blessing. They are very popular, they provide more flexibility in searching than their paper-based counterparts, and they allow for remote access 24/7. While they do not reduce library operating costs, they do present new challenges for public service staff (e.g., constantly updating holding information and troubleshooting access problems), and electronic systems fail as do power supplies, causing user and staff frustration. Also, as anyone who has spent much time with Internet-based services knows, electronic does not always translate into fast. Waiting for files to load, waiting to have the server "accept" your query, or being abruptly cut off in mid-session are sources of frustration that do not exist with paper-based serials. On the other hand, torn-out articles, volumes not on the shelf, and encountering the library closed for a holiday are not problems with the electronic serials.

CHALLENGES TO COLLECTION CONTENT

We could address the topic of censorship challenges in several chapters of this book; however, this is as good a place as any, as serials generate a fair number of complaints. Anyone who has been in a public services position for any length of time will have had one or more experiences of dealing with someone who objects, often very strongly, to the contents of some item in the library's collections. You may expect any format to become a target of a complaint—audio recordings, books, Internet access, serials, videos, and anything else the library collects.

The only type of library that almost never faces this issue is the corporate/business library. School and public libraries experience the highest rates of challenges from users (or parents of users). Surprisingly, academic libraries also are challenged from time to time. Even special collections/archives occasionally have to address the unhappy user.

What may trigger a complaint? The short answer is almost anything. However, religious or political beliefs are a common source along with sexual content (or the lifestyle portrayed). Very often the underlying factor is the person's belief that she/he is protecting children from inappropriate material. Even issues of cultural sensitivity can become the focal point of the persons/groups concern. (It is often a bigger challenge to handle a formal group's concerns as it often has more resources to pursue decisions it does not like.) Finally, there can be challenges based on national (Children's Internet Protection Act [CIPA]) or local legislation.

From a host of possible examples, we have selected a few to illustrate the range of topics that have arisen in various types of libraries. A recent case (2007) is an interesting and complex situation related to a well-known magazine—*Sports Illustrated*. The problem related to its swimsuit issue; this annual issue has generated any number of complaints to libraries and, apparently, to the publisher. Many parents have asked that libraries restrict children's access to this issue, sometimes successfully, and sometimes not. As Francine Fialkoff (2007) wrote, "It has long been regarded as soft-core porn and a blatant example of the objectification of women in our society" (p. 8). What made the situation unusual was the publisher decided, without consulting libraries, *not* to send the issue to libraries. This upset librarians as well as others. "One of the first critics of *SI*'s misguided move was Lynne Weaver of Randolph-Macon Women's College" (Fialkoff, 2007, p. 8). One suspects the publisher believes it cannot win no matter what it decides to do about future swimsuit issues. Other serials that generate more than their far share of complaints are *The Advocate*, *People*, *Penthouse*, *Reader's Digest*, *Rolling Stone*, and *Young Miss*.

Moving on to other formats, it probably comes as no surprise that *Harry Potter* has endured more than a few efforts to keep the series out of libraries. Laura Mallory has been a persistent detractor and has fought several legal battles to have the books removed from her local school libraries (Gwinnett County [GA] Public Schools) (*American Libraries*, 2007). Her position, which will possibly be used in federal court now that she has lost in state courts, is that "this is not just fiction or fantasy. Witchcraft is real. . . . and we were warned of it from God" (*Library Journal*, p. 22). You might imagine what it was like for the first staff person who had to handle this complaint. You can check the list of the 100 most frequently challenged books at http://www.ala.org/ala/oif/bannedbooksweek/bbwlinks/100mostfrequently.htm.

Recorded music has had its turn under the censor's spotlight. In March 2004, the American Civil Liberties Union sought information from the Kansas

State Attorney General about the banning of more than 30 music CDs from libraries in the state. Naturally musicals such as *Jesus Christ Superstar* have also faced a variety of challenges, as a stage performance, audio recording, or motion picture. The last two are found in a number of libraries of all types.

Needless to say, video recordings are also prime targets for those wishing to protect others from inappropriate material. The academic library where the two authors worked had several complaints about videos that were thought to be un-Christian. The individuals who complained were not affiliated with the university; however, that did not stop them from carrying their concerns to the president of the university. We kept the titles, in part because the institution had a degree program in film. Like books, the typical complaints revolve around the level of violence, graphic language, and sexual content.

Our final example comes from special collections/archives and medical libraries. The situation arose in 1996 and concerned the book *Pernkopf Anatomy: Atlas of Topographic and Applied Anatomy*, which was a critically acclaimed anatomical atlas containing more than 800 detailed paintings of dissections that doctors, especially surgeons, used for many years. The first volume was published in Vienna in 1937, part two was printed in 1943, and the final volume appeared in 1952 (Israel, 1996). Urban and Schwarzenberg of Baltimore issued a two-volume set in 1989; later, Wavery Inc. acquired the rights to the title. Both the original and reissue volumes were (and still are) widely held by medical libraries. Reviewers in 1990 used phrases such as "in a class of its own" and "classic among atlases" (Wade, 1996). Anyone thinking about the date and place of the initial publication probably can guess why the controversy arose. Dr. Eduard Pernkopf was a Nazi Party member from 1933 onward, and was named dean of the medical school at the University of Vienna after the Anshluss of 1938. He also spent three postwar years in Allied prisoner-of-war camps, but was never charged with any war crimes. Some doctors in the 1990s wanted medical libraries to withdraw or at least not allow access to the work until there was an investigation into whether concentration camp victims had been used for the dissections upon which the paintings were based. There were differing responses in medical libraries to requests to restrict access.

The above gives you a brief picture of the range of topics that may generate a challenge and should make it clear that any type of library can have such problems. You never know when someone will arrive at your desk and present you and, of course, the library, with a situation that requires very careful handling. Sometimes the request is put forward quietly and reasonably, and sometimes not so nicely, but often the person wants the immediate removal of the objectionable item(s). What should you do if you find yourself on the receiving end of such as request?

The good news is many libraries have established a policy and procedure to handle the situation. (When there is a policy and procedure in place, study it and, if possible, practice the procedure with some of your workmates.) No matter what, a sound first step, with or without a policy, is to acknowledge the person's right to be concerned. Not doing so can escalate the situation, and you don't want that. Also, an appropriate response to such an individual is to indicate the issue is of such an importance that the director will need to handle the concern. However, it is critical that you not indicate what the outcome may be or when the decision will take place. (Anything you say along those lines can come back to haunt both the library and yourself when in the hands of a good lawyer.)

A great many libraries have a form they ask the person to fill out regarding the objectionable material. (Both the ALA and the National Council of Teachers of English have forms they recommend for this purpose.) As you might expect, some people will react negatively to being asked to fill out "bureaucratic paperwork." You should explain that the reason for the paperwork is because the matter is important and because you must pass the information on to people who can address the concern, to be certain the individual's request is accurately conveyed to senior managers who may not be immediately available. Make it clear you are not empowered to do more than pass the information forward as quickly as possible. After accepting the written form and passing it on to your supervisor, you should be out of the process. Handling this type of situation can be stressful and is never pleasant, so think about how to handle it before the first time you have to confront it.

For libraries having Internet accessibility and have children coming in, even if they are with a parent, there are the aforementioned CIPA issues to address. Although the first word in the title is "children," the act impacts most libraries and everyone who uses them. It was enacted in December 2000 to address concerns about offensive content over the Internet on school and library computers. CIPA imposes certain requirements on any school or library that receives federal funding for Internet access (E-rate program).

Both school and public libraries face the biggest requirements from CIPA. Some academic libraries that have access programs with local high schools for honor students also have had to think carefully about the issue—often the reason high schools want these students to have access is the depth of electronic serial databases that the academic libraries have available. The Federal Communications Commission lists three broad requirements (see its Web site for the precise wording and details—http://www.fcc.gov/cgb/consumerfacts/cipa.html):

- Have technology protection (block or filter) against sites that are obscene, contain child pornography, or are "harmful to minors"
- Schools are to "monitor online activities"
- Implement policies that address minors' access to inappropriate Internet material; safety and security of minors using e-mail, social sites, and other forms of direct electronic communications; "hacking" and other unlawful activities by minors; unauthorized disclosure of information about minors; and restricting minors' access to material harmful to them

Public service staff "may disable blocking or filtering measures during any use by an adult to enable access for bona fide research or other lawful purposes." However, for many libraries, this provision of CIPA means extra work for the staff. Libraries with limited resources, including computers, generally cannot afford to set aside some computers for minors and others for adults. Even when they do have separate machines for minors, there is the challenge to "monitor" the usage. When it comes to machines that you enable and disable, staff time goes with this process and there is always a chance a minor may get on a disabled machine. Libraries have also had trouble with the concept of adult "bona fide research."

CIPA does not require tracking Internet use by either minors or adults. However, as we will discuss in the chapter on security, the USA PATRIOT Act presents some countervailing issues. Three rather different CIPA-related Web sites to check out are the ALA's CIPA page (http://www.ala.org/cipa/), the Public Library Association's "Internet Filtering Software" site (http://www.ala.org/ala/pla/plapubs/technotes/internetfiltering.cfm), and an offering by an ethics professor titled "Libraries Internet Use Policies" (http://www.kardasz.org/libraries_policies1.html).

STAFFING

All public service staff are likely to have some involvement with serials. Reference staff direct users to serial resources as well as assist in locating and/or retrieving digital copies of desired items. Document delivery staff members have much of their work generated by requests to borrow or loan articles from serials. Circulation staff will probably have requests to borrow serials and need to understand and effectively explain the library's serials circulation policy. Staff responsible for stack maintenance and reshelving materials will get to know the serials more thoroughly than they might like, especially if serials do not circulate. The entire public service staff will need to monitor the use of serials, with the goal being to keep theft, loss, and damage to a minimum, and to collect usage data for collection development purposes.

Three types of record keeping are important for serials. Accurate records of losses and damaged items can assist the library and its funding sources by showing whether or not more security measures are needed. Increasing security costs money. Before committing to some new security program, there should be an assessment of the total cost of lost and damaged serials. Too often libraries only consider the cost of the replacement and place no value on staff time spent locating, acquiring, and processing the replacements. While it is hard to provide an accurate monetary value for user inconvenience, some record of the number of people seeking the missing item will help in the assessment process. Also, a thoughtful assessment of how effective a new security system or procedure may be in controlling the type of losses being experienced is necessary.

A second important record of serial use is for ILL borrowing. The U.S. copyright law has provisions (Section 109C) that limit the number of times a library may borrow articles from a single serial title in a given year (see the chapter on ILL/document delivery for details). Keeping track of ILL transactions, even if not a legal requirement, helps the library provide better service. When a number of users request material through ILL from a single title, it is time for the library to at least consider subscribing to the title.

Thirdly, the number of times serials are used is an important metric in deciding whether to cancel a subscription to a title or perhaps replace the paper version with its digital counterpart. For paper serials these statistics are often gathered by staff when they pick up and reshelve the publications. For digital titles, the publisher or vendor usually compiles and makes the data available to the library.

SUMMARY

Serials are complex publications, and the public depends on libraries to supply most of their serial needs. Serials present many challenges for public service staff. Knowing more about the nature of serials and their publication helps in understanding the importance of these items, if not reducing some of the frustration and work they create.

Chapter Review Material

1. What are five important characteristics of serials?
2. List three areas in which serials generate work for public service staff.
3. List Machlup's serial categories and the special characteristics of each that have an impact on public service activities.
4. Describe the methods of organization that can be used to keep periodicals in order in the stacks.
5. What are the primary areas of digital serials that appeal to users? What are the challenges for public service staff?
6. Discuss the sources that most often trigger complaints about items in a library's collection.
7. What are some steps to take when a person comes to a service point to complain about an item?
8. What are some of the ramifications of the Children's Internet Protection Act and U.S. copyright laws in terms of serial services?

REFERENCES

American Libraries. "Harry Potter Wins Third Challenge," 2007. 38, no. 1: 25.

American Library Association. 1983. *ALA Glossary of Library and Information Science.* Chicago: American Library Association.

Birney, Ann E., and Sara R. Williams. 1985. "Mutilation and the Folklore of Academic Librarianship," *Library & Archival Security* 7, no. 3: 41–47.

Brady, Eileen, Sarah McCord, and Betty Galbraith. 2006. "Print versus Electronic Journal Use in Three Sci/Tech Disciplines," *College & Research Libraries* 67, no. 4: 354–363.

Brett, Simon. 2003. *Murder in the Museum.* New York: Berkeley Prime Crime, Inc.

Childers, Scott, and Charity Martin. 2006. "Popular Serial Selection Bias and Central Mid-Western metropolitan Libraries," *Nebraska Library Association* 37, no. 3: 34–46.

Fialkoff, Francine. 2007. "SI vs. Librarians," *Library Journal* 132, no. 6: 8

Hahn, Karla. 2006. "The State of the Large Publisher Bundle," *ARL Bimonthly Report* no. 245: 1–6.

Israel, Howard. 1996. "Nazi Origins of an Anatomy Text," *Journal of the American Medical Association* 276, no. 20: 1633.

McElfresh, Laura Kane. 2006. "The E-only Experience: Moving Beyond Paper," *Technicalities* 26, no. 4: 1, 11–13.

———. 2007. "Going E-only," *Technicalities* 27, no. 2: 1, 11–13.

Machlup, Fritz.1978. *Information Through the Printed Word.* New York: New York University.

Sylvia, Margaret. 2005. "E-Serials, How To," *Library Journal* 130, no. 7: 128.

Wade, Nicholas. 1996. "Doctors Question Use of Nazi's Medical Atlas," *New York Times,* November 26, 1996: C1.

SUGGESTED READINGS

Bocher, Bob. 2003. "A CIPA Toolkit," *Library Journal* 128, no. 13: 35–37.

Corbert, Lauren. 2006. "Serials," *Library Resources & Technical Services* 50, no. 1: 16–30.

Eberhart, George. 2005. "Books and Serials Face an Uncertain but Exciting Future," *American Libraries* 36, no. 11: 34–35.

Kranich, Nancy. 2004. "Why Filters Won't Protect Children or Adults," *Library Administration & Management* 18, no. 1: 14–18.

LaRue, James. 2004. "Buddha at the Gates, Running: Why People Challenge Library Materials," *American Libraries* 35, no. 11: 42–44.

McElfresh, Laura Kane. 2007. "When a Journal Isn't Journal," *Technicalities* 27, no. 1: 1, 11–13.

McMenemy, David, and Paul F. Burton. 2005. "Managing Access: Legal and Policy Issues of ICT Use." In *Delivering Digital Services* Alan Paultez, ed. London: Facet Publishing.

Millard, Scott. 2004. *Introduction to Serials Work for Library Technicians.* New York: Haworth.

11

Media Services

Videos are the "Twinkies" of library collections.

—Will Manley, 1991

It is counterproductive to stigmatize one format while deifying print. We dilute our energy by imposing such artificial distinctions.

—Myra Michele Brown, 2006

Our opening quotations suggest media collections in libraries have had a somewhat checkered history including varying attitudes about their value. Changing community values and young staff, who grew up in a more visual environment, are key factors in today's more positive perception of media in libraries. There was at one time a school of thought that nonprint materials were inappropriate for libraries, especially public libraries. Followers of this philosophy held the attitude that nonprint materials were distractions from the library's primary mission—the promotion of life-long reading and especially reading quality literary titles. Further, such collections drained essential resources from print material. Essentially, such people viewed libraries as being in the 'book" rather than the "information" business.

Most libraries today do have at least some small collection of nonprint items and there is a recognition that other media do play an important role in having an informed society. Anyone reading *Publishers Weekly* (*PW*) or shopping on Amazon.com knows publishers and booksellers no longer limit themselves to just books and magazines. They see themselves as being in the information business. Regular columns in *PW* on audio as well as video releases indicate that both producers and vendors view this field as an important market. The use of computerized typesetting and scanning equipment, which produces a record of the text in a digital format, opened up a number of options for

241

delivering the information, including the Internet. We will explore this topic later in this chapter.

ROLE OF MEDIA IN PUBLIC SERVICES

In the not-too-distant past, many libraries treated media as marginal, if they stocked them at all; they were viewed as a way to get people into the library and then getting them "hooked on books." Many libraries—except media centers in schools and community colleges—only saw recreational or entertainment value in nonprint materials.

Primary school, secondary school, and community college libraries lead the way in incorporating all formats into their service programs. These institutions used media for instruction and recognized that many ideas are best expressed using a form other than the printed word. Schools regularly use media in what is called *resource-based education.* Further, the media are integrated into the library's collection. Undoubtedly one reason for this, at least in the case of schools, is the relatively small size of the organization and the need to keep things simple from an administrative point of view. Why have two units, one for books and magazines, and one for media, when one unit could handle the workload for both? Use of media in classrooms has been a long-standing tradition in these institutions, unlike four-year colleges and universities.

In academic institutions, the pattern was to establish separate units to handle media needs. Academic institutions tended to view media, essentially films, as solely classroom material; even then there were doubts about its real instructional value. Some professors believed, and a few still do, that use of media in the classroom was the lazy person's way of not "doing" the teaching himself or herself. Certainly, art, film, music, and theater departments were exceptions, but they often created departmental collections, independent of the library, only available to staff and departmental majors.

For many colleges and universities, the notion of media only in the classroom resulted in the creation of a "media services department" that usually operated during classroom hours, basically 8:00 A.M. to 5:00 P.M., Monday through Friday. The reason was that the department provided the equipment, the material/film, and the operator for the instructor. Given the complexity of operating the equipment as well as potential damage to the material from mishandling, neither the instructor nor the department was too interested in having the material used outside the classroom. There was a steady change in attitude as equipment became easier to use and younger faculty began to give assignments that involved use of media and/or truly incorporated media into the instructional process so students who missed a class had to have access to the media outside of the classroom. Integration of all formats will be what most people will demand and expect in the future.

Public libraries were early collectors of sound recordings, and a number also developed film collections. Sound recordings circulated and over time expanded from just classical music to all forms of music and the spoken word. Motion picture films attracted groups for in-house showings and were also available for loan to groups such as scouts, churches, and occasionally schools. Nowadays only specialized film libraries collect reel films. However, there are relatively few libraries that do not have at least a few videos or DVDs in their collections.

Media play an important role in meeting the educational and recreational needs of the service community. Some people are print-oriented, while others prefer audio or graphic presentations of information. For many types of information a print format is inappropriate. Limiting a collection to one or two formats seldom provides the range of services appropriate to the service community's needs.

Sally Mason (1994), although specifically addressing public libraries, summed up the situation for all types of libraries when she wrote: "Clearly, the visual media will only become more important to library service in the future. . . . It is not enough for librarians to 'capitulate' on the issue of visual media. We must become leaders and advocates . . . helping the public to learn what is available, to sort through multiple possibilities, and offering guidance in the use of media to obtain needed information" (p. 12).

All one has to do is think about the growth of Web 2.0 and sites like MySpace and YouTube to realize the importance of visuals and interaction to youth. "Social media" or "social networking" is a tool for sharing one's personal experiences through text, visuals, and sound. A library of any type that ignores social media does so at its peril, at least from a long-term point of view. For effective outreach, libraries need to focus their communication on "people like us" rather than the traditional "top down"/"organizational format." We explore this aspect of media service later in this chapter.

Digitization has to a large degree made the old media formats less significant from a public service point of view. However, for the near term, libraries will have legacy media collections that contain material that is not available in a digital form. Thus, staff may still have to understand how to operate "old" equipment.

The bottom line is technology has reduced media to its basics of visual and audio, but from the perspective of many staff members, it has done so in more complex ways. As Howard Story (2004) wrote, "Many of us long for the way we were or what we think were simpler days. Phonograph records, audio cassettes, film, color television, video cassettes, all at one time were classified as new technology and during their introduction caused someone great anxiety. Digital technology is no different" (p. 12).

MEDIA SERVICES

Not many years ago, media equipment came in a variety forms of because the media content was also varied in format. Sometimes this was due to lack of standards and sometimes it was because of changing technology. Whatever the situation, there was a significant amount of staff time spent on supporting the public in their use of media.

One goal of media services is to make the use of the equipment so simple that it is transparent, whether it is old or new technology. The goal is to let users focus their attention on the information presented rather than on working the equipment. Younger staff members have no trouble with the "new" technology (it's not new to them), but can have trouble with the "old" technologies. Just the opposite is the case for older staff. One important issue in keeping equipment simple to use is maintaining it in good working order.

In addition to making operations simple, most media specialists recommend integrating media with other services. The OPAC should reflect the total holdings of the library regardless of format. Thus, a subject search for Native American basketry would produce a listing of books, journals, videos, oral histories, and, perhaps, in a special collections or museum setting, even some indication of holdings of actual baskets.

Another goal of media service is to collect and provide access to all the appropriate formats. This means the public service staff must know and appreciate the value of all the formats collected. Recognizing that some individuals have strong preferences for one format or another is also important, as well as not letting the staff's personal preferences influence the service provided. Some time ago Ranganathan (1952), a leading figure in librarianship, proposed five laws of librarianship. Media services staff might add a sixth law ("Each user her/his format"), or perhaps modify Ranganathan's law, "Each book its user" to "Each format its user."

One area where media personnel must play a role is in assisting instructors/teachers in their efforts to integrate technology/media into the classroom. Evans and Gunter (2004) make the case that there is a need to "emphasize the exploration, integration, and evaluation of technology in core subjects" (p. 326). We explore some of the ways to provide such assistance in this chapter as well as in the chapter on programming.

MEDIA FORMATS

As we have stated, a given in media services is changing formats, which will keep your work life interesting. The pace of change of 40 years ago now seems slower than a snail, while today's pace seems to be light-speed. As Alan Kaye (2005) wrote, "Now picture and sound seem to be having their way with computers and the Internet. Multimedia information has become almost native to computers, collapsing the market for analog formats and creating a digital world" (p. 62). He went on to discuss how libraries like his have already or are in the process of eliminating filmstrips, slide sets, 16-mm and 8-mm films, Super 8 films, and all phonograph and music audio cassettes. Not all libraries have gone that far and many still have some of these legacy collections. Thus, we briefly mention such formats in what follows; if you are interested in more information about such formats, consult the previous edition of this book.

Video

As suggested by Kaye, today most libraries have or are weeding their film collections in terms of 16- and 8-mm formats. About the only environment in which you find such films are special collections and archives. Like many of the other formats we cover in this chapter, film content has migrated to a digital form (DVDs and increasingly to streaming video). Video cassettes (VHS) are still in collections and are available for purchase, primarily because the content is not yet available in a digital form.

Format battles in the video field have been ongoing for some years now. Perhaps the battle between Beta and VHS is best known. When we prepared this chapter, in late 2007, the video fight was between Blu-ray, HD DVD, and DVD. Once again, Sony Corporation was involved (its Beta format lost the last time). Libraries may once again be caught in the middle of a commercial battle where they must bet on a winning side or spend limited funds duplicating the same content in competing formats. (A few libraries may still have Beta cassettes left from the last time companies could not agree on a single standard.) Prices for Blu-ray and HD DVD players were still substantial in late 2007, so there was not too much demand from users. Some of the most expensive players that could handle either format were not exactly flying off store shelves.

Not withstanding the Blu-ray/HD DVD issue, most libraries have substantial collections of VHS tapes and DVDs. According to Norman Oder (2005) in late 2005, many libraries were still purchasing VHS cassettes in large numbers. By 2007, DVDs had overtaken VHS, at least for feature film titles. "Part of the growth in the DVD era comes down to simple economics. They can buy more movies with their budgets than they could in the VHS era" (Netherby, 2007, p. 5). Most of the video circulation comes from movies in the public library setting, while curriculum-related videos dominate educational library usage. However, the acquisition patterns vary greatly as some public libraries believe they compete with local video rental outlets if they offer movie titles. Another factor is they require even less shelf/storage space per title.

One factor in the continued acquisition of VHS titles is many people still have VHS players at home as well as a small personal collection of cassettes. The reason for the retention by both libraries and individuals is that some content of interest is still only available in that format.

DVDs do present two different and significant service challenges for libraries—damage and security. Damage to DVDs is very high. One librarian in responding to Oder's 2005 survey said of DVDs, "They are used for coasters and Frisbees" (p. 39). One obvious factor in the damage is that, unlike a cassette, the operating surface is fully exposed during handling of the disk. Scratches, chips, even warping are problem areas. Thus, the expected circulation life of a popular DVD is low. For many libraries, if they get 15 to 20 circulations, they think they are lucky. Replacement cost can become significant.

Because of their small size, theft is a much greater problem for DVDs than is true of the VHS cassette. How to display available titles is also a challenge. Some libraries just put out empty cases. Others have tried locking display cases similar to those used in commercial outlets. A few display color photocopies of the cases and keep everything behind a service desk. (All these options clearly have staffing implications.) Libraries that try employing security strips usually drop that approach as thieves merely take the disk and leave the empty case. (We explore the use of security strips/systems in the chapter on security.) So far, the use of RFID (radio frequency identification) tags has not proven any more effective. Oder (2005) reported that one library indicated it had experienced losses in excess of $90,000 in less than five years of offering DVDs (p. 39). Until someone comes up with a real solution, public service staff will find they spend a significant amount dealing with DVD security matters.

DVD collections, given the quick release after the film is in theatres, generate some of the same issues as the best-seller book. Everyone wants it NOW, not next month after all the talk has faded. In terms of circulation, feature film videos beat nonfiction hands down; theatricals represent roughly 68 percent of the collections, 72 percent of the expenditures, and 80 percent of the circulations (Oder, 2005, p. 40). Unfortunately, as of 2007, there is no DVD equivalent of the McNaughton book rental plan where a library can lease multiple copies of a popular title for a short time and return all or some of the copies after the demand has died off. Some libraries attempt to establish a ratio of copies to requests (holds). The problem with purchased multiple copies is they occupy valuable storage space after the demand has died off and scarce money has been expended on the same content. However, not having the material available when the demand is high can have negative consequences in the form of unhappy users.

Perhaps there is a solution on the horizon; that solution is downloadable video. E-video (downloadable) is being tested by some larger public libraries as of 2007. They use services such as OverDrive (movies and concert videos), CallMyLibraryDVD (movies and educational videos), and RecordBooks (books and movies). The Denver Public Library reported they had over 1,200 downloads of their "e-Flicks" while having only 82 titles available (Kim, 2006, p. 62). In 2007, the content available for downloading was limited, but will probably increase rapidly as the demand grows. One appealing aspect of the service is people can download the movies from their homes. Yes, titles are limited and most of what is available are "indies" (independent productions) or special interest, but the "majors" are not likely to miss an opportunity to increase revenue from controlled sites. Most of the services charged the library a fee based on the community's population. One issue for the staff is assisting individuals who are unfamiliar with downloading files. Another concern may be monitoring who is doing the downloading; some libraries have restricted e-movie files to just residents of the service area. Finally there may be fees to collect—in late 2007 they ranged between $2.99 to $49.00 for libraries that do charge a fee (Spielvogel, 2007, p. 12).

Video in the educational environment is becoming ever more central to teaching. Children and youth today are MTV and X-Box oriented, which means things like overhead transparencies, chalkboards, and even simple PowerPoint® presentations just don't hold their attention. No media center/library can afford all the potentially useful videos or, for that matter, maintain such collections. What can you do to meet a need for access to the huge universe of educational videos and still maintain fiscal responsibility? Video streaming may be a way to accomplish both goals.

One of the educational usage issues with video is that frequently an instructor only wants access to a segment from several videos in a single presentation. While it is possible to have several video players available, having all the equipment present and having all the videos properly queued is a nuisance and distraction. With streaming video it is possible to select the desired segments and put them together in the desired sequence. An example might be demonstrating how different actors/directors interpret a scene for a Shakespeare play. With video streaming it is possible:

- To select segments for an entire class or an individual student
- For teachers or students can select segments for presentations
- To bookmark segments for future use
- To control the video the same as on a player (play, pause, rewind, and fast forward)
- To use selected elements in student assignments (Redden, 2005, p. 15)

Video streaming is reaching all levels of education from kindergarten to Harvard Business School. School media centers and academic libraries can use programs such as Windows Media Player®, RealTime®, or Quicktime® to deliver the material to the classroom. The difference between streaming and downloading is with streaming one has the ability to immediately view images as they arrive rather than waiting for an entire download to be completed before viewing anything. (Teaching time is a factor for instructors.) Some educational video content providers offer streaming video services and occasionally material from other producers who are not yet offering such service. Generally the charge for the streaming service is an annual fee based on enrollment.

Movie Ratings and Libraries

One concern, especially for public libraries, is the potential for complaints/ censorship challenges to its video collections. While we explored the issue of censorship challenges in the serials chapter, here we need to note the issues of movie ratings and how they may impact public services. Public libraries usually address the ratings in their collection development policy statement(s). School library media centers have somewhat less exposure to challenges due to the instructional nature of the collections; however, even in these libraries it is possible to have a parent complain about a video, such as one dealing with evolution. Very often individuals will raise a question about the suitability of certain titles for young viewers and the need for "protecting the children." This was the major factor in the creation of the movie rating system.

As most people know, for better or worse, the Motion Picture Association of America (MPAA) has a rating system for its releases—the familiar G, PG, PG-13, R, and NC-17 one sees in the movie section of the newspaper. The Classification and Rating Administration (CARA) within the MPAA handles the establishment of each film's rating. While these ratings have no legal force and, in fact, are based on the somewhat subjective opinion of the CARA rating board, the general public accepts them as appropriate. The key is the content of each film in terms of its suitability for children.

Although the ALA has issued a statement opposing labeling, the majority of public libraries that responded to a national video survey indicated the MPAA/CARA ratings did influence acquisition decisions (Lore, 1994, p. 25). The unfortunate fact is that even a collection of G and PG rated titles does not ensure there will be no complaints. One possible way to handle the situation, although not always easy to accomplish, is to create two sections for video, one in the children's/young adult area and another in the adult area. Again, this will not forestall all complaints, but it could help. From the staffing point of view, making certain that the videos are in the proper section will be something of a challenge, unless the cassette boxes are clearly color-coded or marked in some way that makes sorting easy.

The Indianapolis-Marion County Library developed a video policy after several individuals expressed concerns about the "potential effect on minors" (Lore, 1994, p. 25). The library formed a "Community Video Task Force" to review the existing policy and make recommendations, if any, for changes. Their report concluded that the policy should retain the parent's right to restrict a child's borrowing to the juvenile videos, and that the staff should continue to receive training in the current policy. The basic policy is that anyone can borrow any video, unless it is a child with a card stamped "JV," which indicates a parental restriction. The person who raised the issue wanted the policy to require the parents to *give written permission* for a child to borrow anything but juvenile titles. You might want to check the video polices of some other libraries (e.g., http://www.brookstonlibrary.org/html/videos.html or http://www.lagrange.lib.in.us/policy.html#video).

Videos are an important source of programming for the public library's service community, especially for children. Programming can be something of a problem because of something called "performance rights." We address that and other legal issues in the chapter on programming.

Video and Copyright

Although there are a considerable number of substantive copyright questions relating to print material, they are even trickier when it comes to nonprint, especially in educational libraries. A full discussion of copyright is not possible or appropriate in this book, but some discussion is relevant to this chapter. Please note that what follows *is not legal advice*; it is merely a brief review of the issues and ALA guidelines and position regarding copyright. When in doubt about what is or is not legal, get legal counsel. Copyright holders can, do, and have enforced their rights in court. Institutions and libraries, both public and private, have found this to be true and, more often than not, have lost the suit.

The purpose of copyright is to promote the development and distribution of information while assuring the individual or group developing the idea or information has exclusive rights to profit from that activity. In addition, society, through its copyright laws, reserves for itself the right to use the material developed within limits without violating the copyright holder's right. The labels for the concept vary; in the United States it is "fair use," in the United Kingdom "fair rights." The problem is, what is fair?

Section 107 of the U.S. Copyright Law (Public Law 94–553, Title 17 of the *U.S. Code*), while legally establishing the doctrine of fair use, is short and fairly nonspecific. The doctrine relates to copying, reproduction (multiple copies), and actual use. It indicates that use for criticism, comment, news reporting, teaching, scholarship, and research are reasonable purposes. Further, as pointed out earlier, it specifies four criteria to consider in determining if the use is fair:

1. The purpose and character of the use, including whether such use is of a commercial nature or is for nonprofit educational purposes;
2. The nature of the copyrighted work;
3. The amount and substantiality of the portion used in relation to the copyrighted work as a whole;
4. The effect of the use upon the potential market for or value of the copyrighted work.

Clearly there is room for interpretation and argument. Guidelines developed by educators, publishers, and authors provide some indication of what various parties believe(d) reasonable for fair use. The guidelines are not part of the statute, but they were part of the House Judiciary Committee's report on the copyright bill. They are *Guidelines for Classroom Copying in Not-for-Profit Educational Institutions* and *Guidelines for Educational Uses of Music* (U.S. House of Representatives, 1976). It is important to remember that copyright protection extends to literary works; dramatic works; pantomimes and choreographic works; pictorial, graphic, and sculptural works; motion pictures and other audiovisual works; and sound recordings (Sec. 102).

Some of the media discussed in this chapter are specifically covered in several sections of the copyright law. The following are a *few* of the items and relevant sections of the law.

Audiovisual	108 (f) (3)
Audiovisual work other than news	107, 108 (h)
Book	107, 108
Graphic work	107, 108 (h)
Importing copies from abroad	602 (a) (3)
Instructional transmission	107, 110
Motion picture	107, 108 (h)
Musical work	107, 108 (h)
Periodical article	107, 108
Pictorial work	107, 108 (h)
Public broadcasting program	107, 108 (d) (3)
Sound recording	107, 108, 114

Libraries providing classroom media support face significant copyright questions. Teachers and professors want to use "a personal tape I made" in class using the school's equipment. Is that legal? The answer depends on many factors. A key issue is, when did the taping occur? Few tapes the teachers want to use are home videos; most are copies of a broadcast program the teacher made using a personal video recorder. "Off-air" recordings may be legally used, if they are 45 days old or less and played in the classroom with a teacher present. Such tapes must be erased after 45 days to comply with the guidelines.

An article by Jill Rooker (1991) included some suggested guidelines for off-air taping for educational purposes that we believe are a sound starting point for developing a library policy, which the library should have its legal counsel review:

1. An off-air recording, made at the request of an individual teacher, may be retained for 45 days, but then must be erased or destroyed immediately.

2. The teacher can use the recording once in the classroom or similar place devoted to instruction and repeat such use once during the first 10 days of the 45-day period for instructional reinforcement, but the remainder of the period the recording can only be used for teaching evaluation purposes.

3. A specific program can be recorded off-air only once for the same teacher.

4. Additional copies may be made, but are subject to the same restrictions applicable to the original recording.

5. All recordings and copies must include the copyright notice as broadcast.

6. Programs need not be used in their entirety, but must not be altered, combined, or merged with other recorded material. (p. 51)

When the library has advance notice, or even after the fact, it is possible to contact the network that broadcast the program and receive permission, for a fee, to make a permanent copy that is not subject to the same type of 45-day limitation.

There is also a question of when one can use a video in a "program." For public libraries this can be an issue because there is something called *performance rights*. The issue is too complex to explore in this book, but performance rights are part of the mechanism by which all the people involved in the production of the video receive compensation. The easiest way to think about it is in terms of book royalties: each new copy sold means a small payment is due the author(s). For performance rights each "performance" should mean a small payment is due each of the participants involved in the production of the video/film. To cover such costs the producer/distributor of a video may or may not include "performance rights" in the price. (Essentially performance rights pertain when there is a presentation to a number of people at the same time, such as a children's program in the library.) The best approach is to acquire videos with performance rights; this will almost always mean a higher price than listed, unless it is clearly stated that the price includes performance rights.

Other Image Formats

As we mentioned earlier, many libraries, due to space, maintenance, and low user interest, are disposing of their collections of reel film, filmstrips, slides, and flat pictures. (We hope they do so with care and don't discard items of long-term societal value due to storage space concerns.) Most filmstrips were designed as instructional material and required special projectors. Many of the items are now digitized and available online. The same is true of many of the slide sets. Flat pictures have always presented challenges in organization and access. Scanning images is an approach to keeping pictorial materials in order and increasing access, especially if available via the library Web site, assuming there are no outstanding copyright issues. However, it does little to improve access, unless you engage in a significant amount of indexing. (It is possible to create a Word file of terms and use the "Find" capability to create a very simple digital search function.) The process of scanning is more complicated than placing the item on a scanner and "clicking start." One needs to verify that there is a match been the scanned and original image. Images also require substantial amounts of disk memory and high-end computers (and occasionally printers) to make effective use of them.

Maps

Maps are a form of pictorial material, and most libraries have traditionally held at least a small collection, in addition to atlases in the reference collection. Internet map sites, such as MapQuest, Google Maps, or Multimap, have significantly reduced the demand for road maps in libraries. Information found on such sites provides what the majority of people were seeking when they came to the library "looking for a map"—street/highway information.

Maps actually come in a variety of forms and content. Large public libraries, academic libraries, and many business and industrial libraries have extensive collections. Maps take the form of graphic representations of such things as geological structures, physical features, economic data, and population distributions. They may be folded, sheets, raised relief, globes, and even aerial/satellite images. Any major map collection must determine its scope and define what to collect. While most collections would incorporate aerial photographs, including satellite photographs, should they also house the remote sensing data from satellites? Are raised relief maps worth including, or are they a commercial product of no real informational value? Clearly the users' requirements will determine the answers to these and many other questions about the collection.

Depending on the collection's purpose, maps may be organized in a simple geographic location sequence or by some more complex system. "Do you have a map of X?" may (and usually does) mean a map showing streets, roads, and other cultural features. It could mean a topographic map, which provides elevation information in addition to cultural features. Or the individual may really want a soils map to get information for agricultural or construction purposes. Most map users who want a contour map, however, will ask for "the topo map of X." Normally the person with specialized map needs is knowledgeable about maps and will be precise in his or her request. In a large collection, it is common to keep types of maps together, for example, topographic, cultural, political, and geologic maps. In addition to content, factors such as projection and scale may be important in the organization and storage of maps. Staff working with large map collections will need special training to handle this format properly.

A relatively new service in some larger academic and public libraries is GIS (Geographic Information Services). Rhonda Houser (2006, pp. 318–320) outlines some of the types of user queries a GIS program might assist with:

- Identifying a specific geographic data set
- Creating a map or image from a spatial dataset
- Converting spatial data from two or more formats to a single form
- Cropping spatial data to generate a new map
- Creating data and applying it to a map,
- Taking GPS (geographic positioning system) data and creating a map
- Creating a map from tabular data
- Linking an image to a GIS using geographic coordinates
- Performing spatial data analysis

Audio Recordings

Returning to a widely held format, audio recordings, you again encounter great diversity and incompatibility, at least in terms of the legacy collections found in many libraries. Sound recordings were among the first nonprint formats collected by libraries. In public libraries, the recordings are usually part of the circulating collection. For educational libraries the purpose is usually instructional, with limited, if any, use outside the library. This is the media category that most clearly reflects the long-term influence of a changing technology on a library collection.

Audiobooks are today's most common audio recording purchase in libraries. The widespread use of Internet audio streaming, iPods®, and other electronic gear has made music recordings very low use in most libraries. Many libraries retain their older recordings because often the performance on the disk/tape has not yet migrated to a digital form. These can take the form of 78, 33 1/3 rpm phonograph records, cassettes, and CDs. Naturally each format requires its special playing equipment. Usually someone interested in hearing such material has some familiarity with the equipment, so assisting him or her is not a great problem. A few libraries are purchasing relatively low-cost equipment and software that allows one to convert phonograph records to an MP3 format. Naturally, the library must be careful to do this in compliance with copyright laws.

For public libraries, audiobooks have become almost as important as the video collection. Automobile players and portable handheld DVD players have created a major market for audiobooks. Even reading a small paperback on a crowded subway or bus can be difficult. Listening to a player that fits in one's pocket with a headset allows one to close out the noise, to some degree, and enjoy a favorite piece of music or listen to a best seller. The same is true for those commuting in their cars or just out for their "power walk." Another value of audiobooks is providing those with vision impairments additional opportunities to enjoy "print" material that goes beyond those available through the National Library Service for the Blind and Physically Handicapped (NLSBPH).

Books on tape cassettes, CDs, and DABs (digital audio books) are very popular. The cassette still has a niche in the audio collection (at least as of late 2007) for commuters whose vehicle CD player does not provide dependable playback (road bumps can translate into sound "bumps," perhaps skipping the "key" information in the "whodunit"). Tape decks do not suffer from this problem, but fewer and fewer vehicles have them as a standard feature of their audio system.

Many libraries have formed or are forming collaborative DAB services. Some examples of existing programs, in 2007, are Califa (www.califa.com), Illinois Kids Zone (www.ilkidszone.info), ListenIllinois (www.listenillinois.org), ListenOhio (www.listenohio.org), and Michigan Library Consortium (www.mlcnet. org). Unlike the digital music field, DAB is much more stable and does not, at least in 2007, face the copyright issues of music. In late 2007, there were four major vendors offering DAB products—Audible (www.audible.com), OverDrive (www.overdrive.com), NetLibrary/Recorded Books (www.oclc.org/audiobooks), and TumbleBooks (www.tumblebooks.com). Tom Peters and colleagues (2005) provided an overview of the differences between the services (p. 62). There are other smaller services, offering very few titles, but as they grow they may well become significant market players.

For public service staff there may be a learning process in order to assist users who are unfamiliar or uncomfortable with downloading. Many libraries offer two options for accessing their DAB service—a link from the title's MARC record or a link on the library's Web site. Almost all impose a "loan period" and a limit on the number of titles a person may have at any one time. At the time we prepared this chapter, the major issue was DAB incompatibility with the iPod.

There are major advantages to having DABs as part of a library's audio service program. Most notably, DABs:

- Are available 24/7
- Are never lost or damaged (at least for the library)
- Require no processing
- Require no shelf space
- Never require overdue notices or fines (files automatically delete at the end of the loan period)
- Provide the visually impaired another means of access to popular titles
- Allow for simple weeding
- Allow for easy collaboration
- Their vendors provide usage data

In the past, academic libraries rarely offered audiobooks. DABs may change that fact. If nothing more, the fact that there is no storage space required may make the format attractive. Robert Fox (2004) explored the question of offering audiobooks in academic libraries. He found a few libraries had small collections, more through donations than an active collecting plan, but none viewed them as central to their service goals. His concluding statement was, "audiotapes *do* have a place in academic libraries" (p. 11).

Donna Holovack (1996) published an article outlining the popularity of audiobooks in *Public Libraries.* She suggested that audio books are "a good marketing aid, a loss leader extraordinaire" (p. 115). She noted that libraries have supplied recorded books (and we note current magazines as well) for the visually impaired for some time. (The Library of Congress's service for the visually and physically impaired, NLSBPH, is a most valuable program, and one that perhaps led publishers to think there was a bigger market for audiobooks.) The question of the "suitability" of libraries making abridged versions of works of fiction available is one for the profession; some people prefer the abridged version. The idea that people are only looking for the latest work of fiction is belied by the data from *PW* that show nonfiction does equally well. If you have doubts about the interest in nonfiction audiobooks, just check out the audiobook section at a store like Barnes & Noble.

One of the drawbacks of audiocassettes, spoken word or music, is that they have a relatively short life span, five to six years, even under optimal usage conditions. They are also small objects that have few places upon which a library can attach a security strip/device, so their loss rate ("shrinkage" in retail terms) can be rather high. Nor, for that matter, is there much room to apply bar codes or other property markings. Replacing lost items can be costly. From both the public's and the staff's point of view, the fact that an unabridged audiobook can have as many as four to six cassettes means that keeping everything sorted in its proper order can be a problem. Certainly the staff must check each title that has multiple cassettes each time it is returned. If in fact a person is listening to the cassettes in the car and there is more than one title, there is a very good chance a cassette will end up in the wrong container. No one wants to have the ending of a "whodunit" delayed because the last cassette is for Shakti Gawin's *Creative Visualization Meditations* (New World Library).

Games and Realia

School and some public libraries are the primary collectors of games and realia. Public libraries sometimes have loan collections of games and toys that may attract new people to the library. The loaning of games often proves to be a problem for the circulation department, because staff needs to go through the returned game to be sure all the pieces are still there. Naturally, it also means there must be some easily available record of what should be there. All this takes time and effort away from other activities. When the staff views the process as getting in the way of their "real" work, check-in becomes perfunctory. That view usually results in games with missing pieces and a "service" that is no longer a service. School library media centers collect educational games for use in the classroom or in the media center. While the checking for missing parts must still take place, the losses are usually minimal and the learning value of the game far outweighs the cost of staff time for checking the returned games.

Teaching realia, test kits, and models can range from samples of materials, such as rocks or insects, to working models, to large, take-apart anatomical models. Scientific and technical supply houses offer a variety of large-scale models for use in the classroom. Because the models are expensive, few teachers can afford to buy them and the instructional media center is the usual source for these, except where there is a large biology or physics department that acquires the items. Even in the case of large departments, students get better service if the models are in the media center where they can examine the material at any time.

Today the vast majority of games children and young people play are electronic. Heather Wilson (2005) stated, "When trying to figure out how to make libraries more attractive to teens, young adult librarians might ask themselves: 'what are teens doing when they aren't at the library?' Part of the answer is likely, they are playing games" (p. 446). In her article, she discusses computer/video, role playing, miniatures, collectable/trading cards and board games. She interviewed teens at a gaming conference; as one might expect computer/video games were the dominant type of game played by teens followed some what surprisingly by board games. Her suggestion was, if you want teens back in the library, offer teen-oriented games as well as books and magazines related to games and other teen interests. Further, she acknowledges that having space for board game playing as well as appropriate consoles for video game "tournaments" may be a space challenge, but a great way to get the young people back into the library.

Microforms

Microformats are something of a challenge both in their use and where to discuss them. They require equipment to use them, but almost all of their content is textual in character. We decided to place them in this chapter based on the equipment aspect. Although libraries currently acquire very little in the way of microforms, most of them have substantial legacy collections which contain useful information. While it is possible to digitize microforms, few libraries have the funds to cover this process. Also, few commercial firms find it a profitable activity due to low demand. The bulk of the material contained in a microformat is either backfiles of serials or rare/ephemeral information.

One reason libraries acquired microforms was that they save collection storage space, especially for low-use materials. There never seems to be enough storage space. Public service staff spend many hours each year shifting collections to make "just a little more room." Thirty years of back issues of a journal, occupying 25 feet of shelving, can be reduced to three reels of microfilm which, in their cardboard storage boxes, requiring less than one foot of space. Anything printed that occupies substantial space and that one can photograph is convertible to a microformat, including items where color is a factor. Microforms may also provide access to primary research material or to items that are very rare and may only be available, in their original form, in one or two libraries in the world. Thus, while many librarians and most of the public view microforms with some degree—or a great deal—of displeasure, they have served a useful function in providing access to materials that might not otherwise be available locally.

The two most common microform formats in libraries are reels and fiche. Reel formats are the older of the two and were widely used for newspapers and serials. Reel microfilms are long strips of film on the appropriate size reel and have traditionally been available in several sizes: 16 mm, 35 mm, and 70 mm. The film can be positive (clear with black text) or negative (dark with white text). Public service staff need to know about these different types because microfilm readers require adjustment for different film sizes and types. Failure to use the correct size take-up reel can damage film. Failure to adjust the reader for positive or negative film will make it difficult to produce a readable paper copy on a reader-printer machine. (Most people prefer not to read at the machine, but rather to make paper copies and leave the machine as quickly as possible.)

Most libraries tried to confine the microfilm collection to one or two sizes (35 mm and 70 mm) and one type (positive). With any large-scale collection, however, more variety is inevitable, because the information needed by the library was only available in a particular size and type of microfilm. The choice was either to accept yet another variation or forego having the information. Individuals who regularly use microforms are aware of many of the problems and can make the proper machine adjustments without staff assistance. Most individuals, however, will avoid microforms and use them only as a last resort; these people will need assistance.

Microfiche are sheets of film with the images of the original document arranged in columns and rows. Fiche were primarily employed for materials that might have a number of simultaneous users of the collection/title, such as college catalogs or telephone directories. Fiche can be a great space-saving device while providing much greater access by breaking up the file into smaller units, somewhat like drawers in a card catalog.

Like other media, microfiche come in a variety of sizes as well as reduction ratios. Common sizes are 3 by 5 inches, 3 by 6 inches, and 6 by 7 inches, while reduction ratios range from 12 to over 200. The greater the reduction ratio, the more information the producer could fit on a single fiche. Many commercial publications were "48x" (the "x" equals the reduction ratio), but the other relatively common ratio is "16x." The reduction ratio is an issue for public service staff because the reading machines seldom come with a single lens capable of handling all the reductions. Some of the most expensive readers have a lens capable of "zooming" from 10x to 75x. Such units were very costly, in the tens of thousands of dollars. Most libraries must get along with readers that have interchangeable lenses, that is, one lens for each of the common reduction ratios. These lenses need to be available at a public service desk and the staff needs to know how to change them. Using the wrong lens with the wrong type fiche will not damage the equipment or the fiche, but it will increase user resistance to microforms. While a 16x lens with a 48x fiche will produce a very fuzzy image that, with effort, a determined individual can read, that person will be certain that microforms are a form of library torture. A 48x lens with a 16x fiche will produce a very sharp image of a very small part of the text. Reading the text will tax the patience of the most friendly user, as very small shifts of the fiche carrier result in substantial shifts in the text.

One unfortunate characteristic of fiche is that they do not indicate on the eye-legible header what the reduction ratio is. If they did, it would be a great help to the library staff assisting the public. Lacking accepted standards, commercial vendors selected the size and ratio most convenient for them, perhaps to maximize their income if they produced enough material that libraries believe they must own.

Public service staff may not have to handle any of the other media formats discussed in this chapter, but it will be the exceptional library that does not have at least one type of microformat. Microforms, like serials, require substantial staff time in assisting users, who often require help with the equipment, from loading the film/fiche to focusing and getting the image "right-side up," to making a paper copy of the image needed. The staff must also refile the microforms, because allowing users to do this only creates problems later.

ACCESS, STORAGE, PRESERVATION, AND CIRCULATION

Throughout the preceding section we mentioned variations in size and shape of the media formats. This variety has implications for storage and access. While it is possible to use standard library bookcases to house these materials, even with adjustable shelves such storage wastes space. Library equipment and supply houses offer a wide range of cabinets and storage units designed for the different formats. What type of storage unit to use depends on decisions made regarding circulation of the material and direct public access. Two media formats discussed earlier, microforms and video/films, have special storage considerations we will touch on briefly here.

Microform

Very few libraries have circulating microform collections and most use cabinets with drawers designed to hold either fiche or reels. The cabinets are multiple-drawer units, which are very heavy even when empty and exceedingly heavy when filled. Moving a filled storage cabinet is something to be considered carefully. Because library staff are often the ones to have to move library furniture and equipment, long-term need should dictate the placement of microform storage cabinets.

Normally libraries store their microfilm rolls inside a small cardboard container that has a small identification label. It is rare for the reel of film to carry identification information. Sometimes the film leader will have legible identification information. When users leave a number of reels out, the area staff must be certain each reel is in the correct box, sometimes by putting the film in a reader, if the leader does not provide identification information. Failure to return the reel to the correct box can effectively lose the reel. Often a good way to locate a lost reel when a person says the reel in the box is not what the label indicates is to look for the box for the reel in hand. With luck the desired reel will be in that box. Careless reboxing of reels by staff and/or users can unnecessarily add to the staff's workload.

Microfiche may or may not be stored inside a protective cover, such as an envelope or notebook. They are filed in order, in a fiche cabinet, or notebook.

This allows the user to see a large number of fiche headers without handling several fiche before locating the one needed. Unnecessary handling increases the chances of damaging the fiche. Microfiche, like many of the other media discussed in this chapter, are physically a series of layers. That is, there is a relatively thick, strong carrier base, often acetate or polyacetate, with a very thin surface layer that contains the image. The surface layer is very susceptible to damage. There are two common types of fiche, diazo and silver halide. Silver halide is archival quality, but very easy to scratch. The diazo, although not considered a permanent film, is harder to damage, but is still susceptible to scratching. Most damage occurs during the filing and refiling process. Damage to a corner of the fiche can put a scratch down the entire surface of the fiche behind it. Depending on the film's reduction ratio, the amount of information lost may be little or great (the higher the ratio, the more data will disappear).

Film and Video

Standard library shelving can house the films and videos and make them more available for "browsing," but it wastes space. Library equipment vendors sell storage cabinets designed to store various types and sizes of media material. Video cabinet drawer depth, length, and width are such that three or four rows of cassettes will fit into the drawer. A storage problem does arise with a mixed collection of VHS, Beta, three-quarter-inch cassettes, and DVDs.

In terms of care of these materials, one should rewind and inspect each videocassette and film (if still in the collection) at least once every six months, even if unused. In an environment where there is high temperature (over 80 degrees Fahrenheit) and humidity (65% and higher), the thin image-bearing layer (emulsion layer) becomes soft and somewhat sticky. Films and videos left in such conditions for long periods, without use, become so sticky the image-bearing layer pulls off when use finally occurs.

EQUIPMENT USE

From a public service point of view, locating all of the public access media equipment in one area is best. An area near a service desk with staff on duty full time is ideal. In the past, it was necessary to place microform-reading machines in low-light areas for people to read the screen easily. Today, that is no longer necessary, which makes it reasonable to have a single equipment area. Staffing the area will assure minimal damage to both equipment and the "software" and reduce user frustration. It also means the staff in the area can and should have more knowledge about how all of the equipment works than when it is just one of many public service duties.

While it may be nice to have individual and small group listening and viewing rooms, it is not necessary. Securing the equipment to study carrels and issuing earphones allows individuals to listen to something without disturbing anyone. The less frequently used equipment can be stored in a nonpublic area and set up in public areas when needed. Space always seems to be in short supply in libraries; using public table space for little-used equipment goes against most libraries' service policy.

LIBRARY WEB SITES

A chapter on media is as good a place as any to address public service aspects of a library's Web site. Easy to navigate sites are a given as they are more and more the "face" of the library. With the growing importance of "social sites" (Web 2.0), libraries ought to devote some time assessing the "sociability" of their sites. Ignoring this aspect of the site will, in all likelihood, have a negative impact on the younger segment of the service community. One way to assess your library's site in terms of the social media landscape is to monitor what, if anything, is said about the library's reputation. It may be better to have a "scar" or two rather than not be mentioned at all. Clearly the goal is to earn "stars," but to do so probably will call for greater social interaction capability for the library's Web site.

Darlene Fichter (2007) suggested five social media tools to consider to improve a library's site. An obvious place to start is to use a Weblog (or blog) where comments are encouraged. A library might have two or more such blogs—children, YA, and adult. Wikis, message boards, or forums are other ways to generate user feedback and commentary. Inviting ratings of services and collection content is still another method for engaging the service population. Podcasting, moblogs (mobile-enabled blogs), and vlogs (video) are other options for enhancing interactivity of a library Web site.

Knowing what you hope to accomplish from having a more social site is critical—increased traffic, greater awareness of services, better "branding," stronger community ties, and more user participation are some examples of possible goals. The library's goals will help determine what approach(es) to take. Certainly being more interactive on the Web will call for staff involvement on an ongoing basis. Where will the time come from? That may be *the* question and not an easy one to answer in most situations. Having an answer before starting down this path is very important.

Having a mix of library and user-generated content is a desirable goal. However, inviting user feedback will, at some point in time, generate some less than favorable comments. It is inevitable. When it does occur, being defensive will not be well received. Instead, listen and respond thoughtfully. Making it clear the library is interested in improving and takes all comments seriously is a good approach.

Reviewing how "bookmarkable" the library pages are is another way to assess the site's user-friendliness (it probably will require some technical assistance to make all of them possible bookmarks). A good Web site to check out for additional ideas is Social Media Optimization (http://social-media-optimi zation.com).

Laurie Charnigo and Paula Barnett-Ellis (2007) explored the impact of Facebook.com on academic libraries. They surveyed 126 academic librarians regarding the sites' implications for academic libraries. Perhaps the most interesting finding was that only 12 percent of those surveyed believed Facebook had any conceivable academic value (p. 30). Despite this, some academic libraries are creating Facebook profiles as a way of "connecting" with students.

Diane Ketelhut and her colleagues (2005) wrote an intriguing article about the potential of interactive media for library services, in particular the multi-user virtual environment interface (MUVE). Although their focus was on a school library setting, their discussion could apply to any library wishing to provide a more attractive Web site for younger users. The work was based on Harvard's Graduate School of Education project to develop MUVEs for middle schools. The authors made the point that MUVEs lead to "students highly engaged by this approach" (p. 31). Will this be the future of public service? Who knows, but given the orientation of today's young people some variation seems rather likely.

STAFFING

Any library with a substantial media collection, other than microforms, needs a few staff members who have a background in media. When the library has the responsibility of meeting the classroom equipment needs of 100 or more teachers, it is cost effective to have at least a part-time equipment technician on the staff who can carry out most repair and maintenance work.

Media have an important role to play in any library's service program. The entire public service staff needs to understand that role and not view media services as a stepchild to other services or as an unreasonable burden on staff time.

SUMMARY

One given of media services is they will change at almost the same speed as technology in general. Keeping up-to-date with development is a challenge, especially for staff who have more than enough work to occupy their attention. It seems rather likely that media services will play an ever-growing role in the overall service program of most libraries.

Chapter Review Material

1. What role do media play in public service programs?
2. What are the common problems for media use?
3. Videos present some special problems for the staff. What are these problems?
4. In what ways has technology changed media services over the last five years?
5. Legal use of media is circumscribed by the copyright law. List the major issues.
6. Pick a library you know and go to its Web site. How "social" is it? What might be added?

REFERENCES

Brown, Myra Michele. 2006. "Video Libraries: More Than a Lure," *American Libraries* 26, no. 11: 41.

Charnigo, Laurie, and Paula Barnett-Ellis. 2007. "Checking out Facebook.com," *Information Technology and Libraries* 26, no. 1: 23–34.

Evans, Brandi P., and Glenda A. Gunter. 2004. "A Catalyst for Change," *Journal of Educational Media & Library Services* 41, no. 3: 225–236.

Fichter, Darlene. 2007. "How Social Is Your Web Site?" *Online* 31, no. 3: 57–60.

Fox, Robert E. 2004. "Do Audiobooks Belong in Academic Libraries?" *Georgia Library Quarterly* 40, no. 4: 9–11.

Holovack, Donna. 1996. "The Popularity of Audiobooks in Libraries," *Public Libraries* 35, no. 2: 113–117.

Houser, Rhonda. 2006. "Building a Library GIS Service," *Library Trends* 55, no. 2: 315–326.

Kaye, Alan. 2005. "Digital Dawn," *Library Journal* 130, no. 9: 62–65.

Ketelhut, Diane, Jody Clarke, Chris Dede, Brian Nelson, and Catherine Bowman. 2005. "Extending Library Service through Emerging Interactive Media," *Knowledge Quest* 34, no. 4: 29–32.

Kim, Ann. 2006. "The Future Is Now," *Library Journal* 131, no. 9: 60–63.

Lora, Pat. 1994. "Public Library Video Collections." In *Video Collection Development in Multitype Libraries,* G. P. Handman, ed. Westport, CT: Greenwood.

Manley, Will. 1991. "Facing the Public," *Wilson Library Bulletin* 65, no. 6: 89–90.

Mason, Sally. 1994. "Libraries, Literacy and the Visual Media." In *Video Collection Development in Multitype Libraries,* G. P. Handman, ed. Westport, CT: Greenwood.

Netherby, Jennifer. 2007. "Slow to Become a Shelf Staple, DVD Is Still Growing," *Library Journal,* June 1, supplement: 5–6.

Oder, Norman. 2005. "The DVD Predicament," *Library Journal* 130, no. 19: 35–40.

Peters, Tom, Lori Bell, Diana Sussman, and Sharon Ruda. 2005. "An Overview of Digital Audiobooks for Libraries," *Computers in Libraries* 25, no. 7: 7–8, 61–64.

Ranganathan, Shiyali R. 1952. *Library Book Selection.* New Delhi: India Library Association.

Redden, Linda. 2005. "Videostreaming in K-12 Classrooms," *Media & Methods* 42, no. 1: 14–15.

Rooker, Jill. 1991. "Federal Copyright Law: How It Affects Academic Video Services," *Indiana Libraries* 10, no. 2: 48–51.

Spielvogel, Cindy. 2007. "Libraries Lead the Way to Movie Downloads," *Library Journal* 132, no. 10 (supplement): 11–12.

Story, Howard. 2004. "The World Is Going Digital! How Do I Cope?" *Library Mosaics* 15, no. 2: 12–13.

U.S. House of Representatives. 1976. *Omnibus Copyright Revision Legislative History.* 94th Cong., 2d sess. H. Rept. 1476. Washington, DC: Government Printing Office.

Wilson, Heather. 2005. "Gaming for Librarians," *Voice Youth Advocates* 27, no. 6: 446–449.

SUGGESTED READINGS

Behler, Anne, Beth Roberts, and Karen Dabney. 2006. "Circulating Map Collections at Pennsylvania State University," *DttP, Documents to the People* 34, no. 4: 33–36.

Caron, Susan. 2004. "Transiting to DVD," *Library Journal* 129, no. 9 (supplement): 4–5.

Chase, Darren, 2007. "Transformative Sharing with Instant Messaging, Wikis, Interactive Maps and Flicker," *Computers in Libraries* 27, no. 1: 7–8, 52–56.

Cogdell, Edna. 2003. "School Library Media Management Skills," *Knowledge Quest* 32, no. 2: 21–22.

Cosentino, Sharon L. 2008. "Folksonomies: Path to a Better Way?" *Public Libraries* 47, no. 2: 42–47.

Lee, Scott, and Carolyn Burrell. 2004. "Introduction to Streaming Video for Novices," *Library Hi Tech News*, no. 2: 20–24.

Smith, Angel, and Claudene Sproles. 2004. "Don't Get Lost: The Basics of Organizing a Library's Map Collection," *Kentucky Libraries* 68, no. 2: 22–27.

Snow, Maryly. 2004. "Learning from Latern Slides, 1979–2004," *Visual Resources Association Bulletin* 31, no. 1: 45–50.

Stoltenberg, Jaime and Abraham Parish. 2006. "Geographic Information Systems and Libraries," *Library Trends* 55, no. 2: 217–360.

Government Information

A popular government without popular information, or the means of acquiring it, is but a prologue to a farce or a tragedy; or perhaps both. . . . And
a people who mean to be their own governors, must arm themselves with
the power that knowledge gives.

—James Madison, 1832

The ongoing dialog surrounding free access to government information is
balanced against the, at times, compelling need for security and privacy.

—Linda Johnson, 2007

September 11, 2001, brought about significant changes for many people and
organizations in the United States. Government information also experienced
changes, some large, some small. Initially librarians thought they observed a
significant tightening in what government agencies made available. One factor
in that perception was the ongoing move to a digital format. This process had
been under way for some time, but when some materials were pulled the sense
was the changes were greater than they actually were. It is also true that there
was some tightening in what was released, not an unreasonable reaction to
what had happened. By 2007, some of the concern had abated, but lingering
questions (security vs. access) still remain the subject of strong debate during the time we prepared this chapter, as our opening quotation from Linda
Johnson suggests.

Although you might think access to government information is a relatively
new concern, the opening quote from James Madison shows that interest in
and concern about society's access to government information has a long history in the United States. How to achieve a balance between the access Madison believed in and the much-needed added security in today's very different
world is a challenge for everyone. In this chapter, we explore the nature of

what, not all that many years ago, was referred to as government documents and which today is more realistically labeled government information. We also examine the challenges of achieving a proper balance between access and security.

Citizens, if they are to participate meaningfully in their governance, must have some free access to information about government activities and processes. In the not too distant past, print documents provided that critical information and libraries filled the role of both of acquirer of government material as well as providing assistance in accessing the information. Today there is a vast universe of that information available through the Internet. A significant difference exists between the two means of access. With print you may not have the most current information, but you know what you are looking at has not been modified by some unknown, perhaps third nongovernment party. Also it is not likely to vanish in the blink of an eye. Neither is true of the digital format. Kathy Dempsey's (2004) editorial "The Info Was There, Then—Poof" sums up the issue of permanence and digital information. Her editorial prefaced a themed issue dealing with government information, in which she highlighted a key concern: "Where do you draw the line between which data should be public and which should be kept private?" (p. 4). We might add, "and who should make that critical call?" Dempsey related how one of the articles intended for that issue went "poof" when the White House requested a final review process. (The authors of the article in question worked in a federal information center and their piece was to describe the factors that determine what information is deemed classified.)

For a number of years the idea of an "electronic democracy" has been discussed and debated—long before there was a World Wide Web. The idea was/is that it would "enable citizens to participate more efficiently in civic life, as well as make the public bureaucracy more 'business-like' in the delivery of its programs and services" (Shuler, 2003, p. 107). Certainly most government bodies have a Web presence today; just how that presence has or has not modified programs and services is an open question. "E-government" is a term you see and often appears to have a number of meanings depending on who is talking about the concept. At its most basic level, the term relates to a government's employment of technology to provide information and services to its citizens. You can gain a sense of the variations in meanings when some people view it as a means of emergency communication while others see it as a way of gaining access to reports and minutes of meetings. The latter view makes it clear that libraries, especially public libraries, could/should have a significant role to play, as not everyone has Internet access in their homes.

The Economist (February 16, 2008) published an 18-page supplement entitled "The Electronic Bureaucrat: A Special Report on Technology and Government." The introductory essay to the supplement ends with: "Although hopes have been high and the investment huge, so far the results have mostly been disappointing. That reflects a big difficulty in e-government (and in writing about it): it touches on so many other things. What exactly is it that public organisations are trying to maximize, and how can it be measured?" (p. 4). This has been and still remains an issue: what is the role/purpose of government information and e-government? And that in turn raises the question of what role libraries can and should play.

A 2007 *Library Journal* news note (p. 17) reported on an effort to secure funding for public libraries to provide access to e-governments. Presumably, the focus would be on federal government information as part of a plan to create a national network of public libraries designated as "E-Government Information and Service Centers" (EGISC). We cannot help but wonder if this might be the start of the end of the Federal Depository Library Program (FDLP) for federal information as we have know it (more about FDLP later in this chapter).

Defining what is government information is not always easy. Are reports prepared by nongovernmental agencies, but required by a government agency, "government" information? What about short- and long-term multijurisdictional groups that produce reports? Government information comes from local, state, federal, and international bodies. In today's digital world, there is undoubtedly more government information, regardless of source, available to more people than in the past—if you know how to get at it. Almost all government material is "born digital," which allows jurisdictions to make it inexpensively available on the Web, if they wish to do so.

HISTORICAL BACKGROUND

Michael White (1996) suggested that society's right to government information, at least in the English-speaking world, has its origin in the English *Magna Carta* of 1215. Expanding on this right, the U.S. Constitution (Article 1, Section 5) contains the requirement that Congress shall "keep a journal of its proceedings, and from time to time publish same, excepting such parts as may in their judgment require secrecy; and the yeas and nays of the members of either house on any question shall, at the desire of one-fifth of those present, be entered on the journal." Thus, from the outset some federal information could be legally withheld.

By 1813, selected libraries were part of a depository program that covered congressional materials. Later, in 1857, the program expanded to cover items produced by the executive branch. The program continued to grow over the next 120 years, both in types of material distributed and in the number of libraries receiving all or some of the available material.

At some point, in small steps, the government decided that citizens needed easy access not only to information about government activities, but also to information that would improve the economy or enhance daily living. How-to publications, such as those on gardening and carpentry, became part of the government's publication list. Thus, a second purpose of a government publication program was to help people improve the quality of their life. As Bruce Morton (1987) wrote, "The consumption of information, like the consumption of food, is vital to the nourishment of the pursuit of life, liberty and happiness in a democratic society" (p. 54).

In some cases, government publications covered topics that no commercial (for-profit) publishers would handle because the market was too small or the cost of production too high. Many of the statistical compilations are possible only due to governmental authority, resources, and support. The primary user groups, and often the only ones of such compilations, are scholars and researchers. As part of the federal government's review process, some people are questioning the role the government should play in producing such publications. Morton (1987) summarized the situation as follows:

> The first information obligation of the government of the United States is to produce the information it needs to effectively govern, and in so doing provide accurate information about its activities for itself and so it can be held accountable to, and by, its constituents . . .
>
> The government, however, is neither obliged (nor should it feel so) to produce, let alone provide it, based on the needs of the researchers who occupy the nation's libraries. One neither disputes the needs of these researchers nor their researches. (p. 53)

By the time the Reagan administration began in 1980, there were over 1,300 full and partial depository libraries of U.S. government documents. (Today the number is only somewhat lower.) During President Reagan's first term, the Office of Management and Budget (OMB) received authorization to develop a federal information policy as the result of the passage of Public Law 96–511 (Paperwork Reduction Act [PRA] of 1980). OMB had the responsibility to minimize the cost of collecting, maintaining, using, and disseminating information. One of OMB's initiatives supported the concept of disseminating federal information as raw data in an electronic format, often without software for using or searching for desired data. Despite this drawback in providing the mechanism for access, certainly OMB's role in shifting the emphasis from paper to electronic means of dissemination has been significant.

A major problem with the implementation of the PRA was that the necessary national, much less local technological infrastructure that would make the concept viable did not yet exist. Another significant issue was the lack of government-wide standards for making information available electronically. That remains something of a problem in 2008. Only a few individuals who could benefit from government information have the skills to locate and retrieve what might be useful without some assistance. Realistically, until there is a true single standard, most people will have to depend on either their place of employment or libraries to provide the needed assistance. Perhaps this is another factor in the effort to create the EGISC network that we mentioned earlier.

From a public service point of view, providing such assistance for all the variations in U.S. government databases is a challenge that few libraries can fully meet. We do agree with Golderman and Connolly's (2002) statement that "Whether you are inspired by the dynamic expression of democracy at work in Washington or believe that our politicians must be closely watched at all times, keeping track of how our officials carry out their constitutional mandated mission has been made easier thanks to online resources" (p. 50). However, we have a long way to go before it is truly easy. As you will read shortly, finding your way through the options to get to the desired information calls for patience and persistence. Users will need all the assistance you can provide when they are seeking government information.

Efforts by the government as well as private groups to improve access have a mixed track record. Such projects as GovBot, USGOVSEARCH, and Web-Gov, all intended to improve access, have come and gone since the late 1990s

(Notess, 2003, pp. 263–264). In late 2000, FirstGov—now called USA.gov—went live as the federal government's Web portal. We cover this site in more depth later in this chapter.

PHILOSOPHY OF LIBRARY GOVERNMENT INFORMATION SERVICE

Free unrestricted access is the cornerstone of library public service programs, at least for the library's primary service population. In the case of government depository libraries, there is a legal requirement that the documents collection be open to *all* persons, not just the primary service population. Thus, privately funded libraries that have depository status must allow anyone to come in and use the government material, even if the library limits access to its other collections. This requirement can create some problems for public service staff, especially if the library requires the user to show a valid identification card to enter the library. Staff operating the entrance control desk must understand that they must admit anyone requesting access to the depository collection.

It is unlikely that the founders of the depository system envisioned the federal government becoming the country's largest publisher, or really debated which documents should or should not be available to the public. By the 1950s, there was growing concern about who could gain access to what material in a depository collection. So, even before 9/11, there was debate regarding what and how much information should be available to those outside the government. That debate has only escalated.

Access to scientific and technical information, provided by the National Technological Information Service (NTIS), has been one such focal point of debate. The government discussed and to some extent acted to limit access to NTIS information, particularly scientific and technical material. Many people, including most librarians, think complete freedom of access to unclassified government information is vital to scholarship and to the well-being of society. Others think that access to scientific but unclassified information leads to increased security risks for the country.

As Klein and Schwal (2005) discuss, there is a delicate balance that society must achieve between maintaining some degree of security and free access to information in this troubled world, if its citizens are to effectively participate in a meaningful democracy. Libraries play a significant role in providing such access. When it was just a print world the process was complex, and often painfully slow for the person seeking access. Libraries and their staff were an essential part of the process. Something that is frequently overlooked in the debate about security and access is the fact depository libraries (the largest holders of print government publications) do not *own* the material. Although they invest significant sums of money in the long-term storage of the material as well as in staff effort to service the collections, they do not have ownership. The government can and has, at various times, withdrawn material from depository collections—it is not a post-9/11 phenomenon. Further, it can do so without consultation, and libraries have no recourse.

Klein and Schwal (who themselves are federal government employees) in their concluding section make the following points; "Newly generated government information will be evaluated against established criteria for review for public release, the same as always. There is no core group making these decisions, although there may be a tendency on the part of those responsible to err on the side of caution" (2005; p. 23).

Staff members who work regularly with government information also believe that better and more frequent use of government information would benefit most library users. They believe that if individuals understood the broad range of information and subjects available, usage would increase. It is interesting that several studies of the use of government information as reflected in citations have shown usage remaining constant, even in an Internet world—"despite this increased visibility and access, the use of physical documents and citation patterns indicate that government is not being used or cited more frequently than it was in the 1980s" (Cheney, 2006, p. 303).

It is incumbent upon the public service staff to remind users about the potential value of government information. Unfortunately, this is not always done. This forgetfulness is not only because of the location of the print material (which often is a separate and less central area), but also due to the difficulty in identifying appropriate material. Public service staff need to make a conscious effort to be more involved in identifying and using government information.

As a result of congressional consideration of the Government Printing Reform Act of 1996, various library associations (for example, the ALA, the American Association of Law Libraries, and the Association of Research Libraries) became active in attempting to influence the final form of the legislation. One of their efforts was to create a list of basic principles:

- The public has a right of access to government information.
- The government has an obligation to guarantee the authenticity and integrity of its information.
- The government has an obligation to disseminate and provide broad public access to its information.
- The government has an obligation to preserve its information.

Government information created or compiled by government employees or at government expense should remain in the public domain ("Statement on H.R. 4280, the Government Printing Reform Act of 1996," 1997, p. 11).

Current federal policy essentially has been to maximize the usefulness of information, within limits of security concerns, while minimizing costs and recovering some of the costs of developing the information. How the issues are resolved will have implications for public services staff.

A hint of where the process may be going appeared in an article by Wayne P. Kelly (1998). Kelly served as superintendent of documents from 1991 to 1997. In the article, he discussed the question of privatization of traditional Government Printing Office (GPO) publications. His case study was the sale of one of the best-selling titles produced by the GPO, *U.S. Industrial Outlook*, to McGraw-Hill. Kelly raised several points: (1) that there was no empowering legislation allowing for the privatization of government-produced information; (2) that there was no debate about the new policy; and (3) that agencies were becoming more restrictive in their distribution arrangements or were charging use fees. One of his concerns about privatization was the fact that what one could use in the past without permission was now copyrighted: was this in the public interest? Another concern was accountability; Kelly noted that McGraw-Hill printed a disclaimer of responsibility for the accuracy and completeness of the material, apparently even for the work compiled by McGraw-Hill. His final concern was who profits from such activities, in the sense of how much revenue is actually coming back to the government. Citing what happened when the *Journal of the National Cancer Institute* was privatized in 1997, he expressed concern that such privatization activities create the potential for conflict of interest, especially if the details of the transaction are secret. Such privatization raises the cost for libraries when it comes to providing access to such data.

Reference service in this "new age" of electronic government information presents some challenges for the staff. There is much to learn about the idiosyncrasies of the various agency databases and Web sites, even in terms of such basics as how to search, display, and print/download. Also, some agencies provide different or more information in the electronic format than they did/do in the print version. The result is that the public services staff and users alike must remember which version supplies this or that type of information.

We conclude this section with a news note from *American Libraries*. Much has been written, over the last seven years, about the federal government restricting access to its information. In an interesting turnaround, the GPO notified an academic library it had no authority to restrict access to depository items, in this case Nuclear Regulatory Commission (NRC) material. In sum, "only the Superintendent of Documents has the authority to request that depository libraries withdraw or secure publications in their collections. No such official request has been made" (*American Libraries*, 2007, p. 16). The statement was issued by the GPO due to a documents librarian sending an e-mail to a number of depository libraries asking that they carefully screen requests for access to NRC material in order to protect national security. This is an interesting twist in trying to achieve "the delicate balance."

TYPES OF GOVERNMENT INFORMATION

Federal Information

Without question, the U.S. government produces a prodigious amount of information every year, even if agency staff err on the side of caution when it comes to what may be released to the public due to security concerns. Although more and more is only released in a digital form, print, videos, maps, and other formats are still produced. You should keep in mind that it is not just the three branches that generate public information; there are a very large number of independent agencies (such as the Federal Communications Commission) adding to the daily flow of information.

One very rich source of information about many topics of current interest is the series of congressional committee hearing reports. These documents almost always present pros and cons about the subject of the committee hearings, thus making the report a single source for expert opinion and information on both sides of an issue. Another characteristic of the hearing reports is their sheer volume, because they contain all the transcribed oral presentations (testimony) as well as written statements and any insertions. Because of the volume of material and their relatively low use, paper-based committee reports are usually only found in full depository libraries. With a degree of patience and persistence you can find many of them online. Your first step is to go to USA.gov, click on "federal government," then "legislative," followed by either "House" or "Senate." (Needless to say you can check out executive or judicial branches of government from this site as well.) Once you get that far, you need to know the committee's name. Eventually you will get to the hearings. Another method is to go to GPOAccess (http://www.gpoaccess.gov/) and click your way down. Since the process at either Web site can yield a large number of results, many users will get frustrated unless they get some assistance from library staff.

One frequently used publication is the *Congressional Record* (*CR*). *CR* is a semi-verbatim record of the floor proceedings of both houses of Congress. It is "semi-verbatim" because a member of Congress may add to or delete information from the *CR* after the fact. Most individuals are unaware of this editing process and accept the material as an accurate account of what transpired. Because of its wide appeal and fairly heavy use, many medium-sized public and academic libraries have the *CR* in their collections, as do the large libraries. The *CR* is also available online (http://www.gpoaccess.gov/crecord/index.html). Another good source is the *CQ Electronic Library* (http://library.cqpress.com), which contains *CQ Weekly*. As Golderman and Connelly (2002) state, the *CQ Weekly* is a "true record of the workings of Congress" (p. 50), which, unlike the *CR*, is not modified. The service is subscription based, so it may not be available in some libraries.

The GPO home page (GPOAccess) allows you to search recent publications as well as which depositories selected the item. Some of the databases one will find on GPOAccess are *Code of Federal Regulations, Commerce Business Daily, Congressional Bills, Congressional Record, GAO Reports, Monthly Catalog of U.S. Government Publications, Public Laws*, and the *U.S. Code*.

Earlier we mentioned that end users face the prospect of losing their favorite publication as federal agencies move into electronic dissemination of their information. Joe Morehead (1997), certainly one of, if not *the* leading scholar of government publications and their distribution, wrote an article about the migration of federal periodicals from print to electronic format. He labeled the electronic versions "govzines." His baseline was the Congressional Information Service's *U.S. Government Periodical Index* and information taken from the University of Memphis Government Documents Department's Web site, in particular its database of "migrating government publications" (the site no longer exists). In all, Morehead discussed 14 govzines. When describing *The Third Branch*, he noted, "however, with this govzine (and others, especially *FDA Consumer*, encountered in my cybersurfing expedition), the print version turned out to be considerably more current than the electronic version, a refutation of a guiding Internet principle, the rapid access to information" (p. 25).

An ongoing concern about electronic resources, government and commercial, is how permanent is permanent? Who will archive and assure continued access to electronic information as operating systems, software, and hardware change time and time again? In classic Moreheadian prose he concludes his "preachment" with: "It seems that while the GPO gets a grand makeover, the using public suffers a bad hair day. To change the metaphor, the migration to the Internet and the concomitant extirpation of print-equivalent sources will falter if it proceeds with the frenetic exigency exhibited by the thundering herds of wildebeest across the Serengeti plains" (p. 29).

We wish to note that for all its problems, USA.gov *has* made it much easier to identify useful federal information, regardless of how far one may be from a depository library. It has some user-friendly topical categories (for example, Consumer Information and Kidsgov). Naturally, there are links to federal agencies (either the A–Z index or "Federal Government"). You can also sign up to receive updates to the site via e-mail or RSS feed. The move away from agency-only access to subject-based makes locating useful information much more likely for the general public. However, as Patricia Fletcher (2003) stated, "FirstGov does not remediate these age-old problems with access to data. It does not mean all government information will reside in one format, in one location. Rather, FirstGov makes use of existing federal agencies for its content" (p. 279).

When the public services staff is aware of the variety of information contained in federal information sources, they can direct the public to these useful sources. All types of libraries can find some useful material for users in the annual pool of federal information.

State Information

Several differences exist between state and federal information. One difference is that there is still a strong print orientation at the state level. Certainly there is a movement to have more and more state information available through the Web. Unlike federal information, states often and frequently do copyright their publications. Many people, including librarians, believe that state publications are public domain (not copyrighted) items, similar to federal publications. Because it is an option that some states elect to use while other states do not, it does cause some confusion. In Michigan, for example, the state *may* copyright materials, while in Pennsylvania state law *requires* copyrighting. Some shared characteristics between state and federal information are diversity of subject matter, relatively low cost, and increasing difficulty in identifying what is an official publication. From a library point of view, state documents are no different than any other copyrighted material. The staff and the public should assume the concept of fair use applies to state publications rather than the concept of public domain.

As is true of the federal government, most states now produce materials mandated by law. Many of the federal statistical publications are compilations of state data, which means the most current information, by as much as two or three years, may be in the state publications. The volume of general information and how-to publications from states is low compared with federal output.

Access to state publications is often difficult. There are two good online resources for state government information—a link from the USA.gov home page (state government) and State and Local Government on the Net (www. statelocalgov.net/).

For most libraries with only occasional requests for state publications, the Web sites cited above are good options. Using the Center for Research Libraries (CRL) for older print material is a probably the fastest option. Since 1952, when CRL started actively collecting documents from all the states, it has gained the reputation of having the most comprehensive state documents collection in the United States. Any library can borrow materials from CRL, for a fee, through the regular ILL system. Using CRL may provide users with more cost-effective access to state documents than if a library attempts to build up its own collection.

Local Government Publications

Collecting local documents is something almost all public and academic libraries do, if not through intent then by serendipity. Even if there is nothing about acquiring local documents in the library's collection development policy, local governments often view the library as a distribution mechanism. A better approach is to plan on collecting local documents, as they are often high-interest items for the community. One consideration in planning is the retention policy: How long should the library retain such documents? Collecting and retaining the local city and perhaps county documents is reasonable for a central public library and perhaps a local academic library.

Normally the public learns about local government publications through newspaper articles and/or local news broadcasts, not from indexes. While almost all local governments produce budgets, minutes of meetings, annual reports, and so on, the problem for both the public and library staff is learning what appeared and when. Tracking down reports of various departments and programs is obviously time consuming. Adding to the problem are various short- and long-term associations formed by several local governments.

Where would you go to get a copy of the 1987 survey of visitors to the Monterey Peninsula produced by AMBAG (Association of Monterey Bay Area Governments)? For that matter, how would anyone learn about such a publication? We found our example in an article about the Monterey Peninsula published in an issue of United Airlines' magazine *Vis à Vis*. Local area documents are often high-interest items. They also will represent a major challenge for library staff to identify and obtain.

As one would expect, local and regional governments' use and organization of electronic information is highly varied. Although the "State and Local Government on the Net" does have links to cities, the sites tend to be more like chamber of commerce Web sites in nature rather than those of the local government. The site provides a wide variety of information, but the ones we checked did not get you to the city government. Your best bet is to try to find an official city Web site for the community of interest.

International Documents

National governments in almost every country issue at least a few publications each year and a great many now have Internet sites. In many countries, the government publication program equals the U.S. program in volume and complexity. The good news is that these large-scale programs generally have an agency, like the U.S. GPO, that is the primary distributor of the publications. Very few countries offer a depository program to foreign libraries. Only the large research libraries actively collect foreign documents because few users need the material. If the public service staff knows the location of the nearest foreign document collection, they can adequately serve the few users with an interest in or need for these publications.

International documents, especially United Nations publications, however, do have a wider appeal. The major sources of international publications/information are intergovernmental organizations (IGOs). The Union of International Organizations site, http://www.uia.be, may be useful for information on free online resources from such bodies. The usual definition of an IGO is a group of three or more member countries working together on one or more long-term common interests. Without doubt, the largest IGO is the United Nations. There are also nongovernmental organizations (NGOs), such as the World Health Organization, that issue publications and information of interest to many library users. A good starting point for such organizations is the Geneva International Forum (http://www.intl.ch/), or the U.N. Non-Governmental Organizations database, available from the U.N. Office at Geneva (UNOG) Web site (http://www.unog.ch). Yahoo!'s Government: Countries (http://www.yahoo.com/Government/Countries) provides links to more than 100 countries' Internet sites. Some of these sites have little information, but have some links to other helpful electronic resources.

The United Nations has an extensive publications program, and like other governmental bodies issues material in electronic formats. The U.N. Web site provides a variety of information about the organization, such as the U.N. Publications site (http://unp.un.org), which includes ordering information. Additionally, a list of U.N. depository libraries worldwide is available online (http://www.un.org/Depts/dhl/deplib/countries/index.html). For most libraries that have some U.N. documents, the material is part of the regular collection, circulating or reference, rather than held in a separate document area, simply because they do not acquire very many titles. As a result there are few, if any, public service implications, other than knowing the location of a more comprehensive foreign and international collection.

PUBLIC ACCESS AND THE FEDERAL DEPOSITORY LIBRARY PROGRAM

We've mentioned depository libraries several times in this chapter. Here we focus on the Federal Depository Library Program (FDLP) and its long history. It has been very successful in getting government information to the public. As of late 2007, there were 1,250 such libraries. To locate the one nearest to you, go to http://www.gpoaccess.gov/fdlp.html.

There are two types of depository libraries: full and selective. A full depository agrees to accept all items available to FDLP participants, while selective institutions take only a portion of the material. The selective libraries are encouraged to take at least 15 percent of the items available. (Note: The depository program does *not* include all publications issued by federal agencies and organizations.) The GPO provides government information products at no cost (at least at present) to members of the FDLP. Member institutions are, in turn, required to provide local, no-fee access in "an impartial environment" to the public and to provide professional assistance in using the material.

The composition of the FDLP is heavily weighted toward academic libraries (50%), with public libraries a distant second (20%). The breakdown for the balance of members is 11 percent academic law libraries, 5 percent community college libraries, 5 percent state and special libraries, 5 percent federal and state court libraries, and 4 percent federal agency libraries.

As the federal government moves toward greater and greater dependence on electronic dissemination of information, questions such as the following have been raised:

- Is the FDLP still necessary?
- Is the FDLP a remnant of the nineteenth century?
- Is it really the best way to get information to people in the twenty-first century?
- Is there a way to change the system to make it more cost-effective?

In the mid-1990s, questions such as the above were actively debated. Patrick Wilkerson's article "Beyond the Federal Depository Library Program" (1996) explored the challenges facing the FDLP. Wilkerson concluded, "The traditional FDLP is dead. . . . The new entity will be created to fill the country's need for free and open access to government information in the twenty-first century" (p. 417). On the other hand, Prudence Adler (1996) believed that FDLP "has stood the test of time because of the role that it has played in promoting access to government information, and in support of teaching and learning and in stimulating economic development. That role continues and, indeed, should be strengthened and reaffirmed" (p. 441).

John Shuler (2004), a noted government documents librarian, in writing about FDLP and its economic realties in today's electronic world indicated, "No matter how GPO rethinks its content management responsibilities, there has to be clear acknowledgement that there are just too many depository libraries. . . . What's more is the notion of a depository library as local institution valid any longer?" (p. 249). Shortly after this statement was made, Miriam Drake (2005) concluded her article about FDLP with the observation that "depository libraries and librarians should not and are not going away. Depository librarians provide safety net and expertise so that people have free and permanent access to the records of their government and its activities" (p. 50). What the future will hold for FDLP is impossible to correctly predict; whatever it may be it seems likely that some form of e-access will play an ever greater role for new information and some libraries will have very large legacy collections of print materials that they do not own.

A reminder about public access to federal documents is appropriate here. Any depository library, partial or full, *must* allow anyone access to the federal documents, regardless of the library's policies about public use of its other collections. (The U.S. Code, Title 44, § 1911 (1944) states, "Depository libraries shall make government publications available for free use of the general public.") In the *Instructions to Depository Libraries* (1992), "free use" is further defined and the *Federal Depository Library Manual* (*FDLM*) (1993) addressed issues of access to electronic materials. If the library restricts public access to its general collections and few people request access to the documents collection, staff members, especially new staff, may unknowingly deny legally required access. It is important that all public service staff understand this legal requirement.

Another requirement is that there be a library staff member primarily responsible for handling the depository material, but this does not necessarily mean a public service person. Very often, when there is just one person, the staff member is part of the technical services section because of the high volume of record keeping and processing associated with maintaining a documents collection. In such cases, occasional "mini-workshops" for the public service staff on use of government publications and access tools (indexes, abstracts, etc.) will help increase the use of the material.

FDLP members have an obligation to promote their federal information collections and services. The *FDLM* states that when it comes to promotion the "most important group to target for public awareness is the general public" (1993, p. 112). In essence, the library's primary service population may not be the target group the GPO is interested in reaching.

Another aspect of the depository program is mandated retention. Adequate collection space is a chronic problem in most libraries. One method for gaining space is deselecting material from the collection. A traditional "weeding"/deselection technique is to remove the lowest-use items and either store them in less expensive space or discard the material. Government publications more often than not fall into the low-use category, yet the depository may not be as quick to remove these items as it might be with low-use purchased materials. All depository libraries must retain items for at least five years after receipt. Regional (full) depositories *must* retain their collections, and selective depositories must offer items identified as discards to the regional library and local partial depositories before discarding. On the plus side, periodic reviews of the documents collection may also encourage a review of the general collection low-use items that also occupy valuable shelf space.

Preservation problems are the same as in the general collection. Paper-based government publications are just as likely to be on acidic paper as their commercial cousins. There was, in 1990, a congressional resolution under consideration to encourage, if not require, all publishers to use acid-free paper for important publications. The nonprint government materials also suffer from the same problems as their commercial counterparts; for example, poor processing—especially microformats—and poor bonding of the emulsion layer to the carrier film base in both photographs and motion picture film. All the materials need the same care in handling by staff and patrons as well as the appropriate environmental controls (temperature and humidity) as discussed in other chapters.

Use of microformats for distributing government information, which was a significant factor in the recent past but has been decreasing, presents another challenge for service and access.

STAFFING

In an integrated collection situation (where all government publications are included in the general collection) all public service staff will need some training and understanding of government publications. Here, we are assuming the library is a partial depository and receives a substantial number of publications. Obviously, in libraries (nondepository status) that acquire just a few items per year and handle these items as they do any other collection material, no special training is necessary.

When the collections are separate the situation changes. One decision to make is whether the staff responsible for the collections is to be public service only or a combination of public and technical services. The idea is that the recording of depository items and their associated processing is best handled in "the backroom." It is not uncommon for smaller partial depository libraries to divide the duties. Because of the complexity of indexing and other access tools, a common practice is to assign to a reference librarian the primary responsibility for keeping current with the tools. The same person usually suggests what items to add or drop from the depository collection. This person must also become the staff training officer for government publications. If the separate collection is modest, all public service staff may have to shelve government publications, which may require special training in the system used to organize the collection.

With large collections, one or more full-time librarians plus support staff usually handle all aspects of document work. Even with a full-time staff in documents, however, there is a need to provide some background and training for the rest of the public service staff. Without such background they are not as likely to refer users to the collection.

When a library becomes a federal depository it takes on certain obligations, including one of having a full-time staff member responsible for the service. This does not mean a full-time documents staff, just a full-time staff member who is responsible for documents.

We agree with the thoughts of Bertot and colleagues (2006) but believe their comment also relates to academic libraries and their staffs as well: "The increased role for public libraries—often the only place for public Internet access with trained staff—has not been accompanied by additional funding" (p. 35). The need for funding and more training is essential, if libraries are to fulfill their key role in providing access to government information.

SUMMARY

The Internet has changed the way governments provide information to the public about their activities. On the one hand, people can get to information from their homes that in the past they had to travel to a depository library to access. Doing it from home or the office does mean going it alone and, as we noted earlier, that can be an activity laced with frustration. Being able to go to a local library where navigational help is available should mean more people have more access to more government information than any time in the past. It does mean public service staff will need more training and understanding of how to access the information than in the past was well.

Chapter Review Material

1. What role do public service staff play in helping citizens understand their government?
2. What role does the public service staff have in maintaining the delicate balance between security and access?
3. How has the Internet changed access to government information?
4. What do you see as the future of FDLP? How will it impact other libraries?
5. What types of information can you locate on the Internet about your hometown government? How does that compare to what you can find out about you state government?
6. Where would you look for information about UNESCO programs on the Internet? The World Health Organization's publication program?

REFERENCES

American Libraries. 2007. "Superintendent of Documents Sends Letter to Library," 38, no .4: 16.

Adler, Prudence. 1996. "Federal Information Dissemination Policies and Practice," *Journal of Government Information* 23, no. 4: 435–441.

Bertot, John, Paul Jaeger, Lesley Langa, and Charles McClure. 2006. "Public Access Computing and Internet Access in Public Libraries," *First Monday* 11, no. 9: 1.

Cheney, Debra. 2006. "Government Information Collections and Services in the Social Sciences," *Journal of Academic Librarianship* 32, no. 3: 303–312.

Drake, Miriam. 2005. "The Federal Depository Library Program: Safety Net for Access," *Searcher* 13, no. 1: 46–50.

Dempsey, Kathy. 2004. "The Info Was There, Then—Poof," *Computers in Libraries* 24, no. 4: 4.

The Economist. 2008. "The Electronic Bureaucrat: A Special Report on Technology and Government," 386, no. 8567 (supplement): 1–18.

Federal Depository Library Manual. 1993. "Reference Service and Policies for Electronic Publications." Washington, DC: Government Printing Office.

Fletcher, Patricia. 2003. "Creating the Front Door to Government: A Case Study of the FirstGov Portal," *Library Trends* 52, no. 2: 268–281.

Golderman, Gail, and Bruce Connolly. 2002. "Government Information Online: Tools for Democracy," *Netconnect* (a *Library Journal* supplement) 5, no. 2: 50–55.

Instructions to Depository Libraries. 1992. "Physical Facilities." Washington, DC: Government Printing Office.

Johnson, Linda. 2007. "Content and Access Remain Key," *Library Journal* 132, no. 9: 52–53.

Kelly, Wayne P. 1998. "Keeping Public Information Public," *Library Journal* 123, no. 9: 34–37.

Klein, Bonnie, and Sandy Schwal. 2005. "A Delicate Balance: National Security vs. Public Access," *Computers in Libraries* 25, no. 3: 16–23.

Library Journal. 2007. "E-Government and Libraries," 132, no. 5: 17.

Morehead, Joe. 1997. "Govzines on the Web: A Preachment," *Serials Librarian* 23, no. 3–4: 17–30.

Morton, Bruce. 1987. "The Depository Library System: A Costly Anachronism," *Library Journal* 112, no. 15: 52–54.

Notess, Greg R. 2003. "Government Information on the Internet," *Library Trends* 52, no. 2: 256–267.

Shuler, John A. 2003. "Citizen-Centered Government," *Journal of Academic Librarianship* 29, no. 2: 107–110.

———. 2004. "New Economic Models for the Federal Depository System," *Journal of Academic Librarianship* 30, no. 1: 243–249.

"Statement on H.R. 4280, the Government Printing Reform Act of 1996." 1997. *DttP, Documents to the People* 25, no. 3: 11.

White, Michael. 1996. "The Federal Register: A Link to Democratic Values," *The Record* 23, no. 4: 6–11

Wilkerson, Patrick. 1996. "Beyond the Federal Depository Library Program," *Journal of Government Information* 23, no. 3: 411–417.

SUGGESTED READINGS

Allmang, Nancy, and Jo Ann Remshard. 2004. "Leading the Pack," *Online* 28, no. 1: 34–37.

Arrigo, Paul. 2004. "The Reinvention of the FDLP," *Journal of Government Information* 30, no. 5–6: 684–709.

Church, Jim. 2005. "Official Record Only," *DttP, Documents to the People* 33, no. 3: 11–13.

Devakos, Rea, and Annemarie Toth-Waddell. 2008. "Ontario Government Documents Repository D-Space Pilot Project," *OCLC Systems & Services International Digital Library Perspectives* 24, no. 1: 40–47.

Jacobs, James A., James R. Jacobs, and Shinjoung Yeo. 2005. "Government Information in the Digital Age: The Once and Future Federal Depository Library Program," *Journal of Academic Librarianship* 31, no. 3: 198–208.

Marcum, Brad. 2003. "Preserving Government Documents," *Kentucky Libraries* 67, no. 2: 16–20.

Missingham, Roxanne. 2008. "Access to Australian Government Information: A Decade of Changes 1997–2007," *Government Information Quarterly* 25, no. 1: 25–37.

Oliva, Victor T. 2000. "Bringing Federal Documents to the Forefront for Library Users," *College & Research Libraries* 61, no. 6: 555–564.

Rossmann, Brian. 2005. "Legacy Documents Collections: Separate the Wheat from the Chaff," *DttP, Documents to the People* 33, no. 4: 8–9.

———. 2006. "Promote Your Documents Expertise," *DttP* 34, no. 1: 5–6.

Seavey, Charles A. 2005. "Musing on the Past and Present and the Future of Government Information," *American Libraries* 36, no. 7: 42–44.

Smith, Lori, and Maureen Olle. 2004. "Government Documents." *Louisiana Libraries* 66, no. 3: 3–35.

Chapter **13**

Archives and Special Collections

Secondary sources are a cornerstone of undergraduate education. But where do secondary sources come from?
—Shan Sutton and Lorrie Knight, 2006

Imagine the impact of your lesson on students if they could see an original Ansel Adams print or a handwritten letter by Mark Twain.
—Michelle Visser, 2006a

Libraries that have an archive or special collections unit are very fortunate. These two units, often combined, play an important role in the library's public service program. Beyond the immediate impact on quality service to the general public, under controlled conditions, these units play a societal role that goes far beyond the library they are housed in. Their major purpose is the preservation of the original materials (primary material) that make up a society's patrimony. The vast majority of library collections are secondary items of which many copies exist. Most if not all of the items in an archive or special collections unit are unique in some way and therefore irreplaceable. Unlike other public service units that focus on current needs, these units take a long-term view (forever). Dr. Errol Stevens, the retired head of Archives and Special Collections at Loyola Marymount University (LMU), wrote (2007) commenting on this chapter, "Digital materials are wonderful, especially for access, but we should not forget that digital materials are surrogates. If no one preserves the original materials, there is nothing to make digital copies of. Digital copies can be tampered with and no one is wiser. We need to keep the originals to be sure the digital copies are accurate. That is why libraries have to go to the trouble and cost of preserving the originals even when they are not used much" (2007, personal communication).

Just because the goal is preservation does not mean the material cannot be used; rather it means items are used under highly controlled conditions. In the past, these units were places very few people visited or knew much about. Today, there is growing usage of these collections, as we will discuss later in this chapter. One factor, mentioned by Dr. Stevens, for the increased awareness and usage is digitization and Web access. Through careful and selective digitization projects the units are able to post material so people can access it through the Internet. Often the individual can retrieve the information they want without the need to handle the original item, or just enough to be assured that the digital and original are identical.

Archives and special collections play an unusual role in public services. They are a source of pride, image and, occasionally, value to both the library and the community the library serves. Even small public libraries open only a few hours a week often have one shelf, in a secure area, where one or two books of special value to the library reside. The value is not always monetary; it can be informational or even psychological in nature. Like the old family Bible, retained because of age and its record of the family, communities and organizations frequently have materials that carry special meaning and that may only exist in one copy. And, unlike the old family Bible that is coming apart from too much handling and mishandling, communities and organizations make a significant effort to properly preserve and protect such items.

IS THERE A DIFFERENCE BETWEEN ARCHIVES AND SPECIAL COLLECTIONS?

We have used the terms archives and special collections several times and, if you visit a number of libraries, you will find a number of instances where both terms are employed for a single physical unit. In a general sense, they are very similar while being different. There is a third unit that you may encounter, especially in museums, not-for-profit organizations, and corporations, which is usually labeled records management. The Society of American Archivists (SAA) defines *archives* as:

(also **archive**), n. ~ 1. Materials created or received by a person, family, or organization, public or private, in the conduct of their affairs and preserved because of the enduring value contained in the information they contain or as evidence of the functions and responsibilities of their creator, especially those materials maintained using the principles of provenance, original order, and collective control; permanent records.—2. The division within an organization responsible for maintaining the organization's records of enduring value.—3. An organization that collects the records of individuals, families, or other organizations; a collecting archives.

Records management, n. ~ The systematic and administrative control of records throughout their life cycle to ensure efficiency and economy in their creation, use, handling, control, maintenance, and disposition.

The SAA's entire glossary of terms is available online at http://www.archivists.org/glossary/index.asp. It contains hyperlinks that help fill out the picture of what an archive is and what it does.

Joan Reitz's *Online Dictionary for Library Science* (http://lu.com/odlis/ odlis_g.cfm#govarchives) uses the following definitions to categorize the topic of this chapter. The definitions reflect dictionaries produced by the ALA over the years:

Archives

An organized collection of the noncurrent records of the activities of a business, government, organization, institution, or other corporate body, or the personal papers of one or more individuals, families, or groups, re- tained permanently (or for a designated or indeterminate period of time) by their originator or a successor for their permanent historical, infor- mational, evidential, legal, administrative, or monetary value, usually in a repository managed and maintained by a trained archivist (see this example). Also refers to the office or organization responsible for apprais- ing, selecting, preserving, and providing access to archival materials.

Special Collections

Some libraries segregate from the general collection rare books, manu- scripts, papers, and other items that are (1) of a certain form, (2) on a certain subject, (3) of a certain time period or geographic area, (4) in frag- ile or poor condition, or (5) especially valuable. Such materials are not allowed to circulate and access to them may be restricted.

Records Management

The field of management devoted to achieving accuracy, efficiency, and economy in the systematic creation, retention, conservation, dissemina- tion, use, and disposition of the official records of a company, government agency, organization, or institution, whether in physical or electronic form, usually undertaken by a professionally trained *records manager* on the basis of a comprehensive and thorough records survey. Security and disaster preparedness are essential elements of a good records manage- ment program.

Like the SAA glossary, the Reitz dictionary has a host of links within each of the above definitions that you may find useful to follow.

You can probably see that there is some overlap in the definitions for these units. From a practical point of view, based on an examination of the types of materials held, archives and special collections are very similar. Both may have collections of printed material, photographs, digital material, handwrit- ten material, art works, audio and video recordings, and objects. Both have the same primary purpose—preserve their collection of original materials indefinitely. Both limit access and handling of these materials. Both do not allow users to "browse" materials in the sense normally thought of in terms of libraries—staff brings to the user specifically requested files a few at any one time. Users are *not* allowed access to the storage areas, except on a guided tour. Both have similar environmental control issues related to their preser- vation mission. They may organize the materials in different ways depend- ing upon the person's training/background—archivist or librarian. We try to explore the major commonalities in this chapter. (Records management files are different in that they are held for a specified time and then either destroyed or transferred to the archives or special collections unit.)

One trend in this area, especially in academic libraries, is combining the institutional archives program with special collections. This makes sense, especially in an era of limited funding, as both functions have many common elements. Combining the staff of the two functions often results in increased service capability. Preserving institutional history is often a challenge due to the need to create and maintain a balance between being a "dumping ground" for overflowing office file cabinets and assuring that the important documents do become part of the permanent collection. A factor in this challenge is the fact that many organizations do not have a records management program. The result is confusion in the mind of the user between archival functions and those of records management. A records management program assures that the institution complies with a host of laws, codes, and regulations that *require* the organization to retain certain types of documents for prescribed periods: personnel records, invoices, accounting records, and so forth. Records management retention schedules also provide guidelines for the timely destruction of records no longer needed. Many organizations dispose of the records as quickly as possible. We will return to the records management issues later in this chapter.

THE ROLE OF SPECIAL COLLECTIONS

Preservation and controlled access to original materials of unusual value (not just monetary) are the major functions of archives and special collections. An important secondary role is to assist in or be the focal point of the library's overall preservation program. The unit(s) can and should house and provide access to those materials requiring special handling and treatment. This may include housing contemporary materials that may have restrictions on access such as parental permission. This is most likely to happen in public libraries where space is limited; in academic libraries for general collection items that need some level of control because of the likelihood of mutilation or theft, the best location is the reserve unit rather than archives and special collections.

While much of the material housed in or acquired for archives/special collections is old; age alone is not the deciding factor for housing material in this department. Something may be more than 100 years old and yet not be appropriate for the collection, while something produced yesterday may be more appropriate. The two basic factors for inclusion are, first, the item's suitability for the library's collection (which should, of course, reflect the parent institution's mission) and, second, its need for special handling to assure long-term preservation. If an item fits both criteria, it should be in special collections.

Staff who work in special collections are custodians in the same sense as conveyed by the old phrase for a librarian, "keeper of the books." In the majority of the libraries with special collections, the area does not constitute a separate administrative unit or an area with a significant expenditure of money, except for medium-size (research-oriented) or larger libraries.

One example typical of hundreds of libraries is the Molokai Public Library (part of the Hawaii State Library System), which just has a special locked glass case that contains a few hundred items. Most of the items relate to Molokai, but a few are general Hawaiiana. In essence, it is a small local history collection containing primarily commercial publications. It also is probably the world's only collection of publications produced by Molokai service clubs. What other agency is likely to care about, much less acquire, a copy of the Molokai Lions Club's recipe book? For the residents of Molokai, the library's glass-case special collections is a source of local history and information. The items in the case do not circulate and customers surrender their driver's license or library card before they may use the books. Often there is a second copy of the item in the circulating collection which, if dirty and worn pages are valid evidence, receives heavy use by the community. This pattern, with minor variations, occurs in thousands of libraries across the United States and around the world.

At the other end of the spectrum are the large libraries. The Newberry, the Huntington, and the Folger Shakespeare libraries, for example, are, for all practical purposes, solely special collection operations. In between the giants and dwarfs are hundreds of general libraries with separate special collections units with budgets, modest or not, for the purchase of materials for inclusion in their collections. It is this mid-range group that we address in this chapter.

Archives and special collections activities are the area where one sees the difference between contemporary public service philosophy and the pre-twentieth-century library philosophy. Earlier we mentioned the phrase "keeper of the books," which was used for the people in charge of libraries until well into the nineteenth century. All too often today "keeper of the books" generates a negative image or reaction. Such a response is unfortunate and inappropriate. What we have are two different, and equally valid, philosophies about the purpose of libraries and their primary societal role. As the former head of the LMU Archives and Special Collections, Dr. Stevens said in a personal communication to the authors (2007), "It has been my experience that users do not resent this (very controlled access) but seem to feel they have been privileged by gaining access to something important and special."

Today the predominant philosophy is that general collections are for use; the materials should be as accessible as possible. The general attitude is that using a book to pieces is better than having it sit unused on the shelf. However, in special collections the goal is to preserve the work, both its physical being and its information, by limiting access to essential, rather than casual use.

The role of the keeper of the books was to preserve what was a scarce commodity. And, while it was true the keeper's primary duty was to know where every book in his care was, providing some access to these materials was also part of his duties. (Note: in the case of pre-nineteenth-century keepers, the pronoun "his" is correct both literally and grammatically, because almost all of them were males.) Kenneth Carpenter (1986) recounted what is very likely an apocryphal story of an encounter between Harvard librarian John Sibley and President Charles Eliot in 1858. The story is that one day President Eliot met Librarian Sibley briskly walking across Harvard Yard. Mr. Sibley was smiling and when asked where he was going, he supposedly said, "The library is locked up and every book is in it but two, and I know where they are and I am going to get them." Mr. Carpenter's comments about that story clarify the role of the nineteenth-century librarian: "To see it as a symbol of a librarian delighting in having the books all locked up and unused is false. Sibley was doing exactly what was expected of him. It was an ancient practice that all books were to be in the library at the time of the examination by the Visiting Committee" (p. 68).

It is also important to note that the men who were the keepers of the books were also, in most cases, scholars. Thus, they brought to their work the attitudes and views of the working scholar. Until the late nineteenth century, this was the normal pattern and it was only after the first library school opened at Columbia University in 1876 that there was an opportunity to have formal training in library operations. Library school graduates brought different attitudes and views about the role and purpose of the library to the job. Roderick Cave (1982) described this when writing about the establishment of some of the large rare-book rooms and special collections libraries: "In selecting their librarians and curators the benefactors usually consciously avoided the 'professional librarian' and chose men and women who were sympathetic with the humanistic and bibliographic motives behind their collections to carry on the humanistic traditions of librarianship" (p. 14). While we disagree with the implied suggestion that "professional librarians" are not humanistic in their approach to librarianship, the point is that there *is* a difference in philosophy. It is worth mentioning that today archives and special collections place much more emphasis on proper conservation and preservation activities than was true in the past.

What it all comes down to is that there are different classes of material in library collections. One class consists of heavily-used materials (circulating materials). Another class, such as microfilm, are used only in the library due to special equipment requirements. Then there are those materials requiring special handling and preservation, where staff must control and monitor use. It is a question of balancing two priorities, use and preservation. Both circulating and special collections work involve both use and preservation, as we point out throughout this book. For the circulating collection, use is first priority, then preservation, with the reverse true for special collections. One might also say that circulating collections are for present use, while special collections are for the ages.

COLLECTIONS AND STORAGE

Before discussing preservation, it is appropriate to describe briefly the types of material found in special collections and their storage. This discussion is necessarily brief because the range of materials seems limited only by a donor's imagination. As an example, the LMU library's special collections department contains printed books ranging from several incunabula and the four Shakespeare seventeenth-century folios to contemporary books. In addition there are manuscripts, maps (from hand-drawn maps on goat skin to early twentieth-century developer maps used to promote various areas of Los Angeles), photographs, sketches for movie sets, paintings, sculptures, furniture and rugs, two gold records, medals and awards/trophies, and hundreds of thousands of postcards. There are even two of the masks used in filming the movie *Planet of the Apes.* To the above mix you can add a host of electronic media. The range of materials is not atypical for a medium-sized library with a special collections unit. Obviously, storing this range of material safely requires time, thought, money, and equipment.

One might think that the mélange listed above sounds like a museum collection, not a library's, and one would be right. Many special collections take on the characteristics of a museum, especially in small communities lacking a museum. Even when a museum exists, donors may, for a variety of reasons, decide to give their collections to a library. More often than not special collections, other than those of local or regional history, start through more or less chance donations to the library. It is important for the library to place limits on the scope of the collection(s) to avoid becoming society's "attic of the unwanted."

Most archives and special collections attempt to limit the scope of their collecting activities. While one does not always have the ability to choose what one can accept (for political and other reasons), libraries generally attempt to retain the right to dispose of materials that fall outside the primary collecting areas. Disposal may be by sale, gift, or trade to another institution that actively collects the material. Part of the idea behind such exchanges is to concentrate materials at institutions that have a strong interest in an area. Such concentration makes the work of the researcher less time-consuming, expensive, and frustrating. Monies raised as a result of such sales provide funding for acquisition of materials central to the library's collecting interests.

Donations for tax purposes and "house cleaning" frequently result in special collections departments receiving a conglomeration of unrelated materials—even if some of the items may be valuable from either the intellectual or financial point of view. Because of this fact the library must have a clear collection policy statement, as well as a gift policy, that makes it apparent that the library has the right to dispose of "out-of-scope" materials. Of course, special collections staff and library administrators, for political and other reasons, may not be able to refuse the gift or dispose of materials. This can lead to problems. For example, a former president of a public university once accepted a large collection of travel films with the attached condition that the gift could not be sold, given away, or otherwise disposed of. As of this writing, the collection has not found a permanent storage place on the campus.

In time the library will, or should, decide to concentrate its efforts in only a few areas. After considerable thought and discussion, the LMU special collections staff identified four areas of existing strength in which they could reasonably expect to acquire additional material: (1) Saint/Sir Thomas More: more than 1,500 volumes with many items from the sixteenth and seventeenth centuries; (2) a collection of rare and fine editions of Oliver Goldsmith's books, and especially of his *Vicar of Wakefield*; (3) materials concerning Southern California Catholic families and political papers; and (4) the Werner and Florence Kit Von Boltenstern Worldwide Postcard Collection.

Several of the collecting areas involve traditional book materials and pose no unusual problems, at least in terms of typical special collection materials. The California Collection includes manuscripts (unbound) and maps requiring special storage units together with the normal preservation and conservation needs of special materials. The postcard collection, which may be one of the largest in the United States, consisting of over 1 million cards, requires numerous special filing cabinets.

When a library begins to accept and collect in contemporary areas, such as theater and film, storage problems can multiply. For example, when the LMU Library accepted the Arthur P. Jacobs Collection (Jacobs was producer of such films as *Play It Again Sam, Doctor Doolittle, Good-bye Mr. Chips, Tom Sawyer*, and the *Planet of the Apes* series) it contained 4,500 books on film and film history, 3,000 audio disks, 115 audiotapes, 2,300 issues of serials, movie scripts, gold records, plaques, awards, set drawings, storyboards, musical scores, scrapbooks, film stills, costumes, feature-length films (some on unstable nitrate stock), signed costume designs, books of autographs, and much assorted paraphernalia. Usually the donor, either the collector or his or her family, does not want the "collection" broken up, so, in essence, it is a matter of accepting everything or nothing. Although the gift arrived in 1984, the department is still working through the material and buying the appropriate equipment to house the collection.

PRESERVATION

Providing the appropriate storage units for archival materials is only the first step in what must be a never-ending process of preservation and conservation. Reducing the issue to its most basic components, the problem is how to preserve paper, wood, fabric, leather, plastic, metal, and digital materials. Each of these has slightly different ideal storage conditions. If special collections is just a room or two—which is usually the case—there is a problem in just accommodating a growing collection. For most libraries, the collection is confined to a relatively small area, making it much too costly to create a number of mini-climates with major differences in temperature and humidity. Even if a library could afford to do this, the materials do not always lend themselves to such simple divisions. Most are composites of different materials; for example, many early bindings consist of leather stretched over wooden boards, the boards caparisoned with metal bosses. And of course, between these boards are the sections of paper or vellum sewn together with thread. All these elements form an integral bound unit, one whole book. All of this makes it difficult, or impossible, to achieve anything but a compromise environment.

All the handling do's and don'ts described in other chapters apply even more to special collections. Materials must be handled gently and carefully at all times. Piling books on top of one another, tugging at headcaps (the top of the book spine, where so many people unfortunately hook their fingers and yank), laying open books down spine-up, mixing large and small or heavy and fragile materials together, and any other (unfortunately) common practice can have dire consequences.

Manuscripts and other archival materials deserve a brief mention in this section. One can minimize damage to such collections by storing them properly. Placing manuscripts in alkaline or neutral folders is the basic first step.

A second step is to place groups of related folders into archival boxes. When the group of folders does not fill the box they have a tendency to go into an "archival slump," the curving of folders one often sees in partially filled filing cabinets. The archive goal is indefinite preservation, and such slumping can cause damage to materials over time. A simple solution to slumping problems is to fill the space with crumpled-up, acid-free paper or containers. There are also nonacidic multi-ply spacers available commercially to keep materials upright and flat. When handling manuscript materials, the person should wear gloves (in past they were cotton, today the preferred type are the one-time-use nitrile exam gloves) to protect the items from harmful skin oils and dirt. Even when delivering a box that might not require gloves, a staff member who is wearing gloves sends an important, if silent, message to the requester about the need for proper handling.

Monitoring the condition of materials is an important aspect of special collections work. Noticing any change in condition, such as cracking leather or paint, warping boards (book covers), splitting vellum, or just new abrasion from reshelving, is an important habit. Clues like the above might call for anything from minor treatment or protective enclosures to major conservation work. The person in charge of the department or section should be notified of any such indication of change. Of course, a professional conservator should be contacted in the case of significant changes in important items. Library preservation workshops are a good way to help staff learn to identify potential problems.

As in the rest of the library, basic good housekeeping practices are vital, but even more so in special collections. Proper temperature and humidity control are important for a circulating collection, but are critical for the survival of special collections. Special air filters can reduce the dust and other airborne particles that act like sandpaper on items. For libraries, historical societies, and the like that must live with ordinary filter systems (or none), storing the books in half-sized record center boxes on industrial shelving units will offer protection from particulate matter in the air, as well as offering some protection from sprinkler systems that might go off, or even damage from falling off the shelf in an earthquake. If you do employ boxes, be certain the books are packed spine down. Special Collections at the California State University at Northridge, seriously affected by the 1994 earthquake, has been using such boxes and reports that they can hold between 10 and 25 books each.

Pulling a book off the shelf or pushing it across a work surface causes abrasion from the dust and grit particles. A better practice is to *lift* books rather then pull them and *place* materials where wanted rather than drag or slide them. Regular cleaning of both work and storage surfaces increases the useful life and maintains the value of the items in the collection.

Metal shelving is superior to wood because the stains, varnishes, and paints used on wood can damage bindings. Wooden shelves are really unacceptable; however, if wooden shelves are a given, insulate materials by lining the shelves with chemically inert material, such as buffered paper board. On the other hand, be sure that metal shelves and file cabinets are not painted with "never-dry" paints that out-gas (give off fumes) indefinitely, which can affect paper, photographic negatives, and other materials. Metal storage units should have only an original layer of inert, baked-on enamel finish.

If there is no special collections room and storing the materials in locked glass cases is the only option available, be certain there is a way to control heat and humidity inside the case. (The same caution applies to exhibit cases.) If nothing else is possible, drilling some ventilation holes in the back of the case will help, as long as the air can circulate throughout. If there is no space behind and in front of each shelf, it will be necessary to drill holes in each shelving segment to assure the required airflow, but be sure no harmful insects can crawl or fly through these holes! Small pieces of fine mesh screening will help keep the critters at bay.

The lower the temperature, the better it is for paper and fabrics, but low temperatures can damage leather and plastics. Professional standards suggest 68 plus or minus 2 degrees Fahrenheit and 45 percent plus or minus 5 percent humidity as a reasonable compromise. Many people, however, find 68 degrees Fahrenheit too cool for prolonged sedentary activity. Ultimately, there has to be a compromise between ideal conditions for housing the material and the conditions for people to sit and work with the materials. For archives and special collections, the needs of the collection take priority over people comfort.

One other important fact to keep in mind is that the temperature and humidity should be constant 24/7/365. Often, meeting such a requirement is almost impossible to achieve with existing equipment. Maintaining levels close to the ideal is expensive. A constant level, even at higher temperatures and humidity than indicated above, is less damaging to the material than are roller coaster changes, or cycling, especially on a daily basis. When a library is able to achieve the ideal in temperature and humidity control, it may have to set up a separate work area with higher temperatures for people. In this case, it is necessary to provide for a slow warm-up period for the materials before handling them, as well as a slow cool-down period before shelving. This will preserve the materials, but does add to the time expended by users and staff.

It is preferable to provide special collections with an independent heating, ventilation, and air conditioning system (HVAC). Such systems are very costly if installed as a remodeling or renovation project; they also add to the cost of new construction, but at a much lower per-foot cost. Oil, water, or electronic air filter systems can be part of the system. Depending on the system chosen, these special filters can remove particles down to less than one micron in size. (A micron is 1/25,400 of an inch.) Such a filter system would effectively remove lint, fly ash, dust, pollen, fungus spores, fog and mist, the majority of the bacteria present, and a fairly high percentage of tobacco and oil smoke, any of which can pose problems for the material in special collections.

There are several good Web sites, such as Conservation Online (http://palimpsest.stanford.edu/), that provide authoritative information on a wide variety of preservation and conservation topics, ranging from guidelines for special collections exhibits to environmental control to disaster recovery.

REACHING OUT

Michelle Visser (2006b), who we quoted on the opening page of this chapter, conducted a survey of special collections and archives in the Association of Colleges and Research Libraries (ARL) regarding their "outreach" activities. (Over the past 15 or so years, archives and special collection units have become increasingly active in drawing in new users. As we noted earlier, part of the trend comes from technological capabilities that did not exist earlier.)

Some special collections/archives departments make an effort to reach their K–12 audience. Seventy-six percent of the responding ARL departments indicated they hosted class visits from K–12 (Visser, 2006b). Certainly high school visits are the most common, but even kindergarten classes make occasional visits. As Visser stated, "The generally positive response to K-12 visits on the part of special collection libraries would seem to belie the historical stereotype (often much deserved) of special collection libraries as inhospitable places staffed by formidable persons who protect the collections like dragons sitting on treasure" (p. 316).

Another factor, in an academic setting, is proving the value of the unit by finding ways to link up with regular course offerings. LMU's archives and special collections department has been actively engaged in working with faculty to incorporate archival or special collections elements into their courses. Most of the courses that deal with Shakespeare come to the department to see his folio editions. The history department also makes use of the department's collections for its historical methodology course—students are required to prepare a paper based on the archival holdings. English department faculty make extensive use of the T. Marie Chilton Collection of fine first editions of British and American novelists (over 2,500 volumes) when teaching British or American literature. The children's literature course has one or two sessions in the department during the year. Even the postcard collection has it uses in the graphic design as well as tourism courses.

Our second opening quote (Sutton and Knight, 2006) came from their article that described how they incorporated special collections into the regular bibliographic instruction course at the University of the Pacific. Their focus was on helping students understand the difference between primary and secondary materials. Another interesting article is Steven Escar Smith's "From 'Treasure Room' to 'School Room:' Special Collections and Education," (2006). In it, he noted, "we are more involved than ever in reaching out to our traditional constituencies and in creating new ones. . . . There also are many exciting examples of courses and innovative programs all around us" (p. 31).

This changing emphasis means departmental staff will be dealing with an ever growing number of visitors, many of whom have little understanding of the nature of the unit they are visiting. That in turn translates into the need for all staff to fully internalize all aspects of how people may, or may not, have access to the collections and how to monitor usage.

ACCESS

Like all other units in public service, the materials in special collections are available for use. At the same time the special, if not unique character of the materials suggests that limited access to them is prudent. Cave (1982) clearly set out the problems we address in this section:

> In organizing rare book collections for use, the librarian is subject to a sort of professional schizophrenia. On the one hand, guided by his role as conservator, he is concerned to devise methods of control over the use of materials in his care, hedging them around with various restrictions so they will survive for the enjoyment of posterity even at the inconvenience of present users. At the same time he must be conscious that the collections represent considerable capital investment which can be justified only by use: use for general cultural purposes at a popular level as well as for research by scholars; to strike the right balance between conservation and current use is not simple, but is essential if the collection is to continue as a lively service. (p. 100)

Finding a way to place a value on long-term preservation has proven difficult, but one must make the effort in this day of "bottom line" management. If you don't do so, it may become ever more difficult to secure proper funding.

Relatively recent developments in electronic technologies are providing a way to overcome the "professional schizophrenia." Storage capacity for PCs has escalated and the cost has fallen just as dramatically. Digitizing equipment and software likewise have improved in quality and dropped in price. While we are not aware of any empirical study on the subject, it seems very likely that the vast majority of researchers only need access to the *content* of the materials in special collections and archives. That is, they do not need to handle the original item as long as the digitized record is an accurate reproduction of the original material. Certainly there are occasions when the physical properties of an item require examination to determine, for example, specific printing or state, but such events are relatively rare, at least in our experience. Institutions with users who are specialists in descriptive bibliography or the history of printing see this type of hands-on examination more regularly.

Museums, archives, and special collections departments are digitizing more and more of their collections: print, photographs, and other graphic materials, as well as three-dimensional objects. Such projects accomplish several goals and help assure the long-term preservation of the original material:

- Less handling, therefore better preservation
- Less restrictive—often unrestricted—access
- Less time and expense to researchers who can access the material remotely, often through the Internet
- More service to customers on their own terms
- More security for the materials by limiting the use to only those times it is essential to have the original

Many of the projects relate to unique materials that only a few people might be able to consult in person. All such projects greatly enhance the visibility of special collections and archives for the majority of library customers. It also means an ever-increasing role in the overall service program of the library. Keep in mind that digital copies are only *surrogates*; the originals must be preserved. They are the "gold standard" in case the digital copy should be altered or lost when technology crashes, as it does from time to time.

While some special collections have been fully cataloged, with their records in printed catalogs and in databases such as OCLC, the increased security arising from digitized materials has substantially increased posting to such bibliographic utilities. Because the "content" of the digitized item is more readily available, very few people will have a legitimate need to handle the original material, which in turn means greater security for the item. Such postings assist researchers in quickly locating material of interest.

Restrictions on access may be no more than the Molokai Public Library's requiring a driver's license before letting a customer consult their special collections. At the other end of the spectrum are sophisticated electronic security systems, with motion detectors and the like, and the completion of several checks before granting a person access.

Another form of access, a well as promotion and publicity for special collections, is the use of special collections materials in exhibitions. If the exhibition is housed in the library, proper display cases may already be available. It is essential that such display cases be secure and suitable for use with a theft detection system and have a micro-environment that controls temperature, humidity, and lighting. Because both natural and artificial lighting have an aging effect and because book structures, even if properly supported, can become stressed over time, special collections materials should not be on exhibit for long. Materials loaned to other institutions for exhibits should be dealt with just as safely and securely.

Access and security involve three issues: admission to the area, rules regulating use of materials, and the physical protection of the collection. The staff must constantly strive to address and balance all three.

Admission and Use

Regulating admission ranges from no restrictions to requiring a written request in advance of using the materials (sometimes with personal references) explaining why it is necessary to use the collection. Although costly, the more screening carried out before a person gains access to the collection, the less likely the library is to have problems with misuse—but it is also less likely that the collection will be used. However, for "libraries of record," that is, research libraries that have the responsibility of preserving one copy of each important book or other material for posterity, the extra procedures make perfect sense. Library-of-record materials do not circulate outside the library except for exhibit, and so are almost always available.

A few examples of forms related to reader access to special collections, including making copies of materials, are shown in Figures 13.1 to 13.4. The list of rules for researchers (Figure 13.1) lays out the basic requirements for using special collections materials, including restrictions and basic handling guidelines. Additional handling guidelines based on the nature of the material may be given when the requested material is delivered to the researcher.

The reader registration form (see Figure 13.2) is useful as both a vetting (screening) instrument and as a permanent record of a reader. Admission is granted for various lengths of time, according to established need.

1) Normal operational hours are 9:00 a.m. to 4:00 p.m. Monday through Friday. Although an appointment is not required it is highly recommended as many items are stored in a remote facility and require 24 hour retrieval time. Please call (111.111.1234, ex.789) to schedule a visit or discuss your research needs.

2) Researchers must complete a registration form and provide identification on their first visit prior to receiving any material. Later visits only require signing the registration book.

3) All outerwear, personal belongings other than paper and pencils (pens are not allowed) must be stored in the lockers provided. Laptop computers are allowed, but carrying cases must be left in the locker.

4) The collections are non-circulating and must be used in the reading room under staff supervision. Researchers may only consult the finding aids; we do not allow researchers to "browse" in the storage areas.

5) A request form must be completed, including a signature, for each item the researcher wishes to view. The staff may limit the number items the researcher may have at one time based the nature of the material and research interest.

6) Researchers must wear gloves when working the material and maintain the order the material was in when delivered. (Note: the staff will check the material before and after use to ensure that everything is in order and complete. Any researcher who repeatedly fails to keep the original order may be refused further access to the collections.)

7) Cameras (still or video) may only be used with prior permission from the department head.

8) Copies or digital scans *may be* done by the staff, depending on the item's condition, for a fee.

9) Materials in the department's collections may be subject to restrictions on how or when it may be used and in a few cases the classes of researchers who may access the material. Also, materials may be subject to copyright limitations. Researchers must secure the necessary permissions from the copyright holder. The department will assist, to the best of its ability based on its records, in identifying the copyright holder(s). *In no case, will the department assume any responsibility for copyright infringement.*

10) Researchers wishing to publish information from the collections must acknowledge the source.

Figure 13.1 Sample Researcher's Rules

The call slip shown in Figure 13.3 is a two-part no carbon required (NCR) form. When a book is paged, the shorter original (paper) slip is separated and inserted in the book, or clipped to the manuscript box. When the book or material is placed on the reader's table, the slip is put in a box on the desk of a staff member charged with monitoring the reading room. Thus, at any time, this staff member knows what items, and how many, are in use. The carbon (thin alkaline card stock) is left in the empty shelf slot where the material belongs, so the identity of items not returned to the shelf at the end of the day is evident, initiating an immediate search. In some libraries, a reader's driver's license or other identification is clipped to the call slip in the monitor's box and is only returned to the reader when the library material is returned and inspected.

The Archives and Special Collections department of the Museum of Transportation is a private, non-circulating, reference collection that is used by the Museum staff, qualified researchers. The general public may also use the resources of the department to the extent this does not interfere with the work of the staff or researchers. The public is welcome to browse through the finding aids for the manuscript and the photograph indexes.

Please complete all following sections.
Date:_____
Name:_____
Permanent address: _____

_____

Telephone number _____
E-mail address _____
Organizational Affiliation: _____
Address: _____
City: _____ State: _____ Zip: _____

By signing below, you agree to not remove any library materials from the library reading room, not write upon, tear, cut or otherwise alter or damage any material.

Signature:_____ Date: _____

Briefly describe your reason(s) for needing access to our materials.

Figure 13.2 Sample Registration Form

CALL NUMBER	LOYOLA MARYMOUNT UNIVERSITY
	Charles Von der Ahe Library
	Archives and Special Collections
	AUTHOR
	TITLE
VOLUME/YEAR	NAME (Please Print)
STAFF DATE	SIGNATURE

Figure 13.3 Archives/Special Collections Call Slip

By permission of Loyola Marymount University Library.

Use of the manuscript and audiovisual collections entails more detailed vetting, as shown in Figure 13.4. Often the researcher or other user wishes to use an image for some purpose. A signature confirming the reader's awareness and cooperation regarding copyright limitations on use and publication restrictions is required before any material is paged.

The complex issue of access via duplication of special collections materials is too broad to address in detail in this book. A good quality copy (paper

The Archives of _____ hereby grants permission for **ONE-TIME, NON-EXCLUSIVE USE** to:

Name: _____   Date: _____

Title: _____   Work phone: _____

Institution: _____

Address: _____

MATERIALS TO BE USED:

Image/negative number: **Description:**

_____   _____
_____   _____
_____   _____
_____   _____
_____   _____
_____   _____
_____   _____
_____   _____
_____   _____
_____   _____

INTENDED USE OF MATERIAL:

Detailed description of use: _____

Author/Producer: _____

Publisher: _____

Projected date of publication/production: _____

Format: ___Book   ___Magazine   ___Film/Video   ___Advertisement
_____,   ___Postcard, poster, calendar   ___Exhibition   ___Motion
Picture/TV_____,   ___CD ROM ___Computer interactive display   ___On-line
exhibit_____

Estimated print run of edition and expected distribution: _____

1) All requests to reproduce images from the Archives of_____ Photographic department must be submitted on this application. By signing this application, the applicant agrees to abide by

Figure 13.4 Sample Image Photo Request

or electronic), however, may provide a satisfactory and cost-effective solution to the problem of access, supervision, and preservation. In such a situation, the library makes a paper, microform, or digitized copy of the item, which the reader may take away to use at his or her leisure. Thus, the material is not handled unnecessarily and the staff need not engage in all the activities required when the reader uses the physical item in special collections. Obviously, copyright restrictions apply and often donors impose additional restrictions upon both the use and duplication of their gifts.

Photography, photocopying, or digitizing are some of the means by which special collections departments can generate revenue. Many archives and special collections units have a two-tiered pricing system—one for nonprofit noncommercial use and one for commercial use. Generally the cost is somewhat lower if the unit can do the work itself. When that is not possible, locating a service that can do the work properly, at a reasonable cost, and in a timely manner can be a challenge. Prices for such duplication are often set at a level to discourage excessive and often unnecessary copying. All such handling and copying places stress on the material. Staff should refuse to copy fragile items.

Even if you allow people to come to special collections without prior screening, you must still ascertain that the general, circulating collection is unable to supply the desired information. A major purpose of special collections is to preserve and conserve the materials in these collections; if the same information is obtainable from a nonrare or a nonspecial source, so much the better. This is especially true for libraries of record. Thus, students who come to a library of record to use books available at their institutional library might be turned away.

The vetting of prospective users is important, and individuals who need access rarely resent the precautions. Naturally, the process requires tact and respect for the applicant as well as the staff's understanding of the reasons for the importance of the process.

Monitoring Users

Once a prospective user becomes an approved user, other conditions regarding use apply. The ACRL (2006) guidelines for the security of rare book, manuscript, and other special collections outline the major areas of concern in terms of monitoring researchers: "Staff should observe researchers at all times and not allow them to work unobserved behind bookcases, book trucks, stacks of books or other obstacles that restrict staff view. Researchers should be limited at any one time to having access only to those books, manuscripts or other items which are needed to perform the research at hand. . . . Researchers should not be allowed to exchange materials or have access to materials brought into the room for use by another researcher." These relatively few words have significant implications for staffing and operational procedures in special collections. Providing adequate, secure storage space for the users' personal property may present a problem if there is a lot of it, but is essential if one is to maintain collection security. Checking each item before and after each use for "condition, content, and completeness" will add a significant element to the workload. Not doing the checking, however, can result in the loss of plates, charts, maps, pages from books, or important pages from manuscript collections. Having a staff member present in the reading room when researchers are present is mandatory, even if that means some other tasks may not be completed.

Few departments have the luxury of staffing such that the reading room monitor can do nothing else. However, the physical presence of a staff member who clearly is monitoring user activities does increase security. Closed-circuit television cameras and recorders provide even more security, but cannot replace the presence of a staff person. Although somewhat dated, a good discussion of monitoring is Anthony Amodeo's (1983) "Special Collections Desk Duty: Preventing Damage." Limiting the number of items a reader may have at one time certainly adds to the workload. The proctor, however, helps assure that users cannot build up visual barriers that impede monitoring their activities and use of the materials. Carefully planned placement of user stations can help staff monitor use of the materials. Maintaining checkout records indefinitely presents few problems, except in large, heavily used collections where eventually storage space may become a problem.

Why maintain usage records? Few if any special collections have enough staff to literally check every page of every item after every use. When a user reports something missing, having past use records may allow the library to recover the missing material. Occasionally, these records also help identify and convict a thief. One such case occurred in Norway some years ago (Thompson, 1984). In that instance, a high government official had been stealing rare plates and maps from special collections around the country. The records of his use of rare items, which had missing plates and maps, helped convict the man.

SECURITY

The challenge facing special collections and archives staff is how to preserve the collections while providing access to them. Pre-use screening is expensive and suggests the collection may be monetarily valuable; that can help the professional thief identify potential targets. Requiring letters of introduction and other forms of identification is a helpful practice, but presents no problem for the professional thief.

As the LMU head of Archives and Special Collections noted when reviewing this chapter, "It is not possible to verify IDs by telephone or FAX. Professional thieves may carry forged IDs, but this does not mean that it is not important to ask for identification. The amateur thieves can be screened out or at least discouraged." Even though theft is a real threat, it is hardly possible to turn away a researcher who claims to have a legitimate need to look at material. It is important to follow procedures carefully and to treat all collection items equally. If we did not value it, it would not be here. All researchers should also be treated equally. Many thefts are by the "trusted" researcher. For theft to take place, the opportunity for theft must exist. Our job is to reduce the window of opportunity.

Certainly there is a public relations value in showing a casual visitor some of the *special* items in the collection. You need to balance the public relations value against the remote, but nonetheless real danger that the visitor is a professional thief. The 1990 arrest of Stephen Blumberg in Iowa with over 16,000 books, manuscripts, and other special collections items, worth over an estimated $20 million, taken from libraries across the United States illustrates the point: professional book thieves *do* exist. In all probability, prescreening would not detect many professional thieves because they know how to circumvent such procedures. And the sad truth is that many of the thefts are a result of library or institutional staff activities. *American Libraries* ("Philadelphia Archives," 2007) carried a story about the sentencing of a former National Archives and Records Administration intern who had stolen 164 historical documents from the Philadelphia facility and sold them online.

A final note about theft and thieves relates to security systems. As the market for home security systems has increased, the cost of the systems has decreased. At the same time, the monetary value of special collections has escalated. These facts combine to create a situation in which it may even be cost effective for the library to install such a system. Generally such systems will lower the cost of risk insurance. Certainly, that reduction will not cover the cost of the system, but it helps make it more affordable. Truly professional thieves will know how to defeat such systems; however, when faced with a choice between a protected versus an unprotected collection, their decision is easy: "Why make life more difficult than necessary?"

It is important that all public and technical service staff have a sound understanding of what kinds of materials are in special collections and know how to recognize these items. Processing for most special collections items is different from general collection materials. General collection items are heavily stamped, folded, spindled, and mutilated. That is, they carry property stamps, have call number labels, contain pasted-in book pockets and date-due slips, and more often than not have security targets, so there is no doubt they belong to a library.

Special collections items may be cataloged, but they rarely carry obvious library property marks. To mark special collections materials in the same way as circulating materials would greatly detract from their value. They may or may not have an electronic target that sets off the library's security system. Call numbers appear on acid-free card stock strips inserted into the book, or perhaps the library has had a special box or container made to house the item and the box has the call number or location information on it. The point is that special collections items are particularly susceptible to theft because they do not have the usual ownership markings. If the staff is not well aware of what is and is not in special collections, a thief could openly carry off items without challenge. This is another reason why detailed cataloging is necessary. Most special collections materials are unique in some way and detailed catalog descriptions can be helpful in tracking them down, if they do go "missing."

As we have shown, a comprehensive plan to protect the collections will encompass several topics. We have already covered some aspects of protection from the forces of time and use (environmental and handling concerns) and concerns about theft and mutilation. We review natural forces such as mold, mildew, insects, and dust in Chapter 14. Preservation specialists must also deal with some less natural forces, such as the tendency of certain materials to break down on their own ("inherent vice") in a "normal" environment. One inherent vice is acidic paper. There are, however, even more dramatic things against which libraries, and particularly special collections, must protect themselves, including fire, flood or water damage, earthquakes, and other disasters, natural or man-made.

Specialized building construction can generate the greatest increase in security from disaster. Construction costs may be higher than one would like, but long-term security and maintenance costs will be lower. Many special collections areas have bank-vault-like rooms that are highly fire-resistant and provide a measure of theft protection as well. Fire-resistant vaults are not necessarily burglary-resistant and vaults designed to slow down burglars do not always provide more than minimal fire protection. Basically, vaults buy time, whether one hour, two hours, or longer—perhaps enough time for the police or fire department to arrive and solve the problem. The longer the period of protection desired, the higher the price. Many vault units are extremely heavy and require extra supports under the floor or must be housed in the basement of the building. Basements, however, are not good locations for special collections because the location increases their susceptibility to flooding and mold. Burglar or fire vaults have an additional advantage: they increase the level of protection to the collection during earthquakes and other natural disasters, provided interior storage support is adequate. The vaults provide more protection from falling ceilings and walls because they are self-contained units. In earthquake-susceptible areas, some sort of restraining system, especially on the upper shelves, can prevent materials from falling to the floor. Protective enclosures, such as fitted alkaline book boxes, can protect materials that do fall, as well as provide some protection from sprinklers. Even without a disaster, enclosures can mitigate damage from ordinary environmental changes.

Having a written plan for handling a disaster is also a key element in any special collection security program. (See Chapter 15 for a full discussion of disaster and security plans.) Even if the rest of the library does not have a plan for handling disasters, special collections units should. Trying to decide what to do *after* a disaster strikes usually compounds the disaster. In many disasters, time becomes the main enemy; a few hours' delay can increase losses significantly. With a disaster plan in place all the library staff need to do is follow the steps already outlined and use material already stockpiled or readily available.

PUBLIC RELATIONS

While both patrons and staff take pride in the library's special collections, they require promotion to grow and thrive. Special collections are costly in terms of materials, labor, and maintenance of proper preservation and security. Publicity reminds everyone about the collections' existence and helps in obtaining the necessary funds to maintain and expand the program.

Exhibitions in the library are one of the most common methods for maintaining public and staff awareness of special collections. Frequently the person in charge of special collections is also responsible for scheduling, if not actually preparing library exhibitions. When that is the situation, one can expect that at least one of the exhibitions each year will feature special collections. An important goal for exhibitions is to educate and inform the viewers, not just to display "treasures." Linking exhibitions to special community or institutional events can pay off in unexpected support at a later date.

A second method, which is now almost mandatory, is to have a special collections Web page. Web pages provide an excellent means for promoting services as well as describing the content of special collections. They also may become more heavily used than the reading room, if major segments of the collection are digitized.

Within the limits of good security and conservation practice, allowing the special collections area to serve as a background for receptions or special meetings also draws attention to the program. Balancing the value of such attention against potential problems of security and conservation can be difficult. For example, can you control smoking, eating, and drinking in a party atmosphere? Pressure to use "that lovely room" for any and all functions can be hard to resist when it comes from members of the library's governing board or the library's funding body. Public service staff should refer all such requests to the head of special collections or the library director—even those requests that start with, "The Mayor (or President) requests you reserve. . . ."

Lectures and publications about the contents of the collection are both good methods for promoting the program. Occasional carefully planned and monitored "open houses" or tours can bring about greater awareness of contents and activities of the area. Such activities often attract a number of members of the library staff who seldom, if ever, have a chance to visit the area. This in turn gives the staff an opportunity to better learn and recognize special collections items—not only, as mentioned above, to thwart theft, but also because there are always a few items in the general collections that probably deserve inclusion in special collections, especially in libraries of a venerable age.

One obvious purpose in promoting special collections is the desire and necessity to raise money. Many libraries have a group of supporters, frequently called "Friends of the Library," that assists in fundraising. For many such groups the special collections unit is the focal point of interest. In addition to raising money, the group may be a source of volunteer assistance for special collections. The library should limit these volunteers to housekeeping activities; only the most trusted and knowledgeable volunteers should have direct contact with the special collections materials, and then the contact should be limited and with direct supervision.

STAFFING

Archives/special collections staffing requirements are quite distinct, varying considerably from the rest of the library. Clearly the security aspect of special collections work suggests that careful staff selection is necessary. It is not inappropriate to require in-depth background checks and even to require bonding of staff working with the collection(s). As we reported, an intern at the National Archives managed to steal and sell documents from its collection. The authors had the shared experience where a work study student who was working in the archives/special collections unit stole baseball trading cards. A part-time staff member noted his taking some cards; in cooperation with the campus public safety office, the next time the young man came in he was again observed taking cards. A search of his room turned up over 3,000 cards with a value of $15,000. A sad footnote is he had worked in the department for over a year and had been taking items for most of that time.

As the above story highlights, student workers and volunteers need a more in depth review before you allow them to handle materials than is required in other areas of the library. All staff working in the area should have more assessment than usual before hiring; just how far that should go is, in part, dependent upon the nature of the material with which they will be working.

While maintaining good employee relations is a goal of any good supervisor, a disgruntled special collections staff member can cause havoc even with a security system in place, as was the case with the National Archives intern. The rules for users should apply to staff as well; that is, staff should only take needed supplies into special collections. In general, personal belongings should remain outside. It is important to maintain records of staff use of materials; the record should list who used what, when, and why. It is standard procedure to require at least the same degree of preservation-mindedness in staff that one expects from users, such as care in handling, prohibition of food and drink, use of pencil rather than ink pen when working with special collections materials, and so forth.

Naturally, staff members require special training in security matters. Knowing their own legal rights as well as the users' rights and obligations can make the staff's work in maintaining security easier. It will also generate fewer problems because the staff can more effectively relate the rules and regulations to the users before the individuals start using materials.

Archives/special collections areas often have limited staffing. Perhaps the person responsible for the area also has other duties. In any case, that person is responsible for establishing policies and rules of use. In addition, the individual will make decisions about preservation and conservation issues. Support staff often will be in a position of dealing with requests to use the collection. When the request fits into the policy guidelines, support staff can move forward with the vetting process. When there is *any* question about the appropriateness of the request, the person responsible for special collections should make the decision. Normally the special collections support staff deliver the requested material to the user, monitor usage, and also check the material when the user finishes. All staff members are responsible for the security of the collections and, as noted above, bonding may be a requirement for anyone working in the area.

ETHICAL AND LEGAL CONSIDERATIONS

A number of legal and ethical issues affect special collections and their operations. We mentioned some legal issues earlier without identifying precise areas of interest. Staff need to know the state and local laws related to theft and damage of library materials.

Dealing with Theft

Some jurisdictions have laws that expressly cover library issues, while others simply treat library materials as general government property. In either case the laws are general in nature and normally cover all materials, not just special collections. Web sites such as Incidents of Book Theft (http://www.museum-security.org/booktheft2.html) provide useful information and can alert staff of recent problems. Reporting tools such as the Antiquarian Book-seller's Association Stolen and Missing Books database (http://www.abaa.org/books/abaa/database/stolen_search.html) may also be of use. Of course the ACRL Rare Books and Manuscripts Section Web site is also worth consulting (http://www.rbms.info/).

Staff members should also know their own legal rights in stopping a suspected thief, what they can and what they shouldn't do. When is it appropriate to call the police or security officers? May staff members attempt to detain a suspected thief? Should the library try to detain such a person even if it is legal to do so? These are just a few of the questions that need answers. Clearly the issues go beyond special collections staff and are important for all public service personnel. The law is especially important to know if, in your particular state or local jurisdiction, laws about presumption and liability exemption sections dealing with shoplifting also apply to libraries. Naturally, it is essential to check on the current status of the law in your state before deciding on the library's policy in this area. A library should never operate on the basis of unwritten policies, and this is one area where an unwritten policy could lead to legal problems.

Copyright Issues

While how people use copyrighted materials is an overall library concern, it takes on extra importance in special collections. In part, the issue comes up because of the close monitoring of the readers' use of every item they handle. Many people think of copyright only in terms of published material: books, journals, sound recordings, and so forth. The present U.S. copyright law includes any unpublished work in "tangible form." Tangible form includes handwritten material as well as any other form another person can use. In many special collections, unpublished works represent one of the most frequently used classes of material. Certainly experienced researchers understand the law, but most inexperienced users are not aware of the copyright coverage on unpublished materials. Thus, it is the library staff's responsibility to communicate this information to the user. A simple form explaining the copyright facts can be given to anyone asking to use unpublished material.

The creator or author (or the author's heirs) holds the copyright on unpublished works. In the United States, copyright duration for published written materials includes the lifetime of the author plus 95 years. In the case of unpublished works created before January 1978, statutory coverage lasts up through the year 2002, but by publication before the end of that year it may be extended another 25 years (that is, until 2027). Unpublished works created after January 1978 are protected for the creator's lifetime plus 50 years. All of these guidelines are subject to constant modification in the courts as well as legislatively.

As you might expect, researchers often ask for help in tracking down the copyright holder to get permission to use the material. Maintaining files on donors of material is a common practice, but it is not very common to try to maintain current addresses of such donors. Even if the library could maintain such a file it might not always provide the desired information. A donor may not be the author or creator of the material in question and thus not be the copyright holder.

In addition to the copyright concerns, donors of unpublished materials often place restrictions on access. Common restrictions include how soon people may see the material and who may see the material. Time restrictions are relatively easy to handle as long as the items have labels clearly indicating when the public may see and use them (for example, "Not to be examined until A.D. 2025" or "Not to be examined until 25 years after the author's death"). In some instances, donors will allow scholars to examine items for information, but will not allow the user to publish or quote from any part of the item. Restricting certain classes of users creates problems for the staff. Keeping track of who may use what material adds to the workload. How much checking should you do to determine if the requester is eligible to handle the material? Although special collection department heads attempt to limit restrictions they are not always able to do so for a variety of reasons.

Occasionally a worried donor sends someone to test the library's enforcement of the restrictions (as one of the authors of this book learned—we passed the test, but it did come as a surprise). Failure to enforce the restrictions—and the donor decides what failure is—can lead to the withdrawal of the donation.

RECORDS MANAGEMENT

As we noted earlier, many special collections and archives departments are taking on or are assigned the duties of managing an organization's records management program. There are certain similarities between archives and records management (RM) processes. The major difference is that the goal of archives is to preserve records indefinitely, while records management's purpose is to ensure the required records of an organization's day-to-day activities remain available as long as legally required. In essence, RM's concern is retaining material for finite periods.

Retention schedules identify the legal time frames for various classes of materials. The *Federal Records Management Glossary* defines a records schedule as: "Also called records disposition schedule, records control schedule, records retention schedule, records retention and disposition schedule, or schedule. A document that describes agency records, establishes a period for their retention by the agency, and provides mandatory instructions for what to do with them when they are no longer needed for current Government business" (http://www.epa.gov/records/gloss).
Thus, schedules are the guidelines for what to retain and for how long and what to discard. (*Note:* There are often federal, state, and even local government requirements to consider.)

The first step in creating a program is to survey existing records and note types of records, how they are currently organized, and where they exist. Using the survey data and schedules, one can systematically identify the records that must be retained and the appropriate time period. One can then review the balance to determine which, if any, the organization may wish to retain for its own purposes. Most RM specialists agree that there are five primary reasons to retain materials: administrative, fiscal, legal, historical, and informational value. Generally, retention time increases as one moves through the list. In some cases the form in which one retains the material is also a matter of law (what format will be acceptable in court should it come to that).

RM activities do require time and effort. Combining them with archives and special collections programs *may* achieve some economies of scale. But, given the requirements of staff time and space, expecting an existing special collection and/or archive staff to take on RM as an additional duty or without additional staff, funding, and space is unrealistic.

SUMMARY

Working in an archive/special collections is interesting as well as challenging, especially if you have an interest or expertise in history or in the subject areas of the particular collections. Doing so requires constant attention to and a talent for detail. Environmental conditions, users' and one's own habits regarding careful handling of materials, and collection security are main concerns in this area.

Chapter Review Material

1. Discuss the differences between general and special collections materials.
2. What are some of the characteristics of special collections materials that can create complications in storage?
3. Outline the major aspects of a sound environmental control program in special collections.
4. What kind of normal library procedures might present a preservation or security problem if used in special collections? How would you guard against these problems?
5. What factors distinguish access to special collections from access to the general collection?
6. Describe the legal issues related to special collections work.

REFERENCES

American Libraries. 2007. "Philadelphia Archives Thief Gets 15 Months," 38, no. 8: 22.

Amodeo, Anthony. 1983. "Special Collections Desk Duty: Preventing Damage," *College & Research Library News* 44, no. 6: 180–82.

Association of Colleges and Research Libraries (ACRL). 2006. *Guidelines for the Security of Rare Books, Manuscripts, and Other Special Collections.* http://www.ala.org/ala/acrl/acrlstandards/securityrarebooks.cfm.

Carpenter, Kenneth E. 1986. *The First 350 Years of the Harvard University Library.* Cambridge, MA: Harvard University Library.

Cave, Roderick. 1982. *Rare Book Librarianship,* 2nd rev. ed. London: Clive Bingley.

Smith, Steven Escar. 2006. "From 'Treasure Room' to 'School Room:' Special Collections and Education," *RBM* 7, no. 1: 31–39.

Sutton, Shan, and Lorrie Knight. 2006. "Beyond the Reading Room: Integrating Primary and Secondary Sources in the Library Classroom," *Journal of Academic Librarianship* 32, no. 3: 320–325.

Thompson, L. S. 1984. "Biblioclasm in Norway," *Library & Archival Security* 6, no. 4: 13–16.

Visser, Michelle. 2006a. "The Real McCoy," *School Library Journal* 51, no.12: 33.

———. 2006b. "Special Collections at ARL Libraries and K-12 Outreach: Current Trends," *Journal of Academic Librarianship* 32, no. 3: 313–319.

SUGGESTED READINGS

ACRL Rare Books and Manuscripts Section. Security. http://www.ala.org/ala/acrl/acrlstandards/securityrarebooks.cfm.

———. Transfer of Collections. http://www.ala.org/ala/acrl/acrlstandards/selec transfer.cfm.

———. *Guidelines for the Loan of Rare and Unique Materials.* http://www.ala.org/ala/acrl/acrlstandards/borrowguide.cfm.

Association of Records Managers and Administrators. 2003. *Vital Records: Identifying, Managing, and Recovering Business-Critical Records.* Prairie Village, KS: ARMA.

Bachman, Konstanze. 1992. *Conservation Concerns: A Guide for Collectors and Curators.* Washington, DC: Smithsonian Institute Press.

Bansa, Helmut. 1987. "Conservation Treatment of Rare Books," *Restaurator* 8, no. 2–3: 140–150.

Basler, Teresa, and David Wright. 2008. "Making of a Collection of Mesoamerican Manuscripts at Princeton University," *Libraries & the Cultural Record* 43, no. 1: 29–55.

Blumenstien, Lynn. 2006. "Special Collections at Risk," *Library Journal* 131, no. 1: 26.

Brooks, Charmaine. 2007. "Records Management," *AIIM E-Doc Magazine* 21, no. 3: 16–18.

Goodbody, Margaret, and Jennifer Evans. 2005. "Protecting Access and materials in Public Library Special Collections," *Technical Services Quarterly* 22, no. 3: 19–28.

Huntsberry, J. Steve. 1989. "Forged Identification: A Key to Library Archives." *Library & Archival Security* 9, no. 3–4: 69–74.

Pugh, Mary Jo. 1992. *Providing Reference Services for Archives and Manuscripts.* Chicago: Society of American Archivists.

West, Jessamyn. 2007. "Saving Digital History," *Library Journal Net Connect* 132, Spring: 2–4, 6.

Whittaker, Beth M. 2006. "Get It, Catalog It, Promote It: New Challenges to Providing Access to Special Collections," *RBM* 7, no. 2: 121–133.

———. 2008. "Using Circulation Systems for Special Collections: Tracking Usage, Promoting the Collection, and Addressing the Backlogs," *College & Research Libraries* 69, no. 1: 38–35.

14

Programming

To effectively serve 21st century library users, librarians must strongly challenge their current assumptions about patron needs, service programming, and about their own roles as information professionals.
—Daryl Youngman, 2002

The feeling that libraries are central to healthy communities is even more common among those who are most actively engaged in communities: the voters, volunteers, and contributors who make communities strong and can usually be counted upon to raise a ruckus when things go wrong."
—Ruth Wooden, 2006

All of the foregoing chapters dealt with a more or less single, traditional service that one finds in any type of library. In this chapter, we explore a variety of services; several of which are only seen in one or two types of libraries. Our choice of the term "programming" required some debate on our part. We settled on it because it is broad enough to cover the services we discuss and it is not library type specific.

Very often the services we cover in this chapter are the ones people mention when asked, "What makes your library special?" Certainly such services by themselves cannot transform a poor service reputation; however, they almost always enhance a good reputation. Knowing what "special" service(s) to offer requires careful thought, planning, and resources in order to "get it right." Programming options are only limited by staff imaginations. What is important is not so much what the staff thinks would be good to offer, but what the service community is interested in using and willing to support.

No two service communities are identical. Those of us working in libraries sometimes forget that fact and think "I just read about this very successful program at library X; I think we should try it here." Since each service community is slightly different, there is no guarantee someone else's program will translate effectively to your library. How do you learn about what services are desired/wanted/needed in your service community? Part of the answer lies in conducting a study such as a community analysis, needs assessment, or marketing project.

Libraries must provide useful/wanted services due to today's highly competitive information delivery environment. It is no longer a matter of if they should; they must do so, if they hope to have long-term viability. Public service staff play the lead role in the library's service program. (Yes, those working in technical services start the service process, but the quality of those in public services through their daily work will make or break a library's reputation and any effort to promote the service.)

QUALITY SERVICE/PROGRAMMING LINKAGE

As our opening quotation by Daryl Youngman states, today's libraries must rethink their assumptions about user needs, wants, and desires. Youngman (2002) went on to suggest: "As fewer patrons avail themselves of traditional desk-based reference services, increasing numbers of users are taking advantage of remote-access library services that often served with no option to seek librarian help. Libraries must be positioned to deliver services to this new generation of academic library users whose expectations and use patterns differ markedly from their predecessors" (p. 1).

The fact is, all types of libraries, not just academic, face the same situation. Leigh Estabrook and colleagues (2007) reported, "Young adults in Generation Y (ages 18–29) are the heaviest users of libraries when faced with these problems" (p. iii). The "problems" the authors referenced related to the use of the Internet, libraries, and government agencies information. The authors later noted, "Use of libraries as a source for dealing with these matters is higher among those who are younger and those with lower incomes" (p. 18). Assuming their data are an accurate reflection of how younger people solve problems, libraries ought to better position themselves to meet the needs of these computer/technology-oriented individuals.

We noted earlier that one element in a market assessment is gaining an understanding of what the various segments of the service population are interested in, what they want, what they expect, what they need, and how they make use of the information/material they access. Such data should assist libraries as they shift their services to an ever more user-centered approach. (In the past, libraries often appeared to be more profession-oriented rather than user-focused; one example is the old card catalog with its complex filing rules that often even baffled staff members and few if any users ever mastered.)

Some years ago, when teaching in library school, one of this book's authors had a student who conducted a study of which library staff categories—librarians, support, and part-time—had the most accurate sense of what services were most desirable from the service community's point-of-view. The student developed a list of potential services based on a literature review and discussions with 15 public library directors. The resulting questionnaire was mailed to the residents of three communities, and each of the staff categories in the public libraries serving the communities. Somewhat surprising at the time was the fact that the part-time staff (pages, volunteers, etc.) most accurately reflected what the residents stated they would like to see offered. The librarians' assessments were the furthest removed from the residents' thoughts on the matter. The study emphasized the importance of conducting a marketing assessment whenever thinking about expanding one's services—guessing or just going by press releases about the newest and best is not a good idea.

We wish to stress that rethinking does *not* mean that all the standby services are relegated to the dustbin. Far from it; most if not all services are still highly regarded by users. Some services, such as reference, are morphing into more virtual forms, but the basic reference procedures remain at the heart of the process regardless of the delivery mechanism. We touch on a variety of old and new services in this chapter. We cannot predict what new services will become "new standbys," even in the very near future. Public service staff members just have too active imaginations to make any accurate predications

PROGRAMMING

It should go without saying, but we will emphasize the idea, that whatever services are offered are or ought to be closely linked to the library's mission, goals, and objectives. Sometimes ideas and services get ahead of the formal documentation; rarely does this cause a serious problem, but it is always wise to check your idea(s) against the stated library purposes before going too far into the planning process.

Obviously, the library's environment plays the dominant role in the selection of what services to offer. What is desirable in a school media library setting is most unlikely to be appropriate for a special/business library. However, you should not dismiss out of hand a service just because you've only read about it being offered in another type of library. The underlying concept may well become suitable, if one thinks about it and "tweaks" it a little.

Tailoring services to user needs is much easier when you have access to marketing/long range planning data. Often such data focus on what exists rather than new service ideas; however, they can provide a sound starting point for thinking about new approaches. Some of the more traditional services include:

- Consumer information
- Career/business information
- Referral services
- Lifelong learning
- Literacy programs—adult/children
- Computer/information literacy
- Homework assistance
- Cultural awareness
- Government data
- Group use space
- Genealogical
- Outreach services
- Mobile services
- Story hours

Although the above are traditional or at least long-standing services appearing in one or more types of libraries, they can and do take on a variety of shapes and forms. Using marketing/community analysis data you can make adjustments in these activities to keep them alive and vibrant.

There may be better ways to structure a discussion of the services, but we elected to employ a three-category approach—educational, recreational, and outreach. We fully recognize that dividing lines are blurry, but the approach does provide a means of grouping more or less similar activities.

Some years ago Charles McClure and colleagues (1987) outlined a variety of roles for public libraries. With only a slight rewording, most of those roles could apply to any type of library. The following is our reworking of the original set of roles:

- Activities center (meetings, collaborative programs, etc.)
- Information center (community data, referrals, etc.)
- Education support center (homework assistance, language materials, etc.)
- Independent learning center (career development, updating skills, etc.)
- Preschool learning center (story hours, early literacy training, etc.)
- Recreational materials center (books, videos, maps, etc.)
- Research materials center (data sets, primary and secondary sources, etc.)
- Reference center (in-person and remote assistance, etc.)

The last three are "core" services that we covered in earlier chapters. The balance of this chapter addresses other services.

EDUCATIONAL SERVICES

Robert Martin (2004) wrote that public libraries are "agencies of public education, fundamental to the education infrastructure of our society" (p. 84). Rabner and Budd (1998) made much the same point in writing about public libraries as "a place that links education and entertainment" (p. 183). The educational role goes back to the founding of public libraries in the United States. One of the earliest references to such a role is found in the document that created the Boston Public Library, when the founders indicated its primary purpose was to provide a source of self-education for Boston's citizens (Crowley, 2005, p. 48).

Today the educational role is paramount for almost every type of library, when one takes the broadest view of "education." They perform this function in a variety of ways. Some view it as providing the means for those interested in lifelong learning while others offer basic services in language literacy; still others view the process as being a "university for the people." Such programs cover all age groups from infants to seniors. Even special/business libraries engage in at least some "education" as they provide training in the use of online resources to their target audiences.

Lifelong Learning

Life-long learning is a widely used phrase. When one explores what people mean when using it, there are dozens of definitions; however, there do appear to be three core elements on which most people agree. One element is that it is often informal; the individual decides what and how to learn about something. A second aspect is that it is often sporadic in nature; the individual can start and stop at will and there can be long and short pauses between those activities. Finally, it is personally driven; no outside agency or person directs the process. The underlying key is it is open to anyone willing to make the effort, not just those matriculated in an educational program, nor does it require any level of attainment.

The public libraries' concept of the "university of the people," which was promoted in the late nineteenth and early twentieth centuries became rather diluted over time. Recently, post-2000, the idea has regained some of its former prominence. A 2007 essay by S. Randle England reviewed the educational role of public libraries. Essentially, the concept of free access to libraries has and does mean that anyone, regardless of social or financial status, may use public library resources and services to acquire skills and/or knowledge in order to become a more informed citizen or more productive member of society. At the same time libraries are under pressure to keep costs as low as possible and even to generate income. Thus, what was once free has become less so as fees for this and that service increase. There may even be limits on who may use certain resources—we mentioned the limiting of downloading videos to local residents in the media chapter. Many academic libraries limit access to their electronic resources to members of the institution, even in tax-supported institutions.

Lifelong learning, to be effective, requires collaboration between educators and libraries. Sara Gillis and Julie Totten (2006) describe a highly successful collaborative program in the Halifax Public Library and the school district. On the other hand, Alan Bundy (2006) suggested that educators often seem more concerned with teaching a curriculum rather than lifelong learning. (There are some significant reasons for that focus, at least in the United States. One of the reasons is schools can lose funding when their students don't achieve certain levels on standardized tests.) Perhaps curriculum focus is an opportunity for libraries where they can, with educator input, take on some of the broader aspects of lifelong learning. Bundy went on to say. "So what is meant by education? Is it learning the three Rs? Is it learning physics, chemistry, and maths? Is it learning languages or about a country's history and politics, geography and economy? Is it about value development?" (p. 128). No matter which of his questions, or the host of others, one focuses on, libraries are one of the places where independent learning can occur. One of the roles the public service staff can and must play in the process is to assist the individual in identifying the most appropriate resources for what the person wishes to learn about. Bundy ended his article with a plea for greater cooperation and coordination between educators and libraries.

Literacy Programs

One significant educational issue is just how much concern society should have about the level of reading literacy. Computers and related technologies may be what today's youth focus on and understand and those technologies are likely to increase as factors in our daily lives. However, people who never read a book and only use computers must be able to read and understand the written words that appear on the screen. In 2007, the National Assessment of Adult Literacy (NAAL) issued a report on adult literacy in the United States. The study looked at three types of literacy (Kutner et al., 2007, p. iii):

- Prose (the knowledge and skills needed to search, comprehend, and use information from continuous text)
- Document (the knowledge and skills needed to search, comprehend, and use information noncontinuous text, such as labels on medicines, job applications, and tables)
- Quantitative (the knowledge and skills needed to identify and perform computations using numbers that are embedded in printed materials, such as calculating discounts and handling a checking account)

The report compared data it collected in 1992 with data from the current study (2003). Overall, the results were rather disappointing, if not surprising. "White and Asian/Pacific Islanders adults had higher average prose, document and quantitative literacy than Black and Hispanic adults. Black adults had higher prose and document literacy than Hispanic adults. . . . A higher percentage of adults with below basic prose, document and quantitative literacy lived in households with income below $10,000 than adults with higher levels of literacy" (Kutner et al., 2007, p. v). The proficiency levels measured were "Below Basic," "Basic," "Intermediate," and "Proficient."

Another key finding of the study was that parents with higher proficiency levels read to their children five or more times a week. Many public libraries have story hours for preschoolers to encourage such reading. For example, the Flagstaff City-Coconino County Public Library offers an eight-level program each week:

- Infants to eighteen months
- Eighteen months to two years old
- Infants to two-year-olds
- Two- and three-year-olds
- Three- and four-year-olds
- Three- through five-year-olds
- Four- and five-year-olds
- Families

In addition, it has a "PALSmobile," a small scale bookmobile (PALS stands for Preschoolers Acquiring Literacy Skills). The service visits preschools, day care, and Head Start centers throughout the county (http://www.flagstaffpublic library.org/services/palsmobile.html).

Nicole Whitehead (2004) noted "that frequent reading is directly related to higher performance in reading" (p. 165). One of her findings was that "the groups that visited the library eight to twelve times within the six month study period had higher averages in most of the areas measured (5 out of 7) in comparison to the group that did not go the library as a class" (p. 172). The areas she examined were reading performance, attitudes toward reading, time spent reading at home, number of books in the home, family and class visits to the community library, and the child's "ownership" of a library card. At least in this study, the public library did help improve classroom performance in reading, especially when the child had library card and the family and class visited the library.

An interesting program that involved both parents and children is the Boulder Public Library's "Reading Buddies" (Sherry, 2005) (http://www.boulder reads.org/services/buddies.html). The idea grew out of the fact that many of the adults who took part in the library's adult literacy program had child care issues. The library and the local university's school of education developed a program where a student teacher became a "buddy" to one of the children with a parent in the literacy class. The service, while encouraging the children to read with their buddies, also wished to help the children with their homework. Mentors helped the children find material in the library, played word games with them; a few even wrote a "book" with their buddy. Because the student teachers receive service-learning credit they proved reliable and motivated. Their buddies were very enthusiastic and regular in their attendance as well.

ESL Programs

Another educational area that libraries assist in is ESL (English as a Second Language). In part, these services arise from the fact that most schools, of all types, have full courses and waiting lists. Many libraries employ technology to provide a structured, but self-paced means of learning English. There are downloadable programs for learning English based on the native language of the learner—for example, Pimsleur Language Program and Rosetta Stone. There are, of course, the PC-based programs in many libraries that offer the learner/user the opportunity to get assistance from the library staff. This does of course require the public staff members to be familiar with the programs, or at least the basics of using them. To date, we are not aware of any challenges to offering such programs, unlike some of the concerns about print materials.

Homework Assistance

Perhaps one of the most popular services is homework assistance. Pamela Warton (2001) suggested that homework, for parents, teachers, and students, is "a source of considerable difficulty and conflict at home and school" (p. 155). Public libraries are well positioned to help reduce the stress of homework. Often there are partnerships with after-school programs with assistance being available both in the library and at a learning center. Many programs are tiered—elementary, middle, and high school. A few not only actively partner with a school district, but gain the involvement of a local academic institution (Brooke and Ryan, 2007). The St. Paul (Minnesota) Public Library, offers "Zone Homework Help Center" in conjunction with Metropolitan State University. Students in the University's Urban Teachers Program volunteer to become mentors. Late in 2007, the "Zone" went live on the Web after several years of just being offered in the main and branch libraries (http://www.stpaul.lib. mn.us/homework/thezone.html). Zone provides one-on-one tutoring for individuals from fourth grade through lower division course work in college. The Web service came into being through the support of the mayor, the president of Metropolitan State, and the director of the library. Both the mayor and the university president were so impressed with the quality and effectiveness of the face-to-face program that they provided funding to launch the Web program. A follow-on article about the service describes some of the government support it has received, such as additional funding earmarked for the homework program and enhancing the technical capabilities of the Web site (Confer et al., 2007).

College Access Programs

Our final example of "educational" services is related to homework assistance. Some libraries have an active service, not just a collection of books about financial aid and college catalogs, but one that assists high school graduates to gain access to and be ready for a post-secondary educational experience. One interesting article, both for its content and because its author went to work for a college after being a school librarian, is Ellysa Cahoy's "Will Your Students Be Ready for College?" She suggests that the best way to improve students' chances of "being ready" is for school and academic librarians to work together at the high school level "to start learning about students potential needs in the local high schools as well as what the high school library(ies) are capable of offering" (p. 15). Her main focus in the article is on the ACRLs' "Information Literacy Competency" standards and how school and academic librarians need to work together in developing realistic expectations for what school libraries are capable of doing in terms of information literacy competencies given their limited resources (http://www.ala.org/ala/acrl/acrl standards/informationliteracycompetency.cfm).

It is one thing to be information literate, and quite another to be interested in going on to college. College access programs help spark students' interest in higher education as well as assisting parents in negotiating the issues of financing and supporting the student once admitted. Although in an unusually rich academic environment, the Boston Public Library's "Higher Education Information Center" (30-plus institutions take part in the program) does provide insights into student higher education life. It also provides advising and referral services, identifying scholarship opportunities, the application process, and educational requirement information. June Eiselstien's article (2003) describes the Boston program and explores the issues related to college access programs. She notes collaboration is the key to success.

Many academic libraries provide a related service for some high school students along the lines of "advance placement (AP) student access." Most of the libraries offering such services enter into an agreement with each high school wishing to have their AP students have access to the library's resources. In turn, the participating high school agrees to be responsible for any fines/fees generated by the students—they have an easier means for recovering the costs than do the academic libraries. The school then supplies a list of the eligible AP students. Generally the agreement allows AP students access to all resources in the library, and limited borrowing privileges, but not to document delivery services (ILL) or other remote access that generates individual use fees. A few even offer special instructional classes for the AP students; generally they do so because they believe in the long run it will save staff time when working with such students. High school students are different from freshmen, even if they are enrolled in "college prep" classes; thus anyone teaching library instructional classes for AP students needs an understanding of teenage development and interests. To be effective, AP library programs require close cooperation between the two parties; the most successful are when the high school principal and library director meet once or twice a year to discuss the program.

A good essay that covers one such program is Debra Pearson and Beth McNeil's (2002) "From High School Users College Students Grow." Pearson and McNeil review the past and current practices in the University of Nebraska—Lincoln library's AP program. The library had employed the AP as part of its outreach program since 1980. From the outset it had been a collaborative program with local school librarians teaching high school students about research and how to use a university library system in that process. Not long before they published their article, the university library modified its lending rules for the AP students; the student had to get a receipt for each item returned. The change substantially reduced the "I know I returned it"/missing rate for the program. Other changes focused on the changing formats the library made available to the students. The authors concluded by stating, "Regardless of whether or not participants decide to attend the University of Nebraska, the librarians have helped prepare young Nebraskans for their college experience and their future information needs" (p. 26).

RECREATIONAL SERVICES

One person's recreational activity may be someone else's educational experience and vice versa—sometimes it is both for an individual. Thus, we know our division is a matter of convenience rather than clear-cut differences. However, we have tried to place the services where the educational or recreational value is highest.

Meeting Rooms

A long-standing service, especially in public libraries, is to provide meeting rooms for various activities. Some libraries even have an auditorium/lecture hall facility. Events may be library sponsored or solely supported, other than the meeting space, by outside groups. Community service clubs and interest groups are often the beneficiaries of such room use (charity groups, garden club, chess club, etc.) Libraries have learned, from sometimes bitter experience, that there must be a clearly stated and governing board-approved policy and procedure for the use of the space. Lacking such documentation there is likely to be problems, with the public service staff often caught in the middle.

In the past, there were few issues arising from having a meeting room available. Today, the issue of who may make use of the space could end up at the U.S. Supreme Court, even with a policy/procedure in place. The following three examples provide some perspective on the complexity of having a meeting room available to the public.

Our first example took place in Colorado Springs (*American Libraries*, 2005). The Rampart Library District had a board-approved policy that stated if the rooms were used by religious or political groups, the meeting must provide a balanced view. Early in 2005, a religious group asked to use a room and the request was turned down because it would be a religious service. Shortly after the use denial took place the library received notice that a lawsuit was being filed by Liberty Counsel (a religious rights defense organization located in Florida) against the library district for denying use of the room for a religious program. The Rampart District decided to modify their use policy because they did not have the funds to engage in a legal battle. (Liberty Counsel has filed at least seven such suits since 2000. They won some of them for the same reason that Rampart conceded—lack of funds to engage in a legal battle.)

Early in 2006, the Montana State Library cancelled an ACLU film screening that was critical of the USA PATRIOT Act due to some complaints that the program did not list a speaker who would support the Act. Rather than file a lawsuit, the ACLU booked a room in the Lewis and Clark Library (the local public library). The difference between the two libraries, according to *American Libraries* (2006c), was the presence and absence of room usage policies. Lewis and Clark had a policy that stated as long as a program dealing with a controversial topic provided most, if not all points of view on the topic, the meeting room could be booked. The State Library had no policy and reacted to several telephone calls complaining about the program. The article did note that the ACLU had invited a representative from U.S. Attorney General's Office to speak by the time they applied to Lewis and Clark. However, no such representative came to the meeting.

Our last example took several years to resolve (2004–2007). It started in 2004 when the Antioch branch of the Contra Costa County (California) Library system rejected a room request from the Faith Center Church Evangelistic Ministries. The denial led to a lawsuit. The denial was based on the library board's policy that stated that rooms cannot be used for religious services—separation of church and state grounds. Library staff stated the denial was based on the fact that the group indicated it would hold prayer services as part of their program. (They had distributed flyers throughout the area inviting people to attend a worship service at the library.) Interestingly enough, the U.S. Department of Justice took the position that Contra Costa County had to allow the group to use the library room for their service; a somewhat strange twist on the separation of church and state concept. Contra Costa County pushed the case forward, as it viewed this more than a matter of library room use. They had no problem with the group using the space for nonworship service purposes, but not for a religious service. Each side appealed the case; each side won and lost in the lower courts. On the first day of the 2007–2008 term, the Supreme Court refused to hear the appeal of the Ninth Circuit Court of Appeals ruling that the library and county had acted properly. (Note: the ruling only applies to those libraries in the Ninth Circuit Court's jurisdiction.) *American Libraries* (2007b) reported the religious group said they would revisit the case in lower courts using a new set of arguments. Stay tuned; who would guess having a library meeting room could cause so most stress and expense for everyone?

Book Discussion Programs

Originally we thought of starting this section with something like, "Turning to a non-controversial service. . ."; however, we realized one can never be 100 percent certain a service will not generate some type of complaints from someone.

Like meeting rooms, book discussion groups have been a staple of library service programs for a great many years. Sara Stevenson (2005), a middle school librarian, wrote, "My favorite time of day is after lunch when I host our book clubs" (p. 48). She offers four clubs—horror, fantasy, mystery, and "girls time out." Stevenson's ultimate goal is to make the children better students while making reading and thinking about what is read fun. Her article outlines a number of activities that are fun and, at the same time, moving toward her long-term goal.

Book clubs, book discussion groups, or whatever term one employs for the activity more often than not have several common characteristics—they are informal, have no rules/bylaws, have little structure, and have people dropping in and out without notice. Sessions maybe informative or even enlightening, but first and foremost they are to be enjoyable. Many public libraries offer several types of groups—genre based (like Stevenson's), literature of a country or author, and nonfiction topics such as politics or history for example. The process also varies from group to group—some have everyone read the same book; another approach is to have each member read a different book and lead a discussion; still others use a mixed approach. A library staff member often acts as a group facilitator. Occasionally a library is fortunate to secure the volunteer services of a scholar to handle a group.

One concept that has gained popularity is that of the "One Book." An example of this technique in an academic setting is from Loyola Marymount University. Each year a book is selected for the entire freshmen class to read. Titles selected almost always address a social issue. Throughout the year, the freshmen English classes devote some time to discussing the book. In addition, the University brings the author to the campus for several days to meet with groups to discuss the book and give a public lecture. Some larger public libraries have secured funding to do something similar. State libraries as well as local libraries have been employing some aspects of such a program for a number of years.

Book discussions have both an intellectual and a social aspect (chatting over coffee and biscotti). People have an opportunity to exchange/share their views with others, meet new people with similar interests—especially reading, have a chance to explore new ideas, think about what they read in a new manner, and perhaps gain new insights.

Exhibitions

Libraries have probably been putting up exhibits for most of their history. Certainly most of these are not an exhibition in the museum sense; many are nothing more than displaying dust jackets of newly arrived books or a few themed posters on the wall, or pieces of replica sculptures. (Regarding book dust jackets, many libraries are adding the dust jacket image to the record in their OPACs. Essentially the libraries are taking a page out of the online book sellers' and bookstores' playbook, to catch the attention of readers.)

School media centers often have their walls covered with posters intended to encourage reading. Anyone visiting the exhibits area of an ALA convention quickly learns that publishers give away posters that promote some of their publications. Naturally the children's book posters are the most colorful and useful in promoting reading in a school or public library. Thus, there is an annual stream of useful colorful material available at no cost. The ALA also sells a variety of posters promoting reading, many of which feature celebrities.

Research, academic, and larger public libraries are the most likely to mount museum quality exhibitions. Frequently the special collections unit is responsible for planning and executing such shows. A good show is not inexpensive in terms of staff time as well as for the proper materials and security. It may also require substantial planning, sometimes over several years. The person responsible, or curator to use the formal label, picks a topic and begins identifying potential material. Sometimes the exhibition draws on materials from sources outside the exhibiting library. In those cases, the issues of item security become paramount and there are often costs for proper shipping as well as special insurance. See Chapter 7 for more information on loaning archival materials for exhibits.

Exhibitions can be mounted in the library, virtually (on the Web), or both. An example of an online exhibit was the "Great Pianistic Traditions in the IPAM Collections" done by the University of Maryland (http://www.lib.umd.edu/PAL/IPAM/traditions.html). Having an Internet presence for an exhibit assists in publicizing the current exhibition, as well as the opportunity to archive prior shows; one example is also from the University of Maryland (http://www.lib.umd.edu/mdrm/gallery/previous.html).

Susan Swisher (2007) detailed how the Hammond (Indiana) Public Library holds an annual Senior Art Exhibition. Their show had been operational for 16 years at the time she wrote the article and grown in size from a small local exhibition to a regional juried event. The library partners with the Northern Indiana Art Association and significant awards are given to category winners. A not unexpected outcome of the event is an increase in the library's reputation as a major contributor to the region's social programs.

Northern Virginia Community College Alexandria Campus Library mounted a different type of art exhibit (Rortvedt, 2007). It was a collaborative show between the library and the art department. Two art faculty members created a class project "based upon an interpretation of the text using the physical elements of the book as catalyst and structure" (p. 27). Unneeded library donations and withdrawn books furnished the raw material for the students to create their "altered book" art. The end products and exhibition were such a success the show may become a traveling exhibition.

We noted earlier, in the chapter on archives and special collections, that some academic libraries use their exhibitions, along with the broader purpose of informing, to introduce school children to research. A good article discussing this concept is Timothy Young's (2007) "The Young Visitors." Young provides the rationale for such programs and the issues involved in creating a beneficial experience for young people. Further, he discusses 18 lessons learned from the program at Beinecke Library (Yale). His "lessons" included:

- Plan ahead
- Advertise early and in different venues
- Think about sightlines and obstructions for young viewer
- Keep group size manageable

- Work with campus liaisons
- Host previews for teachers
- Develop an alternative storyline when planning for tours
- Have something to give away (flyers, postcards, etc.)

As is true of many library services, exhibitions can lead to complaints as well as praise. Although art shows have the greatest potential for offending someone, even a "Banned Book" exhibit can and has caused problems for a library. The factors we discussed in the section on censorship apply to exhibits as well. *American Libraries* (2008) covered a story about an exhibit in the Kennebunk Free Library and its problems. An artist, G. Bud Swenson, had created a series of collages using pieces of discarded U.S. flags or artwork symbolizing the flag ("American Portraits in a Time of War"). Included in these pieces were images of President Bush and Vice President Cheney. Some users complained. First the library cancelled the show, but reversed its decision after the board met with the artist. The director was quoted as saying, "It's easy to have pat answers, but finding the area in the middle requires courage" (p. 26).

Exhibitions are a good public relations tool and generally are appreciated by the service community. From a public service staff point of view, exhibitions generate many viewer questions and they expect informed answers. A useful activity is to have those who planned the show meet with the staff to discuss the material and address the most likely questions. If the show is on for some time, it is also useful to have a follow-up meeting where the staff can raise questions that have come up and that they did not think they had good answers to.

Summer Reading Programs

Summer reading programs have been a public library staple for a very long time. An equally long-standing question is, which goal is most important in summer reading programs—promoting lifelong reading or providing children with an enjoyable summer activity? We believe the answer is neither—both are equally important. A key method for accomplishing both goals, as well as helping to reinforce reading gains of the past school term, is to work with the local schools. Walter Minkel (2003) acknowledged it requires real effort to develop a sound relationship with the various schools; however, the children are the long-term beneficiaries of the effort. A factor in a successful summer program is getting the word out to parents. If one can get the schools to distribute a flyer about the program near the end of the school year, participation increases substantially. These programs also increase circulation during what can be otherwise slow times.

Many libraries now make the summer program a family affair rather than solely child-focused. With parents involved, children realize reading is important, and it may motivate parents to read more often with their children. One method some libraries employ to keep families active in the program is to have the family "write a book" about their summer experiences and offer some modest prizes for the best stories. Whatever one does it should be fun, first and foremost. While there are innumerable guides and Web sites on the topic of summer reading programs, the Association for Library Services for Children (ALSC), a division of the ALA, has a Web page devoted to the topic that is well worth reviewing from time to time (http://www.ala.org/ala/alsc/alsc resources/summerreading/summerreading.cfm).

Gaming

We mentioned gaming in the media chapter; here we provide a little more depth to the topic. Not surprisingly, gaming is on the rise in libraries. It is well beyond the board game activity of the past—some readers may remember the occasional complaints about allowing children to play "Dungeons and Dragons" in the library during the late twentieth century. Today it is computer games that hold young people's attention, although board games have not completely disappeared. The ALA held its first ever symposium on gaming in mid-2007 ("Gaming, Learning, and Libraries"). Linking learning and fun was a key element in the program. Coverage ranged from traditional board games to "Big Games" (games using an urban location as the game "board"), and, of course, the ever-present computer/online games.

Rebecca Moore (2006) discussed how she combined teaching research skills with middle school students' desire to play and compete. (Note: In her school all the students belong to either a Blue or Gold team that competes throughout the year for points and year-end rewards. Thus, she had existing teams with which to work.) She uses a form of *Jeopardy* in her orientation sessions. In all, she describes 12 games that combine a contest and learning objective.

Can video games support learning objectives such as media literacy? Eli Neiburger (2007) believes they can. She makes the point, which many of us may not recognize, that success in video games, at least initially, requires comprehending both text and game conventions. Squire and Steinkuehler (2005) noted, "Game cultures promote various types of information literacy, develop information seeking habits and production practices (like writing), and require good old-fashioned research skills, albeit using a wide spectrum of content. In short, libraries can't afford to ignore gamers" (p. 38). Academics who studied both stand-alone and multiplayer online games, Squire and Steinkuehler explored the social practices associated with gaming. One of their concluding recommendations was for libraries to carry games, host game nights, have gaming contests, and stock game-related materials.

Not all gaming in libraries is geared to learning. The Flagstaff City—Coconino County Library uses Wii™ bowling as a family outing opportunity. An interesting aspect of the "family bowling night" is it takes place in a branch located in a low-income neighborhood—having a free, fun, and safe family time is a wonderful benefit to the community and good PR for the library.

A few libraries, such as the Austin (Texas) Public Library (APL), have gone beyond having video games and contests. APL, with the aid of a special grant, hired a game developer to work with two groups of children to create their own video game (Minkel, 2002). The program helped the children gain an understanding of game logic and what is involved in coding a game.

Our last gaming item relates to something called "cosplay" (costume and play). In a sense, it is an extension of the Halloween costume contest that some libraries sponsor. Brehm-Heeger and colleagues(2007), young adult staff members of the Cincinnati-Hamilton Library, discuss how they employ this concept with their teen anime (shorthand for animation) club. Each year the club puts on a cosplay event in which members dress in anime costumes for judging by noncostumed members. They are asked questions about the costume, the character represented, and the reason for the choice. In addition, there are two-/three-minute skits by the costumed members. Again they are questioned about their knowledge of the anime and manga (Japanese word for comics) elements in the skit. Through this type of program, members have fun while engaging in research.

Lectures, Concerts, and Film Showings

These are other long-standing service programming, found most frequently in academic and public libraries. In most cases, the events are sponsored by the library, although, as we noted earlier in this chapter, sometimes the library only supplies the space. When the library puts on an event there must be a surprising amount of planning in order to achieve success. A few factors that require thought are:

• Budget	• Audience
• Topic	• Location
• Timing	• Marketing

If a library is fortunate, it may have an endowment to underwrite some of the event costs. Even when that is the case, the available funds are rarely adequate to cover the total costs of the program. Speakers/performers of any merit usually charge a fee, often very large, although sometimes there may be a local connection (personal friend/family for example) that will secure a discounted fee. Speaker fee(s) alone make it challenging to put on a meaningful program at a reasonable cost. Collaborative efforts sometimes work well, as long as the library's role is not lost in the process; for example, joint grant requests for program support.

Just because you think a topic is interesting does not mean it will attract a good audience. Having a group involved in topic selection is often the best means for identifying suitable topics and presenters. This is a place where marketing data can be useful in the planning process. Having some "extra" events such as small group meeting(s) with the presenter can help ensure a good turnout for the main event.

Topics and approaches vary, from single speakers (Robertson, 2007, book collecting) to panel discussions (Howie and Yochelson, 2006, mystery writers). Sometimes the theme is established and the goal is to identify a speaker who can provide new insights on the topic (for example, Cline Library's [Northern Arizona University] Grand Canyon Country Lecture series).

Film programs raise additional issues such as copy/performance rights, even if the producer/director is participating in the program. (See the media chapter for a discussion of performance rights.) Certainly film series are also more likely to generate a complaint or two (*American Libraries,* 2004). There may be pressure to screen only "family friendly" films (Caldwell-Stone, 2004). All in all, film showings require even more thought and planning than traditional lectures.

One academic library (Kansas State University) offers "movies with a conscience." The showings, on a plaza next to the library, include a post-showing discussion with several faculty members of the Institute for Civic Discourse and Democracy. The program is a collaborative activity, with the library playing the central coordinating role (Peairs et al., 2007).

One public library film series example focuses on group discussions (Bence, 2006). The underlying premise of the program is to create "an opportunity for people to connect with one another with the main purpose of fostering meaningful relationships" (p. 4). Bence's program does this by focusing on the issue of diversity. According to Bence, the diversity goal is even reflected in the attendees in terms of age, gender, and cultural and economic backgrounds.

Our last example is one that focuses on an age group (teens) and film type (anime). Jane Halsall (2004) wrote, "How I learned to love Japanese animation and changed our teen video collection forever" (p. 6). She became exposed to teenagers' interest in the film type through her daughter, who made her mother watch several anime videos and tried to explain what teens like about the genre. Halsall's library now has a large collection of such videos. She also has occasional group discussions of individual videos.

OUTREACH

Turning to outreach, a term with a variety of meanings and thus services, we explore a few of the most common activities. For some people, library outreach just goes back to the 1960s. Actually, one can trace the concept back much further to when it was called "library extension." In its early days, library extension focused on providing library service to rural populations. It quickly expanded to urban dwellers lacking transportation. Today's bookmobiles are the direct descendents of the extension service concept. By the late twentieth century, outreach expanded further to providing service to groups with special needs of some type or who were/are "under served."

Determining the appropriate special service(s), like all other programming services, requires a sound understanding of the service community composition, needs, and wants. Looking to other community service agencies may provide unexpected partnership opportunities as well as a way to stretch limited funds. Orange and Osborne (2004) suggested, "If we reframe what we know as 'outreach' so that it is based upon equality rather than underserved populations, we can open a new window to information access and, more importantly, service delivery" (p. 47). The authors agree that outreach is not dead, but rather will be richer if libraries broaden the concept to equality of access for all. One of the authors, Satia Orange, was the director of the ALA's Office of Literacy and Outreach Services when she wrote the essay.

Mobile Services

Essentially, mobile services are branches that move. They are a way to address the "Law of Least Effort." That is, people tend to expend the least possible effort to secure information, even when it is reasonably important to them. Is it in arm's reach? In my office/home? How far away is the most likely source? If not right here, is it worth the effort? These are questions we all ask ourselves—whether we are aware of it or not. The greater the effort required the less likely we are to make it. Thus, reducing the effort, especially for remote users, makes sense for libraries.

Today's mobile rigs are a far cry from those of 20 years ago. It has been a long time since all they carried were books and magazines. Now they may include computer access and employ satellite technology (Knight, 2006). Many draw on travel trailer concepts such as pull-out sections that provide extra space once they open for business. More information on bookmobile services may be found on the ALA's Office for Literacy and Outreach Services Web page (http://www.ala.org/ala/olos/outreachresources/servicesbookmobile.htm).

Not all "mobile" services are confined to wheeled vehicles. For many years, some libraries offered "books by mail"; academic libraries employed this approach in the early days of distance education programs. In the case of public libraries, users receive lists of books that are available; they fill out the form and return it to the library, and the library mails the book(s). A few libraries now use the Internet as the means of communication, but still use "snail" mail for books that are not in an e-format. In remote coastal areas, book boats provide the service, often also serving as the postal service as well. A few countries with large merchant marines, Norway for example, have libraries assemble "book boxes"—today they include all formats—that go to outgoing ships. Ship captains exchange the boxes; the boxes may be at sea for a very long time and sometimes never do return to the home port.

Perhaps the most unique mobile service we are aware of is the "camel-mobile." (It would seem mobile service is only limited by the staff's imagination.) The Kenyan National Library operates a camel book service (Hoffert, 2007) to its remote northeastern areas. The service has even inspired a novel (*Camel Bookmobile*, Harper-Collins, 2007) by Marsha Hamilton; it explores the tension between people with deep traditional values and those who believe the modern world and its books are essential to long-term survival. You can read more about this service at http://www.knls.or.ke/camel.htm.

Services to Special Populations

This is an area where a great many books and articles exist and thus, we will only touch on a few areas. For years libraries provided books in their original languages as a service to those who either spoke the language originally or who had learned it later. There was also the goal of aiding immigrants in becoming assimilated into the dominant society. Edwin Clay (2006) raised the question of if the goal today is integration, assimilation, or multiculturalism. How one answers that question has significant service implications. He made the point that the dialog has gone from "melting-pot" to "mosaic" to, perhaps, "co-existence." Further, he suggested that a new goal might be better thought of as to "foster positive attitudes toward multiculturalism" (p. 12), such as becoming aware of how backgrounds and experience act to form views about cultural diversity and beginning to understand how others view the concept. Essentially he suggested that by understanding how others view diversity there is better chance of having less stressful relations, even in the absence of full acceptance of the differing views.

Whatever the label, libraries did and do attempt to provide appropriate services to a host of people of differing cultural backgrounds as well as classes of people (seniors, youth, institutionalized, and partially sighted to mention but a few types). A good start for developing a useful model for approaching cultural diversity is Geert Hofstede's *Cultures and Organizations: Software of the Mind,* 2nd ed. (New York: McGraw-Hill, 2005). It will provide very useful insights for both thinking about the service community as well as workplace colleagues.

At the time we prepared this edition, a major issue in the United States was illegal immigration, with an emphasis on Hispanic people. Such was the concern that the October 2007 issue of *American Libraries* published two articles offering different points of view regarding library service to illegal immigrants. Julia Stephens took the position that, "By creating bilingual collections, librarians are contributing to a divided America" (p. 41). Todd Quesada's position was, "Eliminating Spanish-language fiction undermines the validity of public libraries" (p. 40). Stephens also stated, "Our founding principles of a unified nation with one language are being cast aside" (p. 43). Letters in the "to the editor section" of the two following issues suggested this was indeed a "hot topic." Although the overwhelming majority of the letter writers were against Stephens' position, not everyone disagreed with it. If nothing else, the articles and the reaction to them demonstrated just how complex outreach can be.

Surprisingly, the issue of providing non-English language materials is not cut and dry, as exemplified in a 2007 article about providing non-English language services that caused no ripples. Nedlina Yelena (2007) described service to Russian speakers and the pros and cons of creating separate sections for different language materials. Libraries have almost always had material in other languages in their collections. Often this was because the item is/was considered a classic in its original language and knowledgeable individuals know that something is always "lost in translation" and they want to read/see it in its original form. Also, there was/is the desire to provide recent arrivals with the opportunity to continue using their mother tongue. There is a question, which Yelena explores, as to the effectiveness of separating materials by their language. (What seems to be currently [2008] driving the Spanish language debate is illegal immigration and national security rather than the desirability of providing non-English materials.)

Academic libraries have long recognized their international students, as well as those with strong different cultural backgrounds, have values/expectations that may call for specialized assistance when it comes to library services. Very often they partner with ethnic studies centers and the international students' office to develop such services—one of this book's authors developed and taught such a program for Native American students at the University of California, Los Angeles. The goal of such services is to assure there are appropriate resources and support for the students. Emily Love's (2007) article provides a good overview of the issues involved in such services. Her major points were the importance of:

- Identifying potential campus partners
- Identifying the needs of student service groups
- Establishing meaningful relationship with such groups
- Actively cultivating those relationships
- Ensuring long-term partnerships
- Engaging in effective publicity that reflects existing partnerships
- Evaluating and assessing the partnerships on a regular basis

A good, well-balanced article about developing multicultural collections in a school library setting is by Denise Agosto (2007). She covers the benefits of such collections and what factors to take into account. Such collections do reach out, in a meaningful way, to children with different cultural backgrounds. Agosto suggested student learning benefits from creating such collections included the following:

- A sense of belonging
- A facilitation of student learning
- An appreciation of differences
- An increased knowledge of the world

Her suggestions for evaluating the quality of multicultural materials are not that different from those you would employ for any item—accuracy, expertise, purpose, format quality, and, most importantly, respectful treatment.

Specialized service to seniors is common in public libraries, if nothing more than large-print materials. Who are seniors? People who are retired? People of a certain age? If so, what age? People who have visual and/or physical limitations? Perhaps the best answer was Alan Bundy's (2005): "the one thing that seniors have in common is they are all different" (p. 158). The problem in defining the group more specifically is that various agencies define it differently. The U.S. Social Security office allows a person to start collecting retirement payments at age 62 and the individual may continue to work. The American Association of Retired Persons starts membership at age 55, whether one is retired or not. Perhaps it would be best to drop the term and just have the services available to anyone who needs them, essentially what happens in any event. In addition to large-print materials, there are "assistive" technologies (text readers and monitor enhancers, for example), homebound services, and basic computer literacy courses. Although a higher percentage of "older" users may benefit from the services, they are clearly not the only group that does so.

Some other outreach services are to institutionalized individuals (long-term care, prisoners, ex-convicts (see Dowling, 2007), for example). Services to government agencies (Davidson, 2006) are not all that common, but also do exist. Providing consumer health information calls for careful planning and some training as there can be some legal issues. Gail Kouam and colleagues (2005) provide a good review of the issues involved in such a service. Our Further

Reading section offers many other articles on topics we covered, as well as some we didn't have room for.

STAFFING

Many of the services we covered in this chapter call for some special skills or knowledge in addition to the basics of library public service. Not everyone is comfortable or effective working with one or more of the groups or activities covered. However, Karen Hake (2000) echoed the point we made in the staffing chapter, when discussing service to children, "To provide good service, the staff must be friendly, committed, enthusiastic, knowledgeable, and reliable" (p. 7).

The ALA's Association for Library Service to Children developed a set of competencies for those going into this area on a more or less full-time basis (http://www.ala.org/ala/alsc/alscresources/forlibrarians/professionaldev/competencies.htm). The set covers such concepts as having an understanding of the theories of infant, child, and adolescent development, the special needs of various cultural groups, and the social development of children. There are seven communication skills competencies listed.

1. Defines and communicates the needs of children so that administrators, other library staff, and members of the larger community understand the basis for children's services.
2. Demonstrates interpersonal skills in meeting with children, parents, staff, and community.
3. Adjusts to the varying demands of writing planning documents, procedures, guidelines, press releases, memoranda, reports, grant applications, annotations, and reviews in all formats, including print and electronic.
4. Speaks effectively when addressing individuals, as well as small and large groups.
5. Applies active listening skills.
6. Conducts productive formal and informal reference interviews.
7. Communicates constructively with "problem patrons."

Beyond those there is the skill of being an effective storyteller.

Language and communication skills are essential in any service area; however, when it comes to outreach to special populations, one may need bilingual skills or at least cultural awareness/understanding abilities as well. When it comes to teaching a class, having the ability to "pitch" the presentation at the proper level for an audience is critical for success, and is a talent that not everyone possesses. Even the availability of staff members who are able to handle a large mobile unit may not as widespread as one would like.

SUMMARY

Knowing the community is the key to offering effective services. Once you have that information you can begin to explore possible new or modified services. Naturally, another important factor to consider is what skills currently exist in the staff that would allow the service to be effective. Sometimes, it is necessary to wait until a new position is authorized or a resignation occurs so you can develop a new job description.

Chapter Review Material

1. In what ways do the services covered in this chapter differ from those we addressed in other chapters?
2. Discuss the concept of lifelong learning and the role libraries can play in that process.
3. What are some of the broad societal benefits from the "educational" services that libraries provide?
4. What are some of the likely causes of problems related to usage of library meeting rooms?
5. Discuss the overlap between educational and recreational services.
6. What are the goals/purposes of outreach programs?
7. Discuss the controversy regarding services for illegal immigrants.
8. What are some other specialized skills/knowledge one might need to be effective in one or more of the services discussed in this chapter?

REFERENCES

Agosto, Denise E. 2007. "Building a Multicultural School Library," *Teacher Librarian* 34, no. 3: 27–30.

American Libraries. 2004. "Libraries Nix Flicks as Patrons Cry Partisanship," 35, no. 11: 18.

———. 2005. "Colorado Gets Meeting-Room Religion," 36, no. 9: 28–29.

———. 2006a. "Boston PL Defends Reputation in Wake of Scathing Report." 37, no. 5: 19.

———. 2006b. "DOJ Supports Prayer Meets," 37, no. 2: 18–19.

———. 2006c. "Montana State Library Pulls ACLU Film Screening," 37, no. 4: 12.

———. 2007. "Supreme Court Won't Hear Meeting Room Appeal," 38, no. 10: 18.

———. 2008. "Bush and Cheney Images Reelected to Exhibit," 39, no. 1/2: 26.

Bence, Tamara. 2006. "Fostering Friendship through Film Discussions," *Kentucky Librarian Association* 70, no. 4: 4–5.

Brehm-Heeger, Paula, Ann Conway, and Carrie Vale. 2007. "Cosplay, Gaming, and Conventions," *Young Adult Library Services* 5, no. 2: 14–16.

Brooke, Joanna, and Rebecca Ryan. 2007. "A Tale of Two Libraries," *Public Libraries* 46, no. 4: 9–12.

Bundy, Alan. 2005. "Community Critical: Australian Public Libraries Serving Seniors," *Australasian Public Library Information Services* 18, no. 4: 158–169.

———. 2006. "Supporting Students," *Australasian Public Library Information Services* 19, no. 3: 126–136.

Cahoy, Ellysa. 2002. "Will Your Students Be Ready for College?" *Knowledge Quest* 30, no. 4: 12–15.

Caldwell-Stone, Deborah. 2004. "Movie Ratings Are Private, Not Public Policy," *Illinois Library Association Reporter* 22, no. 2: 10–13.

Clay, Edwin. 2006. "They Don't Look Like Me," *Virginia Libraries* 53, no. 4: 10–14.

Confer, Sarah, et al. 2007. "Homework Help Is a Click Away," *Young Adult Library Services* 5, no. 2: 17–20.

Crowley, Bill. 2005. "Save Professionalism," *Library Journal* 130, no. 14: 46–48.

Davidson, Robert. 2006. "Serving Government Clients Using Library Electronic Resources," *Florida Libraries* 49, no. 1: 10–12.

Dowling, Brendan. 2007. "Public Libraries and Ex-Offenders," *Public Libraries* 46, no. 6: 44–48.

Eiselstein, June. 2003. "College Access Programs and Services," *Public Libraries* 42, no. 3: 184–187.

England, S. Randle. 2007. "The Consequences of Promoting an Educational Role for Today's Public Libraries," *Public Libraries* 46, no. 2: 55–63.

Estabrook, Leigh, Evans Witt, and Lee Rainie. 2007. *Information Searches that Solve Problems*" http:www.pewinternet.org/pdfs/Pew_UI_LibrariesReport.pdf.

Gillis, Sara, and Julie Totten. 2006. "Creating Lifelong Learning Opportunities through Partnership," *Feliciter* 52, no. 6: 244–246.

Hake, Karen. 2000. "Programming and Children's Services," *Bookmobiles and Outreach Services* 3, no. 2: 7–10.

Halsall, Jane. 2004. "The Anime Revolution," *School Library Journal* 50, no. 8: 4–13.

Hoffert, Barbara. 2007. "Books by Camel," *Library Journal* 132, no. 5: 6.

Howie, Emily, and Abby Yochelson. 2006. "Deft, Daring, Delightful: Popular Mystery Writers Discuss Their Craft," *Library of Congress Information Bulletin* 65, no. 6: 150–151.

Knight, Robert. 2006. "Branches on Wheels," *Australasian Public Library and Information Services* 19, no. 2: 89–96.

Kouam, Gail, Margo Harris, and Susan Murray. 2005. "Consumer Health Information from Both Sides of the Desk," *Library Trends* 53, no. 3: 464–479.

Kutner, Mark, Elizabeth Greenberg, Ying Jin, Bridget Boyle, Yung-chen Hsu, and Eric Dunleavy. 2007. *Literacy in Everyday Life.* (NCES 2007–480) Washington, D.C.: Department of Education.

Love, Emily. 2007. "Building Bridges: Cultivating Partnerships between Libraries and Minority Student Services," *Education Libraries* 30, no. 1: 13–19.

Martin, Robert S. 2004. "Libraries and Learning," *Advances in Librarianship* 28: 81–93.

McClure, Charles, et al. 1987. *Planning and Role Setting for Public Libraries.* Chicago, IL: American Library Association.

Minkel, Walter. 2002. "They've Got Game," *School Library Journal* 48, no. 9: 27.

———. 2003. "Making a Splash with Summer Reading," *School Library Journal* 49, no. 1: 54–56.

Moore, Rebecca. 2006. "From Jeopardy to Microfiction Mprovs," *Voice of Youth Advocates* 29, no. 3: 219–223.

Neiburger, Eli. 2007. "Games. . .in the Library?" *School Library Journal* 53, no. 7: 28–29.

Orange, Satia Marshall, and Robin Osborne. 2004. "From Outreach to Equality," *American Libraries* 35, no. 6: 46–51.

Peairs, Rhondelyn, Ellen Urton, and Donna Scenck-Hamlin. 2007. "Movies on the Grass," *College & Research Libraries News* 68, no. 7: 444–457.

Pearson, Debra, and Beth McNeil. 2002. "From High School Users College Students Grow." *Knowledge Quest* 30, no. 4: 24–28.

Quesada, Todd Douglas. 2007. "Spanish Spoken Here," *American Libraries* 38, no. 10: 40, 42, 44.

Rabner, Douglas, and John Budd. 1998. "Public Images of the Role of Information Technology in Public Libraries," *Public Libraries* 38, no. 3: 180–186.

Robertson, Guy. 2007. "One for the Books," *Feliciter* 53, no. 2: 89–91.

Rortvedt, Sylvia. 2007. "Text, Image, and Form: The Altered Book Project," *Virginia Libraries* 53, no. 3: 27–28.

Sherry, Dianna. 2005. "Providing Reading Buddies for Children of Adult Literacy Students," *Colorado Libraries* 43, no. 1: 40–42.

Squire, Kurt, and Constance Steinkuehler. 2005. "Meet the Gamers," *Library Journal* 130, no. 7: 38–41.

Stephens, Julia. 2007. "English Spoken Here," *American Libraries* 38, no. 10: 41, 43–44.

Stevenson, Sara. 2005. "When Bad Libraries Go Good," *School Library Journal* 51, no. 5: 46–48.

Swisher, Susan H. 2007. "'A' Is for Art Not Age," *Indiana Libraries* 26, no. 2: 38–39.

Warton, Pamela. 2001. "The Forgotten Voice in Homework," *Educational Psychologist* 36, no. 3: 155–165.

Whitehead, Nicole. 2004. "The Effects of Increased Access to Books on Student Reading Using the Public Library," *Reading Improvement* 41, no. 3: 165–178.

Wooden, Ruth. 2006. "The Future of Public Libraries in an Internet Age," *National Civic Review* 95, no. 4: 3–7.

Yelena, Nedlina. 2007. "Public Service to Russian-Speaking Patrons," *Bookmobile Outreach* 10, no. 1: 25–31.

Young, Timothy. 2007. "The Young Visitors," *College & Research Libraries News* 68, no. 4: 235–238.

Youngman, Daryl C. 2002. "Re-Shaping Library Service Programming for the New Millennium," *IATUL Proceedings* no. 12: 1–5.

SUGGESTED READINGS

Agosto, Denise. 2001. "The Cultured Word: Cultural Background, Bilingualism, and the School Library," *School Libraries Worldwide* 7: 46–57.

Alward, Donna. 2008. "Great Stories Club," *Public Libraries* 47, no. 1: 74–77.

American Library Association Advocacy Resource Center. http://www.ala.org/ala/issues/issuesadvocacy.htm.

Arnold, Rena. 2002. "Coming Together for Children," *Journal of Youth Service Libraries* 15, no. 2: 24–30.

Bell, Lori, and Tom Peters. 2005. "Digital Library Services for All," *American Libraries* 36, no. 8: 46–49.

Berger, Leslie. 2008. "All Seasons & All Reasons," *American Libraries* 39, no. 3: 45–48.

Bourke, Carolyn. 2007. "Working with Schools, Parents an Other Community Groups," *Australasian Public Library Information Services* 20, no. 2: 67–71.

Bryan, Robin. 2002. "Darreydog.net: A Homework Assistance Portal for Students," *Public Libraries* 41 no.2: 101–103.

Cavallaro, Nicole, and Jamie Conklin. 2007. "Mobile Gamma," *Florida Libraries* 50, no. 2: 4–6.

Cavanagh, Mary. 2004. "Sense Making: a Public Library's Internet Policy Crisis," *Library Management* 26, no. 6/7: 351–360.

Costello, Joan, Janet Dwyer, Suzanne Harold, Ann Penchacek, Karen K. Peterson, and Sara Ryan. 2001. "Promoting Public Library Partnerships with Youth Agencies," *Journal of Youth Services in Libraries* 15, no. 1: 8–15.

Dewey, Barbara I., and Loretta Parham. 2006. *Achieving Diversity.* New York: Neal-Schuman.

Early Learning with Families (ELF). 2008. http://elflibraries.org.

Forrest, Charles. 2005. "Segmenting the Library Market," *Georgia Library Quarterly* 42, no. 1: 4–7.

Gilman, Isaac. 2008. "Beyond Books: Restorative Librarianship in Juvenile Detention Centers," *Public Libraries* 47, no. 1: 56–66.

Gordon, Carol. 2002. "A Room With a View," *Knowledge Quest* 30, no. 1: 16–20.

Green, Sandy. 2007. "Ten Years of Summer Reading Success," *Australasian Public Library Information Services* 20, no. 2: 55–66.

Herold, Irene. 2006. "Planning and Executing an Annual Library Lecture," *Library Administration & Management* 20, no. 3: 131–134.

Karp, Jane. 2005. "Taking Library Services to Seniors," *Florida Libraries* 47, no. 1: 1, 6–7.

Lee, Deborah. 2004. "Market Segmentation and Libraries," *Library Administration & Management* 18, no. 1: 47–48.

———. 2006. "Check Out the Competition: Marketing Lesson from Google." *Library Administration & Management* 20, no. 2: 94–95.

Makola, Jeffrey, and Rebecca Getty. 2006. "Making Exhibits out of Nothing at All," *College & Research Library News* 67, no. 11: 681–683.

Mellio, Paolo. 2007. "Transforming ESOL-Learning Opportunities Through Technology," *Florida Libraries* 50, no. 2: 11–13.

Mediavilla, Cindy. 2001. "Why Library Homework Centers Extend Society's Safety Net," *American Libraries* 32, no. 11: 40–42.

———. 2003. "Homework: Students Success Is Coming from a Neglected Source," *School Library Journal* 49, no. 3: 56–59.

Peters, Thomas A., Josephine Dorsch, Lori Bell, and Peg Burnette. 2003. "PDAs and Health Services Libraries," *Library Hi Tech* 21, no. 4: 400–411.

Quigley, Thomas. 2003. "How Public Libraries Can Promote Adult Literacy with the World Wide Web," *Feliciter* 49, no. 1: 38–41.

Rockefeller, Elsworth. 2008. "Striving to Serve Diverse Youth: Mainstreaming teens with Special Needs through Public Library Programming," *Public Libraries* 47, no. 1: 5055.

School Library Journal. "Giving Libraries an Edge," 51, no. 12: 50.

Scordato, Julie. 2008. "Gaming as a Library Service," *Public Libraries* 47, no. 1: 67–73.

Selnick, Shari. 2004. "READ/Orange County: Changing Lives through Literacy," *Public Libraries* 43, no. 1: 53–56.

Spellman, Anne, and Paula Kelly. 2004. "In Visible Light: Illuminating Partnerships across Libraries to Facilitate Lifelong Learning for Young People," *Australasian Public Library Information Services* 17, no.1: 4–26.

Steinkueler, Constance. 2004. "Learning in Massively Multiplayer Online Games," in *Proceedings of the Sixth International Conference of the Learning Sciences,* Yasmin B. Kafai, ed. Santa Monica, CA: Mahwah, pp. 521–528.

Taber, Margaret. 2002. "Rite of Passage: A Visit to a University Library," *Knowledge Quest* 30, no. 4: 29–30.

Young, Courtney. 2006. "Collection Development and Diversity on CIC Academic Web Sites," *Journal of Academic Librarianship* 32, no. 4: 370–376.

Youngman, Daryl. 2002. "Reshaping Library Service Programming," *IATUL Proceedings* 12, no. 1: 1–5.

15

Security Issues

Court disaster long enough and it will accept your proposal.
—Mason Cooley, 2000

Public Libraries are more susceptible to patron violence than academic and other special libraries, as their open door policy allows anyone to use the building.
—Sarah Farrugia, 2002

Imagine yourself being sued or disciplined because someone alleges sexual misconduct against you or because a patron was injured in your library.
—Patricia Smith, 2005

How might a library court disaster? A list of all the possibilities would generate pages and pages of text. Some of the broad categories of problem areas we touch on in this chapter are:

- Natural disasters
- Criminal activity
- Human health and safety
- Collection "health" and safety
- Maintenance failures
- Data security
- Legal actions

We all know the typical natural disasters—hurricanes, tornadoes, floods, and earthquakes. Some of the others we overlook are wildfires, mud/landslides, and ice/snow storms. Depending on your location, the odds are fairly high your library will have to face one of these events at some time during your career. Having a plan to handle the occurrence will help get the library back in operation more quickly. Not having a plan is surely courting disaster, as Cooley's quote suggests.

Criminal activity ranges from petty problems such as mutilation of library property, to theft of materials, to violence and even murder. Knowing what steps to take when something happens will help you get yourself and others safely through a trying circumstance.

People issues can range from unhappy users to gang problems. Lacking a proper physical environment can lead to health issues for staff and regular users of the library.

Just as people have better or worse environmental conditions, so do the items in the collections. One challenge for staff is that the two sets of conditions are rather different. Providing ideal conditions for both people and collections is almost impossible.

Maintenance issues are all too common in an era of "deferred maintenance." Funding is almost never adequate to cover everything a library would like to accomplish and often it is easy to put off some of the facility maintenance to save some money for other activities. The outcome of such practices is often a leaking roof, an electrical fire, or a broken water pipe, all of which seem to take place when the building is closed, creating an even bigger problem.

Data security is an increasing problem as more and more of the library's operations are digital in nature, making them susceptible to hacking activities. There are also significant concerns about user privacy.

Finally, in a post-9/11 world, there are legal issues about what type of information about library operations can be shared with what groups, if any. We cover all these topics to some degree in this chapter.

RISK ASSESSMENT AND MANAGEMENT

An excellent starting point to avoid "courting" disasters is to engage in proactive risk management. To manage risk, usually with substantial assistance from the library's "parent" institution, one must understand what the "risks" are and what is involved. Although taken from a business context, Jackie Bassett's (2007) concluding sentence makes the point that sound risk management starts at the lowest operational levels. She notes, "Internal auditors who proactively reach out to senior management through out the entire audit process set the stage for audit success and help to better promote the implementation of security recommendations" (p. 31). Substitute lower-level staff for "internal auditors" and risk assessment for "audit" and you have the picture. Managing risk is an ongoing process, not a one-time activity. People on the floor are in the best position to identify risk issues on a daily basis. They must speak up when the risk issue requires more than their moving a chair away from a fire exit or putting out a sign cautioning about a wet floor.

Thomas Steele (1997) provided a concise description that helps clarify what risk assessment and management is as well as why it is important, noting, "The American legal system has developed a method of allocative responsibility for physical and mental injuries to persons. Personal injury law (or tort)

deals with injuries to individuals, caused either negligently or intentionally"
(p. 94). Steele listed three interrelated issues involved in negligence, whether a
mental, emotional, or physical injury:

1. The cause of the injury must be a person, not an act of God.
2. The person causing the injury has responsibility/duty to the injured
   party.
3. The duty may be one of warning or one of action. (p. 94)

An example of possible negligence would be the failure of the library staff to
put out signs warning of slippery entryway floors on a rainy or snowy day and
a person falling and injuring him or herself.

Within the concept of personal injury law in the United States and England
is a subarea that involves premises, such as the library property. According
to Steele, the courts have divided the "controller" of the premises duties into
three broad categories: invitees (users/staff in public areas), licensees (users
and staff in nonpublic areas such as technical services and administrative offices), and trespassers. There is a descending order of duty to the categories.
Beyond these basic categories, there are special duties to children and persons who are mentally or physically challenged.

All types of libraries, except special libraries and a few specialized research
libraries (such as the Huntington Library in California), must expect a greater
or smaller percentage of their visitors to be children. "Latchkey children" have
been a major challenge for public and academic libraries. (These are children
whose parents expect the child to go to the library after school and wait for
the parent, or children brought to the library by a parent who then leaves the
building to attend to other activities.) There is a question of just how much liability a library has for looking after latchkey children. Can the parent(s) hold
the library and its staff liable for an injury or health problem that occurs when
the child is alone in the library?

Whatever steps the library takes to control this problem, one step is absolutely necessary to prevent even greater problems: have clear policies and a
plan of action reviewed by the legal counsel for the library or parent institution. Some of the options that exist in various jurisdictions are:

- To have academic libraries bar children without parental supervision
- To offer special programs designed for such children
- To have policies requiring staff to call child welfare services or police
  to pick up any unattended child at closing time
- To have policies of allowing staff to contact police/security when a
  child is left unattended for a specified period of time during normal
  school hours

Policies need to be posted in prominent locations, especially at public entrances, and provided to parents when a child is given a library card. The
library Web site is another location for posting such policies. Another important element is not to make it appear that the library assumes any child care
responsibility.

The list of potential problem areas for injury is long; some are ongoing such as stairways, carpets, and furniture, while others are intermittent or rare, for example, weather or construction related. To assure reasonable safety in all areas the library ought to have a security plan. Conducting a security audit is the first step in developing a security plan that helps assure better safety for collections and people.

Our third opening quotation (Patricia Smith) identifies one of many possible legal problems you may personally face some time during your career in a library. Although the chances are not too great of being named in a law suit when you are a front-line staff member, as you assume more senior roles, the risk increases. Where the greatest risk arises is when you were on duty and worked directly with the plaintiff when the incident took place. Lawyers have a tendency in liability suits to name everyone they can identify as having even a slight connection to the event in question. Obviously "the library" and its parent body will be the lead defendants as they have the "deep pockets"; however, individual staff may also be named. While the parent institution is likely to cover legal fees, there may be instances where the individual's liability is such that the person will need to cover legal costs as well as any legal "judgments." As a result, it is prudent to check with one's homeowner/renter's insurance to determine if the liability coverage also applies to one's work activities. If not, it may be wise to see what the cost of workplace liability may be. Some library associations offer such coverage to members.

SECURITY AUDIT/ASSESSMENT

A security audit/assessment can provide essential information about the library's overall security situation. Conducting a risk assessment with a risk professional (for example, someone from the fire/police department or insurance company) will speed the process and provide better data because of the expert's experience in such matters. If the library is part of an organization that carries insurance policies, the risk manager is usually very willing to assist in the audit. Risk managers assess various types of risks for which there is insurance coverage (for example, personal injury, theft, or liability). They also determine what changes in conditions would reduce the possibilities of a loss or claim. Most risk managers welcome the opportunity to do or review a security audit, because such an audit may also reduce the cost of the organization's insurance. At the same time, a review of the library's insurance coverage may show that the collection and equipment evaluation is too low.

Whoever completes the audit will need some background information about the community, campus, or organization, including demographic data and the physical location and relationship to other buildings and activities. Often, branches of public libraries are in park-like settings and, as a result, relatively isolated from other activities. Academic libraries, while often located in or near the center of campus, have long service hours. It is not uncommon for academic libraries to close at midnight or even later. Extended hours result in a form of isolation; no other buildings are open nor are other activities going on at closing time.

A well-known, prominent, or valuable collection, whether in the open stacks or in special collections, increases certain types of risk. Most of the books stolen from libraries are not in special collections, but rather in the circulating collection. Finally, there needs to be some evaluation of staff and user attitudes. If either or both groups have a negative attitude about the library or the institution the library serves, the risks of theft are greater. Preparing the assessment paper can be an eye-opener and may point out potential problem areas.

The audit process consists of two parts: looking for security/risk weaknesses and observing current security procedures. Much of the search for weaknesses involves reviewing the past. Lacking good records makes this a memory exercise that will be selective and subjective. The lack of good security records is itself a weakness. Maintaining a log of incidents and complaints provides better information about the problems and their seriousness and frequency. Some useful questions to explore are:

What evidence of theft exists?

- Are there areas that may create problems?
- Is there a record of user complaints?

What deferred maintenance exists?

What key control plan is in operation, if any?

Is there a procedure for handling terminations of staff and patrons?
    What happens with regards to:

- Materials checked out?
- Fines owed?
- Keys issued?
- Supervised packing up of personal belongings?

Does an emergency plan exist?

Does a disaster plan exist?

Does a security plan exist?

With the answers to these questions and others like them, one will know how vulnerable the library may be. Some problem areas may be inexpensive to correct; others may be too costly given the frequency or volume of the problem. However, one should base such judgments on information provided by a security audit.

The second phase of the audit involves observing how the existing procedures function. This includes things such as the relationship of service points (places where library staff work) and the building's exits. A number of questions arise in this regard:

Are all of the exits equipped with alarms and/or fully observable from a
    service point?

How often is the service desk's view blocked by traffic or people needing
    assistance?

Are there guards for main entrance and exit?

If so, do the guards do full, random, or casual searches? Is there a discernible pattern to the searches? With a full search, do guards check purses? Does the frequency of searches vary with the volume of traffic? What training or instructions have the guards received?

If an electronic security system is in place, is it a bypass unit (materials handed to users after passing through a screening device)?

What are the characteristics of all doors and locks?

Who has keys for emergency exit alarms?

How much visual control is there of loading docks and receiving areas?

What is the relationship of shelving units used to store recently received, but not yet processed materials, such as the holding area for approval books, to exits?

What type of ceiling exists? How much crawl space is there? Is the ceiling on the alarm system?

Are there utility tunnel doors and maintenance areas that are not part of the library key system? If so, who has access to these areas and when?

How secure is the special collections area?

If there is a vault or safe, who has a key or knows the lock combination?

Is there a fire suppression system in place?

Is there an alarm system tied into the police department, fire department, or security office?

What security measures exist for the computer room? Are the audio-visual units, computers, and terminals secured to work surfaces in some manner?

How secure is the after-hours book return?

How effective is the closing procedure in preventing after-hours concealment?

Study the loss and control procedures for office supplies as well. Theft of basic office supplies can cost the library hundreds, if not thousands of dollars per year.

Clearly a security audit takes time to perform, but the results of the time and effort are important to users and staff. The library can put together a comprehensive security plan with the information gained from the audit. Staff, users, and collections will all be safer as a result of the effort invested, even though staff and users may not even be aware that the audit has been done.

SECURITY PLAN—RISK MANAGEMENT

A security plan is actually a combination of plans and activities. The major plans are operational security, a key control procedure, an emergency procedure plan, and a disaster preparedness plan. The operational activities include such things as opening and closing procedures, monitoring library use, and monitoring safety issues. Sometimes an assessment may lead to changing door locks or installing an electronic security system.

Most libraries have some procedures in place to handle emergencies. Supervisors should train new staff members in the procedures for their area. (When the library has waited for weeks or sometimes months for the new person to start work, it is natural to focus on the main duties the person is to perform. The thinking is, "We will get to the minor areas and things later.") Certainly emergencies are not very common in the library and it is not unreasonable to wait a little while, as long as the subject does get covered. To be a new person on duty alone at the circulation desk for the first time and to have a telephone caller say, "There is a bomb in the library" and then hang up can be a frightening experience. Not knowing who to call or what to do until help arrives adds to the stress. Knowing the emergency procedure will not eliminate the worry such a call creates, but it does help a staffer get through the situation more effectively.

Key Control

Key control is a chronic problem for any organization. Who has, who must have, and who wants this or that key are administrative problems; they are also problems of status and ego. In the absence of a clear and enforced key control plan, the status and ego aspects tend to dominate. "May I borrow key X for a while?" is a common request. If someone does not keep track of who has each key and if the keys are, in fact, returned "in a while," there will be no control over the keys.

To control keys there needs to be single office and person to issue and collect keys or otherwise disable (electronic for example) access for a terminated person. Where that responsibility lies varies; three common units are the HR department, O&M (Operations and Maintenance), or the library administrative office. Having such a single source with the responsibility does not absolve supervisors from knowing which keys are held by which people in her/his unit. Tom Teper (2003) reported that in a review of supervisors' knowledge of who held what keys, they could only account for 60 percent of the keys issued to their staff (p. 55). He made a crucial point about the problem that arises from poor key control: "Over time, campus administrators became aware that unauthorized entry and access during non-operational hours and unnecessary access to some spaces affected not only the safety of physical properties and their contents, but also affected the safety of the individuals that worked with the facilities" (p. 54). The latter point is important. Unfortunately, workplace violence is all too common in the United States and libraries have had their share of such occurrences. Often it is an unhappy ex-employee who has the means of access to the work area who causes the trouble. Being certain of all the keys the individual had is only possible when there is a sound key control program in place. (Note: key control encompasses all forms of controlled access, not just what we think of as a "key.")

Almost every library has some form of internal key control, even if some other department makes and supplies the keys. A typical model is to have the supervisor submit an "access" request form to the administrative office that spells out the reason(s) the individual needs a key, or other means of access (pin number, key card, or biometric access for example). The office reviews the request, and if authorized, orders the appropriate form of access. In the case of a physical key, the person who is to receive the key signs for it and returns the key upon termination of employment or after no longer needing such access. The truth of the matter is that the process is seldom as carefully carried out as is necessary for good security

One possibility for avoiding a "key" problem is somewhat expensive, but highly effective: to install electronic locks. These locks allow the institution to issue a code number to each person who needs access to an area. The code number is also put into the lock. When a person needs to enter the area, he or she keys in a personal code number. (There are also systems that use individually coded magnetic keycards. Today even biometric access [finger/palm print or eye scan for example] are becoming much less costly and may be worth the extra cost for areas such as special collections or archives.)

What is especially good about these locks is that one can, using a special infrared scanner and printer, get a list of code numbers used by date and time. Because some staff members might share their code numbers with others, there is no unequivocal proof that a specific person entered the area, but there is no question about the fact someone did use that number. Locks of this type cost hundreds of dollars, so they are not suitable for all areas. However, they are worth serious consideration for certain areas: staff entrances, rooms with expensive equipment, and special collections.

Opening Routines

Opening and closing procedures for the library have a relationship to key control in the sense that some staff will need to have a number of keys to perform their duties. Also, there are times when other staff will have to substitute for a person who is sick, which can result in "borrowed" keys. Opening procedures are simple, but staff should follow the steps consistently and complete them *before* the public enters the library. While different libraries will have slightly different needs, three basic steps are part of any sound opening procedure.

The first step in the opening process should be turning on lights and checking the equipment. In setting up a regular route to follow when turning on the lights, try to include passing by all the areas where there is equipment. Obviously reporting any missing equipment is normal, but noting any unusual arrangement of furniture and equipment may also forestall a problem. Sometimes only part of a piece of equipment is missing.

Checking any coin-operated equipment is another important part of the opening routine. While we were preparing the previous edition of this book, one of the public service staff discovered during her opening routine that all the photocopy coin boxes and change machines were open and empty. Sometime between midnight and 7:00 A.M. someone came into the library and managed to empty all the coin boxes. Unfortunately, this was before we purchased the electronic lock for the library. With such a lock, police could have checked on each code number used during the hours we were officially closed. The sooner an investigation starts, the better the chances are it will have a successful outcome. This is one reason why daily checking is so important.

Next, check the after-hours book return. Pick up the returned books, but also check for vandalism. Graffiti is an all-too-common occurrence in public areas of buildings. Book drops and the exterior walls of libraries receive their share of attention from graffiti artists. As with all vandalism, the quicker the library addresses the issue the more likely vandalism will stop or decline in occurrence. (Many police departments recommend engaging in what they call "the battle of paint cans" to combat graffiti. This means painting over the graffiti as soon as it appears. Continue repainting, washing, or cleaning it up until the "artist" gives up.)

Opening a book drop can be an adventure; you never know what may walk, hop, crawl, or squirm out of the opening. Only the size of the book return's opening and people's (often children's) imagination limits the variety of living things you may encounter. Mice, toads, snakes, turtles, and other living things may startle you when you find them in the return, but they cause no significant harm. It is not living things that create the biggest problems. Liquids like oil, molasses, glues, and just plain water cause serious damage to the items in the return.

The worst form of book return vandalism is arson. Most of the time it is some newspaper or cloth stuck in the return, followed by a few lit matches. Fortunately, such cases usually result in attempted rather than actual arson because the paper or cloth does not catch on fire. The staff member should not simply log the incident, but also report it to the police, fire department, or library's security service. Unsuccessful attempts frequently result in continued efforts until the arsonist succeeds. Serious arsonists often use a flammable liquid that assures a fire and results in costly repairs and replacements for the library. When the book return is inside the library, such fires can cause major damage. Many building codes now require such inside returns be a small fire rated room (four- or six-hour resistance), which is used solely for book return.

Closing Routines

Many complications exist for the closing routine, and it offers additional challenges for the staff because there are usually fewer staff members on duty and some users can be very reluctant to leave. Once a procedure has been set up, have the security department review it for overall safety. Late service hours and isolation make closing the library a little risky, so a knowledgeable public safety officer's review of the plan can help reduce the risks. Establish a written procedure so that anyone on duty can do the job, not just the regular closer. Unless the library is physically small, have three to four people involved in the closing process. There should be at least one person covering the exit to keep people from coming in and to see that those who leave take only their personal belongings and properly checked out materials. Working in pairs is safest, but often there are not enough staff members to do this and still finish the process in 15 to 20 minutes. Working in pairs is essential if the library is in a high-crime area and especially where there is gang activity.

Users should get 10 to 15 minutes' notice that it is approaching closing time. At the official closing time library staff *must* go through the building turning off lights, checking all public seating and stack areas, and occasionally moving people out. After-hours concealment is a problem in many libraries, which means the staff closing the library should check all the possible hiding places. The checking process needs to include restrooms, study and meeting rooms, under stairways, in dark corners, and other places where things can go bump in the night. Staff also must know what to do or not do when they find someone in one of these places. Do they confront the person or call for assistance? One problem for public libraries is finding a child whose parent has not returned or sometimes has "forgotten" a child in the library. After clearing the building, activate any alarms and, if possible, lock the elevators at the main floor. If there are windows that open, someone must close and lock them for the night.

For staff safety, having at least two people on duty for closing routines is the minimum a library should use. After closing, staff should leave together or call for an escort from the security or police department. Well-lighted walkways and parking areas for users and staff are also part of a sound security plan.

The day's cash receipts can pose a problem. Someone must be responsible for putting away the money. Too often there is no safe in the library, other than the vault in special collections. The result is that the cash box gets "hidden" in a lockable file drawer. Frequently the key to the drawer is in a nearby unlocked desk drawer. When staff start putting things (such as cash boxes) away early, the hiding places soon become common knowledge. Having a small safe for public services is a good idea and a reasonably modest investment. (Note: do not write down the combination and leave the information in a "safe place," or there will be no security.) Certainly in high-crime areas the return on investment will be significant; better yet, find a way not to collect cash.

DISASTER PREPAREDNESS PLANNING

According to the Northeast Document Conservation Center (2007, http://www.nedcc.org/resources/leaflets/3Emergency_Management/03Disaster Planning.php), "Disasters can come in all shapes and sizes, from natural disasters (floods, hurricanes, and earthquakes) to emergencies resulting from an accident (bust water pipe), deferred maintenance (leaking roof), or negligence (fire or mold)." The foregoing is a very short list, if the most common, of potential library disasters. Having a plan for how to handle such situations will make a highly stressful event somewhat less uncomfortable.

Disaster recovery planning is a major part of an overall security plan. It is also the part that may take a long time to develop. Such plans require time and very careful thought as well as input from experts such as the fire department. (Some risk management firms require that they have a current copy on file.) One reason it takes so long is that it must involve every department and ought to have wide staff involvement. In large organizations the library's plan must fit into the institution's comprehensive plan; this may require rethinking and rewriting parts of the plan. A small steering committee is essential to keep the work moving, and someone must take on the basically thankless task of writing and rewriting drafts of the plan.

Keys to successful planning are:

- Assessing potential sources of emergencies (fire, tornados, bomb threats, floods, water pipes breaking, earthquakes, and occasionally major vandalism)
- Considering the difference in handling just a library disaster from one that is part of a larger local or regional problem
- Setting collection priorities (that is, what is irreplaceable? What is expensive, but replaceable? What is easy to replace?)
- Determining insurance coverage and access to emergency funds; does insurance include money for recovery? Can the disaster team leader have authorization to commit money to salvage work? Will cash be readily available?
- Preparing summary posters of the plan's steps and posting them in all staff areas
- Developing an emergency telephone tree and keeping the telephone numbers up to date (a telephone tree is simply a listing of calls to make and their priority of placement. The tree's design is such that no person makes more than two or three telephone calls)
- Writing up the plan, reviewing it internally, checking on its agreement with broader-based organization-wide disaster plans, and training the staff in its implementation, which should include a walk-through exercise
- Having floor plans in the document that clearly indicate the first-priority areas for salvage teams
- Collecting supplies for handling the various emergencies
- Having a list of service supply companies and experts that can assist in the recovery work as an appendix to the plan
- Setting up the disaster team, training them, and conducting practices
- Making certain fire and security personnel know where a copy of the plan is and whom to call first; having copies of the plan on and off site
- Sending team members to workshops and conducting in-house disaster-handling programs to keep the staff up to date on developments in the field
- Conducting plan reviews with new employees and yearly plan update sessions for all employees

Probably the most common disaster in a library is water damage. Storms such as hurricanes and tornadoes can cause structural damage to a library and perhaps damage some of the collection. It is, however, the rain that accompanies these storms that causes the most damage. Most of the time water damage in the library results from an internal library problem. A broken water pipe, a ruptured sprinkler system, or an air conditioner located on the roof that springs a leak during the one weekend of the year the library is not open are common water disasters that libraries encounter. While such disasters seldom are worth even passing notice in the local newspaper, they still present the same recovery problems a major storm, flood, or fire would cause.

This is not the place to explore in detail the recovery process for water-damaged material. However, the Western Association for Art Conservation produced a brief, but comprehensive set of guidelines, which appears online as Betty Walsh's "Salvage at a Glance" (http://palimpsest.stanford.edu/waac/wn/wn19/wn19–2/wn19–207.html). Conservation OnLine (CoOL) at http://palimpsest.stanford.edu (the host site for Ms. Walsh's chart) is an exceptionally useful site for authoritative and current information on all aspects of disaster planning and recovery, as well as conservation and preservation topics in general.

Fire Protection

Despite their occasional malfunction, sprinklers in the library are the best fire protection. Properly installed and maintained, they provide a quick response to a fire while it is still small. More than 80 percent of all building fires are controllable by three or fewer sprinkler heads, assuming proper installation and maintenance. Yes, there will be water damage, but not as much as when the fire department turns on its fire hose. (A fire hose puts out 2,500 gallons of water per minute, compared to 100 gallons per minute for a typical sprinkler head.) If the sprinkler system is an older zoned type, where perhaps a quarter or a third of all the sprinklers go off at one time whenever one sprinkler responds to a fire, the damage can be much greater. Together, however, they still will not put out as much water as one fire hose.

Depending on the size of the library, if there is a server room present, an investment will likely need to be made in a separate fire suppression system. In the past, such systems were usually Halon-based, although in recent years Halon has been replaced with another gas called Low Pressure Inergen (Woods, 2002, p. 179). For a good overview of the special issues to consider with regard to computer systems and data, see Richard Boss's (2001) "Disaster Planning for Computers and Networks."

Everyone working in public service should know how to handle a fire extinguisher and how to determine which extinguisher to use on a specific type of fire. There are extinguishers for combustible materials such as paper and wood (Type A), for electrical fires or flammable liquids (Type B), and for any type of fire (Type C). Comprehensive (Type C) extinguishers are the most expensive, but they eliminate worries about which unit to use. In an emergency, the fewer things the staff must worry about the better they will handle the situation. Most fire departments are willing to come to the library to teach people how to put out a fire with an extinguisher. A half-day fire safety workshop with fire extinguisher training is well worth the time lost from regular duties; annual updates and reviews are very useful.

Building Evacuation

Getting everyone out of the library in an emergency is *the* most important aspect of handling a disaster. Because public service staff members work in areas with or near users, they have the major responsibility for clearing the building of people in an emergency. The type of alarm system the library has (or does not have) will determine how hard or easy it will be to clear the building. Many libraries lack public address systems and must depend solely on a fire alarm system's signal. That signal may work well and be appropriate in a fire emergency, but is it good for a bomb threat or other nonfire situation that requires clearing the building? This becomes even more of a problem if the fire alarm system connects directly to the fire department. Another concern is whether or not one can hear the alarm in every location and office. Individual or group study rooms or audiovisual rooms are special problems. People using such rooms may be concentrating so hard (or have earphones turned up so high, or have hearing impairments) that they do not hear the alarm even when it is audible in the room. What this means is that public service personnel must go through the library, almost like the closing procedure, to be certain everyone leaves.

There are two big differences between the closing routine and evacuating the building. The first obvious difference is that, in the emergency situation, speed is important. If the emergency situation arises during a period when there is full staffing, usually only at peak usage times, the process of clearing can go quickly, because there are enough staff members to go to the key areas at the same time. Problems can arise during low staffing periods (for example, nights and weekends). Too often when a library conducts a practice evacuation it is with a full staff. Libraries should plan for and practice both full and minimum staff evacuations.

The second difference from closing routines is that there may be more problems with people. An emergency can occur at any time, but the chances are it will not be just before closing time. This means people may not be ready or willing to leave, especially if they must leave their work behind. Convincing people that there is a problem and that it is important to leave quickly can be difficult. It is particularly difficult when the alarm system is not clearly audible and there is no real indication of a problem, such as the smell of smoke. Knowing how to handle the reluctant individual is a key to quickly clearing the building. Deciding under what circumstances people may or may not pack up their work takes careful planning with the assistance of public safety officials. Another issue that ought to be thought through with public safety officials is what to do about disabled individuals (both staff and users). This can be a challenge in multistory buildings because elevators are generally "off limits" in an emergency.

Shelter-in-Place

A relatively recent phenomenon, at least for libraries, government agencies, and businesses in large metropolitan areas to consider, is the concept of shelter-in-place. The exact opposite of building evacuation, shelter-in-place procedures would come to play as a result of chemical, biological, or radiological contaminants that may be released accidentally or intentionally into the environment. In such an instance, library staff will be responsible for ensuring the safety of patrons by asking that they stay, not leave the facility.

Some institutions have already incorporated shelter-in-place guidelines into their overall security plan. For a review of standard guidelines that can be adapted for your library, consult http://www.redcross.org/services/disas ter/beprepared/shelterinplace.html, from the American Red Cross, or the Department of Homeland Security's "Make a Shelter-in-Place Plan" (http://www. ready.gov/business/plan/shelterplan.html).

Earthquakes

Earthquake preparedness presents several special challenges for public services staff. One is in maintaining the collection stacks in a safe manner. As one begins to run out of shelf space, there is a tendency to look at shelving dust canopies (usually a lightweight metal cover) as extra shelving. Although not as strong as regular shelving material, dust canopies are usually capable of carrying the weight of one row of books. The danger comes from the fact that even a moderate earthquake can throw books in any direction because they are freestanding. A bound volume of *Newsweek* simply dropping from a height of eight feet (the usual height of open stack shelving) can cause an injury. Having it thrown off the dust canopy by a 5.5 to 6.5 Richter scale earthquake could cause a serious injury. The potential for injury is high enough in such an earthquake that there is no need to add to it by shelving materials in an unsafe manner. Even bookends can be an issue; "wire" book supports (those that hang from the bottom of a shelf) tend to allow more books to fall than bookends on the shelf, at least the ones with nonskid bases.

In countries and states where earthquakes are common, there are usually special building code requirements for library stack ranges and other storage units. Seismic bracing adds to the cost of installing shelving. Unfortunately, such bracing does not assure that shelving will not fall or twist out of shape; but it does provide better safety for people. This is because the linked ranges do not normally fall to the floor, but rather twist or lean over as a block and never completely collapse. Certainly, whatever is on the shelves will end up on the floor. Study tables or carrels, however, are likely to avoid being crushed by heavy steel or wood shelving. This is important because hiding under a table or desk gives people some protection during an earthquake.

Libraries in areas of high earthquake potential, especially in large urban areas, need to consider what type of supplies they should have on hand for when a major quake does strike. Earthquake specialists suggest that any earthquake registering over 7.0 on the Richter scale occurring in an urban area will disrupt community services for about 72 hours. This means being without fire, police, or medical assistance for at least three days. Some libraries in earthquake-prone areas set up storage areas for food, water, basic first aid materials, and rescue equipment. One question facing libraries is whether to have sufficient food and water for three days for the normal work force, for all the staff, or for all staff and an estimated number of users trapped at the library. A second question is, who provides the money to pay for these supplies? For libraries in earthquake zones it is not a question of *if* it will happen, but *when.*

FEMA (FEDERAL EMERGENCY MANAGEMENT AGENCY)

After an area in the United States in struck by a major natural disaster, it is often declared a federal disaster area. When that happens, FEMA teams come to the area. FEMA is the federal agency with the power to provide money to assist local jurisdictions in recovering from a disaster. There are two types of funds: loans to individuals and grants to local government agencies. A FEMA representative or team will assess the damage and prepare a Damage Survey Report (DSR) (http://www.dps.state.vt.us/vem/emd/Appendix/appendix_12_05.pdf). DSRs are the basis upon which FEMA determines reimbursement. The second step in the process is an "audit" by other FEMA staff; that is, a second survey. The second survey may approve, modify, or disapprove the first DSR. The last step is a later FEMA visit to determine what was done with FEMA funds. The overall objective of DSRs and recovery money is to return the location/person back to the same condition as prior to the disaster as soon as possible by the most advantageous and economical means possible. There is considerable room for interpretation as to what constitutes the "same condition" and what it will cost to achieve.

FEMA personnel have a responsibility to assure that funds, which are not inexhaustible, go toward warranted recovery efforts. The goal of a representative of a local jurisdiction or "individual" in the case of private institutions is to secure as much of the disaster recovery costs as possible. While these are not mutually exclusive goals, it is clear there is plenty of opportunity for disagreement.

Probably the biggest recent (as of 2007) experience that libraries have had with FEMA was the aftermath of Hurricane Katrina, which struck the Gulf Coast in 2005. Norman Oder (2006) reported on the library experiences in the Gulf Coast region. One key example was the New Orleans Public Library. Pre-Katrina it operated in 12 locations with a staff of 171, post-Katrina there were 40 people operating five locations (p. 39). Most of the libraries that were operating in the months following the hurricane had a dual relationship with FEMA, as an applicant for help and as a service location for FEMA.

One way to reduce some of the uncertainty and conflict is to have good documentation. As the *Earthquake Preparedness Manual for California Libraries* suggests, "Write it down, log it, or photograph it" (California Library Association, 1990, p. 22). Any photographs that are available showing pre- and post-disaster damage will be very useful in *assisting* the FEMA team as they make their determinations. (Note: FEMA does not pay on the basis of photographed damage. However, the library may not be at the top of a long list of sites the inspectors must visit, and some cleanup activities are likely to be underway, if not completed, when the inspectors arrive. An example might be picking up and reshelving materials dislocated during the disaster.)

FEMA will reimburse for the cost of books and other collection items lost in a disaster, if they were in the library at the time and the library can provide author, title, or other documentation. If one has an online catalog and backup tapes are available, the documentation should be available. If all else fails, the library may be able to able to get some useful data from a service such as OCLC or WorldCat.

When it comes to earthquakes, most FEMA inspectors do not know about seismic specifications for shelving. For that matter, they are not familiar with the cost and complexity of library shelving. Having a copy of seismic standards for library shelving and/or a written cost estimate for replacement and repair from a library shelving vendor will help speed the process and reduce some of the conflict between inspector(s) and library staff. Another useful step is to have someone available from the department that maintains the library during the site inspections. As few if any staff members are architects or contractors, having a knowledgeable person available who can point out special structural issues is helpful.

TECHNOLOGICAL SECURITY

Technology has become a key component, if not the critical one after people, in providing quality library service. Libraries have more complex equipment than any time in the past as well as having users who expect to have 24/7 access to library resources and services. Downloading and e-commerce are becoming "standard" services. All of this raises a variety of security issues for both the library and its users.

Technological security begins with risk analysis, just like all other library security concerns. When thinking about technology there is sometimes a tendency only to think about equipment, but the library often has as much or more invested in its own databases and software as it does in hardware. (The safety of user information in the library system[s] is an increasing concern. Terrence Huwe [2005], in writing about security breaches, noted; "In the past year, there have been at least three similar incursions on various University of California campuses, some involving library patron records" [p. 31].) Risk analysis should cover at least three issues: value, dangers, and existing safeguards.

One can group library technology security issues into six broad categories— passwords, backups, viruses/malware, hardware, data privacy, and legal. Staff members know that IT personnel seem to push the importance of passwords and the need to change them on a regular basis. However, few of us really appreciate the full significance of keeping passwords secure. Too often we share passwords with colleagues in our department so they are able to "check on" something when we are out of the office. When IT enforces the idea that you should have different passwords for different applications, as it should, there is tendency to create a list of passwords and "hide" it so we can consult it when necessary. The hiding place is also sometimes shared. Another pitfall to avoid is having a "core" element in the various passwords—such as a last name or easily guessed date; yes, it helps us remember them, but it also makes it easier for the hacker to gain access to multiple applications. Anyone having authorized access to databases with user information must be very careful about their passwords.

Generally there is little need to worry about backing up the major library databases. Given their critical value to daily operations, the IT personnel make certain this is carried out on a regular basis (daily in most cases). The question is, what about your files that are stored on the local hard drive? When was the last time you backed them up? If you are like a lot of us, the answer is probably "never." Certainly not every file is worth backing up. Ask yourself, "What would/will I lose if my hard drive crashes?" "Could I really accurately recreate the important files?" Backing up your critical files really is important and, just as is the case with library-wide backups, be sure to store the backup outside the workplace.

Another area of concern is virus/malware "infections." When purchasing antivirus software, be certain it has the approval certification of the National Computer Security Association (NCSA) and provides for frequent updating. Some of the features that one should look for are signature-based scanning, heuristics-based scanning, memory-resident monitoring, and integrity checking. Of course, the best virus protection software is useless if you don't run it on a regular basis. Again, the main concern is for your PC, as there are usually library-wide virus/spyware programs in place that address network security, but as we sometimes learn our computer can become infected because we failed to run a regular check.

Not all equipment and software is equally valuable or important. The old PC used by a volunteer to do some word processing is not as important or as vulnerable as a high-end machine located at the reference desk or administrative area. Knowing the cost and importance of each piece of equipment helps in setting appropriate levels of security. Another part of determining the appropriate level is an assessment of what dangers exist for the item. (Beyond theft there are the issues of disk crashes, power outages, and "hackers" to consider.) Finally, assessing what safeguards already exist (or are possible) determines what more, if anything, needs to take place. (Here, one can think in terms of protect, detect, prevent, and recover.)

Installing front-end security involves highly visible elements such as cable locks and perhaps motion detectors. Another element in front-end security is a secure menu system, which allows users access to features the library deems appropriate and disables those that may create problems. Back-end security protects data and applications. This type of security protects against hackers.

If the library's network is connected to the Internet, it is advisable to use a "firewall" to provide some protection for the library network. In essence, firewall software only allows "authorized" connections between outside systems and the library network. If the firewall is under the control of an agency outside the library (for example, an academic campus network), there can be delays in getting access to a new Internet-based service. The library must request the firewall manager make the appropriate changes in the firewall to allow the access.

As libraries expand their e-services, they face a number of privacy and legal considerations. Consider the implications when a computer is connected to the Internet and available for public access. There is also the fact that the library collects some data about each registered borrower and stores them in a database. Although no longer the case, in the past libraries frequently used the person's Social Security number as the identifying number. An important question to consider is, have all those numbers been deleted for long-time users? This is critical as hackers have been able to access user information from library databases (Kennedy, 2006).

Some individuals frequently use library computers for personal activities. Some examples are online shopping, bill paying, online banking, and even paying taxes. If the library has posted policies regarding user confidentially, people may assume they do not have to worry about using the computers. The postings should make it clear the library has no liability when a person uses the public computers for transactions that are not related to library services.

Libraries are engaging in more and more e-commerce, which also raises privacy/data security challenges—online book sales (Gerding, 2007), payment for services such as downloads and document delivery, and overdue fines to name but a few. All these activities call for staff to provide assistance to users from time to time. More importantly, it means protecting personal information is even more complex and essential.

Any time a library provides wireless access, additional security/privacy challenges arise. Some libraries check out wireless security cards or wireless-enabled laptops to those who wish to use them. This will probably mean public service staff will need some understanding of how to configure the laptop to use the card for those who are unfamiliar with the process. Check out Bill Drew's Web site (http://wirelesslibraries.blogspot.com/) for an ongoing discussion of library wireless issues.

Library public service staff must understand and be on guard against "social engineering." (Social engineering has come to mean gaining unauthorized access to information or computer systems.) The process works so well because people generally assume others are honest and provide answers to apparently legitimate/harmless questions. Probably the most common ploy is to pretend to be someone needing to verify some personal information. The social engineer first builds a trust relationship and, with data gathered elsewhere, attempts to secure additional information that can help with identity theft. Although, as we noted earlier, most ILS systems no longer employ user Social Security numbers, they do have addresses, telephone numbers, and occasionally e-mail addresses. "I'm calling for my sick mother (or whoever) to verify you have her current address," may or may not be a legitimate call. Samuel Thompson (2006) provided some excellent suggestions for preventing social engineers from succeeding:

- Be suspicious of unsolicited communications asking for people or operational information
- Never give out passwords no matter who claims to be calling
- Never provide user information to anyone except when the requester comes in and presents proper identification
- Inform supervisors or authorities if you have any doubts about a request for user information
- Document and report suspicious communications (pp. 224–225)

We will explore such legal issues as the USA PATRIOT Act and CIPA later in this chapter.

BUGS AND OTHER NASTY THINGS

Turning to another type of problem, why is it that so many libraries try to prevent people from bringing food and drinks into the building? Perhaps an enlargement of an illustration of a cockroach with a message such as, "If you do not want to share your library space with me, leave your food and drinks outside," would reduce the staff's time spent in trying to enforce a no food and drink policy. Unfortunately, even with completely successful enforcement of such a rule, insects can still be a problem. Book collections, by themselves, represent a fine gourmet feast for several types of insects (book lice, book-worms, silverfish, firebrats, cockroaches, and termites). These insects account for 95 percent of insect damage to libraries and their collections.

Insects

Book lice love to eat starch in almost any form; library paste is the main source in libraries. These pinhead-sized, gray-white insects prefer dark and somewhat damp conditions. While thousands of lice can reside in a single musty book, overall they really don't do that much damage. Their presence, however, is a clear signal that all is not well with the environmental control system. Of all the problem insects, this is the group most likely to be seen. In fact, anyone who is a frequent book user has seen them. (You may not have known what it was, but that faint quick movement on the page you thought you saw when you opened a book was probably a book-louse trying to scurry to safety in the book's gutter.) Keeping the temperature and humidity at the recommended level (70 degrees Fahrenheit and 55% humidity) is the best method of controlling book lice.

Bookworms are even more destructive. These are actually the larvae of bee-tles; there are over 160 species. Adults burrow through covers or the edge of textblocks and lay their eggs in the pages. The hatched larvae feed on the pages. Their excrement resembles a fine dust that cannot be easily differenti-ated from normal dust. However, if some shelves seem more dusty than nor-mal, especially under the books, open some of the volumes. If pages are stuck together, there is probably a bookworm problem. When the larvae feed they secrete a glue-like substance that causes pages to stick together. Good climate control can help prevent the problem, but, once it has arisen, professional help is the best way to resolve an existing problem.

Silverfish and firebrats enjoy late-night dinners or at least eating in the dark. Firebrats prefer hot and dry conditions, while a cool and moist environ-ment is ideal for silverfish. Pages that look like lacework or the work of a Chi-nese papercutter probably are the result of these insects. Seeing one silverfish or firebrat usually means a major infestation because they normally only come out when it is dark. They are long-living by insect standards (two to three years) as well as tough, being able to exist four to five months without food or water. Because they attack the inside of books, the first sign of trouble will be small dark lumps (feces) on the shelves, which shelvers may notice when shifting materials.

Cockroaches feed on almost anything: paper, cloth, or leather. Some can even exist inside electronic equipment. A problem with cockroaches requires regular visits from a professional exterminator service. Cockroaches are resilient and seem at times to be immune to insecticides. Like many problem insects, they prefer to move about in the dark unless the population is large, when some risk moving about in the light. Not only are they destructive, but they also can transmit diseases. An early warning sign of cockroach problems is discoloration of shelves, furniture, and cabinets. Cockroaches secrete a dark liquid that discolors surfaces across which they crawl.

Termites attack wood and wood products. Books and other paper materials on steel shelving are fairly safe as long as new additions to the collection, especially gifts, are screened. Naturally, they can be very destructive to the building and furniture. As with most insect damage, termite damage occurs inside the material and the surface offers few clues that a problem exists. Although primarily tropical and subtropical insects, they do exist in areas with extended periods of damp heat. Again, their eradication requires professional services.

What can be done? Circulation staff, especially shelvers, need training in identifying signs of insect damage. Make it clear that the reason for having no food and drink in the library is to help reduce the possibility or level of cockroach and other insect problems. Emphasize the fact that cockroaches can transmit diseases. Maintaining sanitary conditions is the best insurance against cockroaches and other insects. Naturally, keeping the temperature and humidity in balance and at the recommended levels for libraries creates conditions that discourage insects. When signs of trouble do appear, set some traps, especially glueboards. This will help establish the areas and degree of trouble. While small insect outbreaks may be suitable for in-house treatment, if there is any doubt, call in the experts and do not wait too long to make the call. If the library staff tries treatment on its own, it is better to use a bulb applicator rather than spraying. Powders are longer lasting, do not stain materials, provide a more precise application, *and* afford less danger of inhaling the poisons. To be effective the material must be highly toxic, and improper handling can lead to real trouble. Whenever possible, leave this work to those trained to do it safely, even if this means waiting a little longer to solve the problem.

When you encounter infected or infested books, isolate them in sealed plastic bags. Freezing the material for a week usually solves the insect problem. A few people suggest that 60 seconds in a microwave oven on high will also do the job. Be aware, however, that heat ages paper. If the materials are worth saving, send them for professional treatment rather than attempting in-house cures.

Fungus

Fungus is another problem that increases when environmental control is poor. Damp, warm conditions not only encourage insects, but also speed up the growth of molds and mildew. Anyone living in tropical or subtropical areas knows the situation is normal and deals with it on a daily basis. Elsewhere, people often don't worry about the problem, but anytime there are damp conditions the problem can arise. After a fire or water leak in particular, molds and mildews can grow on anything that got wet. Information about this aspect of the fungi problem can be found in many sources about library conservation. On example of the leak-mold problem was reported in the January 2008 issue of *American Libraries*. The article indicated all the books in a small branch library had to be discarded due to mold that developed as the result of a leaky roof.

Another concern is for human health ("Mold at Santa Fe Main: Staff Relocates," 2001; "Mold-Affected Missouri Library Reopens," 2006). Three basic factors influence the level of health danger. The first factor is the concentration of fungi spores in a specific area; as the concentration rises, so do risks to health. The second is that the environmental conditions that lead to increased spore production (warmth and moisture) also enhance the chances of health problems. Finally, there is the level of personal susceptibility, which varies from person to person. For a few unfortunate individuals even small concentrations of fungi spores in a relatively cool environment can cause an illness. At the other end of the susceptibility spectrum are those individuals who never seem to get sick. In between there are the majority of staff members, who can and will get sick if the spore count becomes too high.

Almost all of the health problems resulting from fungi will be of an allergic nature. Some can be mycotic (disabling) and a very few toxic (fatal). Rhinitis (asthma) is a fairly common allergic reaction in workers in libraries: they are allergic to book dust. By itself this reaction is not fatal, but it can cause severe discomfort (dry coughing, wheezing, and shortness of breath) and it will also complicate other pulmonary disease problems. Most of the fatal reactions to fungi are the result of ingesting the spores as food (mushrooms) or with food. It is possible to transfer spores from your hands to your food and then eat them.

We will only mention a few examples of fungi found in libraries that, under *some* circumstances, can cause health problems. *Aspergillus fumagatus* can cause pulmonary aspergillosis. *Aspergillus niger* can cause ear infections. *Geotrichum candidum* may cause geotrichosis, which can take the form of an oral, intestinal, bronchial, or pulmonary infection. Certain strains of *Pricillum* can cause pericillosis, which affects the bronchial and pulmonary functions. It is also a possible cause of some eye, ear, and urinary tract infections.

Good air filtering systems will help control spore levels, but the best control is maintaining proper temperature and humidity. Good housekeeping and sanitary practices further reduce the potential for trouble. We point out these potential health issues not to frighten people or raise undue concern, but rather to emphasize that control of fungi in the library does have implications beyond a little mildew on a few books.

CRIME IN THE LIBRARY

Table 15.1 lists the most common crimes that occur in the library. Many of the problems on the list we covered either earlier in this chapter or in other chapters.

Robert Doyle (2006) noted that in 2005, public libraries had 1.3 billion visitors and only a tiny fraction of those visitors caused a problem. Generally

TABLE 15.1 Crimes in the Library

1. Intentional book damage	11. Drug use by staff or patron
2. Book theft	12. Drug sale by staff or patron
3. Reference material stolen	13. Verbal abuse to patron
4. Equipment stolen	14. Verbal abuse to staff
5. Other thefts	15. Indecent exposure
6. Vandalism outside the building	16. Assault on patron
7. Vandalism inside the building	17. Assault on staff
8. Vandalism of patron's car	18. Arson
9. Vandalism of staff cars	19. Trespassing
10. Vandalism of equipment	20. Disorderly or menacing conduct

libraries are very safe, but as public facilities, anyone can come in. The vast majority of public libraries, as well as others, have written and posted policies regarding access and what is acceptable behavior. They also should have guidelines for when the staff should call the police as well as providing training in handling disruptive situations. Doyle suggested seven situations (p. 16) that should result in a call for assistance:

- When a person threatens to or engages in physical harm to a user or employee
- When a person threatens to or damages physical property, whether the library's or a user's
- When a person refuses to leave the library after being asked to do so
- When a person sells, uses, or possesses illegal drugs
- When a person views or prints pornographic material on a library or personal computer while in the library
- When there is a missing or abandoned child in the library
- When a person engages in public indecent acts

If you think about each of the above, you can imagine many variations when assistance might not be needed as well as other situations not listed that could be very serious without assistance. That is why training and guidelines are so important.

Four categories of people commit the majority of library crimes. Regular users are usually the source of most of the deliberate damage done to books and library property. Unfortunately, many of the thefts are committed by staff members (everyone who has a work reason to enter the library). This includes security staff, maintenance personnel, and even some contract maintenance and repair people. Professional thieves seldom bother with libraries; when they do, they usually steal valuable books, bookplates, and occasionally equipment—although theft of purses, briefcases, and other personal belongings of the staff and public is probably the result of at least semiprofessional thieves. Most of the disruptive behavior, vandalism in and outside the library, as well as breaking into cars of users and staff are usually acts of individuals who do not use the library.

One form of crime seldom reported because it is difficult to detect is skimming. Whenever an organization collects cash the opportunity for theft is present. Coin-operated photocopiers, microform reader-printers, and networked printers are services that can generate significant amounts of money. In moderately busy libraries a single photocopier, at $.15 per copy, can generate from $28,000 to $36,000 per year. That amount may approach the salary of a full-time staff member. Certainly, there are ways to control or monitor use and income, but they are complex and require checks and balances. If the library collects fines and other fees, using a numbered duplicate receipt system is the first step in monitoring the process. That is, one receipt is for the person paying the fee and the second remains in the library as a record of monies received. With each set of receipts serially numbered, there is a way of checking on missing numbers. Using a cash register or recording receipts in an automated circulation system also provides some control. No system is foolproof, but most staff members are honest and such systems help trustworthy people stay honest.

Spending a little money on cables and special locking devices to secure equipment also helps honest people stay honest. Popular equipment, such as DVD players, laptops, and PCs, left unsecured will probably disappear. On the other hand, microform reader-printers, overhead projectors, and 6mm film projectors probably are safe without any special security. Security locking devices are not too expensive, but even the most expensive and extensive will not stop the professional thief. In educational libraries, bolting equipment to tables and special media carts is done as much for safety reasons as it is security. If the library delivers equipment to various locations, fastening the equipment to the cart provides increased safety for both the equipment and the person moving the equipment. Where substantial numbers of children or young people gather in the library and media equipment is on tables and in study carrels, bolting is a good idea. Accidents will happen, but it will be harder for bolted equipment to fall to the floor.

One question to consider is how much collection security is appropriate. Almost every library has some loss of books and other items as well as some mutilation of materials. A common approach to securing the collection is to employ an electronic exit control system. The system operates on the basis of a "target" attached to collection items and sensors located at the exit. When an item is properly discharged, the target becomes inactive and the user exits. When the item is not properly checked out and a person takes it through the exit gate, an alarm will sound. Library systems are a variation of the systems used in many retail stores to control theft.

Electronic systems are expensive to purchase and annual expenses for targets, staff time to attach them to new acquisitions, and system maintenance can be substantial. Knowing the magnitude of the theft problem in the library can assist in determining if or how much security is necessary. Some of the steps to take involve the following:

- Staff searches for missing books
- Inventories/random sampling of the collection are done

- Physical evidence (torn-out book pockets, missing date due slips, and so forth) is found

What percentage of missing books are theft candidates? Consider books such as the following:

- Books with color plates
- Books that are costly to replace
- Books that are difficult to locate
- Books with unusual characteristics
- Special-collection-type material in the open stacks

How often have people been stopped for forgetting to check out an item? What patterns exist, if any, in past losses?

- Journal articles?
- Media software?

What types of ownership markings are in place? Are they

- Highly visible?
- In permanent ink?

Are emergency exits fitted with alarms so staff knows when one is used? How often does an alarm sound, or are doors found open? How many staff access doors are open all day? Are they visible to one or more staff members at all times? Do the library windows open? If so, are the screens nonremovable except by maintenance staff? How much vandalism does the library experience, including mutilation to:

- Books and items in collection?
- Furniture, walls, stack areas?
- Restrooms?
- Book drops?
- Exterior walls?

What types of vandalism are present? Is it:

- Directed at the library?
- Directed at other users or the institution the library serves?

Are there discernible patterns to the vandalism in terms of:

- Place?
- Time of day or season?

Creating a situation with complete collection security is perhaps possible, but it would be so costly that it would not be practicable. Also, it would go against the basic user-friendly service concept of most libraries. On the other hand, having no security will be equally unsatisfactory for those wanting to use the materials. Thus, most libraries must try to find a balance among security, user access, and reasonable costs.

The authors of this book have told staff, only half in jest, that if a library wishes to identify its true core collection, all it has to do is prepare a list of all the lost and missing books and mutilated journal titles. Normally, these are the items that, for one reason or another, are (or were) under pressure from users, including high-use or, in the case of missing books, potentially high-use materials.

Every library loses books each year to individuals who, if caught by a security system, say they forgot to check the material out. Journals and other noncirculating material are subject to some degree of mutilation. Each incident of theft and mutilation means some small financial loss for the library, if nothing more than the cost of the material and the labor expended to make the item available. Other costs are the cost of staff time to search for the item and to decide how or whether to replace it and the replacement and processing costs. Although one incident seldom represents a significant cost, the total annual cost may be surprising, even if one calculates only the amount paid for replacement materials.

Despite high-quality electronic security exit systems and targeting every book and every issue of every journal that goes into the collection, a library will have some "shrinkage"(as retail stores identify such losses). Needless to say, time and money expended to prevent theft or replace materials is time and money not spent on expanding the resources available to users.

Some libraries have taken to using a technology called RFID (radio frequency identification), which that may present some challenges in terms of user privacy, at least as it has been presented in the press (for one such discussion see Butters, 2007). Originally employed as a very effective method for inventory control, item identification, and self-checkout, in the unlikely event that its capabilities are extended outside the library building, problems might arise.

An embedded RFID chip identifies a specific item and its location, unlike the magnetic strips commonly used in libraries in conjunction with their exit control system. (The magnetic strip is not item specific and only indicates if the item has or has not been properly checked out.) The RFID can track locations over a substantial distance—far beyond the library building. Some states have proposed banning or at least greatly limiting the use of RFID chips due to their tracking capabilities. (The concern is not particularly directed toward libraries because the typical library RFID is only capable of being read from about 3 feet. The concern is over commercial interests that claim knowing where and when a consumer uses their products is important to delivering the "best" products; their tags apparently are more far-reaching than library tags.)

What the long-term outcome will be is impossible to accurately predict. Used for their original purposes in a library there should be no major concerns in implementing RFID—beyond the high cost of the chips and the labor required to "embed" one in each item in the collection. The use of tracking capabilities beyond the library proper seems problematic. One easy way to keep up on the topic of RFID in libraries is to monitor the ALA's RFID page, available from the ALA Web site.

Regardless of the security mechanism employed, there are several givens to any security program. First, there will be some level of loss no matter what the library does. Second, the systems really only help basically honest people stay honest. A professional thief will circumvent almost any library security system, as Stephen Blumberg demonstrated a few years ago (Allen, 1991). Therefore, the library must decide how important the problem is and how much loss it can tolerate. The goal is to balance the cost of the security program against the losses. The less loss the library will accept, the higher the security costs, so finding the proper balance is important.

Most libraries employ some mix of people-based elements and electronic systems for security. Door guards or monitors who check every item taken from the library are the most effective and most costly option. This works well only when the person doing the checking is not a peer of the people being checked. That is, using students to check fellow students, much less their teachers, does not work well. Retired individuals are most effective. They interact well with users, but also do the job without favoring anyone. The major drawback to exit monitors, after the cost, is that when there are peaks and valleys in the exit flow there can be long queues during the peaks.

Electronic systems are common and may give a false sense of security. Although studies show that the presence of such a system may deter theft, every system has a weakness that the person who regularly "forgets to check out books" eventually discovers, and the professional thief already knows. Also, some materials, for example, magnetic tape and videotape, cannot be deactivated without possibly damaging the data on tape, and some materials simply do not have a place for a target. Such systems are susceptible to electronic interference, such as frequencies generated by computers or even fluorescent light ballasts. Finally, the inventive thief can jam the operating frequency and no one on the staff will know the difference.

Mutilation is another ongoing problem which, over the course of a year, can generate a surprisingly large loss for the library. There are few cost-effective options for handling this problem. Having copy services available and at competitive prices will help. Monitors walking through the building will solve or reduce many other security problems, but will do little to stop mutilation. Studies suggest that even users who see someone mutilating library materials will not report the activity to library staff (Pederson, 1990). One option that users do not like, but that does stop the mutilation of journals, is to supply only digital or microform backfiles of journals that are subject to high mutilation. This option does not safeguard the current issues, and it requires providing microform reader-printers, which are more expensive than microform readers. Today's online databases, with back files, help reduce the problem, but only if the library can afford to acquire the back files.

Theft and mutilation are a part of doing business. How much they cost the library depends on the local situation. Those costs come at the expense of adding greater variety to the collections and, in the long run, they hurt the user.

"PROBLEM" USERS

As our opening quote from Sarah Farrugia (2002) suggested, "Public librar-ies are more susceptible to patron violence than academic and other special libraries, as their open door allows anyone to use the building. This can some-times invite trouble from asocial citizens who can cause disruption and un-easiness amongst staff and patrons and even lead to acts of extreme violence" (p. 309). As we noted earlier, staff need to have policies regarding acceptable behavior and when to call for backup help.

Disruptive behavior is a problem all public service staff experience at one time or another. It is especially disconcerting when it is a fellow staff mem-ber. With a colleague, however, one usually has a baseline for judging what is wrong. With the public there is less basis for knowing what is wrong and what to expect. Unfortunately, today the behavior may be drug related; this applies to all types of libraries, even those in middle schools.

When does unusual or strange behavior become disruptive? Every library must decide the answer to that question. Certainly, you cannot call security every time someone exhibits slightly different behavior. Like the boy who cried wolf, you might not get help when it is truly necessary. Workshops conducted by professionals specializing in human behavior and substance abuse can help prepare the staff to handle such problems safely. They also help set up reasonable guidelines for when to call for assistance. Also helpful is training from specialists in mental health. After training, the policy guidelines should be written down for later consultation when the need arises. (An increasing percentage of homeless or street people in the United States are individuals who, in the past, would have been hospitalized and on medication. Most of them are harmless, but without their medication their behavior can be erratic and often disruptive.)

Although most libraries are open to the public, many private academic li-braries also allow limited public access. If the library posts reasonable rules regarding access, hours, and behavior, it may legally remove anyone violating those rules. The two key considerations are reasonable rules and posting. The rules should reflect existing laws and should have been reviewed by an attor-ney. Both conditions must be present for removal from the library to be legal. Repeat offenders can face legal action, if the library wishes to press charges.

American Libraries (2006c) reported on a problem with the "reasonableness" of library access/behavior polices of libraries. In one instance, the Dallas Pub-lic Library's plan to ban persons "emitting odors (including bodily odors or perfumes) which interfere with services by other users or work staff" was chal-lenged. Homeless advocates questioned the fairness of such a rule. The ACLU filed a lawsuit in Massachusetts over a rule that limited a homeless person to checking out only two books at any one time (*American Libraries*, 2006a). These two incidents illustrate the fact that just having written rules regarding access/behavior does not end controversy.

One type of disruptive behavior is the user who becomes verbally abusive about a library issue, such as a fine or policy. How much verbal abuse must one tolerate? F. J. De Rosa (1980) commented: "People in all areas of public service, and librarians in particular, seem resigned to the opinion that abuse from their public is inescapable and there is not much they can do about it. Much of this misconception is due to the fact that many people do not realize the point when disruptive behavior becomes antisocial behavior and when antisocial behavior becomes criminal behavior" (p. 35). An excellent book to consult on handling problem behaviors of all types in libraries is Mark Willis' *Dealing with Difficult People in the Library* (Chicago: ALA, 1999). It addresses just about any type of "difficult person" category you can think of in a library setting.

LEGAL CONCERNS

We have mentioned CIPA several times in this book. Here we just wish to mention some of the software packages that allow you to comply with Internet filtering for children's access.

"Deep Freeze" (Faronics Technologies, USA, Inc.) automatically resets a computer to the library settings no matter what changes a user may succeed in making—which can be a real staff time saver. "Total Traffic Control" (Lightspeed Systems) offers monitoring, reporting, and filtering, which is also a staff time saver. "Bees" (Secure Computing) allows for customizable control lists that can allow students to gain access to such topics as breast cancer, something some of the packages don't allow. "Cyber Sentinel" (Security Software Systems) offers not only monitoring of the Internet, but all Windows applications. "pro 5060" (SonicWall, Inc.) is a security gateway for medium and large networks and allows for establishing different user groups. "iPrism" (St. Bernard Software) has a high filtering accuracy rating in terms of schools needs.

In late 2007, *American Libraries* reported a public library system had started blocking access to social Web sites. The Kent District Library system decided to block access to such sites on all but the six computers facing the reference desk so staff could monitor Internet activity. Blockage arose from a request by city officials because the library had become involved, unknowingly, in a teenage gang "turf war." Police said gang members were using the library's computers to access sites such as MySpace in order to intimidate rival gang members. During the first six months of 2007, police investigated eight cases of gang vandalism and fifteen complaints about disorderly conduct at the library. The library was also told to hire full-time security guards to help control the problems (p. 41).

First enacted in October 2001, the USA PATRIOT Act has been a concern for libraries. An outgrowth of the events of 9/11, the acronym stands for Uniting and Strengthening America by Providing Appropriate Tools Required to Intercept and Obstruct Terrorism. Section 215 of the Act allows the government to secure secret warrants to obtain "business records"—this includes library records as well as from library database vendors. The Act also authorizes the issuance of National Security Letters (NSLs), which do not require a judge's review, that require organizations to secretly provide information. At least one library has been on the receiving end of such a letter. (Between 2003 and 2006 the FBI issued over 140,000 NSLs [Pike, 2007, p. 18]).

If you are on duty when an agent arrives, just direct the person to the administrative office and let that office handle the situation. Do not offer assistance, even if the "admin" office is closed, in the unlikely event you are asked to assist.

SUMMARY

When a disaster strikes or a security problem comes up, all staff members should know what to do and know that they do have the authority to act. There should be no hierarchy of decision making at the moment a problem comes up. All staff should take part in an annual disaster-handling drill and fire safety updates.

Chapter Review Material

1. What are the major elements of a security plan?
2. Outline the steps in a safe closing routine.
3. What are the key elements in having an effective disaster plan?
4. Why is it important to maintain a no food or drink policy in the public areas of a library?
5. What are some the most significant crime problems in libraries? Do you agree with Farrugia's quote at the beginning of the chapter indicating public libraries are more susceptible to patron violence than academic/ special libraries? Why or why not?
6. What are some guidelines for when to call for assistance when you face disruptive behavior?
7. How should you handle requests for user information, especially when asked for the information by properly identified law enforcement officials?

REFERENCES

Allen, Susan. 1991. "The Blumberg Case: A Costly Lesson for Librarians," *AB Bookman's Weekly* 88 (September 2): 769–773.

American Libraries. 2001. "Mold at Santa Fe Main; Staff Relocates," 32, no. 9: 25–26.

———. 2006a. "Homeless residents Sue over Borrowing Limits," 37, no. 7: 18.

———. 2006b. "Mold-Affected Missouri Library Reopens," 37, no. 9: 11.

———. 2006c. "Stir Raised by Dallas Body Odor Rule," 37, no. 2: 11.

———. 2007. "Patron Abuse Prompts Trial of Social-Network Filter," 38, no. 8: 41.

———. 2008. "Leaky Branch's Future Uncertain after Administrators Dispose of Moldy Collection," 39, no. 1: 21.

Bassett, Jackie. 2007. "Security in Management's Terms," *Internal Auditor* 64, no. 3: 27–31.

Boss, Richard. 2002. "Disaster Planning for Computers and Networks," *Public Library Association TechNotes*, http://www.ala.org/ala/pla/plapubs/tech notes/disasterplanning.cfm.

Butters, Alan. 2007. "RFID Systems, Standards and Privacy within Libraries." *Electronic Library* 25, no. 4: 430–439.

California Library Association. 1990. *Earthquake Preparedness Manual for California Libraries*. Sacramento, CA: author.

Cooley, Mason. 2000. *Aphorisms of the All-to-Human*. New York: Ragged Edge Press.

De Rosa, F. J. 1980. "The Disruptive Patron," *Library & Archival Security* 3, no. 3/4: 29–37.

Doyle, Robert P. 2006. "Libraries as Sanctuaries for Criminals?" *Illinois Library Association Reporter* 24, no. 6: 12–17.

Farrugia, Sarah. 2002. "A Dangerous Occupation? Violence in Public Libraries," *New Library World* 103, no. 1180: 309–319.

Gerding, Stephanie. 2007. "Online Books Sales for Libraries," *Public Libraries* 46, no. 1: 23–35.

Huwe, Terrence. 2005. "New Technology's Surprising Security Threats," *Computer in Libraries* 25, no. 2: 30–32.

Kennedy, Shirley Duglin. 2006. "I've Been Violated," *Information Today* 23, no. 6: 17–18, 20.

Oder, Norman. 2006. "How'd You Come Out?" *Library Journal* 131, no. 10: 38–41.

Pederson, Terri. 1990. "Theft and Mutilation of Library Materials," *College & Research Libraries* 51, no. 3: 120–128.

Pike, George. 2007. "The PATRIOT Act Illuminated," *Information Today* 24, no. 5: 17–18.

Smith, Patricia. 2005. "An Ounce of Prevention Is Worth a Pound of Cure," *Texas Library Journal* 81, no. 1: 22–23.

Steele, Thomas M. 1997. "Managing Legal Liability," *Library Administration & Management* 11, no. 2: 94–101.

Teper, Tom. 2003. "Re-establishing Key Control as a Security Measure," *Library & Archival Security* 18, no. 1: 53–61.

Thompson, Samuel T. 2006. "Helping the Hacker?" *Information Technology and Libraries* 25, no. 4: 222–225.

Woods, Chris. 2002 "Meeting the Montreal Protocol: Alternative Fire Suppression Systems for Archives," *Journal of the Society of Archivists* 23, no. 2: 179–186

SUGGESTED READINGS

Alao, I. A. 2004. "The Effectiveness of Library Measures against Theft and Mutilation," *Library & Archival Security* 19, no. 1: 29–37.

Alire, Camila. 2000. *Library Disaster Planning and Recovery*. New York: Neal-Schuman Publishers, Inc.

Airoldi, Joan. 2004. "One Book, One County, One Subpoena," *Alki* 20, no. 3: 19–20.

———. 2006. "A Grand Jury Subpoena in the PARTIOT Act Era," *Library Administration & Management* 20, no. 1: 26–29.

American Libraries. 2008. "Security Revisited after Child Is Assaulted," 39, no. 4: 24.

American Library Association Office for Intellectual Freedom. 2007. "Model Policy: Responding to Demands for Library Records," *American Libraries* 38, no. 8.

Baker, Whitney. 2001. "Mold in the Stacks: A Universal Problem," *Kentucky Libraries* 65, no. 3: 20–22.

Beaty, Kathy. 2005. "How Safe Are Rural Libraries?" *Rural Libraries* 25, no. 1: 57–72.

Brown-Syed, Christopher. 2004. "Law Enforcement Agencies and Library Records," *Library & Archival Security* 19, no. 1: 53–57.

Burkhead, Keith. 2007. "Problem Patrons, or How I Learned to Quit Worrying and Love the Ban," *Public Libraries* 46, no. 5: 28–30.

Corcoran, Mary. 2002. "How to Survive and Thrive in the New Economy," *Online* 26, no. 3: 76–77.

Falk, Howard. 2004. "Privacy in Libraries," *Electronic Libraries* 22, no. 3: 281–284.

Gelernter, Judith. 2005. "Loss Prevention Strategies for the 21st Century Library," *Information Outlook* 9, no. 12: 12–22.

Gudsen, Neil. 2001. "Legal Liabilities in Handling of Problem Patrons," *Library & Archival Security* 17, no. 1: 17–31.

Gelernter, Judith. 2005. "Loss Prevention Strategies for the 21st Century Library," *Information Outlook* 9, no. 12: 12–22.

Howard, Linda, and Max Anderson. 2005. "RFID Technology in the Library Environment," *Journal of Access Services* 3, no. 2: 29–39.

Kahn, Miriam B. 2008. *Library Security and Safety Guide to Prevention, Planning, and Response.* Chicago: American Library Association.

Martin, Susan H. 2006. "Streakers, Stalkers, and Squatters: Dealing with Problem Patrons," *Tennessee Libraries* 56, no. 2: 135–140.

McCarty, Laura. 2005. "Libraries through the Eyes of E-Commerce," *Alki* 21, no. 1: 7–9.

Rogers, Michael. 2006. "When in Doubt, Throw 'em Out?" *Library Journal* 131, no. 10: 82, 84.

Security Guidelines Subcommittee of the Buildings and Equipment Section, Safety & Security of Library Buildings Committee. 2001. *Library Security Guidelines Document.* Library Administration and Management Association. http://www.ala.org/ala/lama/lamapublications/librarysecurity.htm.

Shuman, Bruce. 1999. *Library Security and Safety Handbook.* Chicago: American Library Association.

Weessies, Kathleen. 2003. "The Secret inside Your Library's Atlases," *American Libraries* 34, no. 9: 49–51.

Weihs, Jean. 2007a. "Theft in the Library, Part One: Problem Users," *Technicalities* 27, no. 4: 7–10.

———. 2007b. "Theft in the Library, Part Two: Library Staff," *Technicalities* 27, no. 6: 9–11.

———. 2008. "Theft in the Library, Part Three: Conclusions," *Technicalities* 28 no. 1: 8–11.

Chapter 16

Assessment

What is a cynic? Someone who knows the price of everything and the value of nothing.

—Oscar Wilde

The truth is that librarians have failed to explain to those outside the field what contributions they and their institutions actually make to society at large.

—Joan C. Durrance and Karen E. Fisher, 2005, p. 4

The measurement and assessment of library services has long been important to libraries. Managers use this information to plan and improve services, to justify to their funding authorities the financial and staffing resources allocated to libraries, and to prove the worth of library services by their frequency of use. As Brophy (2006) states, "Performance measurement is central to library management since without a firm grasp on what is actually being achieved it is impossible to move forward to improved service—or even to maintain the status quo" (p. 1).

Managers have attempted to evaluate library services by collecting statistics on the inputs and outputs relating to services delivered. These data include statistics such as the number of reference questions answered, the number of items checked out, the number of information literacy lectures delivered, and the number of ILLs obtained for library patrons and loaned to other libraries.

In the years since the publication of the last edition of this text, the evaluation or assessment of library services has assumed increased importance. As the costs of education have increased, school and college administrators; federal, state, and local governmental authorities; parents; and the general public are demanding that institutions be accountable, that the money they are spending for educational activities is being well used. Libraries are attempting to address the accountability challenge through new and more purposeful assessments that go beyond quantifying inputs and outputs in order to demonstrate the library's support of the parent institution's goals and objectives. As an LMTA you may well be involved in one or more of these assessment activities. This chapter will introduce you to the topic of measurement and assessment, explain why assessment is important, and illustrate some of the ways assessment is used to justify and improve library performance.

WHAT IS ASSESSMENT/MEASUREMENT?

Assessment is defined by Dugan and Hernon (2002) as documenting "observed, reported or otherwise quantified changes in attitudes and skills of students on an individual basis because of contact with library services, programs, or instruction." Substitute the word "patrons" for students and this definition applies to public and special libraries as well as to educational institutions.

Internal Focus

What we know as assessment today began in most libraries with an irregular collection and compilation of statistics. Initially, libraries undertook evaluation of their services for internal reasons. They wanted to use the information gathered from evaluation to improve library efficiency or effectiveness. Internally, the increasing complexity and cost of library operations, along with increasing demand for services, requires good information to assess and plan for. Managers need objective, standardized data on which to make decisions. The assessment of use statistics describes current performance and allows staff to see where improvements are needed. Assessments help managers allocate resources and plan their operations and services, and to make better decisions in general. The data also help to assess the success of new programs and services.

Weiss (1982) described a number of decisions such internal uses of evaluation data might inform (pp. 244–245):

- To continue a program. For example, should a middle school library continue purchasing extensively in the field of mathematics if the material is rarely used?

- To institute similar programs elsewhere. Should a public library expand the practice of filtering all public terminals to all its branch libraries, or just to those with no separate children's room?

- To improve practices and procedures. How can corporate library staff improve their recall rates for online searching, for example, without overloading company researchers with irrelevant citations?

- To add, drop, or change specific program strategies and techniques. Should an academic library expand its evening hours when requested to do so by the sophomore student government?

- To allocate resources among competing programs. Should the budget allocation for books be reduced in order to increase the amount spent on online databases?

- To accept or reject a program approach or theory. Would students be more likely to read and view reserve materials available in a digital reserve system than they are through the traditional service?

A further reason for libraries to undertake evaluations of their programs is to publicize their worth to the greater public. Libraries and library staff have generally done a less than stellar job of educating their publics about the library's contributions to society. Durrance and Fisher (2005) state the problem succinctly: "The truth is that librarians have failed to explain to those outside the field what contributions they and their institutions actually make to society at large." (p. 4). Experts, legislators, and decision makers often ignore the vital role libraries play in supporting learning and developing an informed citizenry. This is seen no more clearly than in the perennial struggles for funding faced by public, school, and academic libraries, particularly in times of budget constraints.

Quantity rather than quality was the focus of most library assessment efforts, although levels of quality were often inferred from quantitative measures, and the techniques were primarily mathematical. Circulation counts, reference questions asked, and books purchased and cataloged were among the kinds of statistics collected. Often, however, there was no analysis of these data in terms of what they meant for the quality of the library program, and the information was frequently filed away, unused.

User Focus

In the 1980s came an interest to go beyond assessment using internal library data alone and to involve users in the assessment process. Focusing on the user was hardly a new concept in libraries. It was expressed early in the twentieth century by the Indian librarian S. R. Ranganathan (1931) in his "five laws of library science":

- Books are for use
- Every reader his book
- Every book its reader
- Save the time of the reader
- A library is a growing organism

Assessment techniques like surveys, distributed to students, faculty, and other library users, were often used to find out about programs and services. The number of these user studies increased greatly in the 1990s. The increasing use of information technology to compile and share data gave rise to the use of benchmarking as a means to judge quality based on comparison of output data with that of carefully selected institutions.

Inputs and Outputs

Before the decade of the 1990s, measurements of library quality were generally limited to looking at inputs and outputs. *Inputs* may be considered the raw materials of a library's services. They include such things as the library budget, amount of available space, the size of collections, amounts and kinds of equipment, and the number of staff. But in terms of assessing libraries it is more important to measure how libraries use these inputs in order to deliver services. *Outputs* are the quantifiable products of the inputs, like the number of books circulated, reference questions answered, number of children attending story hours, and ILLs borrowed for a library's patrons. Outputs indicate the degree to which the library and its resources are being used. Measuring outputs is important for planning and making decisions about such things as staffing levels, hours of service, and so forth.

Benchmarking

Library managers use both inputs and outputs to infer quality in a process called *benchmarking*. Benchmarking involves a library assessing its operations by detailed comparisons with the same operations in other libraries or against professional standards. Often a comparison library, or libraries, is chosen based on the perceived high quality of the library's resources and services, which the library doing the benchmarking wishes to aspire to. This allows a library to evaluate its own operations based on the perceived "best practices" of the comparison library or group.

Both input and output measures allow libraries to judge the effectiveness and efficiency of their programs by comparing themselves with other institutions and with standards developed by the library profession. For example, the ACRL *Standards for Libraries in Higher Education* (2004) suggests the following comparison points for inputs:

- Ratio of volumes to combined total student (undergraduate and graduate, if applicable) and faculty FTE.
- Ratio of volumes added per year to combined total student and faculty FTE.
- Ratio of material/information resource expenditures to combined total student and faculty FTE.
- Percent of total library budget expended in the following three categories:

  1. materials/information resources, subdivided by print, microform, and electronic
  2. staff resources, subdivided by librarians, full and part-time staff, and student assistant expenditures. Federal contributions, if any, and outsourcing costs should be included here. When determining staff expenditures care should be taken to consider comparable staff (i.e., including or excluding media, systems or development staff) and fringe benefits (within or outside the library budget)
  3. all other operating expenses (e.g., network infrastructure, equipment)

- Ratio of FTE library staff to combined student and faculty FTE
- Ratio of usable library space (in square feet) to combined student and faculty FTE
- Ratio of number of students attending library instructional sessions to total number of students in specified target groups
- Ratio of library seating to combined student and faculty FTE
- Ratio of computer workstations to combined student and faculty FTE (consider that institutional requirements for student ownership of desktop or laptop computers could affect the need for workstations within the library).

Standards also suggests using the following outputs for comparisons:

- Ratio of circulation (excluding reserve) to combined student and faculty FTE.
- Ratio of interlibrary loan requests to combined student and faculty FTE (could be divided between photocopies and books).
- Ratio of interlibrary loan lending to borrowing.
- Interlibrary loan/document delivery borrowing turnaround time, fill rate, and unit cost.
- Interlibrary loan/document delivery lending turnaround time, fill rate, and unit cost.
- Ratio of reference questions (sample week) to combined student and faculty FTE.

Gathering data to do benchmarking studies used to be a time-consuming task, but for public and academic libraries, Web-based comparison tools make the task much easier. Data from the annual Public Libraries Survey are made available at the Institute of Museum and Library Services (IMLS, 2005) Web site (http://harvester.census.gov/imls/publib.asp). The database allows library staff to choose a comparison library, or libraries, based on one or more variables such as city, state, collection size, or income per capita. Data from more than 9,000 libraries are included in the database. Staff can then compare their own library's inputs and outputs, such as operating revenue, FTE staff, collection size, reference transactions per capita, children's program attendance per 1,000 population, and so forth. A similar Web site exists for academic library benchmarking, maintained by the National Center for Education Statistics and based on the biennial Academic Library Survey (http://nces. ed.gov/surveys/libraries/compare/index.asp?LibraryType=Academic).

An example of how benchmarking can be used by managers to improve resources and services may be offered by one of the authors of this text. In advance of an impending visit by a regional accrediting agency, the author used the academic library Web site to compare his library's staffing, collection size, and budget per FTE student with those of a set of peer institutions long recognized by the college. The comparisons showed the library's staffing and collections budget to be far below the mean for the other institutions. These data helped convince the college to adopt a multiyear plan to increase staffing and collections budgets to the mean level of the other institutions (and earned a commendation from the accrediting agency).

But with the increasing interest in and need for demonstrating account-ability, a shift is occurring in how the quality of a library and its services is being measured. The effect of a library's programs and services on its users is becoming a more important measure of library value. Traditional inputs and outputs are still valuable measures as ways to determine if a library is func-tioning effectively and efficiently. They can be especially useful when enabling a library to compare its program with professional standards and to bench-marking data provided by other libraries.

ACCOUNTABILITY AND ASSESSMENT

Since the 1990s there has been a conceptual change in the way libraries evaluate themselves. Doing evaluation for internal reasons is still commonly done in libraries, however recently there is impetus from both inside and outside libraries to measure and assess their performance. Outside forces, summarized by Nitecki (2004), are especially driving the trend towards more assessment. The recent trend towards increased accountability, driven largely by increased economic pressures and corresponding interest by funding au-thorities, has increased pressures on libraries to adopt measures of assess-ment. The 1993 federal Government Performance and Results Act requires annual progress reports from every government agency towards achieving performance goals. This has affected publicly funded state and local libraries. Major foundations are also requiring greater accountability for how their funds are being used. Some state libraries, like Florida's, expect libraries submitting grant proposals to use outcomes assessment as a measure of accountability. The IMLS, through grants and awards, encourages the adoption of outcome-based evaluation in both libraries and museums.

Many libraries are moving towards more patron-centered assessments that measure how a library affects its users. Most notable in this change is the growing popularity of assessing the quality of library services. To do this many libraries are moving towards assessing *outcomes*, especially in the context of how the library program affects users.

In higher education, for example, the regional accrediting associations have modified their standards to include requirements to document learning out-comes as evidence of student learning, and libraries are called on to provide evidence of their contribution to the teaching and learning mission of the par-ent institution.

OUTCOMES

Outcomes were defined by the 1998 report of the Task Force on Academic Library Outcomes Assessment (ACRL, 1998): "Outcomes, as viewed by the Task Force are the ways in which library users are changed as a result of their contact with the library's resources and programs. Satisfaction on the part of a user is an outcome. So is dissatisfaction. The Task Force considers simple satisfaction a facile outcome, however, too often unrelated to more substantial outcomes that hew more closely to the missions of libraries and the institutions they serve. The important outcomes of an academic library program involve the answers to questions like these:

- Is the academic performance of students improved through their contact with the library?
- By using the library, do students improve their chances of having a successful career?
- Are undergraduates who used the library more likely to succeed in graduate school?
- Does the library's bibliographic instruction program result in a high level of "information literacy" among students?
- As a result of collaboration with the library's staff, are faculty members more likely to view use of the library as an integral part of their courses?
- Are students who use the library more likely to lead fuller and more satisfying lives?

Questions like the above are difficult to answer. That is to say, empirically rigorous measurement of academic library outcomes is hard to do. This Task Force firmly posits, however, that it is *changes in library users* such as the ones addressed in these questions that comprise the outcomes with which academic librarians should be concerned. It may be that these outcomes cannot be demonstrated rigorously, or in a short period of time, or even by very many institutions. The Task Force believes that they can be measured, however, and their relationship to resource inputs and program inputs can be meaningfully determined through careful and lengthy research."

Good outcome measures are based on specific library objectives and help determine if these objectives have been achieved. They are not concerned with how much library patrons like a particular service or resource, but how much it benefited them. An important part of successfully using outcomes to ascertain the impact of resources and services is planning. Before embarking on outcomes measurement library staff should develop an assessment plan that identifies what changes in patron skills, values, and perceptions the library wishes to produce. These should then be expressed as outcomes. The plan should also articulate the measures that will be used to determine if the outcomes have been achieved. This assessment plan should not be static, but should evolve and change to reflect modifications based on the extent to which the assessment reveals progress, or lack of it, towards the desired outcomes (Hernon and Dugan, 2002).

Academic Libraries

In colleges and universities, the primary impetus for assessing outcomes is the changes in the criteria used by regional accrediting agencies to evaluate the quality of educational institutions. The accrediting agencies have incorporated increased accountability into their standards in the form of evidence of the effectiveness of student learning. Before the 1990s accrediting agencies based their evaluations on the assumption that an educational institution's quality of outcomes was directly related to the amount and quality of institutional inputs. Library standards, for example, often included input measures like number of books circulated, number of reference questions answered, number of ILLs, and so forth. Today accrediting associations are more concerned with evidence of a library's effects on its users. For example, the Western Association of Schools and Colleges (WASC), one of the six regional accrediting associations in the United States, revised its accreditation standards in 2001. Included as one of the "questions for institutional engagement" is the following: "To what extent does the institution provide an environment that is actively conducive to study and learning, where library, information resources, and co-curricular programs actively support student learning?" (WASC, 2001, p. 22).

External constituencies, including segments of the public such as the business community and funding authorities, have become skeptical of the social model that higher education benefits individuals directly and society indirectly. They are looking for evidence that higher education is adequately preparing students for careers and to participate in society. An economic model is now prevalent that demands evidence of a return on investment. As Hernon and Dugan (2002) state: "Federal and state government, the private sector, and the consumers of higher education (students and parents) want educational institutions to be more accountable for the funds, time, and other resources allocated and expended in the education process, especially when the pursuit of an undergraduate degree is often expensive" (p. 2). This produces pressure on the institution as a whole, and the library in particular in the case of information literacy, to assess the positive impact they have on student learning (Matthews, 2007, p. 20).

Another definition of outcomes is offered by the IMLS: "benefits or changes for individuals or populations during or after participating in program activities, including new knowledge, increased skills, changed attitudes or values, modified behavior, improved condition, or altered status (e.g., number of children who learned a finger play during story time, number of parents who indicated that they gained new knowledge or skills as a result of parent education classes, number of students whose grades improved after homework clinics, number of children who maintained reading skills over the summer as a result of the summer reading program, number of people who report being better able to access and use networked information after attending information literacy classes). While outcome measurement may at first seem very different from the traditional program or service model, in fact it incorporates all of the elements of traditional library measurement (inputs, activities, outputs) while adding only the element of outcomes" (IMLS, 2001, p. 20).

The last sentence in the IMLS definition above is important. Libraries continue to measure inputs and outputs, both to assess their programs and services and to benchmark their outputs against peer institutions as a measure of quality, but they now try also to relate these and other measures to changes in their users.

Public Libraries

Public libraries, too, moved towards outcomes assessment as local governments have demanded accountability from public agencies. Prescriptive national standards have been replaced by locally developed effectiveness plans that focus on user services (Hernon and Dugan, 2002). Public libraries are increasingly using user surveys to inform planning and to assess the effectiveness of and improve their services.

In the case of public libraries, Intner and Futas (1994) defined accountability as follows: "Public money supports public libraries. Members of the public are held accountable in their own lives for their actions, including spending money, so they expect the same from their institutions. And this is right and proper. As citizens we want to know where our money goes, how it gets there, and what it buys. We hold government officials accountable for how tax money is collected, contracted, and consumed. Libraries need to show how their expenditures of tax dollars benefit the public" (p. 410).

The Public Library Association (PLA) addresses outcomes in its *The New Planning for Results: A Streamlined Approach* (Nelson, 2001). Prior to this public libraries had only *Output Measures for Public Libraries* (Van House, 1987) to guide their evaluation efforts. While useful for measuring productivity and the success of efforts to attract users, the outputs do not assess the library's effect on its users. The PLA now provides public libraries a list of 13 "service responses," defined as "what a library does for, or offers to, the public in an effort to meet a set of well-defined community needs. . . . [Service responses] represent the gathering and deployment of specific critical resources to produce a specific public benefit or result" (Nelson, 2001, p.146). These are designed to help public libraries and their communities create local standards of library service. The 13 service responses are:

Basic Literacy: A library that offers Basic Literacy service addresses the need to read and to perform other essential daily tasks.

Business and Career Information: A library that offers Business and Career Information service addresses a need for information related to business, careers, work, entrepreneurship, personal finances, and obtaining employment.

Commons: A library that provides a Commons environment helps address the need of people to meet and interact with others in their community and to participate in public discourse about community issues.

Community Referral: A library that offers Community Referral addresses the need for information related to services provided by community agencies and organizations.

Consumer Information: A library that provides Consumer Information service helps to satisfy the need for information to make informed consumer decisions and to help residents become more self-sufficient.

Cultural Awareness: A library that offers Cultural Awareness service helps satisfy the desire of community residents to gain an understanding of their own cultural heritage and the cultural heritage of others.

Current Topics and Titles: A library that provides Current Topics and Titles helps to fulfill community residents' appetite for information about popular cultural and social trends and their desire for satisfying recreational experiences.

Formal Learning Support: A library that offers Formal Learning Support helps students who are enrolled in a formal program of education or who are pursuing their education through a program of home schooling to attain their educational goals.

General Information: A library that offers General Information helps meet the need for information and answers to questions on a broad array of topics related to work, school, and personal life.

Government Information: A library that offers Government Information service helps satisfy the need for information about elected officials and government agencies that enables people to participate in the democratic process.

Information Literacy: A library that provides Information Literacy service helps address the need for skills related to finding, evaluating, and using information effectively.

Lifelong Learning: A library that provides Lifelong Learning service helps address the desire for self-directed personal growth and development opportunities.

Local History and Genealogy: A library that offers Local History and Genealogy service addresses the desire of community residents to know and better understand personal or community heritage. (Nelson, 2001, p. 65)

An example of how output measures may be used to assess several of the above service responses can be found in the study *Counting on Results: New Tools for Outcome-Based Evaluation of Public Libraries* (Lance et al., 2001) http://www.lrs.org/documents/cor/CoR_FullFinalReport.pdf.

School Libraries

School libraries and media centers are also feeling pressure to document the value of the library's program to parents, faculty, and administrators. "Whereas once school librarians would ask *whether* evaluating students was appropriate to their role, now many are intent on learning *how* and *which* evaluations and assessments to use, as well as *what* to assess and *why*, and feeling less satisfied with their final decisions" (Abilock, 2007).

Another factor guiding assessment in schools is the No Child Left Behind (NCLB) Act. NCLB ties federal K–12 educational support to schools meeting national and state content standards. Each state is required to implement a comprehensive accountability system aligned with the state's curriculum and covering all students in the public schools.

The current national guidelines for school library media centers, *Information Power: Building Partnerships for Learning* (American Association of School Librarians and Association for Educational Communications and Technology, 1998), "envisions library media centers transitioning from a focus on providing resources to an emphasis on creating a community of lifelong learners. This transition requires that library media specialists view their 'curriculum' as extending beyond the traditional location and retrieval skills to skills in evaluating, synthesizing, and interpreting information. . . . Importantly, it requires that library media specialists expand their data collection beyond the tabulation of quantitative statistics on collection size and circulation to measures of actual student learning" (Harada and Yoshina, 2005).

Given the expanding role of school library media centers in student learning, the effectiveness of a school's information literacy instruction in the states' accountability systems assumes increased importance. School library media centers in a number of states are responding to this imperative by evaluating how their programs and services positively affect student learning in their schools. Inputs like staffing levels and budget allocation and outputs such as collection size and currency, the number of hours open, number of networked computers available, and the amount of time spent on information literacy instruction are being correlated with learning measures like students' SAT scores. As you might imagine, positive correlations are being found between student learning measures and stronger library programs. Links to descriptions of a number of these state assessment efforts may be found on the Web site for Library Research Service Impact Studies (http://www.lrs.org/impact. php).

Special Libraries

Special libraries, too, are called on to prove their value to their parent organizations. As with academic, school, and public libraries, special libraries have long relied on analysis of inputs and outputs to judge their effectiveness and efficiency. With the increasing strain on library resources and increasing demand for specialized levels of service, coupled with competition from other sources (like Google), outcomes assessment as a means for demonstrating a library's value to the parent organization is gaining popularity. Because outcome measures focus on the impact of the library on the parent organization and its members, they are seen as a good way to demonstrate a library's value.

One method of assessment that is more prominent in special libraries than other types of libraries is calculating a return on investment (ROI). This may be especially true in for-profit institutions. The benefits from using the library are identified by the clients, and the costs for providing library services are known from the library's budget. The preparation of the cost-benefit analysis allows the library to prepare an estimate of the library's ROI. Depending on the approach taken, ROI calculations range from 2.5:1 to 28:1 (the value of benefits compared with the costs of the library) (Matthews, 2003).

TECHNIQUES FOR GATHERING AND ASSESSING DATA

The several converging factors driving library assessment offer an opportunity for library staff to demonstrate the worth of libraries. If libraries can develop assessment measures that prove the value of library services and resources to the missions of their sponsoring institutions, and to the information needs of their users and society at large, the assessment evidence can be marketed to help convince those in authority about libraries' priority in funding decisions.

Assessment needs to be multifaceted, covering a range of indicators, and utilizing multiple methods and strategies to assess the effectiveness of library programs. The more methods used to collect assessment data about a particular service, the more complete, reliable, and persuasive the assessment will be. The following brief description of some of the more familiar assessment methods used in libraries today is not meant to suggest that one or more of these methods will suffice to assess a library service. Rather, the most effective assessments often employ more than one method, often combining a quantitative with a qualitative methodology to get a more complete picture of the phenomenon being studied.

Quantitative and Qualitative

The methodologies used to gather assessment data tend to fall into one of two general categories: quantitative or qualitative. *Quantitative* methods are designed to find out the extent, or the "what," of a particular phenomenon and involve collecting numerical data; for example, the number of hits on the library's Web site, the number of patrons entering the library over a particular time period, or the number of classes using the media center or library. Quantitative data is the most common form collected by libraries, but if used exclusively a manager runs the risk of placing too much emphasis on merely counting things and not enough on assessing quality.

Qualitative methods are designed to find out "why" something is happening, such as the reasons patrons come to the library or what students use the media center or library for. Glazier and Powell (1992) note that qualitative research views "Experiences from the perspective of those involved and attempt to understand why individuals react or behave as they do. They tend to give more attention to the subjective aspects of human experience and behavior." Qualitative measures often involve surveying or interviewing patrons about their satisfaction with the service of the library or media center or to determine how well information needs are being met.

Haynes (2004) argues that neither quantitative nor qualitative methodology makes sense without the other and advocates the use of mixed or "blended" method approaches in assessment. Different methods sometimes reveal different issues and mixed methods help compare the validity of findings.

The following examples from Nitecki (2004) are some of the more prevalent qualitative and quantitative data collection methods LMTAs may be asked to assist with. Each method has inherent strengths and weaknesses. The key is to select the method with the most strengths and fewest weaknesses for the assessment task at hand.

Counting

This is the simplest and most common means for collecting data on service inputs and outputs. Examples of counting library statistics are legion: the number of questions asked at the Reference Desk, including the level of complexity, date and time of day, general subject area, and whether asked in person or by phone, e-mail, text, or IM. Automated library systems have greatly simplified statistical data gathering and analysis, and allow for powerful data mining techniques to discover library use patterns and inform library planning.

Surveys

Surveys or questionnaires are probably the data-gathering methodologies most familiar to library staff. Although most library staff are not trained in survey methodology, such as instrument design, sample selection, and statistical analysis, it is easy to find examples in the library literature of surveys conducted by all types of libraries. Survey instruments may be administered via the Web, mailed, e-mailed, or distributed in person to library patrons. A survey can reach more people than interviews and focus groups, for example, and provides a more valid and reliable statistical sample. Questionnaires can also be administered on a pretest/posttest basis to measure outcomes. This latter application is often seen as part of Web-based tutorials to measure the effect of information literacy instruction.

Interviews

Data gathering via interviews involves an interviewer asking questions of one or more individuals, usually one participant at a time. The questions are predetermined so as to limit data to the questions or areas being evaluated. Interviewing has gained increased popularity as library staff members have become more familiar with focus group methodology.

Focus Groups

Used since the 1920s, focus groups are a kind of group interviewing. They involve open-ended, in-depth discussions with small groups, usually between six and ten individuals. The participants are purposely selected and led (ideally) by a trained facilitator, although resources do not always make this possible. The groups explore a predefined topic in a nonthreatening and semistructured setting, and the goal is to obtain data about a single topic or limited range of topics. The entire group answers questions together (Walden, 2006).

Focus groups are often used to determine patrons' perceptions of library programs and to explore the reasons behind their satisfaction, or dissatisfaction, with library services. While focus groups can provide a rich source of qualitative data about library services, the methodology is labor intensive to perform and that limits its wider use in libraries. Focus groups are frequently used in conjunction with surveys to gather both qualitative and quantitative data about an issue.

Observation

Observation of patron behavior and staff behavior has been a popular data-gathering method since at least the 1960s. One popular method, called unobtrusive observation, involves someone (referred to in the business world as a "secret shopper") posing as a patron and asking typical questions in a reference or other service setting, then judging the quality of the staff member's response. Human subject concerns are often addressed by obtaining permission from the staff members prior to beginning the study. Question content is carefully prepared and tested to insure consistency and the answers are judged against predetermined answers. Some libraries have used extensive observation programs, including videotaping, to assess service behavior. However, observation is most commonly used informally by managers seeking quick information about library operations.

In addition to the popular data collection methods described above, Hernon and Dugan (2002) describe some additional methods you may encounter.

Citation Analysis

The citations of student papers are sometimes analyzed to assess the use of higher level references. This is often used to measure the outcomes of information literacy presentations, especially if compared with the papers of students who did not receive information literacy instruction. The papers of students receiving instruction often show more scholarly resources, less reliance on the Web, fewer incomplete citations, and higher grades from instructors (for example, see Wang, 2006).

Transaction Log Analysis

Looking at the records of patron OPAC searches reveals mistakes patrons make in using the catalog, and unsuccessful searches. One of the most common mistakes revealed by transaction log analysis is misspellings. This information can be used to improve the OPAC (such as including spell checkers and "do you mean" prompts) and suggests frequently searched authors, titles, and subjects for purchasing decisions.

Logs, Diaries, and Journals

Patrons are sometimes asked to keep a record of their information-searching practices in order to allow library staff to discover barriers to the search process. The results allow staff to design programs to help improve patrons' searching experience. For example, Web sites may be redesigned to allow easier access to resources and services. This process may also ask patrons to reflect on their research experience as it progresses and how well they believe they are coping with the process.

Think-Aloud Protocol

Related to logs and diaries, this method asks participants to articulate their experiences into a recorder while accomplishing a particular task. The recordings are later transcribed for analysis.

Standardized or Locally Developed Tests

General, widely disseminated tests like the National Survey of Student Engagement (NSSE) and the College Senior Survey (CSS) are used by educational institutions to evaluate their programs. Some of the questions asked on these assessments are relevant to library support of student learning. For example, the Cooperative Institutional Research Program's (CIRP) *Your First College Year Survey* (YFCY), administered to freshmen, includes the question: "Please rate your satisfaction with this institution on each of the aspects of college life listed below: Library facilities and services." (Higher Education Research Institute [HERI], 2007). Library staff can use these test results to see if student satisfaction improves over time, and to see how student ratings of facilities and services compare with those of peer institutions.

LibQUAL+ (http://www.libqual.org/) is an assessment tool developed jointly by the Association of Research Libraries and Texas A&M University to measure user satisfaction in libraries. The assessment is based exclusively on users' opinions of service quality, gathered via a Web-based survey. The survey utilizes "gap analysis" to identify shortfalls that may exist between the level of services received and the level expected. Libraries have found LibQUAL+ to be particularly useful in that the results can be used to identify specific changes to make in specific services. For example, the University of Pittsburgh administered the study in 2002, and a major complaint was lack of complete journal runs. The library addressed this by purchasing digital back files for many journals, instituting document delivery for faculty and graduate students, and providing a shuttle connection to the off-site storage facility (Saunders, 2007). As of March 2007, more than 1,000 libraries have used LibQUAL+, including colleges and universities, community colleges, health sciences libraries, law libraries, and public libraries (Joubert and Lee, 2007).

What a library decides to assess should be based on the goals and objectives of the individual library. Many libraries design their own assessments, especially survey instruments, to measure their effectiveness. Staff should design these assessments to inform library personnel, students, institutional members, and external constituents of the strengths and weaknesses of the program and the progress being made towards quality outcomes. Locally developed tests need to be checked for reliability and validity.

There is no single recommended method for gathering library assessment data. Instead, experts recommend using multiple methods of evaluation and assessment to determine quality. As Matthews (2007) observes, "Recognizing that learning is multidimensional, it is important to utilize multiple assessment methods. No single method will accurately or fully assess all important student outcomes. A comprehensive assessment program should contain measures that are formative as well as summative, direct as well as indirect, and course-focused as well as institution focused."

Although a library-wide assessment program is the ideal, the reality is that assessment efforts tend to focus on the primary service activities. The following illustrate how assessment has been developed and used in two of the library's most visible services.

REFERENCE SERVICES

In recent years technology has greatly expanded the reference staff's ability to provide quality reference service. Technology has also altered the means by which staff answer patrons' information needs. But improved information technology has also made it incumbent upon reference staff to assess and demonstrate the quality of the services, both new and traditional, that they provide. Although specifically addressing academic libraries, Diamond and Sanders' (2006) observations apply also to public and school libraries: "Delivering consistent, high quality reference service is more important than ever with the increased competition many college and research libraries face from the rise of their patrons' exclusive reliance on Google and other Internet search engines. Consequently, the evaluation and assessment of service is one of the most important issues facing reference departments" (p. 1).

There are many studies of reference service effectiveness reported in the literature. Frequency of reference use is one of the most commonly measured outputs, usually estimated by counting questions, asking users how often they use reference services, asking users whether or not they used reference services in their present library visits, and keeping records of reference questions asked (*Reference Assessment Manual*, 1995, p. 8). For public libraries, Van House and colleagues (1987) recommend counting the number of reference transactions per person in the community served and the proportion of reference transactions successfully completed on the day the question was asked. Additional areas of focus in reference assessment studies include the accuracy of reference answers, user satisfaction, and how accurately reference staff identified the user information need (Jacoby and O'Brien, 2005, p. 325). The behavior of reference staff, for example interest, approachability, and listening skills, has been recognized as having an important impact on the success of the reference interaction. The Reference and User Services Association (RUSA) *Guidelines for Behavioral Performance of Reference and Information Service Providers* (2004a) offer a number of criteria to assess the behavioral quality of reference service.

Desirable outcomes of reference service identified by Saxton and Richardson (2002) are "utility, user satisfaction, and accuracy" (p. 2). Lankes and colleagues (2003) identify six "quality standards" in assessing digital reference services:

- Courtesy of library staff
- Accuracy of answers
- User satisfaction
- Number of repeat users
- Awareness among users that the service exists
- Cost per digital reference transaction

Especially in academic libraries, information literacy instruction is an additional important outcome of the reference encounter.

Since virtual reference services began in the form of e-mail exchanges between library staff and patrons in the mid-1980s, these services have expanded greatly to include such methods as chat, IM, and texting. These methods of providing reference service are especially important to libraries serving remote users, either through distance education programs or people not physically able to come to the library. As libraries work to improve digital reference services to expand the reach of their resources and services, staff have experimented with different ways to assess these virtual services. For the most part these assessment efforts focus on the reference process itself, especially the reference interview, and the content of the exchanges (Smyth and MacKenzie, 2006).

The methods used to measure traditional and virtual reference outputs and outcomes tend to be observations (usually unobtrusive), expert judgment by library staff, and surveys of users after reference encounters. Norlin (2000) described an assessment of reference services using a mix of quantitative and qualitative methods. The evaluation used a combination of surveys, focus groups, and unobtrusive observations. Areas of concern were approachability, ability to answer questions correctly, and skills in offering ideas on how to get started with research. The assessment resulted in several key changes to the service including roving librarians, name tags, and better promotion of technology classes.

With virtual reference services examinations of the transaction logs of chat and IM transactions may be made to ascertain the quality of the reference interview and accuracy of answers. Unobtrusive evaluations, where staff do not know they are being evaluated, have probably been the most common method for assessing the quality of reference service, and this technique is also being used to assess virtual reference service (for example, see Kaske and Arnold, 2002, and Lankes et al., 2003). The results of these assessment efforts are usually judged against the institution's own standards of quality and/or professional standards such as the *Guidelines for Behavioral Performance of Reference and Information Service Providers* (RUSA 2004a) and the *Guidelines for Implementing and Maintaining Virtual Reference Services* (RUSA 2004b).

INFORMATION LITERACY

Library personnel spend a considerable amount of time teaching patrons how to find and evaluate sources of information. With the focus of educational institutions on providing evidence of student learning, assessing the effectiveness of information literacy instruction is probably the most important way an academic or school library can demonstrate its value to the parent organization. Assessing information literacy is particularly important in academic institutions, as most regional accrediting agencies have included information literacy as one of the expected learning outcomes. For example, WASC (2001) includes the following question for institutional engagement in its accreditation standards: "How does the institution ensure that its members develop the critical information literacy skills needed to locate, evaluate, and responsibly use information?" (p. 27). Bonnie Gratch Lindauer (1998) argues that teaching information literacy skills directly affects student outcomes and contributes to the development of critical thinking and liberal arts values such as problem solving and lifelong learning. The best way of assessing the effectiveness of an information literacy program is to measure its effect on the quality of student work. This is easier said than done. As Dunn (2002) states: "The ambiguities in the core information competencies illuminate the assessment challenge. The difficulty in creating concrete, easy to test standards, performance objectives, and outcomes reflect the multiplicity of skills and thought processes needed by people when they attempt to find relevant and reliable information" (p. 27).

Several of the assessment techniques described earlier are being utilized to evaluate the effect of information literacy instruction on student work. These include citation analysis, pre- and posttesting, surveys, and standardized tests. A recent publication (Neely, 2006) identified more than 70 survey instruments to help library staff assess information literacy skills.

Portfolios are an increasingly popular assessment tool in educational institutions, especially in higher education. Portfolios involve collecting examples of student work and self-reflections that reflect the student's progress and achievements in one or more areas. Generally the student has a hand in selecting the examples. The portfolios may be analog, digital, or a combination of the two.

Online tutorials are an effective and popular way of providing information literacy instruction. Although they have particular value in reaching distance students and in allowing staff to stretch their numbers to accommodate large numbers of sessions, tutorials are time consuming to develop and keep up to date. Assessing the effectiveness of tutorials is important in improving their effectiveness and in determining their impact on student learning in order to see if the investment in tutorials is worthwhile. However, there is little information on assessing tutorials as stand-alone instructional programs, rather than being linked to a course or information literacy session (Lindsay et al., 2006). Pretests and posttests often embedded within the tutorials and patron surveys are the most common ways of assessing the outcomes of tutorials.

Standardized tests have been developed to assess information literacy skills. The iSkills (http://www.ets.org) assessment combines information literacy and technology fluency. The test uses scenario-based tasks to measure college students' ability to navigate, critically evaluate, and make sense of the information available through digital technology. Project SAILS (https://www.projectsails.org/) pretests college students' information literacy skills, then delivers instruction based on weaknesses diagnosed in the pretests. Posttests are used to measure students' progress and the effectiveness of the instruction. TRAILS (http://www.trails-9.org/) is a similar program geared for high school students. It is based on the philosophy of *Information Power* and tests skills and concepts deemed essential for information literacy (Morriston, 2007).

Some have argued that standardized tests created by an external agency cannot adequately measure the student learning in local classrooms. Even if an institution is using one of the assessments described above, library staff may need or choose to develop local assessments to evaluate specific aspects of their programs that they consider important for student learning. Staff considering developing their own instruments are advised by Neeley (2006) to first obtain support from administrators and others in their organization, to create goals and objectives that will help drive the process, and to evaluate other available assessment instruments before developing their own instruments from scratch (p. 153).

SUMMARY

Libraries have long collected information on library use in order to measure the amount of work done, improve effectiveness, and demonstrate the value of the library to its parent institution. Originally most of the data collected was statistical, primarily easy-to-count output measures like acquisitions, circulation, and reference statistics.

In recent years library users have become a focus of assessment efforts, both in terms of ascertaining patrons' satisfaction (or dissatisfaction) with various aspects of the library and in trying to measure the effect or impact of programs and services on library users. This latter emphasis has been driven since the 1990s by the public's interest in making institutions accountable for the money invested in them and for accomplishing their goals and objectives. Federal and state government authorities, higher education accrediting agencies, and for-profit businesses are asking for evidence of libraries' contribution to the funding authorities' goals and objectives. As a result, libraries now try to assess outcomes, the ways in which patrons are changed through contact with library resources and programs. These outcomes are difficult to measure accurately and libraries are struggling to find ways to do so in order to prove their value by supporting their parent institutions' goals and objectives.

Libraries use many quantitative and qualitative measures to assess their outputs and outcomes. Staff often try to combine quantitative and qualitative measures in order to get the most complete and accurate picture of an assessment target. LMTAs will often find themselves assisting in one or more assessment efforts no matter what kind of library they are employed in.

Chapter Review Material

1. How would you define "assessment"?
2. What are some of the reasons libraries try to assess their performance?
3. Give an example of an "input" and an "output."
4. What does accountability mean in terms of library performance?
5. How does accountability change the way libraries assess themselves?
6. What are the two primary categories of evidence libraries collect?
7. Give examples of qualitative and qualitative means of collecting data.
8. What are some ways library assess their reference services?
9. How do libraries assess their information literacy services?

REFERENCES

Abilock, Debbie. 2007. "Choosing Assessments that Matter," *Knowledge Quest* 35, no. 5: 8–12.

American Association of School Librarians and Association for Educational Communications and Technology. 1998. *Information Power: Building Partnerships for Learning.* Chicago: American Library Association.

Association of College and Research Libraries (ACRL). 1998. *Task Force on Academic Library Outcomes Assessment Report.* Chicago: American Library Association. http://www.ala.org/ala/acrl/acrlpubs/whitepapers/taskforce academic.cfm.

———. 2004. *Standards for Libraries in Higher Education.* ACRL: 2004. http://www.ala.org/ala/acrl/acrlstandards/standardsguidelines.cfm.

Brophy, Peter. 2006. *Measuring Library Performance: Principles and Techniques.* London: Facet.

Diamond, Tom, and Mark Sanders, eds. 2006. *Reference Assessment and Evaluation.* Binghamton, NY: Haworth Information Press.

Dugan, Robert E. and Peter Hernon. 2002. "Outcomes Assessment: Not Synonymous with Inputs and Outputs," *Journal of Academic Librarianship* 28, no. 6: 376–381.

Dunn, Kathleen. 2002. "Assessing Information Literacy Skills in the California State University: A Progress Report," *Journal of Academic Librarianship* 28, no. 1/2: 26–35.

Durrance, Joan C., and Karen E. Fisher. 2005. *Libraries and Librarians Help: A Guide to Identifying User-Centered Outcomes.* Chicago: American Library Association.

Glazier, Jack D., and Ronald H. Powell. 1992. *Qualitative Research in Information Management.* Littleton, CO: Libraries Unlimited, Inc.

Harada, Violet H., and Joan M. Yoshina. 2005. *Assessing Learning: Librarians and Teachers as Partners.* Westport, CT: Libraries Unlimited Inc.

Haynes, Abby. 2004. "Bridging the Gulf: Mixed Methods and Library Service Evaluation," *Australian Library Journal* 53, no. 3: 285–306.

Hernon, Peter, and Robert E. Dugan. 2002. *An Action Plan for Outcomes Assessment in Your Library.* Chicago: American Library Association.

Higher Education Research Institute (HERI). 2007. *Your First College Year (YFCY) Survey.* Los Angeles: HERI.

Institute of Museum and Library Services (IMLS). 2001. *Perspectives on Outcome Based Evaluation for Libraries and Museums.* Washington, DC: IMLS. http://www.imls.gov/pdf/pubobe.pdf.

———. 2005. *Library Statistics: Public Libraries.* Washington, DC: IMLS. http://harvester.census.gov/imls/publib.asp.

Intner, Sheila S., and Elizabeth Futas. 1994. "Evaluating Public Library Collections: Why Do It, and How to Use the Results," *American Libraries* 25, no. 5: 410–413.

Jacoby, JoAnn, and Nancy P. O'Brien. 2005. "Assessing the Impact of Reference Services Provided to Undergraduate Students," *College & Research Libraries* 66, no. 4: 324–340.

Joubert, Douglas J., and Tamera P. Lee. 2007 "Empowering Your Institution through Assessment," *Journal of the Medical Library Association* 95, no 1: 46–53.

Kaske, Neal, and Julie Arnold. 2002. *An Unobtrusive Evaluation of Online Real Time Library Services.* Paper presented at the Library Research Round Table, American Library Association Annual Conference, Atlanta, GA. http://www.lib.umd.edu/groups/digref/kaskearnoldunobtrusive.html.

Lance, Keith Curry. 2001. *Counting on Results: New Tools for Outcome-Based Evaluation of Public Libraries.* Aurora, CO: Bibliographical Research Center. http://www.lrs.org/documents/cor/CoR_FullFinalReport.pdf.

Lankes, R. David, Melissa Gross, and Charles R. McClure. 2003. "Costs, Statistics, Measurements, and Standards for Digital Reference Services: A Preliminary View," *Library Trends* 51, no. 3: 401–416.

Lindauer, Bonnie Gratch. 1998. "Defining and Measuring the Library's Impact on Campus-wide Outcomes," *College & Research Libraries* 59, no. 6: 546–570.

Lindsay, Elizabeth Blakesley, Lara Cummings, Corey M. Johnson, and B. Jane Scales. 2006. "If You Build It, Will They Learn?" *College & Research Libraries* 67, no. 5: 429–445.

Matthews, Joseph R. 2003. "Determining and Communicating the Value of the Special Library." *Information Outlook* 7, no. 3: 26–31.

———. 2007. *Library Assessment in Higher Education.* Westport, CT: Libraries Unlimited, Inc.

Morriston, Terry. 2007. "Carving a New Assessment Trail," *Knowledge Quest* 35, no. 5: 48–49.

Neeley, Teresa Y. 2006. *Information Literacy Assessment: Standards-Based Tools and Assignments.* Chicago: American Library Association.

Nelson, Sandra. 2001. *The New Planning for Results: A Streamlined Approach.* Chicago: American Library Association.

Nitecki, Danuta A. 2004. "Program Evaluation in Libraries: Relating Operations and Clients," *Archival Science* 4, no. 1/2: 17–44.

Norlin, Elaina. 2000. "Reference Evaluation: A Three-Step Approach," *College & Research Libraries* 61, no. 6: 546–553.

Ranganathan, S. R. 1931. *Five Laws of Library Science.* Madras: Madras Library Association.

The Reference Assessment Manual. 1995. Compiled and edited by the Evaluation of Reference and Adult Services Committee, Management and Operation of Public Services Section, Reference and Adult Services Division (RASD), American Library Association. Ann Arbor, MI: Pierian Press.

Reference and User Services Association. 2004a. *Guidelines for Behavioral Performance of Reference and Information Service Providers. http://www.ala.org/ala/rusa/rusaprotools/referenceguide/guidelinesbehavioral.cfm*

———. 2004b. *Guidelines for Implementing and Maintaining Virtual Reference Services.* Available at http://www.ala.org/ala/rusa/rusaprotools/reference guide/virtrefguidelines.cfm.

Saunders, E. Stewart. 2007. "The LibQUAL+ Phenomenon: Who Judges Quality," *Reference & User Services Quarterly* 47, no. 1: 21–24.

Saxton, Matthew, and John V. Richardson, Jr. 2002. *Understanding Reference Transactions: Transforming an Art into a Science.* San Diego, CA: Academic Press.

Smyth, Joanne B., and James C. MacKenzie. 2006. "Comparing Virtual Reference Exit Survey Results and Transcript Analysis: A Model for Service Evaluation," *Public Services Quarterly* 2, no. 2/3: 85–99.

Van House, N. A., Douglas Zweizig, and Public Library Association New Standards Task Force. 1987. *Output Measures for Public Libraries.* 2nd ed. Chicago: American Library Association.

Walden, Graham R. 2006. "Focus Group Interviewing in the Library Literature," *Reference Services Review* 34, no. 2: 222–241.

Wang, Rui. 2006. "The Lasting Impact of a Library Credit Course," *Portal: Libraries and the Academy.* 6, no. 1: 79–92

Weiss, Carol H. 1982. "Purposes of Evaluation." In: *Strategies for Library Administration: Concepts and Approaches.* Charles R. McClure and Alan R. Samuels, eds. Littleton, CO: Libraries Unlimited.

Western Association of Schools and Colleges (WASC). 2001. *WASC 2001 Handbook of Accreditation.* Alameda, CA: WASC.

SUGGESTED READINGS

Competencies for Information Professionals of the 21st Century. 2003. Revised ed. Chicago: Special Libraries Association. http://www.sla.org/PDFs/Competencies2003_revised.pdf.

Everhart, Nancy. 1998. *Evaluating the School Library Media Center.* Englewood, CO: Libraries Unlimited, Inc.

Heath, Fred M., Martha Kyrillidou, and Consuella A. Askew, eds. 2004. *Libraries Act on Their LibQUAL+™ Findings: From Data to Action.* Binghamton, NY: Haworth Information Press.

Hernon, Peter, and E. Altman 1998. *Assessing Service Quality: Satisfying the Expectations of Library Customers.* Chicago: American Library Association.

Jones, Rebecca, Eileen Abels, John Latham, Dee Magnoni, and Joan Gard Marshall. 2003. "Competencies for Information Professionals in the 21st Century," *Information Outlook* 7, no. 10: 12–18.

McClure, Charles R., R. David Lankes, and Melissa Gross. 2002. *Statistics, Measures, and Quality Standards for Assessing Digital Reference Library Services: Guidelines and Procedures.* Tallahassee: School of Information Studies, Information Use Management and Policy Institute, Florida State University.

National Center for Education Statistics. 2006. *Library Statistics Program.* Washington, DC: U.S. Department of Education. http://nces.ed.gov/surveys/libraries/academic.asp.

Index

About the Authors

G. EDWARD EVANS, renowned Fulbright scholar and sought-after international consultant, is retired University Librarian and Adjunct Professor at Loyola Marymount University, Los Angeles, California.

THOMAS L. CARTER is Dean for Academic Resources at St. Mary's College of California.